Investing Online For Dummies, 5th Edition

D0131631

Online Investor Vocabulary

Active Investors: Frequent traders who make around 12 trades per month.

Block Trades: Usually 10,000 shares of stock or $200,000 in bonds traded by institutions such as pension funds, banks, insurance companies and so on.

Broker/Dealer: An individual or company, other than a bank, that is in the business of buying and selling securities for itself and others. Brokers/dealers must register within the states they conduct business in and with the SEC.

Buy and Hold Investors: Typically mainstream investors who make 20 trades per year or less.

Day Traders: Active traders who hold positions for a very short time (often just minutes) and make several trades per day.

Earnings Announcements: The most recent quarterly financial results of a company. Often this announcement includes revenue, earnings, and earnings per share (EPS) information.

Extended Hours Trading: The trading of securities while exchanges are closed. Today many online brokerages offer extended hours trading that are before and after normal trading hours.

Index Fund: A passively managed mutual fund that attempts to replicate certain stock indexes, such as the S & P 500.

Maintenance Fees: A charge assessed on some types of brokerage accounts at a fixed frequency, usually quarterly or annually.

Odd Lots: Usually less than 100 shares of a stock, sometimes called broken lots or uneven lots; the opposite of round lots.

Options: The right, but not the obligation, to purchase (for call options) and to sell (for put options) a specific amount of a security, such as a stock, commodity, and so on at a specific price (called the strike price) during a specific time period.

Portfolio Management: The process of managing investments; also called money management or investment management.

Round Lots: The usual unit of trading a stock is 100 shares or 5 bonds; also called normal trading unit, even lot or full lot trading.

For Dummies: Bestselling Book Series for Beginners

Investing Online For Dummies, 5th Edition

Cheat Sheet

The Major Components of Investing	Twelve Point Investing Program For Investing Online For Dummies
Select	**I – Investigate investment candidates.** For new or beginning investors ValuEngine refer to Investorguide.com University (www.investorguide.com/university.html) and immediately discover how to get started.
	N – Never consider a deal that looks too good. Check out the latest scams at the National Fraud Center (www.fraud.org) and the Federal Trade Commission for the Consumer (www.ftc.gov/bcp/menu-invest.htm).
Analyze	**V – Value the price of investments using fundamental analysis.** Check ValuEngine for a quick analysis and an easy-to-understand price forecast (www.valuengine.com/servlet/Main).
	E – Evaluate investment candidates using Internet-based information. Investment super-sites like Reuters at www.investor.reuters.com eliminate the need to go to several places to get comprehensive financial information.
	S – Screen investment candidates using online screening tools. MSN Money offers a basic and a deluxe stock screen free of charge at moneycentral.msn.com/home.asp.
Purchase	**T – Trade online using a brokerage that meets your individual needs.** First, determine your investor profile by using the Risk Tolerance Assessor at www.webcalcs.com/cgi-bin/calcs/prod/risk.cgi?client=safecofunds. Next go to Consumer Search at www.consumersearch.com/www/personal_finance/online_brokers/ to read what analysts have to say about the top-rated online brokerages. Finally, select the brokerage that meets your unique needs.
	O – Open your mind to different purchasing methods. Find techniques for purchasing investments at the lowest prices. You may want to try a direct stock purchase plan; NetstockDirect (www.netstockdirect.com) has all the details.
	N – Never pay a brokerage more than you have to. Watch out for hidden costs and compare brokerage prices at SiebertNet (www.siebertnet.com/html/compare_us.html).
Monitor	**L – Letting your portfolio "ride" is a big mistake.** Online portfolio management tools like those at RiskGrades (www.riskgrades.com) can help you increase the value of your portfolio without taking undue risks.
	I – Investigate your portfolio for investment "overlaps." Using the Morningstar.com (www.morningstar.com) online portfolio x-ray tool, check for overconcentrations and avoid investing mistakes.
Sell	**N – Never expect a stock to go straight up.** Gain an understanding of how the economy affects the market and the value of your investments by reading *The Wall Street Journal* (www.wsj.com/public/us).
	E – Establish your personal selling rules and reap your rewards. Read *Investing Online For Dummies,* 5th Edition, and discover how you can make the most of your investments by selling at the right time.

Copyright © 2005 Wiley Publishing, Inc. All rights reserved.

Item 8456-1.

For more information about Wiley Publishing, call 1-800-762-2974.

For Dummies: Bestselling Book Series for Beginners

Investing Online
FOR
DUMMIES®
5TH EDITION

by Kathleen Sindell, PhD

Wiley Publishing, Inc.

Investing Online For Dummies®, 5th Edition

Published by
Wiley Publishing, Inc.
111 River Street
Hoboken, NJ 07030-5774

www.wiley.com

Copyright © 2005 by Wiley Publishing, Inc., Indianapolis, Indiana

Published by Wiley Publishing, Inc., Indianapolis, Indiana

Published simultaneously in Canada

For general information on our other products and services, please contact our Customer Care Department within the U.S. at 800-762-2974, outside the U.S. at 317-572-3993, or fax 317-572-4002.

For technical support, please visit www.wiley.com/techsupport.

Wiley also publishes its books in a variety of electronic formats. Some content that appears in print may not be available in electronic books.

Library of Congress Control Number: 2005923224

ISBN-13: 978-0-7645-8456-5

ISBN-10: 0-7645-8456-1

Manufactured in the United States of America

10 9 8 7 6 5

5B/SZ/QT/QV/IN

WILEY

About the Author

Kathleen Sindell is the author of *Managing Your Money Online For Dummies* (Wiley, 2004), *Safety Net: Protecting Your Business on the Internet* (Wiley, 2002), *Loyalty Marketing for the Internet Age* (Dearborn, 2000), *The Unofficial Guide to Buying a Home Online* (Hungry Minds, 2000), and *A Hands-On Guide to Mortgage Banking Internet Sites*, a separate directory published by *Mortgage Banking Magazine* (2000, 1999, 1998, 1997). Dr. Sindell is a contributing author to the *Encyclopedia of Computer Science* (Groves Dictionaries Inc., 2000) and the online investing columnist for *Investor Direct* magazine (1999). She is the author of *The Handbook of Real Estate Lending* (McGraw-Hill Professional Publishing, 1996). Dr. Sindell is an expert on electronic commerce and is an adjunct faculty member at the Johns Hopkins University MBA program. She is the former Associate Director of the Financial Management and Commercial Real Estate Programs for the University of Maryland, University College Graduate School of Management & Technology.

Dr. Sindell provides consulting and publications about management, finance, security, and real estate in the e-commerce environment. Her goal is to improve the quality of life and economic well-being of people and business organizations by providing information that they might not otherwise have or understand.

She received her B.A. in Business from Antioch University, an MBA in Finance from the California State University at San Jose, and a PhD in Administration and Management from Walden University, Institute for Advanced Studies.

Dedication

This book is dedicated to my dear friends Arlene Meilich and Gail Pasternack.

Author's Acknowledgments

Investing Online for Dummies, 5th Edition, illustrates the latest trends in online investing and represents my desire to help people take control of their finances by accessing high-quality Web-based investing information. My gratitude and thanks to Bob Woerner, senior acquisitions editor, for his guidance. Development editor Mark Enochs made working on this book a joy. My appreciation to Andy Hollandbeck and Teresa Artman for their excellent copy editing. It was a pleasure to work with technical editor Dan Chesler. I am also grateful to the many folks who work behind the scenes at Wiley Publishing.

It was a delight to work with my literary agent, Carole McClendon, and all the folks at Waterside Productions on this fifth edition of *Investing Online For Dummies.*

A very special thank you to my brother-in-law, Gerald Sindell, for his profound counsel on everything relating to the business of publishing.

Publisher's Acknowledgments

We're proud of this book; please send us your comments through our online registration form located at `www.dummies.com/register/`.

Some of the people who helped bring this book to market include the following:

Acquisitions, Editorial, and Media Development

Project Editor: Mark Enochs

Senior Acquisitions Editor: Bob Woerner

Copy Editor: Andy Hollandbeck

Technical Editor: Dan Chesler
`dan@charttricks.com`

Editorial Manager: Kevin Kirschner

Media Development Manager: Laura VanWinkle

Media Development Supervisor: Richard Graves

Editorial Assistant: Amanda Foxworth

Cartoons: Rich Tennant (`www.the5thwave.com`)

Composition Services

Project Coordinators: Emily Wichlinski, Nancee Reeves

Layout and Graphics: Carl Byers, Andrea Dahl, Lauren Goddard, Denny Hager, Joyce Haughey, Barry Offringa, Lynsey Osborn, Melanee Prendergast, Heather Ryan

Proofreader: Kelly Ewing, Leeann Harney, Jessica Kramer, Carl Pierce

Indexer: TECHBOOKS Production Services

Special Help: Teresa Artman

Publishing and Editorial for Technology Dummies

   Richard Swadley, Vice President and Executive Group Publisher

   Andy Cummings, Vice President and Publisher

   Mary Bednarek, Executive Acquisitions Director

   Mary C. Corder, Editorial Director

Publishing for Consumer Dummies

   Diane Graves Steele, Vice President and Publisher

   Joyce Pepple, Acquisitions Director

Composition Services

   Gerry Fahey, Vice President of Production Services

   Debbie Stailey, Director of Composition Services

Contents at a Glance

Introduction 1

Part 1: Online Investing Fundamentals 9

Chapter 1: Finding Investor Stuff on the Net 11

Chapter 2: No Experience Required: Getting Started with Online Investing 31

Chapter 3: Making Your Money Work Harder 47

Chapter 4: Selecting an Online Broker That's Right for You 63

Chapter 5: Getting Ahold of Trading Online 81

Part 11: Finding the Right Investments 97

Chapter 6: The Keys to Successful Internet Mutual Fund Investing 99

Chapter 7: Online Analysis, Buying, and Selling of Mutual Funds 121

Chapter 8: The Basics of Stocks and Rates of Return 141

Chapter 9: Internet Stock Screening 159

Chapter 10: Using Company Information to Make Investment Decisions 175

Chapter 11: Digging Deeper: Advanced Stock Analysis 195

Chapter 12: Going with Fixed-Income Securities:
Which Type of Bond Is for You? 221

Chapter 13: Valuing, Buying, and Selling Bonds Online 243

Part 111: Expanding Your Investment Opportunities 263

Chapter 14: Going International Online 265

Chapter 15: Looking for the Next Big Thing: IPOs, DPOs, and DRIPs 281

Chapter 16: Taking the Option: Alternative Investing 301

Chapter 17: The Internet and Managing Your Portfolio 315

Part 1V: The Part of Tens 337

Chapter 18: Ten Warnings About Cyberfraud 339

Chapter 19: Ten Important Selling Points 353

Chapter 20: Ten Green Flags for Buying 365

Index 373

Table of Contents

Introduction *1*

About This Book 3
Who Are You? 1
How to Use This Book 4
How This Book Is Organized 4
    Part I: Online Investing Fundamentals 5
    Part II: Finding the Right Investments 5
    Part III: Expanding Your Investment Opportunities 5
    Part IV: The Part of Tens 6
What's New 6
Icons Used in This Book 7
Feedback, Please 7

Part 1: Online Investing Fundamentals *9*

Chapter 1: Finding Investor Stuff on the Net **11**

Building Your Own Online Information System 11
    Identifying new investments 12
    Analyzing investment prospects 13
    Purchasing investments 14
    Monitoring investments 15
    Selling investments 15
Setting Up Your Basic Investment Search Strategy 16
    Metasearch engines 16
    Popular search engines 17
    Selecting the best search engine 19
Understanding How Newsgroups Can Help You 20
    Finding the perfect newsgroup 21
    Finally, some investor news reading 21
Getting the Message from Investor Message Boards 22
Uncovering Investor Information from Mailing Lists 23
Using Free and Fee-Based Online Investor Databases 24
    Totally free databases 24
    When all else fails — fee-based databases 25
Getting Online Investor Information Geared to Your Needs 26
    Investor Web sites for children 27
    Web sites for young investors 27
    Other investor special-interest sites 28

Chapter 2: No Experience Required: Getting Started with Online Investing 31

    Getting Smart Online 32
        Online investor tutorials 32
        Web sites for new investors 34
        Glossaries 34
    Maximizing Your Internet Browser with Bookmarks 36
    News You Can Use 37
        Large news organizations 38
        Newspapers 38
        Magazines 39
        Scholarly journals 40
        Multimedia investment news 41
        Electronic newsletters 41
    Practicing with Your New Investment Information 43
        Join the club! Become a member of an investment club 43
        Getting into the game: Online investment simulations 44

Chapter 3: Making Your Money Work Harder 47

    Using the Internet to Make Financial Planning Easier 47
        The joys of compound interest 48
    Moving Some of Your Savings to Investments 50
    Maximizing Your Investments with Tax-Deferred Accounts 51
        Traditional IRAs 52
        Roth IRAs 52
        Online calculators for determining the best IRA account 53
    Deciding How Much Risk You Can Take 54
    Determining How Much You Can Invest 55
    Investing in Securities That Meet Your Goals 55
    Checking Out What the Experts Are Doing 56
        Analyzing the analysts 56
        Getting the opinions of others: Stock-picking communities 57
        Judging who's the real deal 58
    Tracking and Measuring Your Success 59
    Building Your Personalized Investment Plan 60

Chapter 4: Selecting an Online Broker That's Right for You 63

    Is a Traditional Broker Best for You? 64
    Selecting a Premium Online Brokerage 65
    Selecting the Right Discount Online Brokerage 66
    Investigating a Brokerage Before You Invest 67
    Matching Your Needs to the Right Online Brokerage 67
        For beginners 68
        For mainstream investors 68
        For active investors 70
        For affluent investors 70

Getting Online Trading Services for Less.................................72
    Trading online for $15 or less 73
    Finding online brokers with no or
        low initial account minimums 74
Rating Online Brokers...76
Checking Out Hybrid Online Banks and Brokerages 77
Opening Your Online Brokerage Account 79

Chapter 5: Getting Ahold of Trading Online ....**.81**
Understanding the Tax Consequences of Trading Securities...................81
    Special rates for long-term capital gains 82
    Measuring capital gains...83
    What about capital losses? 83
Increasing Profits with Simple Order Specification Techniques.............84
ECNs — It's Not Your Grandfather's Market Anymore.........................86
    How ECNs work 86
    Understanding inside spreads 87
Extended-Hours Trading 88
    Sources for extended-hours stock information 89
    Join the extended-hours club 89
Online Trading and the Active Investor 90
    Active investor trading platforms 91
    You might be a day trader if 93
Going from Hardwired to Wireless Trading 94

Part II: Finding the Right Investments 97

**Chapter 6: The Keys to Successful
Internet Mutual Fund Investing** ....**.99**
Mutual Fund Basics...99
    Discovering the differences between open-end
        and closed-end mutual funds.................................102
    Minimizing fees 103
A Fund for You, a Fund for Me 104
Finding Facts and Figures Online 106
Simplifying Your Investing with Mutual Funds 107
    Discovering index funds 107
    Becoming aware of exchange-traded funds 108
Mutual Funds and Your Risk Tolerance Level 110
How to Screen Mutual Funds Online 111
Locating and Reading the Prospectus................................113
    Checking the facts 114
    Getting it right...115
Analyzing Mutual Funds 116
    Comparing costs and returns 117
    Understanding mutual fund risks................................118

Chapter 7: Online Analysis, Buying, and Selling of Mutual Funds 121

Finding the Right Mix of Investments 121
Using the Internet to Help You Choose
    the Best Funds in Each Class 124
    Following a mutual fund checklist 125
    Reading an online mutual fund listing 126
    Assessing mutual fund performance 127
Using Scoreboards and Ratings 128
The Ratings War 130
    The Morningstar rating system 130
    The Lipper Leader system 131
    The Value Line rating system 131
Buying Mutual Funds Online: Using an Online Broker 132
Commission-Free Mutual Funds 133
Starting Your Mutual Fund Account with as Little as $50 135
Buying Mutual Funds Online: No Broker Needed 136
The Right Time to Sell Your Mutual Funds 137

Chapter 8: The Basics of Stocks and Rates of Return 141

Understanding Stocks 141
Participating in the Market 142
    Common stocks 142
    Preferred stocks 143
Picking the Right Stock for the Right Goal 143
What Does the S & P 500 Have to Do with Anything? 145
Paying the Right Price 147
    Getting down to fundamentals 147
    Using online tools to value stocks 148
    Using the Net to calculate fair value 149
    Valuation model input and results 151
    Analysis for value shopping 153
    Getting technical: Technical analysis 154
    Technical analysis software 156
    Market timing 157

Chapter 9: Internet Stock Screening 159

Finding the Best Stock Using the Net 159
    Choosing the criteria for your first stock screen 160
    Fine-tuning your stock screen 161
    Using your stock screen results 161
    Important ratios for screening stocks 161
Starting with Quick Online Stock Screens 165
Using Those Terrific Prebuilt Stock Screens 166
Locating Those Prebuilt Screens You Can Change Yourself 166

Advanced Techniques for Building Stock Screens 167
    Screening for growth stocks 167
    Screening for income stocks 168
    Screening for value stocks 168
Screening for Investment Bargains 169
    Stocks selling at below book value 169
    Securities selling below liquidation value..............................169
    Stocks with low P/E ratios...170
    Companies reporting deficits 171
    Prospective turnaround candidates 171

**Chapter 10: Using Company Information
to Make Investment Decisions** **175**
    Finding Financial Statements Online 176
    Accessing Web Sites That Specialize in Annual Reports 177
    Using Web Sites That Link to Company Home Pages 179
    Researching a Company's SEC Filing.......................................180
        The Sarbanes-Oxley Act and investors................................180
        Downloading SEC filings in just three clicks 181
        SEC search engines 182
    Dissecting the Annual Report...184
    Analyzing a Financial Statement 187
    You Don't Have to Be a Math Whiz to Calculate Ratios 188
    Utilizing Prepared Online Ratio Analysis 190
    Understanding Bankruptcy..190
        High debt warning signs 191
        Checking out insider trading 192

Chapter 11: Digging Deeper: Advanced Stock Analysis **195**
    Turning Your Hunches into Investment Strategies 196
    Conquering Uncertainty with Online Research.....................................198
        Gaining new investor insights with breaking news........................199
        Business news search engines 200
        Locating company profiles and related data 200
    Gathering Business Economic and Related Data...................................201
        Business economic indicators...202
        Consumer economic indicators 204
        Financial market data 205
    Collecting Market Information...206
        Most active stocks...206
        Market indices 206
    Finding Industry and Statistical Information...............................207
        Checking out analyst evaluations 209
        Following upgrades and downgrades 210

Zeroing In on Earnings 210
    Tracking down earnings estimates 211
    Forecasting earnings and the stock market level...........212
Researching the Background of Corporate Officers 213
Understanding Stock Prices 214
    Understanding Level I stock quotes 215
    Discovering Level II stock quotes 217
    Finding ticker symbols and stock prices online..........218
    Free delayed stock quotes 218
    Free real-time stock quotes 219
    Free wireless stock quotes 219
    Fee-based stock quotes 220

Chapter 12: Going with Fixed-Income Securities: Which Type of Bond Is for You? **221**
Generic Features of Bonds..222
    Special benefits and exposures 223
    Using the Internet to find new bond offerings............225
    Locating those elusive bond quotes 226
    Finding bond indexes and historical data online..........226
    Risks and stability 228
How Small Investors Can Make Money with Fixed-Income
  Investments and Bonds 228
When to Choose a Money Market Deposit Account (MMDA) 231
The Four Basic Types of Bonds......................................232
    Uncle Sam's bonds: Treasury securities 233
    Federal government agency bonds..........................235
    The beauty of tax-free municipal bonds...................235
    Floating with corporate bonds 238
    Using the Internet to screen bonds.......................239
Two Alternate Types of Bonds 240
    Zero-coupon bonds 240
    Eurobonds 241

Chapter 13: Valuing, Buying, and Selling Bonds Online **243**
The Math of Bonds..244
    Calculating bond values 244
    Creating yield curves 245
    The easy way to value your bond returns 247
    Let the Internet do the math.............................248
Trading Bonds Online...249
Nice and Simple: Savings Bonds....................................250
    The good and the bad about savings bonds................251
    Calculating the value of your savings bonds..............252
Just Uncle Sam, Treasury Securities, and You 253

Buying Treasury Securities via the Internet 254
    Opening Treasury Direct accounts 254
    Opening your savings bond Treasury Direct
      account for as little as $25 255
    Treasury bills, notes, and TIPS Treasury Direct accounts 256
    How to buy Treasuries online 257
    Selling your Treasury securities 259
    Online sources for more information 260
Increasing Your Profits with a Treasuries Ladder 261

Part III: Expanding Your Investment Opportunities.......263

Chapter 14: Going International Online 265
Taking Advantage of International Opportunities 266
Getting Started with Online International Quotes and Indexes 267
Gathering International News and Research 268
Acquiring International Company Information 270
Online Trading Abroad 271
Investing in Emerging Markets 272
Problems with Investing Directly in Foreign Companies 273
    Administration troubles 273
    Tax problems 273
    Information difficulties 274
Buying ADRs Is an Easy Solution 274
    The risks of international investments 275
    Online ADR resources and research 276
Indirect Foreign Investing Is a Great Approach 276
    Diversification through foreign funds 277
    Buying shares in multinational companies 278
Finding International Mutual Funds Online 278

Chapter 15: Looking for the Next Big Thing: IPOs, DPOs, and DRIPs 281
Looking for Investment Opportunities: IPOs 282
    Getting the scoop on IPOs 283
    Understanding the limitations of IPOs 284
    Locating IPO online super-sites 285
    The Internet and your IPO timetable 288
Be Your Own Broker with Direct Public Offerings (DPOs) 290
    Recognizing the limitations of DPOs 290
    Buying DPOs 291
Buying Stock in a Direct Purchase Plan (DPP) 292

Profiting with Dividend Reinvestment Plans (DRIPs)............................296
   Additional features of DRIPs 297
   Not all DRIPs are alike..297
   How to get your first DRIP share...298
   Selecting the right DRIP 299

Chapter 16: Taking the Option: Alternative Investing 301

Trading Stock Options...301
   Types of option contracts 302
   Exercising your stock option 302
   Call options 303
   Put options 303
Education and Data Sources...304
   Online sources for option quotes...305
   Online sources for options news and data 305
Option Screeners and Calculators 307
Determining Stock Option Values 308
   Taking a closer look at options...309
   Discovering what your options are worth 310
   Online brokerages and options 311
Software Tools for Options Trading...312
Checking Out the Latest Strategies 314

Chapter 17: The Internet and Managing Your Portfolio 315

Why Manage Your Investments? 316
Tracking the Right Information 317
Balancing Your Portfolio with Web-Based Asset Allocation Tools 318
Using the Internet to Uncover the Risk in Your Portfolio 319
   RiskGrades 319
   FinPortfolio..320
   Morningstar..320
Keeping the Winners and Selling the Losers:
   Measuring Performance 321
Your Portfolio Management Options 322
Purchasing Portfolio Investment Programs..323
Using Web-Based Portfolio Management Programs 324
Following Online News with Portfolio Tracking..327
   Business news...327
   Portal portfolio management...328
   Portfolio management alerts 329
Using PC-Based Portfolio Management Software......................................330
   Personal finance software programs 331
   MS Money 331
   Quicken...332
   Portfolio management software programs 333

Part IV: The Part of Tens 337

Chapter 18: Ten Warnings About Cyberfraud 339
Don't Believe Everything You Read 340
    Multilevel marketing plans and pyramid schemes 340
    Financial chain letters and Ponzi schemes 341
    Cons based on bogus research reports and newsletters.............342
    Phishing for your personal information 343
    Nigerian e-mail letter investment scam.......................................344
    Investment hoaxes designed to get your cash 344
    Bogus IRA-approved investment schemes....................................345
    Guaranteed high returns frauds 345
    Get rich quick with investment seminars 346
    Pump-and-dump schemes..346
If an Offer Seems Too Good to Be True, It Usually Is 347
Checking It Out Before You Put Your Money Down 348
Understanding What Real Financial Disclosures Include 349
Telltale Signs of Dishonest Brokers 350
Where to Complain Online..352

Chapter 19: Ten Important Selling Points 353
Determining Your Personal Selling Rules.................................353
    The stock drops below your predetermined trading range 354
    You discover that the company's relative
        strength is flat or trending downward 355
    You recognize that the industry is in a serious downturn............355
    You determine that the company is in decline...............................355
    You discover that the company's profitability or
        financial health is in trouble...356
    Market experts call the company "steady" or dividend
        increases are behind the general market 356
    Company insiders are selling in the public marketplace.............356
Rebalancing Your Portfolio: Which Winners Should You Sell?.............357
Setting Profit-Taking Goals..358
You Can't Be Right All the Time 358
If the Stock Is Going Nowhere, Get Going 359
Don't Be Fooled by P/E Spurts 359
Watch Interest Rates...359
Keep an Eye on Economic Indicators 360
Sell When the Insiders Sell...360
Get Out if the Company or Fund Changes 361
A Final Word about Stopping Profit Wipe-Outs 361

Chapter 20: Ten Green Flags for Buying 365

Digging Out of a Recession with Dollar-Cost Averaging........................366
Buy If the Stock Is at Its Lowest Price 367
Invest in Companies with Beautiful Balance Sheets 367
Check Out the Earnings Forecast...368
Watch for Stocks That Are Trading under Book Value 368
Look for Strong Dividend Pay-Out Records 369
Seek Out Firms with Low Debt Ratios 369
Invest in Industry Leaders 369
Buy Good Performers 370
Select Your P/E Ratio Strategy...370
    Low P/E and high dividend approach..371
    High P/E ratios are worth the price 371

Index 373

Introduction

*W*elcome to *Investing Online For Dummies,* 5th Edition, and to the exciting world of online investing. Regardless of whether you're a new investor or an experienced trader, this book can guide you to the Internet-based resources that can help you make better, more informed investing decisions than ever before. The Internet offers an astounding amount of financial information, and *Investing Online For Dummies,* 5th Edition, provides clear instructions and ample illustrations so that you don't get lost in cyberspace. With the assistance of this book, you can find up-to-the-second stock quotes, historical financial data on public companies, professional analyses, educational materials, and more.

In this book, I show you how to get started, what you really need to know, and where to go on the Internet for additional information. You don't need to memorize complex commands or formulas. I describe everything in plain English, and I leave the Wall Street–speak out in the street.

Thousands of new Web pages are added each day. Many institutions bring educational and government materials online, large and small commercial enterprises create Web-based services, and individuals also account for much of the content that is posted online. This vast amount of content continues to grow in size and sophistication but still remains user-friendly. New online investor applications are added on a regular basis. Today you can fine-tune your online investing in more ways than ever before because more Internet resources are out there than ever before.

As the amount of online content constantly increases, it also changes. Some sites listed in this book may have changed or gone away due to mergers with larger sites. Some Web sites just vanish for no reason. If a site has moved, you may find a link to the new location. If not, try a search engine such as Google (www.google.com), Yahoo! (www.yahoo.com), or MSN (search.msn.com) to locate the resource you need.

Who Are You?

According to the Pew Internet & American Life Project (www.pewinternet.org), one out of every ten Internet users has bought or sold stocks online. As of September 2002, this number was about 12 percent of all Internet users. The survey goes on to state that

✔ On a typical day, between 1 and 3 percent of all Internet users buy or sell stocks, bonds, or mutual funds online. Additionally, online investing grew by 40 percent from March 2000 (10 million Americans) to September 2002 (14 million Americans).

✔ More men than women are likely to buy or sell stock online. As a matter of fact, the ratio of men to women making trades is two to one.

✔ Age doesn't seem to play a significant role in who's investing online. However, Internet users in the 30-to-49-year age bracket seem to take the lead in this area.

✔ Educated individuals with higher incomes are more likely to have traded online than other online users. As of September 2002, about 17 percent of Internet users with college degrees had bought or sold stocks online. Only 8 percent of those individuals without a college degree had traded stocks online. The study also indicated that individuals with household incomes of $75,000 or more are four times as likely to have traded securities online.

✔ More experienced Internet users are more likely to buy or sell stocks online. Moreover, individuals with high-speed connections (that result in real-time streaming stock quotes and other financial information) are more likely to trade online.

A September 2004 study by J. D. Power (www.jdpower.com) of 4,885 online investors indicated that newer online investors have different characteristics than more experienced online investors: These newer online investors:

✔ **Are younger and female:** Newer investors tend to be 18- to 34-years-old and female.

✔ **Are more conservative:** The volatility of the market and decreased returns on investments have made newer online investors more cautious.

✔ **Have smaller portfolios:** Newer online investors tend to have smaller portfolios and a lower risk-tolerance level.

Throughout this book, I assume that you want to join the ranks of newer online investors or that you already invest online and want to maximize your returns. Therefore, you want to

✔ **Take advantage of all the timely investment information available on the Internet.**

✔ **Get some work done with the Internet.** Online selecting, evaluating, and monitoring of investments can be time-consuming. Online investing really is work.

✔ **Partner with the Internet in making your money work harder for you.**

About This Book

This book has no hidden agenda. It focuses on common-sense ways to create and build wealth with the Internet.

I've designed *Investing Online For Dummies,* 5th Edition, for beginning online investors, but experienced investors can also benefit from it. Each chapter stands alone and provides all the instructions and information you need to solve an investment problem or to make an investment decision.

Most online investors will read this book in chunks, diving in long enough to solve a particular investment problem ("Hmmm, which online brokerages offer wireless trading?") and then putting it aside. However, I've structured the book in such a way that if you want to read it from beginning to end (even though the book's primary function is as a reference tool), you can do so.

I discuss online investment topics in a logical way, from online investing fundamentals through making your own online stock transactions to purchasing bonds online and directly from the federal government.

Here's a quick rundown on some of the topics I cover:

- Building your own online investment information system
- Using the Internet to simplify your financial planning
- Selecting the online brokerage that meets your individual needs
- Finding personalized trading platforms from major online brokerages
- Locating Internet resources for the selection of mutual funds
- Working with Internet tools for analyzing and selecting stocks and bonds
- Using mutual fund and stock online screens to find investment candidates that will help you meet your financial goals
- Trading online or going wireless and paying the lowest commissions possible
- Keeping track of your portfolio and knowing exactly how your assets are allocated (even the holdings in your mutual funds)
- Discovering direct stock purchase and ShareBuilder plans that let you become an online investor for as little as $25 a month
- Uncovering how stock options work and determining the value of your employee stock option plan
- Finding out how to take advantage of international opportunities online

Additionally, I offer warnings to help you avoid dangerous or costly traps, and I point out excellent online investment resources. *Investing Online For Dummies,* 5th Edition, puts you in the driver's seat on the Information Superhighway. It provides the Internet knowledge you need to get the edge on investors who rely solely on newspapers and magazines.

How to Use This Book

If you have a question about an online investing topic, just look up that topic in the table of contents at the beginning of the book or in the index at the end of the book. You can get the help you seek immediately or find out where to look for expert advice.

Investing has evolved into a specialized field and isn't particularly easy for "normal" people. Don't feel bad if you have to use the table of contents and the index quite a bit. Luckily, the Internet offers plenty of sites that let you practice before you buy or trade.

If you want to experience electronic trading (and are concerned that a mistake may cost you money), try practicing at the Investing Online Resource Center, located at www.investingonline.org. The Investing Online Resource Center includes a free stock market simulation center. You can test-drive online investing or try out a new investment strategy without losing a dime or having to register.

If you're new to investing on the Internet, check out the first three chapters in Part I. They give you an overview of the Internet and some important investor tips. To get more familiar with the Internet, try some of the activities that I detail in these chapters.

If you're new to the Internet, I recommend getting a copy of *The Internet For Dummies,* 10th Edition, by John R. Levine, Carol Baroudi, and Margaret Levine Young (Wiley Publishing). This book is great for anyone who needs help getting started with the Internet. *The Internet For Dummies*, 10th Edition, can assist you in hooking up with local Internet providers, surfing the Net, downloading free software, and joining mailing lists or user groups.

If you're a new investor, check out Chapter 18, which offers warnings about online frauds, schemes, and deceptions. When you start subscribing to investor newsgroups, mailing lists, or online publications, you're likely to receive e-mail stock tips and investment offers. Treat these messages as you would any telephone cold call. Thoroughly examine the investment and get a second opinion from an independent investment expert you respect before you purchase.

How This Book Is Organized

This book has four parts. Each part stands alone — that is, you can begin reading anywhere and get the information you need for investment decision-making. Or you can read the entire book from cover to cover. The first part of this book lays the groundwork that beginning online investors need. The next three parts focus on how you can navigate the Internet to get the information you want about specific types of investments, online trading, and portfolio tracking.

Here's a quick rundown of the parts of the book and what they contain.

Part I: Online Investing Fundamentals

In Part I, you find out what investor tools are available on the Internet for special interest groups such as children, college students, seniors, and women. The chapters in Part I discuss important investor uses of the Internet: searches for financial topics, electronic mail, newsgroups, and access to databases that until recently were only available to large financial institutions. You also find out how to make your money work harder and how to find an online brokerage that meets your individual needs. You clearly see how new online trading platforms and technology can make online investing assist you in achieving your personal financial objectives.

Part II: Finding the Right Investments

The chapters in Part II show you how to find the right investments and the best ways of purchasing those investments. This part of the book describes how you can select, analyze, and buy mutual funds, stocks, and bonds on the Internet. The chapters in this part of the book cut through the jargon and get to the heart of what investments are (and what they're not). These chapters help you understand rates of return and what mutual funds, stocks, and bonds are all about. They also cover how to research and analyze stocks and bonds online. I point you to many online sources for annual reports, economic data, analyst recommendations, industry standards, and more. You discover great online investment analysis tools so that you don't have to be a math whiz to determine which investment is best.

Part III: Expanding Your Investment Opportunities

Part III includes a chapter that details how to evaluate international investments. You also find out how to use the Internet to find investment opportunities, such as initial public offerings (IPOs) and dividend reinvestment plans (DRIPs), how to find information about stock options, and how to evaluate the value of your employee stock option plan. This part of the book also covers online portfolio management and explores some of the latest tools available online.

Part IV: The Part of Tens

No more guessing about what to hold and when to fold. Part IV provides handy top-ten lists packed full of ready online references. The chapters in this part cover such essentials as avoiding cyberfraud, knowing when to hold and when to fold, and recognizing buying signals.

What's New

A number of features have been added to this edition that make using *Investing Online For Dummies* an even more exciting and beneficial reference book. Changes throughout *Investing Online For Dummies,* 5th Edition, include new investor-related Web sites and updated information about Web sites that now require user registration. This revised edition shows how some Web sites now charge fees for access and provides alternative Web sites that provide similar content at no charge.

Investing Online For Dummies, 5th Edition, omits obsolete Web sites or Web sites that have gone out of business and includes new online investor Web sites that offer improved content or services. Statistics, tables, and graphs have all been updated. The emphasis of many chapters has changed to reflect current trends in online investing. The following are highlights of what you find:

- ✔ Due to the aging of America, the interest in tax-deferred accounts has dramatically increased. Therefore, you find more information about the benefits of individual retirement accounts (IRA) and how the Internet can assist you in maximizing your IRA returns (see Chapter 3).

- ✔ In the early days of online investing, online stock-picking communities were overflowing with "pump-and-dump" schemes, wild corporate rumors, and other nefarious activities. Today's stock-picking Web sites and stock-picking communities have matured into online resources that can be helpful in identifying securities that are winners (check out Chapter 3).

- ✔ Get introduced to online "bankerages" in Chapter 4. By combining your online banking and brokerage account, you can save time and money, as well as enjoy the flexibility and convenience you couldn't get with scattered services.

- ✔ Is your life too complex? Want a simple way to invest? See Chapter 6 and try online investing in index or exchanged-traded funds.

- ✔ Online investors can now use Web sites to examine and compare mutual fund fees to determine the true cost of a mutual fund. Get the scoop in Chapter 7.

- ✔ See Chapter 8 for new, robust, online stock and bond valuation tools developed by academics and specialists.

✔ Refer to Chapter 10 to discover how you can use the Internet to take a closer look at corporate governance and discover the warning signs of a company's bankruptcy before it's too late.

✔ Get up-to-date information about the dramatic changes in buying savings bonds and Treasury securities online in Chapter 13.

✔ In Chapter 17, discover online asset allocation tools that were previously available only to financial institutions. See how you can use these online tools to make certain that you're adequately compensated for the risk you are taking by making an investment.

And so much more . . .

Icons Used in This Book

Throughout *Investing Online For Dummies,* 5th Edition, I use icons to help guide you through all the suggestions, solutions, cautions, and World Wide Web sites. I hope you find that the following icons make your journey through online investment strategies smoother.

This icon indicates an explanation for a nifty little shortcut or time-saver.

This icon points out riskier investment strategies plus other things to watch out for.

The Technical Stuff icon lets you know that some particularly nerdy, technoid information is coming up so that you can skip it if you want. (On the other hand, you might want to read it.)

The Remember icon highlights information that you should file away for future reference. This is basic information that you need to use over and over again.

Feedback, Please

I'm always interested in your comments, suggestions, or questions. I'd love to hear from you. Please feel free to contact me in care of Wiley Publishing, 10475 Crosspoint Blvd., Indianapolis, IN 46256. Better yet, visit my Web site at `www.kathleensindell.com` or send me an e-mail message at `ksindell@kathleensindell.com`.

Part I
Online Investing Fundamentals

The 5th Wave By Rich Tennant

"The first thing you should know about investing online is that when you see the exploding bomb icon appear, it's just your browser crashing — not your portfolio."

In this part . . .

The chapters in this part help you discover why the Internet should be your starting point for researching investments. You find out how to develop your own online investment information system that is geared to your specific requirements. These chapters point you to a variety of online investor resources and data, including numerous Web sites geared primarily toward the beginning investor. You see how to maximize your returns with tax-deferred accounts. You also discover how online brokerages and banks have combined to save you time and money. Find out how to select an online brokerage or one of these new hybrids. Test-drive trading online and see what's new in customizable trading platforms from major online brokerages.

Chapter 1

Finding Investor Stuff on the Net

- -

In This Chapter

▶ Creating your own online information system

▶ Using search engines

▶ Joining newsgroups

▶ Subscribing to Internet mailing lists

▶ Accessing online databases

▶ Finding Web sites that fit your unique needs

- -

*T*he Internet has more than two billion Web pages and is still growing. This information overload has sent some timid investors to full-service brokers, where they pay high commission fees for brokerage services and investment advice. Smart online investors can avoid information overload by developing their own information systems.

This chapter shows how you can take maximum advantage of the Internet's many investment tools, links, and resources. The chapter explains the Internet basics of using search engines, finding investor newsgroups, subscribing to investor mailing lists, accessing online databases, and using Web sites tailored to your specific needs to maximize your personal wealth.

Building Your Own Online Information System

Investments provide opportunities to make money in both a *bull* market (that is, an up market) and a *bear* (down) market. No one ever knows for certain whether the market will go up or down, but investors can develop an information system to watch indicators for potential price changes and investment opportunities. This chapter introduces the elements you can use for building an online investment information system that meets your specific needs.

Investment indicators often signal future market trends. For example, changes in bond prices and interest rates often reflect trends that may affect stock prices. That is, if bond yields decline, investors often rush to purchase stocks, causing stock prices to increase.

Investors need this information to decide whether they should buy, sell, or hold. Gathering, organizing, and saving this information can be time-consuming. However, using your own online information system can make the process more efficient.

Successful investing involves five basic steps:

1. **Identifying new investments**
2. **Analyzing investment candidates**
3. **Purchasing investments**
4. **Monitoring investments**
5. **Selling investments — and reaping your rewards**

The following sections summarize online sources of the information you need for each step. Knowing what type of information you need and where to get it online can help you build your personalized online information system.

Identifying new investments

Before investing, you need to clearly state your financial objectives and know your risk-tolerance level. This information can help you determine your required rate of return. By doing this type of homework, you can determine which categories of financial assets you may want to consider investing in. For example, if you're selecting investments for your Individual Retirement Account (IRA), you don't want to invest in tax-exempt municipal bonds (because being tax-exempt twice isn't the best way to make use of tax exemptions).

Here are some examples of online sources for identifying investment opportunities:

- **Company profiles** describe a firm's organization, products, financial position, chief competitors, and executive management. (See Chapter 10 for details.)

- **Direct purchase plans** (DPPs) show how to purchase stock in a company without paying a broker's commission. (See Chapter 15.)

- **Directories of investor sources** provide hard-to-find information that's necessary for investment decision-making.

✔ **Dividend reinvestment plans** (DRIPs) describe how to join dividend reinvestment programs to purchase company stock at a discount and without a broker. (Chapter 15 shows you how to get started.)

✔ **Initial public offerings** (IPOs) are new opportunities for investor profits. (See Chapter 15.)

✔ **Investing *e-zines*** (electronic magazines) provide educational articles and pertinent facts for beginning and experienced investors. (See Chapter 2.)

✔ **Mailing lists** provide opinions and investors' insights about investment candidates. (I discuss mailing lists later in this chapter, in the section, "Uncovering Investor Information from Mailing Lists.")

✔ **News reports** on the Net can provide information about new investment opportunities. (See Chapter 11.)

✔ **Newsgroups** are informal, online groups of individuals who share their ideas about a common interest. You can find dozens of investment-related newsgroups with topics ranging from specific types of investments to investor strategies. (See "Understanding How Newsgroups Can Help You," later in this chapter.)

✔ **Online databases** (free and fee-based repositories of information) provide historical stock prices, economic forecasts, and more. (See the section "Using Free and Fee-Based Online Investor Databases," later in this chapter, for examples of what's available.)

✔ **Search engines** (specialized Internet programs that seek the data you desire) provide you with links to the Web pages that have the investor information you want. (I discuss search engines later in this chapter, in the section "Setting Up Your Basic Investment Search Strategy.")

✔ **Stock recommendations** from professionals enable you to find out what brokers and analysts are saying about your investment selections. (See Chapter 11.)

✔ **Mutual fund and stock screens** for selecting specific securities enable you to sort through thousands of investment candidates in seconds to find not only the right investment but also the best investment available. (I discuss Internet-based mutual fund screening in Chapter 6 and stock screening in Chapter 9.)

Analyzing investment prospects

The process of analyzing investment prospects includes examining groups of investments or individual securities. For this task, you need information to forecast the timing and amount of future cash flows of investment candidates. That is, the price you pay today is based on the future income of the asset.

Figuring out what the asset will be worth in the future requires some homework, analysis, and luck. Here are a few examples of online sources for this type of information:

- ✔ **Company profiles and annual reports** often forecast the company's future revenues and earnings. (For more information about finding annual reports online, see Chapter 10. You can find more information about company profiles in Chapter 11.)

- ✔ **Databases** (free and fee-based online sources) provide news, market commentary, historical stock prices, economic forecasts, industry standards, and competitor information. I introduce you to these databases in the section "Using Free and Fee-Based Online Investor Databases," later in this chapter.

- ✔ **Earnings estimates** from brokers and analysts give you forecasts of a company's future earnings. (See Chapter 11.)

- ✔ **Industry or business-sector news** can frequently indicate whether an industry is in a downward cycle. (See Chapter 11.)

- ✔ **National economic data** can point you toward a particular investment strategy. For example, if the country is going into a recession, you may want to select stocks that provide you with some defense. (See Chapter 11.)

- ✔ **News databases** offer breaking news that can help you judge whether your stock purchase is a winner or a loser. (Chapter 2 offers a good overview of online news sources.)

- ✔ **Securities and Exchange Commission (SEC) filings** provide you with financial statements from publicly traded companies. These companies are required to file financial statements every 90 days and more often if big events are happening within the firm. More than 7,000 publicly traded firms are now filing online. (For details, see Chapter 10.)

Purchasing investments

After you decide which investments you want to purchase, you have to decide how you want to purchase them. For example, you must decide whether you want a full-service broker or, for online investing, either a premium discount broker who offers online trades and advice or a discount broker that only executes your trades and doesn't offer any recommendations. (See Chapter 4 for details.)

You may participate in an *automatic investment plan* (AIP). With your approval, this type of plan deducts a certain amount from your checking account to purchase mutual funds, savings bonds, or other investments. (Chapter 7 provides step-by-step directions for opening an AIP account.)

Monitoring investments

If you have more than one investment, you likely want to monitor and compare their performances to the market and to similar investments. Here are a few examples of the information and the software you need to accomplish this objective:

- ✔ Market-monitoring tools send alerts that you determine. For example, if your stock increases by 25 percent, you may want to consider selling it. You can set up an alert that sends you an e-mail message notifying you that your stock has reached this target.

- ✔ The Internet provides many portfolio management programs that let you know when your investments are in the news.

- ✔ Online portfolio management tools can automatically send you an e-mail message at the end of the day to let you know whether your investments gained or lost value.

- ✔ PC-based portfolio management tools are downloadable software programs that assist you in tracking your investments and record keeping.

- ✔ Your online broker may track your portfolio for you and keep records of your profits and losses.

See Chapter 17 for more details about online portfolio management.

Selling investments

You need to decide what proportion of your personal wealth you want to invest in specific assets, how long you want to hold those assets, and whether now is a good time to sell those assets to harvest your rewards. To that end, you need information about the following topics:

- ✔ **Asset allocation methodologies:** You need to determine what portion of your portfolio should be invested in mutual funds, stocks, and bonds. (See Chapter 3 to find a strategy that's right for you.)

- ✔ **Capital gains and tax issues:** The Smart Money Capital Gains Guide (www.smartmoney.com/tax/capital) can assist you in understanding the tax implications of investing activities.

- ✔ **Selling strategies:** Determining when you should harvest your investments requires using specific order execution strategies, mutual fund redemption plans, and analyses. (See Chapters 4, 5, 7, and 17 to explore these topics in more detail.)

Setting Up Your Basic Investment Search Strategy

Search engines are commercial enterprises that collect and index Web pages or Web page titles. You can use them to help you sift through all the Web pages out there so that you can find the information you need.

Some of these enterprises review the sites they collect, and others provide site information unfiltered and unedited. Some search engines (like Yahoo! at www.yahoo.com) are hierarchical indexes and use subject listings that are similar to the card catalog in a library. Often, you can search hierarchical indexes by *keyword* (a word that sums up or describes the item or concept that you're seeking) and by topic.

Knowing how to use a search engine is a basic Internet skill. Currently, more than 600 different search engines exist on the Net. These Internet tools can be divided into two categories: metasearch engines and search engines.

Metasearch engines

Metasearch engines enable you to enter a single search term to query many individual search engines. This kind of all-in-one shopping is used to match your inquiry to the millions of Web pages on the Internet. Metasearch engines often have different approaches to presenting your results. Some metasearch engines just query a wide variety of search engines and report your results without you having to go to several search engines. Other metasearch engines bypass existing search engines and query multiple online sources for your search results. Here are some examples of metasearch engines:

- **Dogpile** (www.dogpile.com) searches the Web, Usenet newsgroups, FTP sites (sites for downloading software and data via FTP — the file transfer protocol), weather information, stock quotes, business news, and other news wires. (For more information about Usenet newsgroups, see the section "Understanding How Newsgroups Can Help You," later in this chapter.) This site also includes a Web catalog.

- **Momma** (www.momma.com) simultaneously queries a series of search engines and properly formats the words and syntax for each source being probed. The search results are then organized into a uniform format and presented by relevance and source.

- **Metacrawler** (www.metacrawler.com/index.html) works like Dogpile but doesn't search Usenet newsgroups and FTP (file transfer protocol) sites. Search results aren't annotated.

✔ **SurfWax** (www.surfwax.com) allows users to put together search sets. For example, an "Investor" SearchSet can include *The Wall Street Journal,* CNNfn, *The New York Times,* and so on. You can also use tools for exploring search results. For example, SiteSnaps allows you to quickly view page content, and ContextZooming allows you to search highlighted terms. FocusWords offers suggestions about how you can narrow or broaden your search. Finally, you can use an InfoCubby to save your search results for later retrieval. SurfWax offers three levels of service (free, silver, and gold). With your free registration, you receive the free level of service that includes three SearchSets of up to 15 sources each. Silver and Gold subscribers pay $24 and $60 per year, respectively. Each registered level has access to all of SurfWax's capabilities; the difference is the extent of permitted uses. (Firm pricing is available on a custom basis.)

✔ **Profusion** (www.profusion.com) allows you to search one, some, or all of the listings from AltaVista, About, AOL, Lycos, Raging Search, WiseNut, Metacrawler, MSN, Adobe PDF, LookSmart, Netscape, Teoma, and AllTheWeb. You can fine-tune your search by selecting your search type, the number of results per page, the number of results per source, and when you want the search to timeout. You can narrow your search by looking into vertical search groups, such as Business or Finance.

✔ **Vivisimo** (www.vivisimo.com) technology was developed by researchers at Carnegie Mellon University. Vivisimo doesn't index the Web; it simultaneously searches several major search engines and directories (such as Fast, MSN, Yahoo!, AltaVista, Lycos, Open Directory, Excite, and WebCrawler). The Vivisimo technology then groups results into clusters of titled folders that best fit the query.

Popular search engines

Search engines are trustworthy Internet programs that match the words in your query to words on the Internet. Each search engine is a competitive, commercial enterprise with different databases, search programs, and features. Everyone has a favorite search engine. The search engine that is best is the one that works the best for you.

Search engines employ *spiders* or *crawlers* (robot programs) that constantly seek new information on the Internet. These robot programs index and categorize their findings and then let you probe their lists with keywords. The engine shows your search results with short descriptions and hyperlinks. Just click the hyperlink to go to the Web page you seek.

Personalized search engines

With more than two billion Web pages, your search for investment information is likely to dredge up many articles that are outdated or simply not relevant. One way to increase your treasure-to-trash ratio is to use a personalized search engine. My Yahoo! (my.yahoo.com) allows users to set up profiles for (among other things) specific news topics and a stock portfolio.

The My Excite Web site (my.excite.com) includes much of the same personalization features as My Yahoo! With your free registration, you can select page colors, settings, content, and layout (two columns or three?).

Here are a few of the more popular search engines on the Net:

- ✔ **Excite** (www.excite.com) enables you to browse many subject categories, such as investing. It uses a combination of concept (a general idea) and keyword (a specific word in the Web page) searches, so the results are usually pretty good. If you're unsatisfied with your findings, click the Excite Metasearch link at the bottom of the page for more results.

- ✔ **Google** (www.google.com) is currently ranked as the number-one search engine. It has the largest amount of the Internet indexed. Google offers the Google Toolbar, a quick-and-easy-to-install toolbar that automatically appears along with the Internet Explorer toolbar to increase your ability to speedily find information on the Net.

- ✔ **MSN** (search.msn.com) enables you to set preferences to automatically correct spelling errors, select the number of results per page, and determine whether search responses should include summaries. Additionally, you can search from any one of MSN's international Web sites. If you're unfamiliar with search engines, click Help to get the advice you need. Additionally, MSN has a new beta that is supposed to be a "Google beater," a search engine, index, and crawler. For more information see beta.search.msn.com/default.aspx?FORM=HPRE.

- ✔ **Yahoo!** (www.yahoo.com) is a popular starting point. This directory search engine includes a vast array of subject directories, categories, and special services, such as People Search, Weekly Picks, What's New This Week, Yahoo! Loan Center, Finance Yahoo!, and Real Estate Yahoo!

Selecting the best search engine

With more than two billion Web pages on the Internet, finding the one page you need to complete your investor research can be difficult. Using search engines is often like a crapshoot. Sometimes you win (and you find the Web page you want), and sometimes you lose (you find no relevant Web pages in your search results). If you lose, you have to go to another search engine and spend more time researching.

Not all search engines are equal. Some have indexed a large portion of the Internet. Others are just starting or are slow in keeping up with the thousands of new Web pages that are added each day. To be competitive, search engines are always adding new features. Some search engine databases include Usenet, mailing lists, news sources, indexes, directories, Web sites, company profiles, and other information. Other search engines include only a portion of this data.

When you evaluate search engines, see how they match up to the following criteria:

- ✔ **Subject directory:** Does the search engine enable you to limit searches to specific subject areas? Searches are quicker if the search engine offers a subject directory because it searches only in the topic area that you specify.

- ✔ **Results ranking:** Does the search engine rate your search results so that you know how likely you are to find what you're looking for? (For example, listings with relevancy ratings of less than 90 percent are usually worthless.)

- ✔ **Web:** Does the search engine look through the World Wide Web for your results?

- ✔ **URL (Uniform Resource Locator):** Does the search engine provide the Internet addresses for your search results? Getting the address can be very helpful; you can save or print the results of your search and then later you can backtrack and get to those difficult-to-find Web sites.

- ✔ **Summary:** Does the search engine provide a short text description of the search results?

- ✔ **Boolean searches:** Does the search engine allow you to conduct more targeted searches?

Portal is another name for search engine. Portals are designed to be the Internet user's first window on the Web. Often, you can personalize portals to get financial news, current portfolio data, and interest rate information before moving on to other Web sites. Examples of portals include CBS MarketWatch (www.cbsmarketwatch.com), Microsoft Network (www.msn.com), and MSNBC (www.msnbc.msn.com).

Understanding How Newsgroups Can Help You

Newsgroups are discussion forums (or electronic bulletin boards) where individuals post messages for others to read and answer. New newsgroups appear — and old, unused newsgroups disappear — almost daily.

The advantage of these groups is that the opinions of authors are disparate and come from around the world. There are between 20,000 and 50,000 publicly accessible newsgroups. Some of these newsgroups are filled with spam (junk mail), and others are inactive shells. Newsgroups range from serious to silly and support almost all religious ideologies, political points of view, and philosophical beliefs. If you want to know what investors think about a particular investment, a newsgroup is a good place to look for the answer. Newsgroup participants aren't necessarily investment professionals, but many of them are savvy investors.

Knowing how newsgroups are named can help you determine whether a certain newsgroup may interest you. Newsgroup names typically have two or more parts. The first section of a newsgroup's name is the most general grouping or topic. Here are some examples of different first names that may be of interest to online investors:

Section	Description
Alt	Alternative subjects, ranging from the serious (investing and finance) to the weird (occult and alternative lifestyles)
Biz	Business subjects, including commercials
Misc	Miscellaneous topics, from items for sale to finance

Newsgroups can have names with two sections. For example the first section can be `alt`, and the second section can be `invest`. The name of the newsgroup then would be `alt.invest`. Some newsgroups do not have any subgroups, but others have 20 or more subgroups under the major topic. One example of a major topic is `alt.invest.real-estate`, which branches into other newsgroups, such as `alt.invest.real-estate.methods`. That is, each component of the name represents a different level in the newsgroup. The last named component is the actual theme of the group. For example, `alt.invest.real-estate` is about investing in real estate.

Subscribing to a newsgroup is easy. With most browsers, you simply click the name of the newsgroup you want to subscribe to. For details, use your Web browser to check out Beginners Central at Northern Webs (`www.northern webs.com/bc/index.html`). Discover how to navigate your browser's newsreader, select a newsgroup, and post to newsgroups.

Finding the perfect newsgroup

The Internet provides various sources for finding Usenet newsgroups. Here are a few examples:

- **Harley Hahn** (www.harley.com/usenet) provides Harley Hahn's Master List of Usenet Newsgroups. The master list includes a short description of each newsgroup, placed in a category and organized in an easy-to-use search list.

- **Yahoo! Groups** (groups.yahoo.com) offers nearly 3,000 investment groups and more than 600 online investing mailing lists. In this population, 60 subgroups focus on e*Trade. Registration is free. You can even start your own Yahoo! group.

- **Robot Wisdom Newsgroup Finder** (www.robotwisdom.com/finder/index.html) enables you to search by historical period, numbers of articles, and country or state locations. This site uses clickable maps of the United States and the world. Responses include the newsgroup name, address, description, charter, and sometimes Frequently Asked Questions (FAQs) if available.

Tired of the same old newsgroups? Discover all the Web's new newgroups by going to Newsville at www.newsville.com/news/newnews.html.

Finally, some investor news reading

One of the easiest ways to find newsgroups is to go to Google (www.google.com). Click Groups, then click Browse all of Usenet. At the next Web page shown in Figure 1-1, to select your topic enter your keyword in the Directory Search or scroll through the Usenet names. Regardless of which approach you select, you'll discover a listing of newsgroups that may be of interest to you. Each group includes the group's name, a description of the group, the group's category, and other characteristics. These characteristics can include information about the number of group members, whether the group is open to the public, restricted, moderated, and so on.

The best feature of this site is that you can post your questions directly to the newsgroup without a great deal of fuss. You can also search newsgroup articles for keywords. For example, assume that you're thinking about investing in Microsoft. As part of your research, you can see what newsgroup members had to say about the company, and when they said it.

Another great feature is that you can research the author of the newsgroup article. Google shows how many articles the author has posted and which newsgroup that author is posting to. This data can indicate which newsgroups regularly carry the type of information you're seeking.

Figure 1-1:
Google has
introduced a
new way to
search for
newsgroups.

Getting the Message from Investor Message Boards

With investor message boards, you can read what other online investors are saying about an investment that may interest you. Overall, these message boards include many honest, knowledgeable investors, with only a few unscrupulous fraudsters with questionable intentions. Therefore, you must determine what is sound advice and what is trash. Make certain that you complete your own research before acting on any message board information. The following are a few of the top-rated investor message boards online:

✔ **Silicon Investor** (www.siliconinvestor.com/stocktalk) has several levels of membership. Basic membership is free with your registration. The free, limited level allows you to post between one and two messages per day. You can't turn off ads and can't make use of advanced features such as Next 10 and Search. Paying subscribers have unlimited posting privileges, the ability to turn off ads, and access to Next 10, Search, and Advanced Search features. Subscriptions are $19.95 per month, $29.95 per $29.95, and $49.95 for six months. Annual subscriptions are $89.95, and a lifetime subscription is $199.95.

✔ **The Motley Fool** (`boards.fool.com`) is free with your registration. Here you find company discussions sorted by name, industry, and market analysis, as well as an investors' roundtable for discussing strategies. Before you post, don't forget to read the "Fool Community Guidelines" at `www.fool.com/help/?display=community04`.

✔ **Raging Bull** (`www.ragingbull.com`), now owned by Lycos, has more than 15,000 active message boards. Participants earn a "power rating" that indicates how much credibility a member has earned with the community. Features include lists of the most active message boards and message boards with the greatest number of posts.

Uncovering Investor Information from Mailing Lists

Mailing lists are e-mail groups that are started by organizations or individuals who purchase mailing list programs. Then they advertise to others who may be interested in joining a topic-specific discussion group. The advertisement usually provides precise instructions for subscribing to the mailing list.

You subscribe to a particular mailing list by sending an e-mail message to the list's moderator. In return, you receive an e-mail message confirming your enrollment. This message typically includes the address you use for posting messages to the mailing list, the rules of the discussion group, and instructions for removing your name — that is, *unsubscribing* — from the mailing list.

Mailing list participants exchange e-mail about issues in their subject areas. If someone starts a *thread,* or topic, that you want to comment on, you post your comments to the list, using the instructions you received when you subscribed.

To answer questions or make comments, subscribers send an e-mail message to the mailing list address (which differs from the mailing list program's address), and everyone gets a copy of the message. Unlike newsgroups, most lists are moderated so that inappropriate messages aren't sent to the group.

Today more than 300,000 mailing lists exist. You may find a mailing list while surfing the Net, but they tend to be private. The best source for finding an investor-related mailing list is Tile.net (`www.tile.net`). Tile.net has more than 66,000 public mailing lists and is growing. Don't despair; the site is searchable and provides information that describes each mailing list and how to subscribe (and, more importantly, how to unsubscribe if it doesn't meet your requirements). Another good mailing list directory is CataList (`www.lsoft.com/lists/listref.html`), which includes more than 66,000 mailing lists. It's searchable by site, country, and number of list subscribers.

(Sometimes knowing how many subscribers will receive your investment question is a good idea.)

Don't lose that information about how to unsubscribe! Mailing list members receive an average of 30 messages per day. If you just signed up for four mailing lists, you may have more than a hundred messages tomorrow.

Using Free and Fee-Based Online Investor Databases

Online investors have their choice of searching free or fee-based online databases. One advantage of both types of databases is that they're constantly open. That is, you can access them 24 hours a day, 7 days a week.

It's a no-brainer that savvy online investors should start with the free databases. If the information you desire isn't available in the free databases, try fee-based databases. If you carefully select a fee-based database for your well-constructed query, you can often get the information you want without paying big bucks.

Totally free databases

The Internet is a network of networks linking millions of computers worldwide for the purpose of communicating. The Internet was originally developed in 1969 for the U.S. military and gradually grew to include educational and research institutions. These colleges and universities have never charged for the Internet they assisted in creating. Consequently, many free reference sources exist online. Here are a few examples:

- ✔ **Federal Reserve Bank of St. Louis** (www.stls.frb.org/research/index.html) provides links to high-quality economic research such as FRED II (Federal Reserve Economic Data), a historical database of economic and financial statistics, and FRASER (Federal Reserve Archival System for Economic Research), a new collection of scanned images of historical economic statistical publications, releases, and documents. Sign up for the mailing list and be notified about late-breaking data or new publications.

- ✔ **The Federal Web Locator** (www.infoctr.edu/fwl/index.htm#toc) is a service provided by the Center for Information Law and Policy and is intended to be the one-stop shopping point for federal government information on the World Wide Web.

✔ **Government Information Locator Service** (`www.access.gpo.gov/ su_docs/gils`), shown in Figure 1-2, contains records of public information throughout the U.S. government. Government Information Locator Service (GILS) records and describes the GILS holdings of a particular agency. However, the GILS database is updated irregularly. Each GILS document is available as a downloadable ASCII text file and as an HTML file.

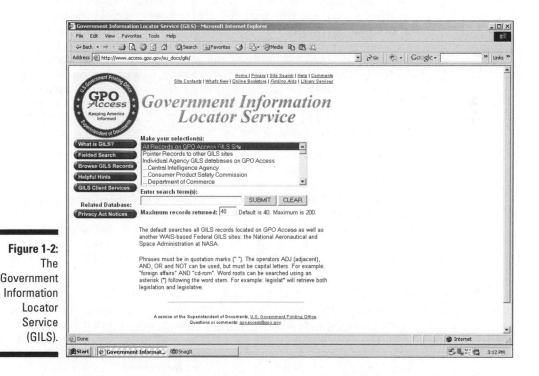

Figure 1-2:
The
Government
Information
Locator
Service
(GILS).

When all else fails — fee-based databases

For specialized investor topics, the only information available may be in an online database that you have to pay for. How each organization charges for database access varies from company to company. Charges can be by query, month, hour, or document. Most firms were designed for large corporate use, and they tend to flounder in their attempts to find equitable ways of charging individuals for private use.

Fee-based databases have several limitations. Often, they use their own search methodologies that require some getting used to, and they can be costly. The fee structure may be geared for corporations and too expensive for individual use. Databases tend to be traditional and may not have that bit of unique information you're seeking.

Here are a few examples of fee-based databases (all price quotes are as of this writing and are subject to change, just like everything else on the Internet):

- **Lexis-Nexis** (www.lexis-nexis.com) includes information from major regional and national newspapers, news sources, company information, and financial information, including SEC reports and proxy statements, in addition to other business sources in English and foreign languages. Find the information you need in one of two ways: select the product or service that you want to subscribe to or choose a particular topic. Lexis-Nexis accepts online credit-card payments. You can pay as you go, $3 for news sources, $4 to $12 for company and financial information. Or you can pay by the day or the week. For example, newspaper, business, and financial databases are $250 weekly or $75 daily. The top 34 business sources are $150 per week or $50 per day. Major papers (such as *The New York Times, The Washington Post,* and the *Chicago Tribune*) are $75 per week or $30 per day.

- **Highbeam Research** (www.highbeam.com/library/index.asp) has, among other things, electronic access to many newspapers, periodicals, and journals that you can search by keyword. Highbeam Research is a good source for background or academic financial research. Basic service is free and limited to previews of articles. Full membership includes unlimited access, lets you archive articles, and provides alerts when new articles about a topic you're researching are posted. A free seven-day trial is available. Full membership is $19.95 per month or $99.95 for 12 months.

- **STAT-USA** (www.stat-usa.gov) is sponsored by the U.S. Department of Commerce. This site includes economic indicators, statistics, and news. It also offers data about state and local bond rates, foreign exchange rates, and daily economic news. Statistics include interest rates, employment, income, prices, productivity, new construction, and home sales. Subscriptions for individuals are $75 per quarter or $175 per year.

Getting Online Investor Information Geared to Your Needs

Today, online investors come from the entire spectrum of society. Online investors range from young to old, beginners to professionals, and so on. Each of these groups has specific needs and interests. Many of the individuals in these special-interest groups are looking to online communities for answers and information about their special investment needs. Others see communities as a way to make online investing simpler because information is geared to their way of thinking. The Internet provides special Web sites targeted to online investors with specific interests. The following is a sample of what you'll find on the Internet.

Investor Web sites for children

Every day you're bombarded with information about the stock market. Turn on the car radio, walk through a hotel lobby, or watch the news on television, and you get updates about the stock market whether you want to or not. In a recent Merrill Lynch survey of 512 teenagers between the ages of 12 and 17, about 9 percent who save their money invest in mutual funds or stocks. How can young people invest? A parent must open a custodial account because a minor can't make securities transactions without the approval of an account trustee. The Merrill Lynch statistic indicates an interest in investing that's supported by a number of online Web sites aimed at children.

Here are a few examples of the wide range of online resources that can meet the needs of even the youngest investor:

- **Big Money Adventure** (`www.agedwards.com/public/content/fcgi/bma/frontpage.fcgi`) is a site in which you select your guides and adventure based on your age: 2 to 6, 6 to 10, and 10 to adult. Visit the Rainbow Castle, jump into a storybook adventure, and learn about investing, or you can play a stock-picking game and win prizes.

- **The Young Investor Web site** (`www.younginvestor.com`) is an interactive community designed for children and parents. Find out the fundamentals of managing money and investing. Don't forget to visit the game room and play a few investing games.

Web sites for young investors

A recent NASDQ (National Association of Securities Dealers) survey showed that college-aged individuals (18 to 34 years old) account for about 20 percent of all U.S. investors. Online brokerages target these investors as their next revenue source. Many online brokerages understand that college-aged investors don't have a lot to invest now but will likely become substantial investors over time.

Here are a few examples of sites that target this group:

- **Edustock** (`library.thinkquest.org/3088`) is an educational Web site designed by high school students for investors young and old. The Web site includes beginning investor tutorials about how to select stocks, company profiles, and a free 20-minute delayed online stock market simulation.

- **Independent Means** (`www.anincomeofherown.com`) is a Web site designed for women under 20 (and their over-20 mentors) to find an income of their own. The motto of the Web site is "girls, money, and power." Discover articles about money and investing, teen business pages, and more.

✔ **TeenAnalyst** (www.teenanalyst.com) is staffed by a group of young investors aged 15 to 16 years old. Using their experience and knowledge of investing, they bring young investors information in a fun and informative manner.

Other investor special-interest sites

Many financial institutions sponsor special-interest Web sites that provide selected groups with the information they need to be educated investors. These and other specialty Web sites (which are often nonprofit) understand that many investor sites attempt to educate online investors but fail to do so correctly because they don't understand the unique needs, top issues, and interests of the Internet users they serve. The following sections present a sampling of the various special-interest investor Web sites available:

Senior investors

Older investors can turn to the following sites for investment information:

✔ **Money & Investing** (www.eldernet.com/money.htm) is geared to senior citizens. You access this site from the ElderNet home page. ElderNet's Money & Investing site provides tutorials on the basics of investing, mutual funds, stocks, and bonds. Also, it includes sound advice on how to select a financial advisor.

✔ **ThirdAge** (www.thirdage.com/money) provides information about investing, money management, and retiring well for adults in their mid-40s through 50s. If you're investing for an early retirement, this Web site can help you.

Socially responsible investors

If you have an active social conscience, consider these sites as starting points for your investment research:

✔ **SocialFunds.com** (www.socialfunds.com) has more than 1,000 pages of strategic content to help investors make informed decisions regarding socially responsible investing. The Web site provides news, information, research, investment analysis, and financial services.

✔ **The Investor Responsibility Research Center** (www.irrc.org) provides research related to corporate governance, social issues, and environmental practices. Get information about corporate benchmarking and environmental indexes.

✔ **The Social Investment Forum** (www.socialinvest.org) offers comprehensive information, contacts, and resources on socially responsible investing. The Web site includes an online guide, financial services, news, and research.

Minority and women investors

The following sites are representative of Internet investment resources targeted specifically at minority and women investors:

- ✔ **The Gay Financial Network** (www.gfn.com) provides free financial news, information, and services. The site also includes articles by featured columnists and a weekly poll.

- ✔ **WIFE.org** (www.wife.org) is the Web site of the Women's Institute for Financial Education (WIFE), a nonprofit organization dedicated to financial independence for women.

- ✔ **iVillage MoneyLife Personal Finance for Women** (www.ivillage.com/money) targets women who want to take control of their finances and start investing. Other topics include handling credit and debt, life and money, and money talk.

Chapter 2

No Experience Required: Getting Started with Online Investing

- -

In This Chapter

▶ Discovering how to get a cost-free investor education online

▶ Locating beginner investor and new online investor Web sites, FAQs sources, and glossaries

▶ Getting expert advice and news from online news sources, newspapers, magazines, and more

▶ Getting investment newsletters automatically sent to your e-mailbox

▶ Investing and earning profits with investment clubs

▶ Practicing what you've discovered with Internet stock simulations

- -

*T*he Internet can assist you in getting the information you need to be a savvy investor. I suggest that you start with one of the many online tutorials for beginning investors. I highlight several helpful online tutorials in this chapter. I also show you the best Web sites for new investors. I continue with directions to online Frequently Asked Questions (FAQs) sources and Internet glossaries to help you with those troublesome investment terms and concepts that the experts use.

This chapter also points out where you can find expert advice and late-breaking financial news from online news organizations, newspapers, and magazines. You discover how you can find scholarly financial journals to research the latest stock-picking methodology that your lunch buddy expounds daily. I even show you how to get specialized investment newsletters automatically sent to your e-mailbox so that you can stay on top of current events. I often give you prices for various services, as well, but these prices may change, so check the Web sites for any updated information.

Finally, this chapter shows you how to practice what you've discovered without losing a dime. First, you can join or start an investment club, which enables you to learn and earn with other folks that are interested in maximizing their investment returns. Second, you can register for one of the many online stock simulation games (some even offer monthly prizes or cash awards).

Getting Smart Online

A study by the Pew Internet & American Life Project (`www.pewinternet.org/reports.asp`) shows that 63 percent of U.S. adults are now online, and many of them — especially those with several years of online experience — have built Internet use into their lives in practical ways. This research indicates that if you start using the Internet to do your own investing, you won't spend a significantly longer time in front of your computer than other people do.

Connecting to the Internet gives you access to millions of documents, a vast variety of software programs, and high-caliber information that in the not-too-distant past only large financial institutions could access. The World Wide Web provides an easy-to-use interface with which you can access the Internet's many financial resources. With your Web browser, you can acquire an education in investing, frequently avoid costly financial services, and conduct high-grade online research.

Online investor tutorials

If you're serious about seeing your capital grow at the fastest rate possible, you need to get smart about investing. The Internet provides many online tutorials, courses, and feature articles that can bring you up to speed.

Avoiding information overload

When you're just starting out on the Internet, you can easily become overwhelmed by the huge amount of business and financial information that's available. The best way to avoid this information overload is to divide these sources into specific categories. You can add these categories to your browser's bookmark file. (Netscape Communicator calls them *bookmarks.* In Internet Explorer, they're known as *favorites.*) For example, this chapter provides information for these bookmark categories:

- ✔ Investment clubs
- ✔ Investment news and market commentary
- ✔ Investment publications
- ✔ Investment simulations
- ✔ Investment tutorials and training

Bookmarks offer a convenient way to retrieve Web pages. When you find a Web page that you know you'll want to revisit, add it to your Web browser's list of bookmarks (or favorites — both terms mean the same thing). The next time you want to visit that page, you don't have to search for it or remember the series of links you followed to reach the page in the first place. Instead, you can simply select the page from your list of bookmarks, and voilà! You're there.

Your Internet browser has menu commands and icons that enable you to create and organize your bookmarks. For more information about bookmarks, refer to *The Internet For Dummies,* 10th Edition, by Levine, Baroudi, and Young (Wiley Publishing, Inc.).

Traditional investment bankers and brokerages that are competing for your investment dollar often sponsor these sites.

These Web sites are usually 80 percent content and 20 percent sales pitch. In my opinion, the ratio makes them well worth the annoyance or inconvenience of having to complete a free registration or read an advertising banner. Here are a few examples of these informative sites:

- ✔ **About Investing for Beginners** (`beginnersinvest.about.com`) is designed to help investors understand why the stock market exists, what makes a stock undervalued or overpriced, and what makes stock prices change. This collection of short online tutorials covers most of the basics and can be very helpful for beginning investors.

- ✔ **Investing Basics** (`www.aaii.com/invbas`) contains feature articles from the American Association of Individual Investors (AAII). Articles show individuals how to start successful investment programs, pick winning investments, evaluate their choices, and more. The articles cost nothing with your free registration. However, higher levels of information require your membership. Basic membership is $29 a year for 10 issues of the *AAII Journal,* the Annual Guide to the Top Mutual Funds, Yearly Tax Planning Guide, Local Chapter Access, AAII Research portfolios, Discount Broker Survey, Guide to Dividend Reinvestment Plans, Guide to Investment Web Sites, and other reports. Enhanced membership is $53 and includes all the Basic membership benefits, plus six issues of the AAII *Computerized Investing* newsletter, member access to the *Computerized Investing* "site-within-a-site," and a 300-page online guide to *Computerized Investing.* The $349 lifetime membership includes both the Basic and Enhanced membership benefits for life.

- ✔ **CNN/Money 101** (`money.cnn.com/pf/101`) is written by the editors of *Money* magazine and includes 23 interactive courses on managing all your finances. Each online tutorial takes about ten minutes. Lessons include calculators, quizzes, and a library for supplemental materials for online investors who want to dig deeper.

- ✔ **NASD Investor Education** (`www.nasd.com/stellent/idcplg?IdcService=SS_GET_PAGE&nodeId=13&ssSourceNodeId=5`), provided by the National Association of Securities Dealers, offers educational materials for investors. In the top margin is information about investor alerts, investment choices, investing resources, investor protection, markets and trading, online tools for research, simulation games, and so on. The left margin shows top links for investors. The center of the page shows what's new for investors, provides quick links, and offers investment tips. The third column includes information about how to check your investment professional's background and an NASD Knowledge Quiz. The Knowledge Quiz includes 18 questions guaranteed to test your investment smarts.

Web sites for new investors

You can find many investor news, finance, banking, and investment organizations on the Internet. Competition is high, so companies are willing to give away a large amount of high-quality information, downloadable software, and online tools for free. These organizations hope that individual investors, like you, will become fans of their great services. This way the online company can become a well-known entity that can charge advertisers for banner ads or require financial institutions to pay high fees for using their services.

To see a few examples of investment sites for new investors, check out the following Web pages:

✔ **MSN Money** (moneycentral.msn.com/investor/research/wizards/SRW.asp), shown in Figure 2-1, shows you how to research a stock. Discover how to determine whether a company is financially sound, how much investors are willing to pay for the stock today, how much investors are likely to pay for the stock in the future, and how the stock compares to the industry.

✔ **SmartMoney University** (university.smartmoney.com) is a great starting place if you're a beginning investor or if you want to look up a specific investing concept. Here, you discover the basics of investing theory, are introduced to the concept of risk management, and get familiar with the major asset categories.

Glossaries

As you cruise the Internet, you may encounter Web sites that discuss stocks, online trading, technical analyses, and derivatives. The language may seem arcane and undecipherable; however, the Internet can help. You can find many online glossaries that can assist you in stretching your vocabulary. Here are a few examples:

✔ **InvestorWords** (www.investorwords.com), shown in Figure 2-2, has more than 6,000 definitions of financial terms and 20,000 links between related terms. This broad financial glossary can save you time and effort.

✔ **Prudential's Glossary of Terms** (www.prufn.com/learningcenter/glossary) provides an online glossary for finding the definitions of financial and investment terms. This extensive glossary offers helpful examples of how investment terms are used.

✔ **Yahoo! Financial Glossary** (biz.yahoo.com/f/g/g.html) is a convenient glossary that includes hyperlinks that define words used in the text. For example, if a definition uses the word *option,* you can click the hyperlink and get the definition of *option.*

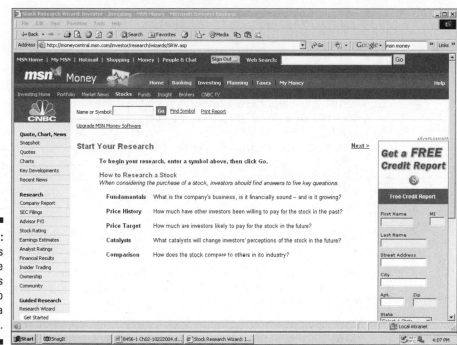

Figure 2-1:
MSN shows new online investors how to research a stock.

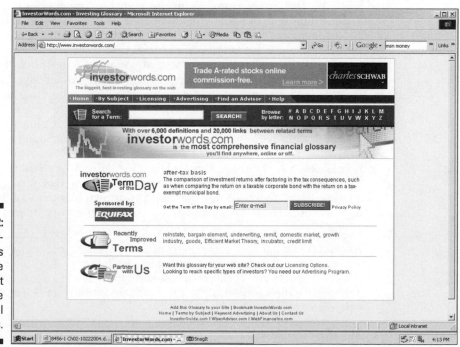

Figure 2-2:
Investor-Words helps take the mystery out of those financial terms.

Maximizing Your Internet Browser with Bookmarks

If you want to return to a first-rate online source, you're likely to use a short-cut, such as a bookmark or a favorite. If you use the Netscape browser, you *bookmark* the Web page. This acts as a shortcut to the online source. If you use the Internet Explorer browser, you save the page as a *favorite.* (I refer to both of these types of shortcuts as *bookmarks* for this section of the chapter.)

If you've used the Internet for a while, you likely have a long list of book-marks. Today hundreds of bookmark managers can help you with the follow-ing problems:

- ✔ **Eliminating dead links:** Frequently, Web sites merge, go out of business, or are redesigned so that the page you have bookmarked no longer exists.

- ✔ **Lessening errors in subfolders:** Sometimes bookmarks are filed in the wrong subfolder or you forget which subfolder contains the specific Web page you're seeking.

- ✔ **Increasing portability:** In many cases, the bookmark you're seeking is saved on your desktop computer and is not accessible from a remote computer, such as at your local library.

- ✔ **Reducing the cumbersome nature of your bookmarks:** Systems that include hundreds of bookmarks in dozens of subfolders often don't allow for easy access to the specific bookmark you seek.

If you want to tame your bookmarks so that you get the most out of your online experience, it's wise to use a free online bookmark management serv-ice. Not only can you continue to create bookmarks to your favorite Web sites, but you often can use the bookmark lists others have created for the topic areas that interest you. This service can shorten your online research time. The following are a few examples of bookmark management services:

- ✔ **FreeLink** (www.freelink.org), shown in Figure 2-3, provides free links (both public and private) with password protection that you can use anytime from anywhere. You can build your own hierarchy of bookmarks or start with one of FreeLink's samples to organize your interests.

- ✔ **Backflip** (www.backflip.com) is listed as one of *PC Magazine*'s top 100 Web sites. Backflip gets you back to the Web pages you have saved and allows you to share your bookmarks with others. Backflip is a free service that lets you organize and search your Web sites in your own Yahoo!-style directory, and you can reach your bookmarks from any-where on the Internet.

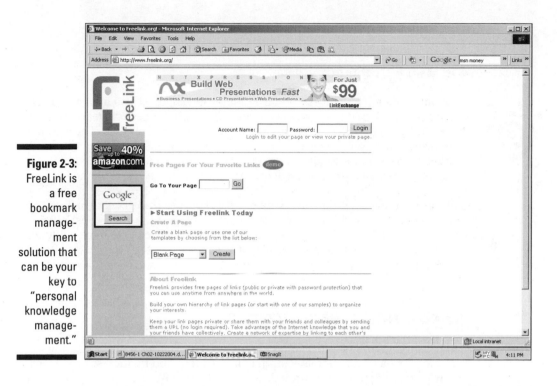

Figure 2-3:
FreeLink is a free bookmark management solution that can be your key to "personal knowledge management."

> ✔ **MyBookmarks.com** (`www.mybookmarks.com`), with your registration, is a free Internet service that allows you to keep your browser bookmarks and favorites online so that you can access them from anywhere. For a quick start, you can import your existing Internet Explorer and Netscape bookmarks and AOL places. You can edit and organize your bookmarks and then export them back to your browser.

News You Can Use

Savvy investors are knowledgeable investors. By using the Internet, you can easily keep informed about fast-breaking business and investment news, as well as stay in tune to the political and economic environment that affects your investments. Hundreds of business and finance Web sites provide compilations of this data, which means that at any time, on any day, you can discover the following by using the Internet:

> ✔ What the experts are saying about the economy

> ✔ Changes in industry trends

> ✔ What's happening at companies that interest you

> ✔ What the experts are saying about your investment candidates
>
> ✔ Forecasts of future earnings
>
> ✔ Historical performance data

Remember, identifying investment candidates doesn't cost you a dime. You can track companies that interest you for several months or several years without being obligated to purchase their mutual funds, stocks, or bonds. The Internet helps you quickly and easily check out how these companies react to a volatile market, what technological changes are affecting their industries, and how shifts in the regional or national economy affect company performance.

This section divides online investment news sources into six categories. The sources that I list in this chapter are a selection of the Internet's best offerings for your daily reading. Be certain to look for features that have value to you, such as breaking news, special features, delayed stock quotes, multimedia news, searchable archives, and newsletters.

Large news organizations

This section contains information about large Internet news organizations and focuses on those that specialize in investment and financial news. Many of these organizations now provide free wireless features so that you can stay in touch with the latest news using your PDA (personal digital assistant) or mobile Internet-enabled telephone. I also include international news organizations that may have affiliations with newspapers, magazines, TV stations, or radio stations:

> ✔ **Bloomberg Personal Finance** (www.bloomberg.com) is loaded with timely news, data, and analyses of financial markets and businesses. Find data on securities, statistics, indices, and research for free. With your free registration, you receive access to Bloomberg University and Market Monitor.
>
> ✔ **CBS MarketWatch** (cbs.marketwatch.com) offers many services with your free registration. You get unlimited use of online portfolio tools, information about indices and the market, and full access to message boards. You can sign up for e-mail alerts to get news as it happens or at the end of the day. You can also retrieve portfolio information using your wireless PDA.

Newspapers

Many of the nation's daily newspapers have online editions that provide fast-breaking news. Frequently, these sources offer online portfolio management, delayed quotes, historical stock prices, and other resources:

✔ *Financial Times* (www.ft.com) provides the latest headlines, special reports, world and company news, market and industry data, and archives with your free registration.

✔ *Investor's Business Daily* (www.investors.com) is a daily newspaper with an online edition that provides facts, figures, and objective news for investors. The online edition has an educational section and a two-week free trial.

✔ *The New York Times* (www.nytimes.com) Business section provides quotes and charts, an online portfolio function, breaking business and finance news, and information about the most active stocks, gainers, and losers. You can receive the daily Business Web page free by e-mail with The New York Times Direct.

✔ *The Wall Street Journal* (public.wsj.com/home.html), considered the granddaddy of all financial newspapers, is now online and better than ever. Free offers include market alerts automatically sent to your e-mailbox. The online edition includes everything the daily edition has, plus a personal journal that enables you to customize your news and track your portfolio. One excellent feature is *Company Research. The Wall Street Journal* has information on more than 8,500 publicly traded U.S. corporations and international companies listed as American Depository Receipts (ADRs). Additionally, you can find quotes, news, and overview information on nearly 20,000 companies that traded on non-U.S. markets.

In the left margin, click Company Research. Next enter the name or up to ten ticker symbols of companies you want to research. If you're researching a mutual fund, enter the name of the fund or up to ten ticker symbols. On the next page, you receive news and quotes, company profiles, financials, analyst ratings, research reports, and Web resources. You can get two levels of service: free and fee-based ($59 per year for nonsubscribers of the print edition). Subscribers can receive articles back to 30 days for free. Articles more than 30 days old are $2.95 for all researchers.

Magazines

Like newspapers, many business and investment publications have online versions that provide the same news and feature articles that their paper-based counterparts do. Often, these online publications include additional features, such as Web-based tools for calculating your investment returns or tracking your portfolio. Here are a few examples of online magazines that are available:

✔ **BusinessWeek Online** (www.businessweek.com) is free to all subscribers of *BusinessWeek* magazine. Free registrants get a daily briefing, special reports, the searchable archive, banking centers, quotes, and portfolio tracking.

✔ **Economist.com** (`www.economist.com`) offers a one-year online subscription to *The Economist* for $89 and a monthly subscription for $19.95. A single pay-per-view is $2.95. Purchasing a subscription provides full access to the entire content of the Web site, 70 percent of which is restricted for subscribers. It includes all the latest articles from *The Economist* newspaper (usually available by 7 p.m. London time every Thursday), as well as access to the archive section allowing you to search and retrieve any of the 28,000 *The Economist* articles published since 1997.

✔ **Forbes.com** (`www.forbes.com`) is the online version of *Forbes Magazine*. You can become a free online member with your registration, which allows you to receive free e-mail newsletters about a wide range of topics. Included in the technology department are columns about e-business, future technologies, networks, science, and medicine. You find timely information about businesses, markets, work, and personal finance. Lists include Forbes 500s, 200 Best Small Companies, 400 Best Big Companies, International 500, and the Global A List.

✔ **Kiplinger.com** (`www.kiplinger.com`) is the online version of *Kiplinger's Personal Finance,* a high-quality combination of personal finance and investment information. The online edition presents news, stock quotes, listings of the top performing funds, mutual fund analyses, online calculators, yield and rate information, retirement advice, Web site recommendations, personal finance information, advice, and an FAQs section.

Scholarly journals

If you really want to check out those newfangled stock analysis methods, you can find lots of scholarly financial journals online. Some articles you can download immediately. Other Web sites provide only abstracts, and you may have to contact the author by telephone, fax, e-mail, or U.S. mail for the complete article. Here's a sampling of the many scholarly financial journals online:

✔ **Financial Economics Network** (`www.ssrn.com/fen/index.html`) resides within the Social Science Research Network. The Financial Economics Network allows individuals to search for information by most requested article, topic, or author. You can download abstracts published in the last 60 days, and subscribers regularly receive e-mailed abstracts of journal articles and working papers. The site encourages journal readers to communicate with other subscribers concerning their and others' research. Membership fees are $25 for students and $80 for professionals. The cost per journal varies.

✔ *The Journal of Finance* (`www.afajof.org/jofihome.shtml`) is the journal of the American Finance Association and publishes leading research across all the major fields of financial research. Online membership is free. Annual membership for individuals is $80, but only $25 for students. Members have access to abstracts and journal articles.

Multimedia investment news

Sometimes it's easier to listen to the latest investment news than to read the small print on your monitor. If you are in a public location, such as an airport, you can use earphones so that you don't disturb other travelers. Most online investment news stations require RealPlayer (www.realplayer.com) or Windows Media Player (www.microsoft.com/windows/windowsmedia/player/download/download.aspx). The following are a few examples of online news stations:

✔ **ABC Stockmarket Broadcasts** (www.abcnews.go.com) offers hourly audio business reports. In the left margin, click Video & Audio to access breaking news stories. The site offers a 14-day free trial, and subscriptions are $12.95 per month with RealOne SuperPass and include CNN, NASCAR.com, the Weather Channel, BBC News, iFilm, and more. ABCNews on Demand is $4.95 per month, uses RealPlayer, and doesn't offer a free trial or any of the SuperPass content.

✔ **Bloomberg.com** (www.bloomberg.com) provides free, up-to-the-minute business news that you're bound to find useful. Click the Bloomberg Media tab on the Home Page to get breaking news stores. In the left margin, click Bloomberg Radio, and you can listen to an update on the major indices, the stocks that are moving the market ,and much more.

✔ **Business TalkRadio Network** (www.businesstalkradio.net) offers free, live, online programs 24/7, demos of programs, and access to archived programs. You need Windows Media Player to listen to live and archived programs. If you don't have the plug-in, just click the Windows Media Player link to get the free download.

Electronic newsletters

The Internet offers investors hundreds of newsletters. For your convenience, these newsletters can be sent to your e-mailbox at regular intervals. Many newsletters are free and require only that you provide your name and e-mail address. Others are fee-based and can cost anywhere from a few dollars to several hundred dollars per month.

The quality of these newsletters varies. Higher-quality newsletters have educational value. Junk newsletters often promote a stock-picking methodology or recommend that you purchase a particular stock. For example, I once received a newsletter encouraging me to buy stock in a gold mine in Bolivia. This e-mail was clearly junk, and I deleted the message immediately.

Sometimes when you visit a Web site or complete a free registration, you may not notice a prechecked box that says something like "Yes, please include me on your mailing list and send me special offers, promotions, coupons, newsletters, and free samples from you and your sponsors." If you don't uncheck this box, you'll start receiving a newsletter from the Web site's sponsor after you click the Submit button. So whenever you register for any online service, make sure that you scroll down and get a look at the entire page; you never know what may be hiding just below the bottom of your screen.

Daily newsletters or alerts from *The Wall Street Journal* (`public.wsj.com/home.html`) or Ziff Davis Publications (`news.zdnet.com`) contain breaking news. Weekly, biweekly, or monthly newsletters tend to focus on larger investor issues and are more educational.

With more than 9,000 newsletters available, Newsletter Access (`www.newsletteraccess.com/investments/index.html`), shown in Figure 2-4, has an extensive searchable directory of investment newsletters. Browse more than 250 listings and get independent investment advice so that you can start to grow your hard earned savings again. If available, information includes newsletter name, description, frequency, subscription price, organization, editor, publisher, address, e-mail, telephone and fax numbers, and Web address.

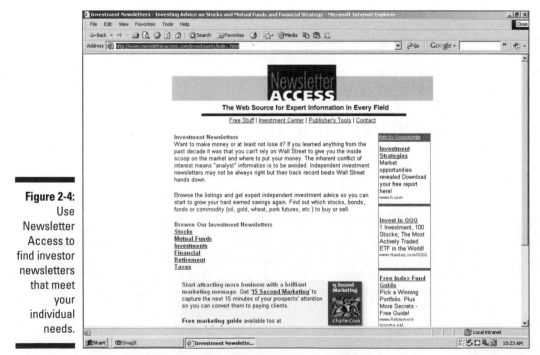

Figure 2-4: Use Newsletter Access to find investor newsletters that meet your individual needs.

As you can see from this section, you can get information in several flavors by going to different online sources. Many of these sources publish news as it develops. Trying to stay tuned to all these sources can lead to information overload, so I suggest selecting two or three sources that agree with your personality and lifestyle. For example, if you check your e-mailbox two or three times a day, an investment newsletter with special alert editions may be for you. If you like reading all the daily news at one time, an online newspaper with a clipping service to personalize the news may be your cup of tea.

Practicing with Your New Investment Information

In the not-too-distant past, only large investment firms had access to the high-quality financial information that's available on the Internet today. Traditional investment bankers use this financial information to pick investments that look promising and then charge their clients substantial commissions to buy or sell investments based on those recommendations. Now you can access the same types of information sources and make your own recommendations, which makes investing less expensive and enables you to take control of your own portfolio. After all, no one is more concerned about your financial success than you.

In previous sections in this chapter, I point you to various online resources that you can use to find out about companies, industries, the economy, and other areas that investors need to know about. However, at this early stage in your online investing career, you may not feel confident enough to start selecting your own investments. Don't despair! You can practice your new investment strategies in two ways and not risk any of your hard-earned savings. First, if you don't have a clue about how to start investing, you can join an investment club and get some one-on-one advice. Second, you can try out your strategies with one or more online investment simulations.

Join the club! Become a member of an investment club

In an investment club, members pay a monthly amount to be invested. The club makes the investments based on member recommendations. The members incur a *pro rata* share of the gains or losses, meaning that each investment club member receives a portion of the investment club's gains or losses and is responsible for his or her share of the taxes on those gains or losses.

In the past, investment clubs often didn't do a lot of research. Members of many clubs purchased only safe, conservative stocks; thus, members made small profits. Over the last five years, however, members of investment clubs have begun taking more risks, resulting in higher profits. Due to this phenomenon, the number of investment clubs is increasing at a tremendous rate.

You can find many investment clubs online. No prerequisites are necessary to join or form an investment club, so investment clubs are great for absolute beginners. Generally, investment clubs have three purposes:

- Finding out about investing
- Having fun
- Making money

The goal of most investment clubs is to help beginning investors become smart investors — that is, to educate investors in a disciplined approach to successful investing, portfolio management, and wealth building. The people who belong to these investment clubs often believe that finding new Web sites and investments, and meeting new people with the same interests, can be very helpful and profitable. For more information about investment clubs, check out the following Web sites:

- **Chicks Laying Nest Eggs** (www.chickslayingnesteggs.com/club/club.html) is geared for women investors and offers general investment club resources and resources for registered investment clubs.

- **InvestorGuide** (www.investorguide.com/clubs.html) provides a listing of U.S. investment clubs, sorted by state. Investors who don't want to leave their computers can also find a list of online investment clubs.

- **The Motley Fool** (www.fool.com/InvestmentClub/InvestmentClub Introduction.htm) offers a short tutorial about investment clubs. Find out how you can start or join an investment club, which resources investment clubs require, and some of the potential pitfalls of being a member of an investment club.

Getting into the game: Online investment simulations

Investment games enable you to invest in a virtual portfolio so that you can test your new investment strategies or try out new theories without losing any money. It's a great way to get hands-on experience with portfolio management. By playing the game, you can find out investment terms, gain confidence in your decision-making, become familiar with financial markets, see how others are faring, and have lots of fun. Your success is measured by how many hypothetical dollars you make each month.

Online investment simulation games are easy to play, and many of the simulation-game Web sites provide helpful investor lessons and insights. You don't need any prior experience to enter the game. Complete the free registration and, in many cases, win prizes for your savvy investment strategies.

Here's an overview of how these games work: After you register, decide how much of your fantasy cash you want to invest. To purchase stock, just click a tab that's named something like Buy Order. To sell, click Sell Order. Enter the quantity and the ticker symbol (the abbreviated name of a publicly owned company that's used when trading on an exchange) of your choice. The program does the rest. When you click Update, the program assigns your portfolio a rank. If your profits pile up faster and higher than other game-players' profits do, you get a better ranking. Playing the stock market for fun in a no-money, no-risk game that can help you get started with understanding the financial market and trading online. Here are some examples of online stock simulation games:

- **Fantasy Stock Market** (www.fantasystockmarket.com) is a free, educational investment simulation game that enables participants to build their $100,000 portfolio by trading stocks and mutual funds on the major U.S. exchanges.

- **Marketocracy.com** (www.marketocracy.com) allows you to create your own mutual fund with a virtual $1 million. Select your fund's name, ticker symbol, and philosophy. The net assets value of your fund will be evaluated every quarter. You also need to stick by your goals and distribution plans. Top funds are rewarded with more virtual cash and interested investors. Membership is free. If you want research, stock alerts, access to stock picks, analyses, and news, you have to pay $60 for a three-month subscription, $180 for a one-year subscription, or $300 for a two-year subscription. A free 30-day trial is available.

- **Virtual Stock Exchange** (www.virtualstockexchange.com) is a free stock simulation game that enables you to trade shares like a real brokerage account. You can test your latest profit-making strategy with stocks you're thinking about purchasing. This Web site also provides research reports, market news, and charting.

Chapter 3

Making Your Money Work Harder

In This Chapter
▶ Using the Internet to simplify your financial planning
▶ Moving from saver to investor
▶ Setting your financial objectives and reaching them
▶ Bulletproofing your investing

*Y*ou may not have a formal investment plan, but you probably do some financial planning, even if it's only noting the bills that need to be paid on the back of your paycheck envelope. However, if you want to be a successful online investor, you need to do a little more homework to get your financial ducks in a row.

This chapter shows you how to make your money work as hard as you do. I explain what you need to do before you begin investing, as well as how the Internet can help you get started. Along the way I spell out how you can move from saver to investor, and I illustrate how you can use an online worksheet to determine your starting point and use an online calculator to compute your personal net worth. From there, you discover how to determine your investment objectives and figure out how much you need to earn to meet those goals. I also provide guidelines for setting a ten-year goal and setting aside emergency funds. And finally, I show you where to go online for financial planning resources, how to determine your risk-tolerance level, and how to start maximizing your personal wealth now.

Using the Internet to Make Financial Planning Easier

Many people find it difficult to shake off the notion that if they're not wealthy, they don't need to do any financial planning. Stock market volatility, inflation, changing interest rates, unemployment, illness, and hard times are part of life. To do no financial planning or to let others (your spouse, employer, broker, or financial advisor) do all your planning is to flirt with disaster. Remember that no one cares more about your financial well-being than you do.

The Internet makes financial planning easier than ever before. The Web has hundreds of online worksheets, calculators, and other tools that can easily put you on the right track. This chapter shows how you can start maximizing your personal wealth by

- ✔ **Analyzing your current financial position:** After all, you can't get to your financial finish line if you don't know your starting point. The Internet provides many online net-worth worksheets and calculators to make this task easier.

- ✔ **Finding out where your cash is going each month:** Your financial well-being doesn't depend on how much you make; it depends on how much you spend. If you don't know how much you're spending, the Internet can help you gain an understanding of your spending habits and assist you in creating a budget you can live with.

- ✔ **Deciding your financial objectives:** Do you want to purchase a house in five years or to retire early? The Internet can help you achieve your goal by helping you develop a workable plan.

- ✔ **Building your financial base so that you can start accumulating real wealth:** This approach to investing offers a diversified system that provides financial growth and protection. Discover how you can build a financial base to maximize your personal wealth.

The joys of compound interest

The most powerful investment returns are stable, compounded returns. Regardless of what's happening in the economy or stock market, you can always count on the magic of compounding. Over time, a modest but steady rate of compound interest can build into a sizable nest egg.

Table 3-1 provides examples of how much you need to save each month to reach a specific financial goal. For example, assume that you need $10,000 for your investment nest egg (retirement fund, house down-payment fund, college expenses fund, or some other large financial goal). If you save $147.05 per month for 5 years at a 5 percent rate of return, you'll have the money you need. The second part of Table 3-1 shows that if you put away only $139.68 a month for 5 years at a 7 percent rate of return, you'll have $10,000. That's the magic of compounding.

Table 3-1	Monthly Savings Needed to Reach Your Financial Goal		
Dollars Needed	*Years to Achieve Goal at a 5% Rate of Return*		
	5 Years	*10 Years*	*20 Years*
$5,000	$73.52	$32.20	$12.16

Dollars Needed	Years to Achieve Goal at a 5% Rate of Return		
	5 Years	10 Years	20 Years
$10,000	$147.05	$64.40	$24.33
$20,000	$294.09	$128.80	$48.66
$50,000	$735.23	$321.99	$121.64
$300,000	$4,411.37	$1,931.97	$729.87

Dollars Needed	Years to Achieve Goal at a 7% Rate of Return		
	5 Years	10 Years	20 Years
$5,000	$69.84	$28.89	$9.60
$10,000	$139.68	$57.78	$19.20
$20,000	$279.36	$115.56	$38.40
$50,000	$698.40	$288.90	$96.00
$300,000	$4,190.40	$1,733.40	$576.00

Want to be a millionaire? Go to Kiplinger's Tools at www.kiplinger.com/tools/planning and click the What Will It Take to Become A Millionaire? link under Budgeting. Enter the required data and then click Calculate. The results show how much you need to invest today to be a millionaire in the future.

The Internet provides many online calculators to assist you with calculating compound interest. To use these calculators, all you need to know is the amount you want to save, the average rate of interest you expect to receive, frequency of compounding (monthly, weekly, and so on), and how long you plan to save. The following Web sites can help you get started:

- **AARP Webplace** (www.aarp.org/financial-investsave/Articles/a2002-10-08-compoundint.html), shown in Figure 3-1, provides information on types of interest and links to a variety of online interest calculators.

- **Dinkytown.net Compound Interest Calculator** (www.dinkytown.net/java/CompoundInterest.html) can show you how the different ways in which interest is calculated affect your savings.

- **Federal Reserve Bank of Chicago** (www.chicagofed.org/consumer_information/abcs_of_figuring_interest.cfm) shows the ABCs of figuring interest. For example, how is the interest you pay or receive calculated? How do these calculations affect your interest? What is the difference between simple interest and compound interest?

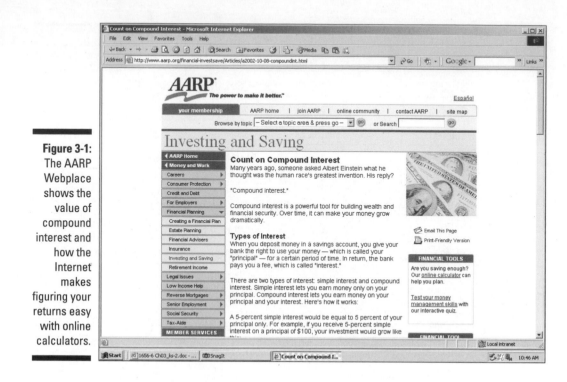

Figure 3-1:
The AARP
Webplace
shows the
value of
compound
interest and
how the
Internet
makes
figuring your
returns easy
with online
calculators.

Moving Some of Your Savings to Investments

Saving and investing are different, although savings are often the source of funds for investing. *Savings* are a set level of funds that you put aside regularly, usually at a low interest rate. You can easily access savings, and often they're insured by a financial institution.

Investment funds are the funds that you don't have earmarked for the rent, groceries, taxes, and so on. You place these funds in securities that can increase or decrease in value. They may earn interest or dividends, but you have no guarantee of increased value or future income. (Investment funds should be free of any obligations. Good examples of investment fund sources are inheritances, gifts, and disposable income.)

The beginning of personal wealth is the accumulation of capital that you can use for investing. This capital often begins with savings and expands into other types of more profitable investments. Savings are the beginning of your capital accumulation. Families need a regular savings program that's between 5 and 10 percent of take-home pay per month. Some people even manage to put away 15 percent. Getting into a regular rhythm with saving is important.

Additionally, individuals and families need emergency funds. Folks with fluctuating income, few job benefits, and little job security may need to have a larger emergency fund. Families with two wage earners may need a smaller emergency fund.

A general rule is to have three to six months of take-home pay in a savings account (or a near-cash account similar to a market fund with check-writing privileges) for emergencies. If you don't have an emergency fund, you need to increase your savings. Payroll deduction plans that divert funds into a savings account or money market fund are often the most painless way to achieve the best results. On the other hand, if you've been saving a surplus, you may want to consider using these funds for investing.

Every successful investor starts with a financial plan. The plan includes clearly stating your financial objectives, saving a certain amount of money each month, developing investment asset allocation strategies, and so on. Here are a few examples of Internet sites that can assist you in building your financial plan:

- ✔ **Charles Schwab** (www.schwab.com) can help your financial planning with online calculators, tools, and advice. Go to the home page and click Planning. You'll discover a step-by-step guide to retirement, estate planning, charitable giving, college, tax planning, and changing employment. Other online planning tools include an investor profile, IRA analyzer, college planner, and more.

- ✔ **GE Center for Financial Learning** (www.financiallearning.com) provides online tutorials, articles, and tools about investing, how to develop the right plan for your situation, and how you can become successful at investing over time.

- ✔ **Vanguard Online Planner** (flagship2.vanguard.com/web/planret/PlanningAdvicePublicOverview.html) has excellent online tools that can assist you in creating a personal investment plan based on the information you enter. Free of charge, Vanguard offers a five-step investment plan to help you map out your financial strategies.

Maximizing Your Investments with Tax-Deferred Accounts

An individual retirement account (IRA) is one of the best ways you can accumulate something to invest because making contributions and earnings is often tax-free. An IRA must be established with a financial institution that has received Internal Revenue Service (IRS) approval to offer IRAs. These financial institutions include banks, brokerages, federally insured credit unions, and savings and loan associations. IRA accounts can be established at any time. Contributions must be made by the IRA owner's tax-filing deadline (usually April 15 of the following year). Tax-filing extensions do not apply.

Traditional IRAs

When you invest in a Traditional IRA, you don't have to pay taxes on the money you earn in your account until you start withdrawing the funds during retirement. You may also be able to deduct your annual contribution to a Traditional IRA from your yearly income taxes. Qualifying for this benefit depends on how much you earn.

Several rules affect withdrawals from Traditional IRAs. For example, you can't begin withdrawing funds without penalties until you reach 59½ years of age. If you withdraw funds before that time, you pay a hefty tax penalty. Additionally, you must withdraw funds when you turn 70½ years old (the time when you can no longer contribute to a Traditional IRA). Keep in mind that you have to pay taxes on the funds that you withdraw. Therefore, spreading your withdrawals across as many years as possible before you turn 70½ years old is a wise choice. For example, if you withdraw a little at a time between the ages of 59½ and 70½, you can keep your taxes affordable. If you wait until you're 70½ years old to withdraw all your funds, the tax liability is similar to paying taxes on a large windfall or lottery win.

Roth IRAs

Roth IRAs were created by Congress in 1997. With a Traditional IRA, earnings accrue on a tax-deferred basis. With a Roth IRA, earnings accrue on a tax-free basis. For most situations, a Roth IRA is a better deal for those individuals who are eligible.

As defined by the U.S. Congress, Table 3-2 shows the annual contribution limits for Traditional and Roth IRAs. It's important to note that contributions levels are higher for individuals who are over 50 years old. This increased contribution level was implemented to assist individuals who didn't start saving earlier to catch up with their wiser peers.

Table 3-2	Annual Contribution Limits for Traditional and Roth IRAs	
Year	*Under age 50*	*Age 50 and older*
2005	$4,000	$4,500
2006–2007	$4,000	$5,000
2008	$5,000	$6,000

Roth IRA withdrawals are tax free if the account is held five or more years and you're 59½ or older. Withdrawals also are tax-free if you become disabled, if you're purchasing a home for the first time, or if the account holder dies. Roth IRA eligibility is based on adjusted gross income (AGI) and phases out for individuals with AGIs of more than $95,000 and for couples who file joint tax returns with combined AGIs of more than $150,000 in 2004.

Keep in mind that as long as you have earned income, you can contribute to a Traditional IRA until you turn 70½. Investors older than 70½ cannot contribute to a Traditional IRA, but can contribute to a Roth IRA. If you don't have earned income but are married and file a joint return, you still can contribute to an IRA based on your working spouse's income.

For more information about this topic, see these Web sites:

- **Employee Benefit Research Institute** (`www.ebri.org`) is a nonprofit, nonpartisan organization that provides information and education about employee benefits. Find the latest information about IRAs.

- **Kiplinger.com** (`www.kiplinger.com/basics/managing/retirement/roth1.htm`) provides a large online retirement center that includes articles, resources, and online calculators.

- **Roth IRA Web Site Home Page** (`www.rothira.com`) offers technical and planning information about Roth IRAs to practitioners and consumers.

- **The Motley Fool** (`www.fool.com/60second/ira.htm`) provides "The 60-Second Guide to Opening an IRA." This online guide offers step-by-step guidance for opening an IRA and a calculator to determine what type of IRA account is best for you. You'll also find suggestions about where to invest your cash and brokerage comparisons.

Online calculators for determining the best IRA account

Several kinds of IRA accounts are available. The Vanguard Group (`flagship3.vanguard.com/web/planret/PTRetireCenterOV.html`) has a Retirement Center that offers an online calculator to help you determine what kind of IRA is best for you. At the Retirement Center, click the I'm Starting To Save For Retirement link and then click What Kind Of IRA Is Best For Me? You'll discover whether you can contribute to a Traditional or Roth IRA, find out whether you're eligible to deduct your Traditional IRA contribution, calculate your maximum allowable contribution, project the long-term returns of each type of IRA, and then compare your options.

Why you should start now

The best argument for why you should start investing is to do the math and compare the results. For example, if a 25-year-old invests about $100 a month (at a 12 percent return) until age 65, the investment will be worth $1 million. It's much harder for someone older to make that much money. To have a $1-million nest egg at 65, a 40-year-old needs to invest $600 a month at a 12-percent return for 25 years (assuming that all returns are reinvested and the investments escape taxes).

The Internet provides other online IRA comparison calculators at these Web sites:

- **Morningstar.com** (`screen.morningstar.com/ira/iracalculator.html?tsection=toolsiracal`), with your free registration, provides an IRA calculator to help you make better IRA decisions. Discover your eligibility, determine your contribution limits for Roth or Traditional IRAs, compare various scenarios to uncover which IRA is best for you, and discover whether you need to convert your traditional IRA to a Roth IRA.

- **Calcbuilder** (`www.calcbuilder.com/cgi-bin/calcs/IRA1.cgi`) offers an online calculator to help you determine which type of IRA account provides you with the most retirement income.

Deciding How Much Risk You Can Take

Your investment decisions need to take into consideration your attitudes about risk. The amount of risk you can tolerate often depends on your knowledge of investments, your experience, and your personality. Each person has his or her own style and needs. Knowing exactly what your risk-tolerance level is can help you select investments that offer the highest return for the investment's level of risk.

The Internet provides many personal investment profiles — for example:

- **Bank of Hawaii** (`www.boh.com/invtrust/invest/calculator/index.asp`) offers a seven-question worksheet to assist you in identifying your investor profile and risk tolerance. (Remember, there are no right or wrong answers.)

- **Mutual of Omaha** (`www.mutualofomaha.com/individual_products/investments/invprov.html`) offers a short investor profile that can assist you in learning about your risk-tolerance level.

> ✔ **Risk Tolerance Assessor** (www.webcalcs.com/cgi-bin/calcs/prod/
> risk.cgi?client=safecofunds) has a questionnaire that can help you
> determine your personal comfort zone with regard to risk.

Determining How Much You Can Invest

Deciding how much you can invest isn't guesswork. It requires some analysis
and setting up a budget. A budget is a blueprint that guides you through the
process of paying bills, purchasing needed items, putting money into savings,
and knowing how much you can invest. Where you can often run into problems
is not budgeting for predictable but occasional expenses. Occasional expenses
can include car repairs, annual life insurance premiums, and tuition.

Gaining a good understanding of how much money you can expect to earn
and understanding where your cash goes are the first steps to determining
how much you can invest. Make a budget using pen and paper, Internet tools,
or personal financial software such as MS Money (www.microsoft.com/
money) or Intuit's Quicken (www.intuit.com/products_services).
Because the pen-and-paper method is too time-consuming, and personal
software programs can be costly and difficult to learn, I recommend using
Internet tools. The Internet offers many online budgeting resources that are
free, easy to use, and quick.

Investing in Securities That Meet Your Goals

Investors often receive hot tips from neighbors, e-mail messages, and message boards or chat rooms. However, studies indicate that chasing these
investments, even if the investments are top performers, rarely produces the
returns investors expect. Keep in mind that each security purchase is part of
your investment plan, which is tied to your long-term goals. Specifically, how
you choose to invest your capital (in mutual funds, stocks, bonds, Treasury
securities, money market funds, and other types of investments) depends on
the following considerations:

- ✔ Your required rate of return
- ✔ How much risk you can tolerate
- ✔ How long you can invest your capital
- ✔ Your personal tax liability
- ✔ Your need for quick access to your cash

Checking Out What the Experts Are Doing

After factoring all the elements of this chapter into your investment plan, you may want to find out which stocks are creating the biggest buzz on the Internet and find out what the experts are doing. The reports that investment analysts offer generally include

- ✔ **A general description of the company and its industry:** Most analysts specialize in a certain industry or sector of the economy, and many visit companies to see operations first-hand.

- ✔ **The analyst's thoughts about the company's future:** Wall Street analysts are supposed to tell ordinary investors when to expect bad or good things with a company. However, the recent dot-com crash shows how shortsighted many experts can be.

- ✔ **The target price or performance prediction for the stock in a year:** Often, different analysts make different price predictions based on their analyses of the economy, the industry, and the firm's capacity and past performance.

- ✔ **A recommendation to Buy, Sell, or Hold:** All ranking methods aren't the same. Many analysts use numbers, but some companies use Buy as the strongest recommendation. Other companies use Strong Buy as the top recommendation. However, according to the Securities and Exchange Commission (SEC), in 2000, less than 1 percent of brokerage house analysts made Sell or Strong Sell recommendations. Common sense dictates that if you execute a security buy, you must sell a security to offset the purchase. Therefore, due to the lack of Sell recommendations, many investors interpret a Hold recommendation to mean Sell.

Analyzing the analysts

Research analysts influence today's marketplace with their recommendations. Nationally televised interviews of a popular analyst's recommendation can temporarily cause the price of a stock to increase or decrease. These price changes can happen even when the financial situation of the firm hasn't changed. Consequently, you must check out exactly who is making a recommendation and what type of analyst he or she is:

- ✔ *Sell-side analysts* may work for the investment bank that underwrites the securities they're analyzing. Additionally, the firm that employs a sell-side analyst may provide other financial services to the companies that the analyst covers.

✔ *Buy-side analysts* advise mutual fund managers, hedge fund managers, investment advisors, and other institutional money managers who purchase securities for their own accounts. As a general rule, these analysts make money when they make good recommendations.

✔ *Independent analysts* usually aren't associated with any brokerage or firm that underwrites the securities they cover. They make money by selling their recommendations in online investment columns sponsored by large organizations or by writing newsletters that are sold on a subscription basis.

Getting the opinions of others: Stock-picking communities

In the early days of online investing, online stock-picking communities were overflowing with "pump and dump" schemes, wild corporate rumors, and other nefarious activities. Now that the dot-com bubble has burst, things have changed. Today, serious investors can frequent several Web sites if they want to share their investment wisdom or learn about new investing strategies to uncover stocks that are winners. The following are a few examples:

✔ **ClearStation** (clearstation.etrade.com) is a free investment analysis and community Web site. ClearStation members can receive e-mailed stock recommendations, customize and add annotations to their views of graphs, create a Watch List, have an unlimited number of portfolios, and participate in stock discussions. Currently, more than 200,000 members are submitting portfolios. Find a "Clearhead" and follow his or her trades and posts and subscribe to e-mail alerts for portfolio changes.

✔ **Marketocracy.com** (www.marketocracy.com) constantly analyzes and ranks the stock-picking ability of its members using a complex algorithm that incorporates long- and short-term performance, as well as an attribution analysis that accounts for market, sector, style, and trading contribution so that Marketocracy.com can isolate comparative returns. Marketocracy.com believes that this process eliminates much of the performance associated with "being in the right place at the right time" and helps identify the truly best investors. Each month, Marketocracy.com uses its ranking methodology to select 100 of its best investors. The top 100 investors are called the Master's 100 (sometimes called the m100). The m100 receive free premium subscriptions, posting privileges, and invitations to special m100 retreats and can earn cash based on the Master's 100 fund's management fee. Membership is free to run a virtual fund. There are currently more than 65,000 funds.

✔ **ValueInvestorsClub.com** (www.valueinvestorsclub.com) accepts only 250 value investors. Membership is free; however, only a select few, based on their investment ability, are allowed to post long and short investing ideas. Applications are judged by an investment manager with one of the top long-term investment records in the United States. Each member, once admitted, must post a minimum of two investment ideas per year at the Value Investors Club site. Because the club's goal is for members to share only their best investment ideas, members may not submit more than six ideas per year. A message board (open only to other club members) allows members to post comments on each submitted investment idea. Investment ideas are shared and discussed on a daily basis. If you want to find out how to analyze value stocks, this site is a great starting place. Each week, $5,000 goes to the member with the best analysis.

Judging who's the real deal

As you study analyst reports, remember that many sources for potential conflicts of interests exist. In some situations, the analyst's firm may be underwriting the offering of the company that the analyst is covering. In investment banking relationships, client companies of the analyst's firm frequently prefer favorable research reports because positive reports often attract new customers. Other types of conflicts include the following:

- ✔ **Positive analyst reports can generate brokerage commissions.** In other words, an analyst's report indirectly helps the firm make money.

- ✔ **Analysts may be pressured to release positive analyst reports.** Sometimes, an analyst's compensation or bonuses are linked to the number of investment deals or new investment clients the firm acquires as a result of the analyst's reports.

- ✔ **Analysts may feel forced to release a positive analyst report to protect their own investments.** For example, an analyst may have *directly* owned shares of the company's stock before becoming the analyst for the company. Owning shares *indirectly* may occur if the employer is a significant shareholder of a company the analyst covers, and the analyst owns shares in the employee stock ownership plan. In other words, the well-being of the shares owned by the analyst's employer may affect the value of the analyst's shares in the employee stock ownership plan.

Securities regulators require analysts to disclose certain kinds of conflicts of interest. Usually, this information is noted at the end of written research analyst reports. For details on this issue, see Analyzing Analyst Recommendations at www.sec.gov/investor/pubs/analysts.htm.

Keep in mind that you can follow investment candidates for years cost-free. The following are a few of the Internet's best analyst Web sites to assist you in starting your Wall Street research:

- ✔ **BestCalls** (www.bestcalls.com) helps investors conveniently track event schedules for thousands of publicly traded companies and helps investor relations professionals promote and disclose their investor events. The BestCalls CallTracker service allows investors to receive automated and personalized e-mail alerts of conference calls. Individual investor subscriptions are $49.95 for one year or $89.95 for two years.

✔ **Reuter's Risk Alerts** (`www.investor.reuters.com`) allows you to access Reuter's useful analyses with your free registration. On the left side of the Web page appears the analysis of each stock, which is divided into four sections (risk alerts, estimates, recommendations, and research reports). If you don't know the ticker symbol for the stock you're researching, you can enter the name of the company.

✔ **StarMine** (`www.starmine.com`) prides itself on providing independent, objective ratings of securities analysts around the globe by measuring their stock-picking performance and the accuracy of their earnings forecasts. StarMine helps professional investors extract more value from outside research in less time by identifying the analysts that add the most value, forecasting potential earnings surprises and shortfalls, and alerting investors to the most important changes in analyst forecasts and opinions. The free version of StarMine is geared toward individual investors and rates only certain analysts.

A research analyst's report may shine a little light on a hot investment candidate, or it may be flawed. Either way, investors need to check several analytical sources and do their own research before investing. (For more information about researching investment candidates, see Chapter 11.)

Tracking and Measuring Your Success

After selecting, analyzing, and purchasing securities, your work still isn't done. Managing your investment portfolio can help you squeeze every bit of profit from your investments and realize your financial goals. You need to find information on changing market conditions, study analytical techniques, and update your financial plan regularly. The Internet provides many portfolio-management tools that include all these features. (See Chapter 17 for more details about online portfolio tracking.)

Calculating your returns or expected returns with pencil and paper is relatively easy, assuming that no additional purchases or redemptions were made during the period you're calculating (other than the reinvestment of dividends, interest payments, or capital gains distributions). To calculate your return, start with the ending balance and subtract the beginning balance. Divide this number by the beginning balance and then multiply by 100 to determine a percentage. This percentage is your return. Here's the formula:

Total Return = [(Ending Balance – Beginning Balance) ÷ Beginning Balance] × 100

Setting realistic expectations

When you start your investment program, don't expect to become a millionaire overnight. History has shown that the market has many ups and downs. However, when looking at the long term (five years or more), investors have been rewarded for their patience. Additionally, riskier investments held over the long term provide higher rewards than low-risk investments. As you can see from the following statistics, less risk equals less return. For example, the 73-year average annual return (1926 to 1998) for U.S. Treasury bills was 5.7 percent, the return for long-term corporate bonds was 5.7 percent, and the return on the S&P 500 Index was 11.2 percent.

For example, suppose that you invest $10,000 in stocks on January 1, 2002, and on December 31, 2002, your account has a value of $12,174:

1. **Start with the ending balance and deduct the beginning balance:**

   $12,174 − $10,000 = $2,174

2. **Divide the result by the beginning balance:**

   $2,174 ÷ $10,000 = 0.21740

3. **Multiply the result by 100:**

   $0.2174 × 100 = 21.74$

   Your return is 21.74 percent.

A return of 21.74 percent in one year is pretty good (by anyone's standard). This rate means that for each dollar invested, you earned $0.22. To determine whether this rate of return "beat the market," you need to compare it to the appropriate *benchmark* (a standard used for comparison). See Chapter 7 for more information on where to find benchmarks and indices online.

Building Your Personalized Investment Plan

In this chapter, I discuss the beginnings of the investment process. Selecting securities isn't the first thing investors do; choosing investments is just one of many elements in the process. To bulletproof your investing, you need to complete the many tasks that I detail in this chapter. The following checklist outlines how you can build a successful investment plan that meets your individual needs and goals:

✔ **Determine where you stand.** Gain a good understanding of what your financial commitments are now and in the future. Make certain that you have an emergency fund and a savings plan.

✔ **Clearly state your financial goals.** How much do you need? When do you need it? How much risk can you tolerate? If you lost the principal of an investment, could you mentally recover and invest again?

✔ **Determine the appropriate allocation of your personal assets for your age (young adult, middle-aged, retiree, and so on).** Develop a regular investing program and stick to it regardless of market volatility.

✔ **Select the investments that meet your financial goals and risk-tolerance level.** How much time do you have (in years) to invest? Should you be an active trader and invest often during the day or a passive investor with a buy-and-hold policy? (See Chapter 4 for details on answering such questions.)

✔ **Analyze your investment candidates.** Before you call your online broker, make certain that you can tell a child in two minutes or less why you want to own a particular investment. Determine how long you plan to hold the security and decide at what price you will sell (and take your profits or cut your losses).

✔ **Select an online broker that suits your needs.** Avoid mutual fund *loads* (a sales charge added to the purchase or sale of a mutual fund) and high fees. Use automatic investment plans, dividend reinvestment programs, investment clubs, and other programs to reduce brokerage commissions. (See Chapter 7 for more information.)

✔ **Monitor your portfolio and reevaluate your goals on a regular basis.** Rank the performance of your investments and make the appropriate changes. You can expect that changes in general market conditions, new products that are introduced, and new technology will change how established businesses operate. Use this information to gain an understanding of when to hold and when to fold.

For more information about the investment process and bulletproofing your portfolio, check out Investor Home at www.investorhome.com/toc.htm.

Chapter 4

Selecting an Online Broker That's Right for You

In This Chapter

▶ Becoming aware of investment brokerages

▶ Selecting a premium online brokerage

▶ Looking into discount online brokerages

▶ Matching online brokerages to your investor type

▶ Paying the lowest commissions available

▶ Opening your electronic brokerage account online or by mail

*I*n this chapter, I discuss different types of brokerages and provide helpful insights about determining what category of brokerage is best for you. *Traditional brokerages* are generally used by investors who are seeking recommendations, advice, personalized service, help with calculating taxes, access to IPOs (initial public offerings), and assistance for other more complex types of financial transactions. *Premium online brokerages* are a hybrid of the traditional brokerage and an electronic brokerage, where they offer referral services to qualified financial advisors, and branch offices, and investors can meet face-to-face with representatives to discuss some aspect of their portfolios. *Discount online brokerages* are designed for the "do-it-yourselfers" who desire barebone brokerages and want to take command of their finances.

I then continue with a discussion of how all premium and discount online brokerages aren't equal. Some online brokerages are better suited for the needs of certain types of investors than others. Next, I explore how to check out prospective brokers and show you where to get trading services for less. I provide a list of where to get on the Internet to see the latest ratings of online brokerages, and I conclude with easy-to-understand instructions about how you can open your trading account online in 15 minutes or by mail in two to three weeks.

Is a Traditional Broker Best for You?

According to the Pew Internet & American Life Project (www.pewinternet.org), one out of every ten Internet users has bought or sold stocks online. Specifically, a recent study indicates that since September 2002, about 12 percent of all Internet users have bought or sold stocks online. This represents a 40 percent growth from 10 million Americans who reported they had completed online stock trades as of March 2000 to 14 million Americans who reported completing stock trades as of September 2002. The downturn of the stock market in recent years has likely had an impact on the conservative growth of online trading. In other words, the growth of online investing was likely dampened by low (or in some cases nonexistent) stock returns.

Investors who don't use the Internet generally want professional, customized advice; they're looking for a brokerage that provides excellent recommendations and has the ability to handle complex financial services for real estate assets or investments in private companies or partnerships. In other words, these investors want a *traditional* broker that makes his or her living by being a financial consultant and knowing an investor's risk-tolerance level. Following are some of the offerings you can expect to find in a traditional brokerage:

- **Recommendations and advice:** Broker advice is supposed to be unbiased and geared toward your best interests. However, brokers make money from sales commissions, so the more you buy or sell, the more money they make.

- **Quality service:** The quality of service for both large and small account holders can be the same. In other words, both types of customers can get red carpet treatment or, in some cases, can be quickly forgotten.

- **Help with calculating your taxes:** As a value-added service, some traditional brokers will determine the amount of taxes owed by the investor.

- **First choice in IPO offerings:** Traditional brokerages can let their customers know about new initial public offerings (IPOs) so that customers can get in on the *ground floor* (the first stage) of a potential investment opportunity.

- **Access to other investment options:** Many affluent investors need help managing their real estate assets and investments in private companies or partnerships.

- **A little peace of mind:** Traditional brokers are paid to watch for changes in the market so that you don't have to. Additionally, if something goes wrong, the investor can always blame it on a bad broker recommendation.

- **Branch offices:** Some investors need to visit their brokers face to face to feel comfortable. Having a branch office in the neighborhood can encourage investor trust.

Getting a little help from an online brokerage

Some investors are uncomfortable with online investing. For these individuals, a hybrid solution may be the answer: trading with a premium offline broker but getting personalized advice online. For example, A. G. Edwards (www.agedwards.com) has more than 7,200 financial consultants and offers AGe-connect, a free online service for A.G. Edwards customers. AGe-connect is customized to meet each client's needs based on his or her investing profile and interests. Some of the features offered include account information, real-time quotes, news headlines, financial-planning tools, interactive charts, research, and account data downloads (which can be imported into personal-finance software, such as Quicken or MS Money).

Selecting a Premium Online Brokerage

In December 2001, there were 19.7 million active online investor accounts, a slight increase from 2000. During the peak of the market in March 2000, there were 12 to 15 million online brokerage accounts, and about a third of all trading on the New York Stock Exchange and NASDAQ systems was attributed to online investors. Since that time, according to Gomez (www.gomez.com), an Internet research company, trading volume has plunged 40 percent, but online brokerages are still going strong.

Traditional brokers don't require their clients to be computer savvy or to go online. However, as the Internet matures and online investing technology improves, traditional brokers have noted that more and more clients are drifting toward the Internet to make an occasional trade. Some traditional brokerages note that they have more customers using the Web-based part of the business than the traditional offline side of the brokerage. In other words, the distinction between online and offline is getting smaller and smaller. To illustrate this point, I include the following as a few examples of premium online brokerages:

- ✔ **Charles Schwab** (www.schwab.com) offers Schwab AdvisorSource. If your portfolio is over $100,000, Schwab will assist you in finding an advisor to analyze your present financial situation and aid you in determining how to construct your financial future. Services include 72 branch offices for one-on-one visits with a broker.

- ✔ **Fidelity** (www.fidelity.com) offers Fidelity representatives who are happy to review your personal investment goals and objectives and to assist you with any Fidelity investments or related financial services.

- ✔ **Merrill Lynch Direct** (www.mldirect.ml.com) is a leading worldwide financial management and advisory company with offices in 35 countries and total client assets of about $1.5 trillion. In the United States, investors can visit any one of Merrill Lynch's over 600 branches to talk with a broker about their accounts.

✔ **TD Waterhouse** (www.waterhouse.com) provides AdvisorDirect to customers who have portfolios of $100,000 or more. This is a free referral service to qualified independent financial advisors. The initial, no-obligation meeting is free. Advisors typically charge an annual fee based on the percentage of the assets under management.

Many premium online brokerages are reaching out to their customers by offering free referral services to independent financial advisors. This additional service is designed to assist more affluent customers in realigning their portfolios to achieve their goals, managing their investments or inheritances, and planning for retirement, college savings, or other goals.

Selecting the Right Discount Online Brokerage

As a general rule, online investors who use discount brokerages aren't seeking the advice of a traditional broker they've known for the last ten years. Most online investors want brokerages that are stable, provide excellent customer service, and offer different types of choices. The following list shows some of the criteria that investors use to judge discount online brokerages:

✔ **Ease of use:** All online investors want their Web-based brokerages to be easy to use. Web sites need to be uncluttered and free of slow-to-download graphics and useless tools.

✔ **Prompt customer service:** When online investors telephone customer service, being on hold for several minutes is unacceptable. Online investors with large portfolios want more sophisticated financial services and advice. Many are willing to meet with financial advisors for that human touch.

✔ **Reliable responsiveness:** System-wide brokerage crashes aren't acceptable. Quick and accurate trade executions are important for all investors.

✔ **Investing options, products, and tools:** Online access to IPO information, options, and other financial products is a must. Many online investors expect research, real-time quotes, and other market information.

✔ **Low fees:** Hidden costs are often associated with online brokerages. These hidden costs can quickly wipe out your profits. Consequently, you need to read the fine print before signing up for a new account.

Investigating a Brokerage Before You Invest

The Securities Investor Protection Corporation (SIPC) provides account protection for brokerage accounts in a way that's similar to how the Federal Deposit Insurance Corporation (FDIC) insures bank accounts. Each customer's account is protected up to $500,000, and some brokerages have additional insurance. If your brokerage firm goes belly-up, you're covered. However, if you make poor investment selections, you can lose all your money.

As an investor, you're wise to look into the background of a brokerage firm before investing. The Central Registration Depository (CRD) — a registration and licensing database used by regulators throughout the securities industry to collect data about securities firms and their brokers — is available at your state securities agency or the National Association of Securities Dealers (www.nasdr.com/2000.htm). Additionally, each month, the New York Stock Exchange releases a disciplinary action list at www.nyse.com. At the home page, search "disciplinary actions" to zero in on the names of brokers, years, and types of actions taken by the Exchange Hearing Panel.

You can check several sources to find out whether the broker you're considering is registered. The National Association of Securities Dealers Regulation Web site (www.nasdr.com) has investor services that enable you to request background information about your broker through NASD Regulation's Public Disclosure Program (called the NASDBrokerCheck). Your state securities regulator can tell you whether the broker you're considering is registered, and some state securities commissions provide cautionary lists at their Web sites — for an example, see the Oklahoma Securities Commission site at www.securities.state.ok.us.

Matching Your Needs to the Right Online Brokerage

Since their inception, online brokerages have continued to evolve to meet the demands of customers by improving the quality and reliability of online services. Recently, many online discount brokerages added more online research, providing consumers with access to a wider range of financial products. This evolution means that some online discount brokerages are better in some areas than in others. Therefore, considering what types of brokerages best meet your investor type is important.

For beginners

Some uncertain newcomers simply want to experience online investing for themselves. Many beginning investors are uncertain about their investment goals and which types of financial instruments are best for their unique needs. These novice investors or beginning online investors frequently want low initial minimum balances and fees. Beginning investors require lots of offline and online customer help and easy-to-use Web site navigation. The following are a few examples of online brokerages that are especially helpful to beginning investors:

✔ **Ameritrade** (www.ameritrade.com), shown in Figure 4-1, requires $2,000 to open a trading account and $1,000 to open an IRA account. Market and limit orders are $10.99. Ameritrade offers a trading demo and investor education center called Investor Basics. Expect to pay a $15 maintenance fee every quarter.

 Note: Market orders are instructions for the broker to immediately buy or sell a security for the best available price. *Limit orders* are trading orders that specify a certain price at which the broker is to execute the order. For more information, see Chapter 5.

✔ **Harris*direct*** (www.harrisdirect.com) is ideal for beginning online investors because it doesn't require any initial minimum deposit for trading or IRA accounts. The more you trade, the lower the cost of each trade. For example, 1 to 17 market or limit orders cost $19.95, 18 to 59 trades cost $14.95, and 60 or more trades cost $9.95. The brokerage offers access to a wide variety of research resources. (Investors with $100,000 or more have direct access to IPOs.) Customers can place trades via the Internet, telephone, or wireless devices in addition to proprietary software.

✔ **E*TRADE** (www.etrade.com) is one of the top-ranked online brokerages. You need $1,000 for the initial deposit. Market trades are $14.95 per trade for up to 1,000 shares. Customers have unlimited access to IPO information, real-time quotes, charts, baseline reports, market news, and more.

For mainstream investors

Mainstream investors are often defined as investors who make between 2 and 20 trades per year and have portfolios valued at between $25,000 and $75,000. Mainstream investors frequently want an online brokerage that is easy to use and has human customer assistance. Additionally, mainstream investors want to be able to get to their money when and how they want it. Mainstream investors aren't frequently concerned about the split-second timing of trade executions. Additionally, they're often well-versed in finding other sources and tools for financial data. The following sites are good for the mainstream investor:

✔ **Ameritrade** (www.ameritrade.com) provides great tools for monitoring your portfolio and analyzing your next investment move. Many people find this site easy to use and reliable when they need to make a transaction.

✔ **Ameritrade** (www.ameritrade.com) provides great tools for monitoring your portfolio and analyzing your next investment move. Reliable and easy to use, Ameritrade can be counted on when you need to make a transaction.

✔ **Fidelity** (www.fidelity.com) provides a newly updated, easy-to-use Web site. Customer service is generally prompt and courteous. On the whole (and thanks to Fidelity's background in banking and finance), customers can easily access their cash in any number of ways and without any difficulty. The initial deposit to open an account is $2,500.

✔ **Charles Schwab** (www.schwab.com) proved its worth to me when I was in Europe and needed to transfer funds from one account to another. The transaction was quick and error-free. Schwab recently lowered the costs of its trades to $9.95 with 30 trades per quarter or a household balance of $1,000,000. The initial deposit to open an account is $10,000.

✔ **TD Waterhouse** (www.waterhouse.com) is ideal for investors who make fewer than 20 trades per year. Customers have online access to IPO information and proprietary research from Goldman, Sachs & Company, a leading investment bank. The initial deposit is $1,000.

Figure 4-1:
Ameritrade provides an investor education center and easy-to-use trading demo.

For active investors

Active investors are often defined as investors who make between five and ten trades per week. These individuals may want to use brokerages that cater to this type of consumer by providing special software, information streams, and commission rates. Overall, active investors want responsive brokerages with fast and cheap trading fees. These individuals frequently don't care about extensive products, tools, or customer service features. As a general rule, the active investor wants an easy-to-use Web site that allows him or her to navigate easily and make a split-second trade, such as the following:

- **A.B. Watley** (`www.abwatley.com`) offers NASDAQ Level II quotes (detailed real-time quotes of the bid and ask prices for each individual market maker), standard real-time quotes, and trades from $10. The initial deposit is $35,000. Minimum monthly balance is $2,000 with a monthly mainte-nance fee of $50. Investors are required to have an annual income of $50,000 and a net worth of $150,000. The more frequently you trade, the lower the cost for each trade. For example, you'll pay $15.59 for up to your first 49 trades per month, compared to $9.95 for 250 to 499 trades per month.

- **Ameritrade** (`www.ameritrade.com`) charges $10.99 for market orders and limit orders. The Ameritrade system is responsive and all trades are quickly executed.

- **BrownCo** (`www.brownco.com`) offers inexpensive $5 market and limit order trades but requires a $15,000 initial deposit and five years of investing experience to open a trading account.

- **Scottrade** (`www.scottrade.com`) is a recipient of the J.D. Power & Associates award for investor satisfaction with online trading services. Scottrade offers trades that cost $7. You don't pay any maintenance fees, and you need only $500 to open a trading account. Additionally, you don't need a trading account (but you still have to register) to receive free real-time streaming quotes and charts.

For affluent investors

Affluent investors often want lots of products and tools. Affluent investors fre-quently use the Internet to monitor the performance of their portfolios, and they expect proprietary customer service in the form of special, knowledge-able customer service representatives. In some situations, wealthy investors expect reduced margin rates. For these investors, system responsiveness and easy Web site navigation aren't issues. The following sites offer the features that affluent investors are looking for:

Which broker is best for you?

In the section "Matching Your Needs to the Right Online Brokerage," I discuss how each individual investor has different needs, wants, and desires. Some investors want quick response times, low costs, and easy-to-navigate Web sites. Other investors want lots of products, tools, and high-quality customer service. The Internet offers many tools for helping you select a broker. One of the best is at SmartMoney at www.smartmoney.com/brokers/yourselfer/index.cfm?story=. This tool ranks characteristics — such as quality of service, costs, access to mutual funds, and so on — to help you determine which online brokerage best suits your individual needs.

- ✔ **Fidelity** (www.fidelity.com) provides many online products and tools. The site was recently revamped, and investors can now quickly find what they want by clicking tabs at the top of a Web page. Affluent investors can personalize the Web site and easily navigate to areas that interest them the most. Clients are divided into three categories: bronze ($19.95 per trade), silver ($14.95 per trade for 36 trades per year and $30,000 in assets, or $100,000 in assets, or 72+ trades per year), and gold ($8.00 per trade for 120+ trades per year and $30,000 in assets or $1,000,000 in assets).

- ✔ **Merrill Lynch Direct** (www.mldirect.ml.com) provides a wide range of customer services. Here you find proprietary research, portfolio monitoring, online trades, cash management accounts, and so on. You can even visit a branch office to discuss your account. Minimum initial deposit is $2,000 for a trading account and $250 minimum deposit to open a retirement account. Online trades of up to 1,000 shares are $29.95 each.

- ✔ **Charles Schwab** (www.schwab.com) provides easy-to-understand online tools and products. Knowledgeable personnel quickly answer telephone calls and refer clients to customer service representatives and others. Premium services, such as access to prescreened financial advisors, and high-level research are available for investors with portfolios of $100,000 or more.

You can easily locate a broker via the World Wide Web. For a good alphabetical list of licensed brokers, see Yahoo! at dir.yahoo.com/Business_and_Economy/Shopping_and_Services/Financial_Services/Investment_Services/Brokerages/Internet_Trading.

Getting Online Trading Services for Less

As I mention at the beginning of this chapter, no two brokerages are alike. Individual brokerages may change their services and fees to keep pace with their competitors. To find the online broker that best meets your needs, you must investigate the prices, services, and features that various brokers offer.

Make certain that your brokerage doesn't charge you for services that are free elsewhere. For example, suppose that an online brokerage charges a flat fee of $15 for your trade. If the brokerage adds a postage and handling fee of $4 for your transaction, your transaction actually costs $19. That's 27 percent higher than you expected. Other hidden fees may include

✔ Higher fees for accepting *odd-lot orders* (orders of less than 100 shares)

✔ Higher fees for certain types of orders (see Chapter 5)

✔ Fees for sending certificates (some firms charge $50 per certificate)

✔ Fees to close your account

✔ Fees to withdraw funds from your trading account

Table 4-1 illustrates some of the fees that you can expect to find with different brokerages. Keep in mind that brokerages are very competitive and are constantly changing their fee structures.

Table 4-1	Sample Comparison of Online Brokerage Fees			
	E*TRADE	*TD Waterhouse*	*Quick & Reilly*	*Charles Schwab*
Quarterly Inactivity Fee	$25	$25	$25	$45/$30
Minimum Balance to Avoid Inactivity Fee	$5,000	$25,000	$25,000	$50,000
Minimum Activity to Avoid Inactivity Fee	2 trades in 6 months	2 trades in 6 months	$25/quarter in commissions	8 trades in 12 months

	E*TRADE	TD Waterhouse	Quick & Reilly	Charles Schwab
Account Transfers	$25 partial, $60 full transfer	$25 partial or full transfer account	$50 full transfer, $50 to close account if	$50 (partial)/ $95 (full) per household assets are less than $50,000*
IRA Custodian Fees	$25 annual maintenance fee	$25 annual maintenance fee (for less than $25,000 in assets)	None	$50 (if total household assets are less than $50,000)*

* Fees vary based on the size of your household accounts and how they are invested. Call customer service at 1-877-832-4330 for exact pricing.

Trading online for $15 or less

The rapid growth of the Internet, technological advances, and more brokerage evolution has led to low commissions for online trading. Generally, all Internet brokers can handle any type of basic transaction with minimal human contact, which lowers the cost of doing business and permits low commissions. Many reputable online brokerages can complete your trade for $15 or less. Table 4-2 lists several brokerages that offer low-cost online trading.

Table 4-2	Trade Online for $15 or Less	
Brokerage Center	**Web Address**	**Commission Structure (Less Than or Equal to 1,000 Shares)**
Ameritrade	www.ameritrade.com	$10.99 market order; $10.99 limit order
BrownCo	www.brownco.com	$5 market, $5 limit
Charles Schwab	www.schwab.com	$9.95 (with 30 trades per quarter *or* household balance of $1,000,000)
E*TRADE	www.etrade.com	$12.99 market, $12.99 limit

(continued)

Table 4-2 *(continued)*

Brokerage Center	Web Address	Commission Structure (Less Than or Equal to 1,000 Shares)
Fidelity Investments	www.fidelity.com	$14.95 (with 36 trades per year and $30,000 in assets *or* $100,000 in assets *or* 72 trades per year)
Muriel Siebert & Co.	www.siebertnet.com	$14.95, $14.95 limit
Scottrade	www.scottrade.com	$7 market; $7 limit
TD Waterhouse Securities	www.waterhouse.com	$12 (with 18 trades per quarter *or* $250,000 in assets)

Finding online brokers with no or low initial account minimums

One of the things that many investors may find prohibitive about online trading is the initial minimum deposit required for opening a cash account. This requirement means that the broker already has your money when you request a trade. However, this requirement is changing, just like everything else on the Internet. Table 4-3 lists several online brokerages that offer cash accounts with no minimum deposit or a low minimum deposit.

Table 4-3	Minimum Amounts to Open Trading Accounts with Some Online Brokers	
Brokerage Center	**Web Address**	**Minimum to Open Cash Account**
Harris*direct*	www.harrisdirect.com	$0
Firstrade.com	www.firstrade.com	$0
SiebertNet.com	www.siebertnet.com	$0
Trading Direct	www.tradingdirect.com	$0
Scottrade	www.scottrade.com	$500
E*TRADE	www.etrade.com	$1,000

Brokerage Center	Web Address	Minimum to Open Cash Account
TD Waterhouse Securities	www.waterhouse.com	$1,000
Merrill Lynch Direct	www.mldirect.ml.com	$2,000
Ameritrade	www.ameritrade.com	$2,000
Investrade	www.investrade.com	$2,000
Fidelity Investments	www.fidelity.com	$2,500
Charles Schwab	www.schwab.com	$10,000

Commission structures change radically from firm to firm. One reason for this wide range is that some Internet brokers include special or additional features. When deciding which broker is best for you, factoring in some or all of the features that I list in this section is probably wise. First, consider whether each broker offers the following features in your cash account:

✔ Low minimum amount required to open an account

✔ Low monthly fees with minimum equity balance

✔ No additional charges for postage and handling

✔ A summary of cash balances

✔ A summary of order status

✔ A summary of your portfolio's value

✔ A historical review of your trading activities

✔ No charges for retirement account maintenance

When comparing brokers, consider whether each broker offers the following account features:

✔ Unlimited check-writing privileges

✔ Dividend collection and reinvestment

✔ Debit cards for ATM access

✔ Interest earned on cash balances

✔ Wire transfers accepted

✔ No IRA inactivity fees

You should ascertain which of the following types of investments the broker enables you to trade:

- ✔ Stocks (foreign or domestic)
- ✔ Options
- ✔ Bonds (corporate or agency)
- ✔ Treasury securities
- ✔ Zero-coupon bonds
- ✔ Certificates of deposit
- ✔ Precious metals
- ✔ Mutual funds
- ✔ Unit investment trusts

You need to determine whether the brokerage offers the following analytical and research features:

- ✔ Real-time online quotes
- ✔ Reports on insider trading
- ✔ Economic forecasts
- ✔ Company profiles and breaking news
- ✔ Earnings forecasts
- ✔ End-of-the-day prices automatically sent to you

Adding new features to Web sites is a routine occurrence in the online brokerage world, as are changes in the online brokerage's internal database for better and more personalized reporting. Therefore, even though an online brokerage doesn't have all the features you desire, that brokerage may offer the missing items in the near future. For example, you probably won't need to contact customer service very often, but when you do, you want excellent service. Frequently, this service means being able to talk immediately with a sales representative. In response to this need, many online brokerages now offer a *Chat button*. Click the button and a chat window opens in which you can talk directly with a sales representative. E*TRADE (www.etrade.com) is one example of an online brokerage that offers this feature, and many other online brokerages are considering adding this feature to their Web sites.

Rating Online Brokers

Online brokerage rankings are often based on the trade execution process, ease of use, customer confidence, on-site resources, relationship services, commissions, and overall costs. The following Web sites offer ratings that can help you determine which online brokerage meets your needs:

✔ **Consumer Search** (`www.consumersearch.com/www/personal_finance/online_brokers/reviews.html`) offers free reviews of online brokers based on articles written by others. Some of the articles used for ratings offered by Consumer Search are more than four years old.

✔ **Kiplinger.com Rates Online Brokerages** (`www.kiplinger.com`) presents an October 2004 survey of the best online stock brokers, with rankings for asset values, commissions, execution times, mutual fund programs, broker research, and tax information. (This article is from the Kiplinger archive and costs $2.95.)

✔ **SmartMoney.com** (`smartmoney.com/brokers/index.cfm?story=2004-intro`) provides free brokerage ratings. Brokerages are divided into full-service, premium online discount, and discount brokerages. The July 2004 comparison articles and tables are easy to read.

Don't assume that you always get what you pay for. The Keynote Web Broker Trading Index (`www.keynote.com/solutions/performance_indices/broker_index/broker_trading.html`) illustrates the average response times and success rates for creating a standard stock-order transaction on selected brokerage Web sites. The sites that appear in the Index were selected based on publicly available market-share information published in *The Wall Street Journal* and other reliable industry sources. Using the Keynote Web Broker Trading Index, you can easily see that some high-priced online brokerages aren't as fast or as reliable as their lower-priced competitors.

Checking Out Hybrid Online Banks and Brokerages

The Financial Services Modernization Act of 1999 allowed banks and brokerages to offer a full menu of financial products and services. This deregulation, among other things, means that your brokerage can offer you the same products and services as your bank, including having your accounts insured by the Federal Deposit Insurance Corporation (FDIC). Combining your bank and brokerage can reduce the amount of fees you have to pay and the time you spend online monitoring your accounts. Kiplinger's (`www.kiplinger.com`) has coined a new name for these combination entities — *bankerages*. Bankerages offer asset management accounts that combine your banking accounts and brokerage accounts. You receive a monthly statement that reflects all the activities of your bankerage accounts (which can even include an equity line of credit with your bankerage).

Banking with your brokerage has many advantages. For example, you can easily transfer money from your brokerage account to your banking account, savings, or money market fund. (I talk more about money market funds in Chapters 6 and 12.) When it's tax time, all the information you need is in one easy-to-find location.

Another advantage of having all your financial asset information at one location is that you don't have to visit Web sites that are scattered around the Internet to determine the status of your portfolio. The following lists several of the attributes you should look at when evaluating a bankerage:

- **Account aggregation:** This trait enables you to see simultaneously all the different types of investments and accounts you have with one financial institution.

- **Low brokerage charges:** Some bankerages offer low-cost commissions for sales personnel. Mutual fund management and brokerage fees charged by bankerages are also low.

- **Wide range of services:** Some bankerages offer incredible amounts of high-quality research. Other online bankerages provide cost-basis information so that you can easily determine your taxable gains or losses.

- **Bill-payment services:** Some online bankerages provide free bill-payment services. (For more about online bill-payment services, see Chapter 17.)

- **Low banking fees:** Banking fees charged by bankerages can vary widely. Some online bankerages offer free or low-fee ATM costs. Some bankerages have *sweep account programs* that automatically transfer funds above (or below) a certain amount to higher-interest-earning accounts at the close of each business day.

- **Good rates:** Some bankerages offer higher yields on certificates of deposit (CDs) than others. Additionally, some bankerages offer higher rates on interest-bearing checking accounts than others.

The following are a few examples of bankerages:

- **Fidelity** (www.fidelity.com) states that applying online takes approximately 10 to 15 minutes. If necessary, you can save your application and return within 30 days to complete it. Fidelity is a winner when it comes to low banking fees, low brokerage fees for index mutual funds, and research.

- **NetBank** (www.netbank.com) offers an online application. If you don't like online applications, you can always download its paper application. Applicants need a U.S. Social Security number to apply for an account.

- **Citibank** (www.citibank.com) requirements to open an account include U.S. citizenship with a U.S. address, a driver's license or state ID, and a second form of identification, such as a U.S. passport, credit card, or U.S. military ID. All applicants must be at least 18 years old and provide a valid Social Security number, mother's maiden name, and employment address. If you're not a U.S. citizen, try calling 800-374-9700.

- **Wells Fargo Bank** (www.wellsfargo.com) allows you greater control of your finances with just one password. With Wells Fargo OneLook, you can securely manage both your Wells Fargo and non–Wells Fargo accounts. You have online access to your bill-paying services, checking, savings, credit card, mortgage, loans, and investment accounts.

Opening Your Online Brokerage Account

Internet brokerage firms are basically cash-and-carry enterprises. They all require investors to open an account before trading — a process that takes from several minutes to several weeks to complete. Account minimums vary from $0 to $100,000.

Investors can open an account in two ways. The first method of opening an account is online. This quick approach takes about 15 minutes. The second way to open a trading account is by mail. This process takes about two to three weeks to complete. All Internet brokers require that you complete an application form that includes your name, address, Social Security number, work history, and a personal check, certified check, or money order for the minimum amount needed to open an account. Some brokers accept wire transfers or securities of equal value. Your online brokerage firm will send you the application materials to complete and return.

Individuals are eligible to open a trading account or IRA account online if they're U.S. citizens or residents and have a valid U.S. address, are transferring the required minimum deposit into the new trading account, and accept the terms of the online brokerage's account agreement. (Check the broker's Web site for details.)

To see exactly what's involved in opening a trading account go to the Investing Online Resource Center sponsored by the North American Securities Administrators Association at www.investingonline.org. Click the Signing Up For An Online Account simulation. The following are examples of some of the questions you're asked when opening an account online:

1. **What type of account do you want?**

   Individual, Joint, Custodial, or IRA?

2. **Do you want a cash or margin account?**

   I explain margin accounts in Chapter 16.

3. **How will you complete your initial deposit?**

   Will you transfer funds from your checking account, send a check via U.S. Mail, or use securities from another brokerage?

4. **What's your personal information?**

   This information includes your name, address, citizenship, Social Security number, and so on.

5. **Are you a broker/dealer, director, or 10 percent (or more) share-holder of a publicly traded company?**

Be wary of new account incentives

Online brokerages offer numerous incentives to attract new investors. For many online investors, it may appear that this is the time to move to a broker that has more of what you're looking for. Some of these incentives are true bargains, while others aren't as straightforward as they appear.

Many brokerage incentives feature offers that are available only for a limited time and require that you keep a minimum balance in your trading account that's much higher than what you may have anticipated. Remember to read the small print before signing your application.

6. **Where do you want to keep your cash between investments?**

   Do you prefer a money market fund, treasury fund, mutual tax-exempt fund, and so on?

7. **How experienced are you with investing?**

8. **What are your investing objectives?**

9. **Indicate your agreement with the terms and conditions of your trading account.**

10. **Congratulations, you can start trading online.**

The simulation takes less then ten minutes to complete. After you have completed the online simulation (and have the necessary funds for the brokerage's initial deposit), go to the Web site of your selected brokerage. Complete the brokerage's online application, and you're ready to start trading online.

Chapter 5

Getting Ahold of Trading Online

In This Chapter
▶ Deciphering the tax consequences in trading securities
▶ Increasing your profits by choosing the right trading techniques
▶ Getting a grip on electronic communications networks (ECNs)
▶ Turning your desktop computer into an effective trading tool
▶ Getting personal with your online brokerage
▶ Getting the most out of wireless trading

*I*n this chapter, I show you how to make more money by using simple order techniques. You gain an understanding of day orders, limit orders, market orders, stop and stop-limit orders, and so on. You discover why electronic communications networks (ECNs) have revolutionized investing.

Next, you find out where to go for extended trading hours information. You become aware of who is an active investor and how this type is different from a day trader. You discover how mainstream full-service and discount online brokerages have special software that can make your PC (or Mac) into a trading cockpit, and how you can see moving charts, breaking news headlines, and streaming quotes all on one screen. You gain an understanding of how active investors can personalize their desktop software and how online brokerages are offering more Web site personalization.

I conclude the chapter with a discussion of wireless trading. I show you which types of devices you can use for wireless trading and what types of brokerage restrictions or additional costs you may encounter.

Understanding the Tax Consequences of Trading Securities

Investors receive two types of income: ordinary income and capital gains. *Ordinary income* includes dividends and interest. *Capital gains* (or *capital losses*) are when you sell capital assets for a profit (or loss). Assets can include stocks, bonds, and real estate. Capital gains are better than ordinary income because:

- ✔ **You can control the timing:** You don't have to pay taxes on your gains until you sell the asset. This delay lets you control the timing of your gain or loss so that you can maximize your after-tax profits.

- ✔ **Long-term gains get special treatment:** Long-term capital gains (from investments held over a year) are taxed at a lower rate than ordinary income. (Short-term capital gains, on the other hand, are taxed at the same rate as ordinary income.)

Special rates for long-term capital gains

In May 2003, new tax laws gave investors a break by lessening the tax liability of dividends and capital gains. For investors holding assets for more than a year, the gain on the sale is taxed at a lower rate than regular income. For investors who are in the top four tax brackets, the long-term rate is 15 percent. Lower-income investors pay capital gains of 5 percent. Dividends and interest, in most cases, are taxed at the same rate as short-term capital gains. The investment tax changes are effective for tax years 2003 through 2008. In 2008, the 5 percent rate drops to zero. On January 1, 2009 the previous capital gain rates are scheduled to return.

Table 5-1 illustrates how investors who hold assets for less than a year must pay taxes on their short-term capital gains at the same rate as their income taxes. Table 5-1 also shows you how investors who hang on to investments for one year (or longer) can pay significantly lower tax rates. Overall, Table 5-1 shows how taking taxes into consideration can dramatically enhance your after-tax investment returns.

Table 5-1		**2004 Federal Personal Income Tax Rates**			
Tax rate	*Capital Gains Tax Rate (ST/LT)**	*Single filers*	*Married filing jointly or qualifying widow/ widower*	*Married filing separately*	*Head of house-hold*
10%	10%/5%	Up to $7,150	Up to $14,300	Up to $7,150	Up to $10,200
15%	15%/5%	$7,151– $29,050	$14,301– $58,100	$7,151– $29,050	$10,201– $38,900
25%	25%/15%	$29,051– $70,350	$58,101– $117,250	$29,051– $58,625	$38,901– $100,500

Tax rate	Capital Gains Tax Rate (ST/LT)*	Single filers	Married filing jointly or qual-ifying widow/ widower	Married filing separately	Head of house-hold
28%	28%/15%	$70,351–$146,750	$117,251–$178,650	$58,626–$89,325	$100,501–$162,700
33%	33%/15%	$146,751–$319,100	$178,651–$319,100	$89,326–$159,550	$162,701–$319,100
35%	35%/15%	$319,101 or more	$319,101 or more	$159,551 or more	$319,101 or more

ST= Short-term capital gains / LT= Long-term capital gains

Measuring capital gains

A capital gain is the difference between the amount realized in the sale and your basis in the asset you sold. Your *basis* is based on your cost (usually the purchase price plus the brokerage commission) but can be adjusted as a result of different events. For example, if your stock splits while you own it, the basis splits, too. (Most brokerage statements and online portfolio track-ing programs can take care of the math for you.)

> **Example:** You buy 100 shares of ABC at $35, paying $3,500 plus a broker-age commission of $15. Your basis is $3,515. Later, you sell when the stock is at $39. You receive $3,900 minus a brokerage commission of $15, so your amount realized is $3,885. Your capital gain is $3,885 minus $3,515, or $370.

Note: If your basis is greater than the amount realized, you have a capital loss.

What about capital losses?

Uncle Sam gives investors a break by allowing them to deduct up to $3,000 in net capital losses each year using the Form 1040 Schedule D. (If married and filing separately, the deduction limit is $1,500.) This tax break can be used to counterbalance capital gains. If you have no capital gains (or if the capital losses are larger than the capital gains), you can deduct the capital loss against your other income. If you lose more than $3,000 in any one year, you can carry over your losses into the next year.

✔ **Net short-term loss, no long-term action:** You can deduct up to $3,000 of the loss against ordinary income. If the loss exceeds $3,000, you can carry over the excess to the next year. *Note:* The carry-over is still considered a short-term loss.

✔ **No short-term action, long-term loss:** You can deduct up to $3,000 of the loss against ordinary income. If the loss exceeds $3,000, you can carry over the excess to the next year. *Note*: The carryover is considered a long-term loss.

✔ **Net short-term loss, net long-term loss:** You can deduct up to $3,000 of the loss against ordinary income. The $3,000 deduction is applied against your net short-term losses first. If you have an unused deduction amount, the deduction carries over to the next year as a short-term loss. Any unused long-term loss carries over to next year as a long-term loss.

✔ **Net short-term loss, net long-term gain:** If the long-term gain exceeds the short-term loss, then the gain is considered a long-term gain and taxed at a favorable rate. For example, if you had a net short-term loss of $2,000 and a net long-term gain of $2,200, you would pay the long-term capital gains tax rate on $200. On the other hand, if the short-term loss exceeds the net long-term gain, the overall loss is considered short-term. This allows you to deduct up to $3,000 against other income and to carry over the excess to the next year.

✔ **Net short-term gain, net long-term loss:** If the short-term gain is greater than the long-term loss, the net gains is considered a short-term gain and taxed at your ordinary income rate. If the net long-term loss is greater than the short-term gain, the loss is considered long-term, and you're allowed to deduct up to $3,000 against other income and to carry over any excess to the next year.

The best time to take a capital loss is in a year with short-term capital gains or no gains. This timing saves you having to pay taxes at your full ordinary rate.

Increasing Profits with Simple Order Specification Techniques

Traditional brokers recommend the order specifications for your stock transactions and confirm that your transactions were completed. (An *order* is a request to buy or sell a specified amount of a certain security or commodity at a specified price or at the market price.) Specifying security execution orders is one of the expert services that brokers use to justify their fees. *Order specifications* define how your request is completed. One type of order specification is called a *day order*. Day orders are good only on the day you place the order.

Another type of order is the *Good Till Canceled (GTC) order.* The GTC order is open until it's executed or canceled. For example, an investor wants to buy a certain company's shares, but not until the shares are a few dollars cheaper. The investor specifies a GTC order and determines when the order will expire. If the company's shares reach the predetermined limit (today, tomorrow, next year, or next decade), the order is filled.

Trading online means that you're now in charge of specifying your stock order. Knowing how to designate the terms of your order can increase your chances of execution at the price you want. As you look over your online order form, you'll notice different ways of specifying how the order should be executed. In the past, your traditional broker decided which approach was best. With online trading, you select the method you feel is best.

Here are four of the more popular ways to specify your stock order:

- **Limit orders:** Orders in which buyers or sellers specify the price at which they're willing to buy or sell. For sell orders, the limit specified is the minimum price at which the investor is willing to sell. For buy orders, the limit is the maximum price that the investor is willing to pay.

- **Market orders:** Any order (buy or sell) to be executed immediately at the best price available. In other words, the investor wants to buy or sell a stated number of shares at the best price at the time the order is placed.

- **Stop orders:** An order to buy at a price above or sell at a price below the current market. This type of order gives investors more control than a market order, which buys or sells a security at any price. Stop orders limit the investor's loss (or locks in the investor's profit).

- **Stop-limit orders:** After a security reaches the investor's predetermined price, the order is activated. The order can be executed only at the set price or better, so the order may not be completed.

You may want to use a limit order when purchasing or selling *odd lots* (less than 100 shares of any one stock). This type of order can increase your chances of getting filled at your price. Odd lots rarely get the best price because they must be bundled with other orders.

The Investing Online Resource Center offers many resources for beginning online investors. One of my favorites is the handy online trading simulation at www.investingonline.org/isc/index.html. This simulation is a terrific risk-free way to find out what it's like to invest online.

ECNs — It's Not Your Grandfather's Market Anymore

Recent changes in SEC regulations and technology have transformed how investors interact with the stock market. I explain these changes in the following sections, and I show you how these changes enable online investors to make more money on their investments. In the following sections, you gain an understanding of what happens after you click your mouse button to execute an online trade. You also discover how you can avoid hidden transaction costs by using an electronic communications network (ECN) and how you benefit from ECNs even if you never use one.

How ECNs work

In 1988, the Securities and Exchange Commission (SEC) began requiring NASDAQ market makers to accept buy and sell orders of up to 1,000 shares via an automated small-order execution system (SOES). This requirement opened the door for the so-called "SOES bandits," who later became known as day traders. It also led to the development of the first electronic communications networks (ECNs), and in January 1997, the SEC approved the first four ECNs. Today, nine ECNs exist.

Stocks are traded by *specialists* on the New York Stock Exchange (NYSE) and by *market makers* in the NASDAQ market. For example, the NASDAQ requires at least two market makers for each listed stock. This requirement creates a market in which the stock is bought and sold. On ECNs, computers replace specialists and market makers. Anyone can purchase NASDAQ-traded equities through a brokerage that uses an ECN. Investors buy stock through an online broker, and if the broker's computer finds a seller in an ECN, the investor's order is executed with no human intervention. (And because computers never sleep, ECNs open the way for after-hours trading.)

To gain some insight into how ECNs work, compare how investors purchase equities on the NYSE, NASDAQ, and ECNs.

Buying stock on the NYSE involves the following steps:

1. **The broker sends a buy order to a specialist on the exchange floor.**

2. **The specialist looks for sellers on the trading floor or in an electronic order book.**

3. **If the specialist finds enough sellers to match the offer price, the specialist completes the transaction.**

Here are the steps for buying stock on the NASDAQ:

1. **The broker consults a trading screen that lists how many shares various market makers are offering to sell and at what price.**

2. **The broker picks the best price and sends an electronic message to the market maker, who must sell the shares.**

In contrast, buying stock on an ECN involves these steps:

1. **The broker sends a buy order to an ECN.**

2. **The computer looks for matching sell orders on the ECN.**

3. **If the computer finds enough sellers to complete the trade, the transaction is executed. Otherwise, the order isn't executed.**

Understanding inside spreads

One of the first steps in understanding trading is to define the players. What day traders really focus on are the activities of market makers. A *market maker* represents an institution (such as Lehman Brothers, Merrill Lynch & Co., Prudential Securities, and so on) that wants to *make a market* in a particular NASDAQ stock. The market maker is a specialist on an exchange or a dealer in the over-the-counter market who buys and sells stocks, creating an inventory for temporary holding. The market maker provides liquidity by buying and selling at any time. However, the market maker isn't under any obligation to buy or sell at a price other than the published bid and ask prices.

The downside of being a market maker is that you're obligated to purchase stocks when no one wants them. The upside of being a market maker is that you get to pocket the profits of a spread. A *spread* is the difference between a bid and ask price. For example, a stock with a bid and ask price of $15 \times 15\frac{1}{4}$ has a spread of $\frac{1}{4}$. The bid price is $15, and the sell price is $15.25. By selling 1,000 shares at $15.25, the market maker profits by $250.

Spreads are often just a few cents for each stock. However, these pennies quickly become dollars because of high trading volume. Last year, NASDAQ market makers earned $2 billion from spreads. Day traders have sliced into some of these profits. Recent reports indicate that market maker spreads are down by 30 percent.

The existence of several kinds of spreads has caused some confusion. The following list defines some of these spreads:

- **Dealer spread:** The quote of the individual market maker. A market maker never earns the entire spread. The market maker needs to be competitive on either the bid or offer side of the market. The dealer is unlikely to be at the best price (the highest price if selling and the lowest price if buying) on both sides of the market at the same time.

- **Inside spread:** The highest bid and lowest offer being quoted among all the market makers competing in a stock. Because the quote is a combined quote, it's narrower than an individual dealer quote.

- **Actual spreads paid:** The narrowest measure of a spread, because it's based on actual trade prices. The actual spread paid is calculated by measuring actual trade prices against the inside quotes at the time of the trade.

Extended-Hours Trading

In the past, the NASDAQ and NYSE were open from 9:30 a.m. to 4:00 p.m. EST. Today, extended trading hours are the result of ECNs handling more and more orders than ever before. ECNs are computers that can work 24 hours a day. All trades placed during these sessions are represented exclusively on ECNs.

ECNs aren't isolated trading islands; rather, they're just like any participant in the NASDAQ market. Most, if not all, NASDAQ market participants, including ECNs and market makers, are linked to a system called Select Net, which automatically reports transactions. As long as ECNs and the overall NASDAQ market are linked to Select Net, ECNs aren't likely to fragment or reduce liquidity in the market. However, extended-hours trading does have some limitations:

- News stories may have a greater impact on stock prices.

- Some stocks will be very liquid (easily convertible to cash) during after-hours trading, and some will not be liquid at all.

- Investors may encounter wider spreads between bids and offers than during traditional market hours. Stock prices may be more volatile.

- Investors may be competing against professional traders with more information and analysis.

Sources for extended-hours stock information

With unprecedented access to information about securities and trading, investors now enjoy narrower spreads, lower execution costs, and faster execution speeds. For example, the average investor can access the following extended-hours market information:

- **NASDAQ** (dynamic.nasdaq.com/dynamic/afterhourma.stm) offers information on the ten most active stocks.

- **CBS MarketWatch** (cbs.marketwatch.com/tools/stockresearch/screener/afterhours.asp?siteid=mktw) offers summaries of pre-market trading. CBS MarketWatch also provides Instinet quotes for actively traded stocks and companies that have released important news.

Some online brokerages provide extended-hours quotes. For example, account holders at Charles Schwab (www.schwab.com) can go to the real-time quote box on the stock trading Web page. When you enter the ticker symbol of the equity that you're interested in, add the letter *e* to the end of the ticker symbol. (For example, type **IBMe** for the extended-hours trading price of IBM.) The price quoted will be the extended-hours price.

Join the extended-hours club

After-hours trading is one way that an online brokerage can increase revenue. As of this writing, the following six brokerages command 80 percent of all online trading accounts. Each of the following online brokerages, listed with their Web sites and the name of the ECNs they use, offers extended traded hours:

- **Ameritrade** (www.ameritrade.com): Island

- **E*TRADE** (www.etrade.com): Archipelago

- **Fidelity** (www.fidelity.com): REDIBook

- **Harris***direct* (www.harrisdirect.com): REDIBook

- **Charles Schwab** (www.schwab.com): REDIBook

Different brokerages offer different extended trading hours, trade different securities (for example, just NASDAQ or certain securities), and have different rules about joining the club. Table 5-2 shows the rules for several major online brokerages.

Table 5-2	Rules for Extended-Hours Trading	
Online Broker- age (URL)	*Limit Order Online Trading Costs for 1,000 Shares or Less*	*Hours for Trading on the NYSE and NASDAQ*
Ameritrade (www. ameritrade.com)	$10.99 per trade	8:00 a.m. to 8:00 p.m. EST
E*TRADE (www. etrade.com)	$19.95 per trade	8:00 a.m. to 8:00 p.m. EST
Fidelity Online (www. fidelity.com)	$19.95 per trade for first 72 trades, with some order restrictions	8:00 a.m. to 8:00 p.m. EST
Harris*direct* (www. harrisdirect.com)	$20 per trade, with some order restrictions	8:00 a.m. to 9:15 a.m. and 4:15 p.m. to 6:30 p.m. EST
Charles Schwab (www.schwab.com)	$20.95 per trade for first 29 trades	7:30 a.m. to 9:15 a.m. EST; 4:15 p.m. to 8:00 p.m. EST
A. B. Watley (www. abwatley.com)	$19.95 + $0.04 per share for first 48 trades	7:00 a.m. to 6:30 p.m. EST

Online Trading and the Active Investor

Today, many mainstream full-service and online brokerages offer active and hyperactive investors special software, amenities, and low trading fees. *Active investors* are often defined as individuals who place at least 36 stock, bond, or option trades per year and have $25,000 or more in assets. Some of the special services these investors receive are

- Multiple order-entry screens that enable active investors to send many trades with just one click of the mouse
- Low trading fees that are often a fraction of the brokerages' normal rates
- Access to IPO information for investors with high balances in their trading accounts
- Access to knowledgeable representatives to discuss margin buying, short selling, complex options strategies, and day-to-day operations of various markets

✔ Customizable software that makes the active investor's workstation fit his or her specific needs

✔ Special technology, such as real-time streaming quotes and Level II NASDAQ quotes

Most investors are familiar with Level I quotes. These quotes are the ones we're all comfortable with: Bid, Ask, Last trade, Volume, and so on. Level II NASDAQ quotes provide investors with a little more information. For active traders, this information is sometimes considered essential because Level II NASDAQ quotes reveal the order book for a certain NASDAQ stock. In other words, Level II NASDAQ quotes show the best Bid and Asking price of every market participant who is publicly posting a quote. For more about Level II NASDAQ quotes, see Investopedia.com's clearly written explanation of electronic trading at `www.investopedia.com/university/electronictrading/default.asp`.

Active investor trading platforms

Today, individual investors have access to new desktop software that can convert your PC into an effective trading tool. Making your workstation into a trading pit by using active trading technology from full-service and discount online brokerages is truly wonderful, but it can't compete with day-trading software that works directly with an ECN.

In other words, you aren't able to aim a transaction at a specific ECN to gain that extra .125 points in 10 minutes. This feature is the one day traders count on for their livelihoods. Active trading software is designed for gains of between 3 percent and 10 percent over several days or weeks.

The following are a few examples of what mainstream online brokerages can offer active investors:

✔ **Charles Schwab** (`www.schwab.com`) offers the *Street Smart Pro* trading platform. The Street Smart Pro trading platform leverages CyberTrader's trading technology (CyberTrader is owned by Charles Schwab) and combines NASDAQ Level II quotes, real-time streaming news, unlimited watch lists, and real-time, streaming, interactive charts with account management features, risk management tools, multichannel access, and personal support. Street Smart Pro allows you to execute your trades through SmartEx, Schwab's proprietary order-routing technology, without having to access another trading program. Commissions are as low as $9.95. For more information and a demo of Street Smart Pro, see `www.schwabat.com/platforms/streetsmartpro/default.aspx`.

✔ **Fidelity** (www.fidelity.com), shown in Figure 5-1, offers *Active Trader Pro,* which is geared for households that place 120 or more trades per year. Fidelity Active Trader Services offers directed trading, streaming market data, depth-of-book Level II quotes, advanced technical filters, and real-time and historical sales figures. *Wealth-Lab Pro* is a complete platform within Fidelity's Active Trader Pro software that allows users the ability to develop and back-test trading strategies based on technical analysis. You receive commissions as low as $8 per trade, as well as guaranteed one-second execution and convenient wireless trading. For more information and an online tour, see personal.fidelity.com/products/atp/content/atsoverview.shtml.

✔ **E*TRADE** (www.etrade.com) offers *Power E*TRADE* for active traders. Power E*TRADE is a consolidated trading command center that offers automatic routing of stock and option orders, streaming NASDAQ Level II quotes, streaming options chains, custom watch lists, streaming intra-day charts, dynamic account positions, and live order status, in addition to real-time buying power, live time and sales views, intelligent alerts, speed keys, high/low ticker, market data ticker, and real-time news. The *Power E*TRADE Trading Desk* is a streamlined one-page trading console that lets you manage multiple stock and option orders from a single trading screen, allows you to prepare multiple orders in advance for rapid-fire trading, lets you create watch lists with customized quote updates, and permits you fast access to open orders account balances and trade records. *Power E*TRADE Pro* is E*TRADE's desktop software that delivers real-time streaming market data, advanced charting, and direct access to three ECNs. For more information and demos of all three active trader platforms, go to the home page at www.etrade.com. In the search box, enter **advanced trading platforms**, and then click the Advanced Trading Platforms link. Commissions are $9.99 with no extra fees for stop or limit orders.

✔ **Scottrade** (www.scottrade.com) offers *ScottradeELITE* for active traders. To download ScottradeELITE, you need to have a minimum account value of $25,000. You also need to maintain a minimum account value of $25,000 or you're no longer eligible to use ScottradeELITE. You're charged $9.95 per month for NASDAQ Level II quotes. Internet trades are $7 per order (add $5 for stop and limit orders). Trades placed by touch-tone phone are $12; broker-assisted trades are $17; and online mutual fund orders have no transaction fees. ScottradeELITE includes advanced charting, integrated trading tools for stocks and options, customer support, streaming NASDAQ Level II and quote grids, real-time streaming news, integrated account management tools, and technical and fundamental research capabilities.

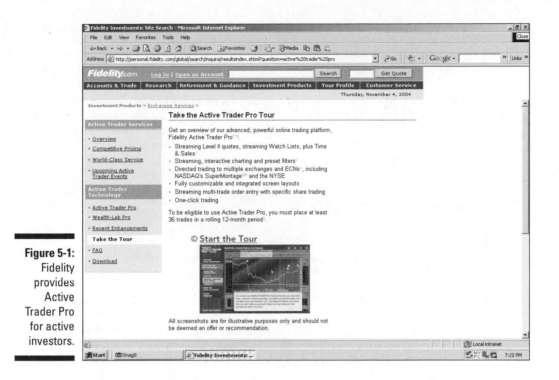

Figure 5-1:
Fidelity
provides
Active
Trader Pro
for active
investors.

You might be a day trader if . . .

The SEC (www.sec.gov) sees *pattern day traders* as investors who trade four or more times in five business days. If day-trading activities don't exceed 6 percent of the customer's total trading activity for the 5-day period, the clearing firm is not required to designate such accounts as pattern day traders. The 6 percent threshold is designed to allow clearing firms to exclude from the definition of pattern day trader those customers whose day-trading activities comprise a small percentage of their overall trading activities.

Additionally, if the firm knows or has a reasonable basis to believe that the customer is a pattern day trader (for example, if the firm provided training to the customer on day trading in anticipation of the customer opening an account), the customer must be designated as a pattern day trader immediately, instead of delaying such determination for five business days.

The benefit of being classified as a pattern day trader is lower transaction fees. The disadvantage of this classification is the requirement for a higher trading account balance. Pattern day traders are required to keep a minimum balance of $25,000 in their brokerage accounts to meet NASD requirements. For details, see an explanation of SEC Rule 2520 at the Securities and Exchange Commission Web site located at `www.sec.gov/rules/sro/nd0003n.htm`. *Note:* This rule was approved August 27, 2001.

CyberTrader (`www.cybertrader.com`), owned by Charles Schwab, is geared toward hyperactive traders. (Trading is so frequent for hyperactive traders that they don't want to reenter their passwords on each order entry.) What makes this Web site unique is the self-paced education and extensive glossary. The proprietary trading system is software-application-based with extras such as charts, NASDAQ Level II data, multiple ECN quotes, and risk-management tools. The software comes in two flavors: CyberX2 for beginners and CyberTrader Pro for the more advanced trader.

Going from Hardwired to Wireless Trading

Many online brokerages offer wireless information to customers. Wireless information allows customers to get the information they want, when they want it, and where they want it. Wireless information can include

- ✔ The ability to execute trades wherever you are
- ✔ Account access to check balances and positions
- ✔ Breaking news stories
- ✔ Real-time quotes and the ability to review the day's trading
- ✔ Notification of price triggers and alerts
- ✔ Trade confirmations or notifications
- ✔ Options assignments for keeping current
- ✔ The ability to receive margin calls

Imagine that you're driving to work when the radio broadcasts news that a company you're interested in has just dropped to $35 a share. You're on your way to the mandatory weekly meeting but want to catch this opportunity. You take out your personal digital assistant (PDA) and log on to your brokerage (pull off the road first!). You get a real-time quote and set up a limit order: If the stock falls to $33, you'll purchase 100 shares. You execute your order and receive a confirmation. Total transaction time: less than a minute.

The Internet revolutionized investing in the '90s by enabling investors to connect with the markets online. The next revolution for investors is the proliferation of wireless, mobile appliances that give you instant Internet connections from the palm of your hand, anywhere and anytime.

Today, the fastest growing categories of consumer electronics are lightweight PC laptops, cell phones, and PDAs — all unwired devices that provide easy Internet and e-mail access. Not only can you send and receive messages and trade stocks while you sit in traffic or on the beach, you can also zap data between devices without a wire. What makes this unwired world possible is highly complex digital and analog technologies on a single chip.

The implications for investors are huge now that wireless devices are available from the major brokerage firms. You don't have to be wired in order to be connected to the stock market anymore! You can be a wireless investor in many ways. Here are a few examples of online brokerages that offer wireless trading:

- **Ameritrade** (www.ameritrade.com) supports Web-enabled phone or hand-held devices. There are no extra charges or restrictions.

- **E*TRADE Financial Wireless** (www.etrade.com) supports AT&T Wireless, Cingular, Nextel Online, Print PCS, Verizon Wireless, VoiceStream, Omnisky, and Palm.net phone systems for your Palm V or Palm VII hand-held devices. There are no extra charges or restrictions.

- **Fidelity** (www.fidelity.com) offers *Fidelity Anywhere,* which supports wireless devices such as Web-enabled phones and personal digital assistants. There are no extra charges or restrictions.

- **Harris***direct* (www.harrisdirect.com), shown in Figure 5-2, supports Web-enabled cell phones, cell phones with text messaging, RIM two-way pagers, and alphanumeric pagers. Harris*direct* also supports PDAs such as PalmPilots, Handspring, and Pocket PC hand-helds. There are no extra charges for trades and no restrictions.

- **Charles Schwab** (www.schwab.com) has developed PocketBroker, a wireless investing service that enables U.S. clients to access account information or place an equity order via PalmPilot, RIM wireless hand-held pager, and Internet-ready cellular phones. There are no additional charges for wireless trades.

- **TD Waterhouse** (www.waterhouse.com) supports your Web-ready phone or Palm- or Windows-powered Pocket PC hand-held. These products require wireless Internet service from a carrier or wireless Internet provider. There are no additional fees.

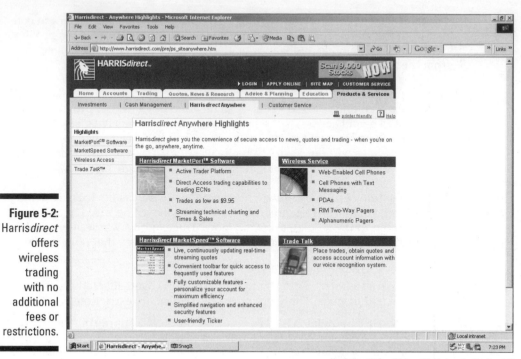

Figure 5-2:
Harris*direct*
offers
wireless
trading
with no
additional
fees or
restrictions.

Harrisdirect LLC, a division of Harris Investor Services LLC

Part II
Finding the Right Investments

The 5th Wave   By Rich Tennant

"I'm not sure — I like the mutual funds with rotating dollar signs although the dancing stocks and bonds look good too."

In this part . . .

The Internet offers plenty of resources that can help you turn your hunches into investment strategies, and the chapters in this part of the book highlight the best Internet sources for tools and information related to mutual funds, stocks, and bonds.

This part of the book shows you how to locate mutual funds online, how to analyze a prospectus, and how you can buy a no-load mutual fund through an online brokerage. Discover how you can simplify your online investing with index or exchange traded funds. Use high-powered online tools to examine and compare mutual fund fees to determine the true cost of a mutual fund. You find out how to use Internet screens to locate stock candidates. You also discover how to use online tools to analyze stocks, as well as how to find earnings forecasts and online sources that can assist you in deciphering company annual reports. Discover the warning signs of a company's bankruptcy before it's too late. Use sophisticated online tools to value securities to determine their fair market value. Discover how you can purchase savings bonds and Treasuries online and directly from the federal government without a broker.

Chapter 6

The Keys to Successful Internet Mutual Fund Investing

· ·

In This Chapter

▶ Understanding mutual fund types, fees, and risks

▶ Using online screening tools to find mutual funds that meet your requirements

▶ Locating and reading online prospectuses and other information

· ·

*T*his chapter provides you with all the basic online tools for identifying mutual fund candidates. I present some general information about mutual fund investment, including types of funds and fees. I include information about what makes exchange-traded and index funds more popular than ever before. I offer suggestions about where to find mutual fund facts and figures online. I also describe several online screening tools that can help you choose the mutual fund that best meets your needs. These mutual fund screens vary from simple to advanced. (By the way, the best online mutual fund screen is the one that includes the investment criteria *you* feel are important.) I conclude this chapter by discussing how you can use new online tools to compare mutual fund costs, returns, and risks.

Mutual Fund Basics

Over the years, the stock market has outperformed any other investment. Unlike a mutual fund, however, individual investors frequently can't purchase a large number of different securities to *diversify* their investment risk. Buying shares in a mutual fund solves this problem. When you invest in a mutual fund, the diversity of the portfolio reduces the risk of losing your total investment. Selecting the right fund may be difficult, but you can find plenty of online help.

Assume that you have $1,000 to invest in a mutual fund. With your investment, you purchase a share of the total assets in the fund. If the share price of the fund is $10 per share, you can purchase 100 shares. The price of each share is the *net asset value* (NAV). The fund manager calculates the NAV of the mutual fund by adding up the value of the securities in the fund and dividing by the number of outstanding shares.

The NAV increases and decreases as the market fluctuates. The SEC requires that the NAV of each mutual fund be calculated and published for investors at the end of each business day. Here are a few examples of online quote servers that provide mutual fund NAV information:

- **Lipper** (www.lipperweb.com), a wholly owned subsidiary of Reuters, is a global provider of mutual fund information and analysis to fund companies, financial intermediaries, and media organizations. Lipper clients manage more than 95 percent of U.S. fund assets. Lipper tracks 125,000 funds worldwide through its offices in major financial capitals in North America, Europe, and Asia. Research mutual funds and check out the 2004 Lipper Fund Awards for investment ideas.

- **CNN/Money** (money.cnn.com) is affiliated with Cable News Network (CNN) and provides links to financial sites, investment articles, market information, and online research sources. Market information shows the current level, amount of change, and time of the last update for the Dow Jones Industrial Averages, NASDAQ composite, S&P 500, Russell 2000, NYSE Composite, Dow Transports, Dow Utilities, Amex Composite, and S&P Futures. For mutual fund data, click "Get a Quote" and then enter the ticker symbol for your mutual fund or stock. CNNfn provides charts and company snapshots of selected firms.

With more than 80,000 funds worldwide to choose from, selecting a mutual fund has become a complex process — meaning that online screening tools are more important than ever before. When you select your investment criteria, you need to consider several factors:

- How long do you plan to own the mutual fund?
- How much risk to your principal can you tolerate?
- Which mutual fund category meets your personal financial objectives?

Which funds you select depends on your answers to these questions. If you need your money in a year and can't afford much risk because, for example, you plan to use the money to purchase a house, you want to consider a safe, short-term bond fund. On the other hand, if this money is your retirement fund that you don't plan to tap into for ten years and you can stomach some ups and downs, you should consider a growth stock fund.

Mutual funds basically come in five flavors. Within these five categories are many different types of funds, so you can find a mutual fund that is tailored to your individual needs. Here's a brief description of the major types of mutual funds:

- **Equity funds:** Mutual funds that primarily include stocks of publicly traded companies. Investing in an equity mutual fund allows investors to quickly create a stock portfolio that matches all their financial objectives. However, a fund can specialize in many different types of companies, which can make selecting the right equity fund (or equity funds) more difficult.

  Equity funds have a higher risk than money market or bond funds, but they also can offer the highest returns. A stock fund's net asset value (NAV) can rise and fall quickly over the short term, but, historically, stocks have performed better over the long term than other types of investments. Not all equity (stock) funds are the same. For example, some equity funds specialize in growth or technology stocks.

- **Bond funds:** Mutual funds that usually invest in the debt instruments of corporations and governments. Investors in bond funds are primarily seeking income with some protection of principal. Frequently, the only way an average investor has access to an expensive bond is through a bond mutual fund.

  Usually, bond funds are conservative and target the payment of dividends. Investors can choose among several types of bond funds. Investment-grade bond funds usually have less risk than funds with stocks, but they aren't risk-free. These types of bond funds are usually good investment choices for short-, medium-, and long-term investors who desire low risk. Investment-grade bond funds focus on current income. For more information on bonds, see Chapter 12.

- **Municipal bond funds:** Mutual funds that invest in local and state governments. The dividends of municipal bond funds are usually free from federal taxes.

- **Hybrid funds:** Mutual funds that invest in both stocks and bonds. Hybrid funds are structured to achieve predetermined objectives such as rapid growth, matching a market benchmark, or investing in one industry. To sum up, hybrid funds use combinations of securities to meet their investment objectives.

- **Money market funds:** Mutual funds that invest in the short-term debts of corporations and the federal government. Money market funds often invest in Treasury bills, commercial paper, banker's acceptances, negotiable certificates of deposit (CDs), and short-term debts of U.S. government agencies such as Ginnie Mae (www.ginniemae.gov). Money market funds provide less return and less risk than other types of mutual funds and are good investments for short-term investors. The principal advantage of these funds is their safety. Also, if you ever need to get to your money fast, money market funds may be the type of fund for you.

Before you start screening mutual fund candidates, you need to understand some general information: the types of funds you can choose, the fees that mutual fund companies charge, the types of risks associated with mutual funds, and how to read a prospectus.

Discovering the differences between open-end and closed-end mutual funds

An *open-end mutual fund* has an unlimited number of shares. You can buy these shares through either the mutual fund company or your broker. The Securities and Exchange Commission (SEC) requires that each mutual fund company calculate the NAV (net asset value) of each fund every day at the close of business.

A *closed-end mutual fund* is a hybrid: part mutual fund and part stock. A closed-end mutual fund is a publicly traded investment company with a limited number of shares. According to the Investment Company Institute (www.ici.org), in August 2004, the combined assets of the nation's closed-end funds were over $232 billion. As of June 30, 2004, there were 604 closed-end funds.

The total of number of June 2004 closed-end funds can generally be divided into two categories. *Bond closed-end funds* totaled 458, and *equity closed-end funds* totaled 146. Specifically, closed fund types include closed-end stock funds (investments in common and preferred stocks), closed-end bond funds (investments in a range of bonds), closed-end convertible bond funds (with portfolios of bonds that can be converted to common stocks), closed-end single country funds (specialize in stocks from one country or geographical region), and so on.

One of the things to keep in mind when you purchase a closed-end fund is that the investment company doesn't stand ready to redeem its own shares from shareholders, and it rarely issues new shares beyond its initial offering. That's why it's a closed fund. You can buy or sell these shares only through a broker on the major stock exchanges. The value of these shares isn't calculated by using the NAV methodology. Instead, shares are valued by using a method similar to bonds and are traded at either a discount or a premium. Market prices of publicly traded closed-end mutual fund shares are published daily.

The Closed-End Fund Center, located at www.closed-endfunds.com, is sponsored by the national trade association of the closed-end fund industry. This Web site offers detailed investor education, a portfolio tracker, and data about specific closed-end funds.

Minimizing fees

Loads are the fees with which mutual fund companies compensate brokers who sell their fund. About half of all stock and bond funds have loads; money market funds normally don't have loads. Loads and other fees are important because they're deducted from your investment returns.

Loading it on

A *front-end load* is the most common type of fee that mutual fund companies charge. Investors pay this fee when they purchase shares in the mutual fund. No additional fees are charged for redeeming or selling your mutual fund shares. By law, front-end loads can't be greater than 8.5 percent. Loads average 5 percent for stock funds and 4 percent for bond funds.

The less common *back-end load* fee is charged when you sell or redeem the shares. Back-end fees are usually based on time, starting at 5 percent during the first year and declining a percentage point a year — by year five, no fees are charged. However, back-end load funds often have Rule 12b-1 fees, which are usually the amounts charged to investors for promoting the mutual fund. Fees range from 0.25 percent to 0.30 percent but can be as high as 1.25 percent. Rule 12b-1 fees are included in the fund's expense ratio.

A mutual fund's expense ratio is the proportion of assets of a mutual fund required to pay annual operating expenses and management fees. For example, if a fund charges an annual fee of $0.50 per $100 of net assets, the expense ratio will be .5 percent. The expense ratio is independent of any sales fees. (For more information on expense ratios, see the section "Analyzing Mutual Funds" toward the end of this chapter.)

If you have to pay a sales charge for purchasing your mutual fund, deduct this amount from your return for the year. For example, if you pay a 5 percent sales charge for your $1,000 investment in mutual funds, the amount invested in the fund is $950. If the fund increases by 10 percent in one year, you have a $1,045 investment. Your true yield is $95, or 9.5 percent (95 ÷ 1,000) — not the full 10 percent. On the other hand, if you purchase a no-load mutual fund, your yield is 10 percent because you don't pay the sales fee. Your original $1,000 investment in mutual funds is now worth $1,100, which is $55 more than the fund with the sales fee.

Share classes

Mutual funds can also be divided into share classes. These lettered share classes indicate the following:

- ✔ **A shares** have front-end loads.
- ✔ **B shares** have back-end loads.

> ✔ **Y shares** are geared for institutional investors and do not have a front-end load.
>
> ✔ **Z shares** are targeted for employees of the mutual fund.

Rule 12b-1 marketing fees increase manager fees and aren't related to maximizing shareholder wealth. As an investor, you need to be on the lookout for these expenses when you read the prospectus.

Generally, funds with back-end fees are more expensive than funds with front-end fees due to the high Rule 12b-1 fees. However, if you're willing to hold your investment for five years or more (which, really, you ought to, if you're investing in stocks), you pay no load because back-end loads usually disappear after five years.

Excluding the maximum fee for front-end loads of 8.5 percent, mutual funds can't charge more than 7.25 percent for the life of the investment. Overall, load fees vary from 4.0 percent to 8.5 percent of the NAV for the shares purchased.

What does all this fee information mean? If you purchase 300 shares at $10 per share with an 8 percent front-end fee, you're purchasing only $2,760 worth of shares. The other $240 goes to compensate the broker who sold you the fund. In other words, your investment needs to increase by $240 just to break even.

Taking it off

Some funds have no loads, which means that they have no front-end or back-end fees. These *no-load funds* generally don't have a sales force, so you have to contact the investment company to make a purchase. Nevertheless, no-load funds do charge service fees, proving that there's no such thing as a free lunch. Mutual fund companies charge annual fees for their management services, deducting these amounts before calculating the NAV.

Annual fees for the fund managers are about 0.50 percent of the fund's net assets. Other service fees include legal and auditing fees, the cost of preparing and distributing annual reports and proxy statements, director's fees, and transaction expenses. When added to the management fee, a fund's total yearly expenses can range from 0.75 to 1.25 percent of fund assets.

A Fund for You, a Fund for Me

You can choose from a wide variety of mutual fund categories. As a matter of fact, so many types of funds are available that you're almost guaranteed to find a fund that is an excellent fit for your personal financial objectives. If you're interested in participating in the stock market, an equity mutual fund may be just right. The following summarizes a few of the types of equity funds available:

- **Aggressive growth funds:** Aggressive growth funds tend to be investments in small, young companies and may involve the use of options and futures to reap greater profits. Aggressive growth funds primarily seek increases in capital gains. If the stock market is hot, these funds often provide the biggest returns of all mutual funds, mostly due to the capital gains of the stocks in the funds. They typically drop the most, though, when the market is cold. Their volatility makes them a poor choice for the short-term investor.

- **Growth and income funds:** Funds in the growth and income category target a steady return with capital growth potential. They often invest in companies that are growing, as well as in companies that are paying high or increasing dividends. Growth and income funds are more diverse than growth funds because they may include bonds, which makes growth and income funds less risky. The diversity also means that growth and income funds reap fewer rewards if the stock market soars and lose less if the stock market drops.

- **Growth funds:** Growth funds are similar to aggressive growth funds but have less risk. They may invest in larger, well-established firms with a long track record of earnings that may continue to grow faster than average. These funds also seek stocks with capital gain potential. In addition to stocks, these funds generally include bonds and cash equivalents. Growth funds are best for investors with medium- to long-term objectives.

- **Value funds:** Value funds include stocks of companies that have low price-to-earnings (P/E) ratios. Usually, value stocks are the *opposite* of Wall Street darlings and may be underpriced. Frequently, value stocks represent mature companies that have stopped growing, companies with poor recent earnings records or troubles, or companies that use their earnings to pay dividends. Value funds offer moderate and less volatile investor returns than growth funds.

- **International funds:** International funds include a mix of stocks and bonds from other nations or governments. These funds are subject to several types of risks that domestic mutual funds don't experience, such as political risk and exchange rate risk (losing money because of changes in the currency exchange rate).

- **Balanced funds:** Balanced funds are a mix of stocks, bonds, and Treasury bills, and possibly some foreign assets. Each fund has a different strategy for determining its asset allocation mix.

- **Dividend funds:** Dividend funds are investments in common and preferred stocks offered by corporations that generate a large, steady stream of dividend income. In Canada, the dividends are usually eligible for the dividend tax credit, thereby increasing the after-tax yield to the unit holder. This credit makes dividend funds attractive to Canadian investors who prefer to pay the lower tax rates on dividend income than the higher tax rates on interest income.

You may be considering purchasing two or three mutual funds. Here's a way to simplify your accounting and reduce your costs at the same time. You can invest in a fund of funds. A *fund of funds* is a fund that invests in other mutual funds in the same fund family, instead of or in addition to investing directly in equity, fixed income or other types of investments. For example, T. Rowe Price (www.troweprice.com) and the Vanguard Group (www.vanguard.com) offer funds of funds that invest only in their own funds. The expense ratios are waived. A fund of fundsis an inexpensive approach to diversifying your portfolio and only paying for the underlying funds.

Finding Facts and Figures Online

This list of online information services can assist you in finding the right mutual fund:

- ✔ **MAXfunds.com** (www.maxfunds.com) features quotes, top mutual fund performers, and lists of mutual funds by name, category, and ticker symbol. Investigate the similarities between two mutual funds by examining recent trends and prices. Brush up on mutual fund basics, create a portfolio, and have e-mail sent to you each month so that you can update your portfolio's performance.

- ✔ **Brill's Mutual Funds Interactive** (www.brill.com) offers tutorials for beginning mutual fund investors, interviews and descriptions of fund strategies with top mutual fund managers, analyses of the mutual funds market, and links to mutual fund home pages.

- ✔ **Standard & Poor's Fund Services** (www.funds-sp.com/registration_features.cfm) offers news on mutual funds from across the globe, up-to-date fund management ratings, and access to fund databases showing the latest performance figures. With your free registration, you receive in-depth fund management ratings analysis, fund news, free access to one of S & P's 23 databases for all sector, fund, and management group fact sheets, a chart comparison tool, quick search, fund management ratings analysis and reports, news, and awards. (I suggest selecting the U.S. mutual fund database.) Prices and products for more in-depth information vary.

- ✔ **TheStreet.com** (tools.thestreet.com/tsc/research_land.html), shown in Figure 6-1, provides information on mutual funds as part of its Research section. This free information includes a fund finder. You can use a ticker, view a list of funds, and sort by type, net assets, or return period. The Annual Reports section provides quick online access to annual reports and other information on many companies. The Mutual Fund Reports section provides quick access to prospectuses, applications, and other information.

Figure 6-1:
TheStreet.
com pro-
vides the
capability to
search for
mutual fund
reports and
statistics.

Simplifying Your Investing with Mutual Funds

At the height of the stock market boom in 1999, a friend of mine complained that he didn't have enough time to do the necessary homework to invest. He felt that investment opportunities were slipping by while his money was gathering dust in a money market account. He could have solved (and simplified) his problem by investing in an index fund or exchange-traded fund.

Discovering index funds

Index funds are sometimes called *passively managed funds*. Index fund managers try to closely track the performance of a target market index. Index funds buy and hold all, or a representative sample, of the securities in a particular index. The composition of the portfolio of the index fund is determined by the index it is trying to mirror. For example, a Standard & Poor's 500 index fund will match the percentage of stocks held in the Standard & Poor's 500 index. In contrast, in an actively managed fund, a fund manager tries to outperform similar funds or an appropriate market benchmark. Actively managed fund managers use expensive research, market forecasts, and their own judgment and experience to buy and sell securities. This expertise makes the operating costs of a managed fund higher than a passively managed index fund.

The operating costs for passively managed index funds are often 0.20 percent. In addition to their low cost, the appeal of index funds is twofold. First, the index fund will match the returns of the index it mirrors. If the market does well and the value of the index increases, the investor does well. The second reason investors like index funds is that some indexes better reflect their individual investing objectives. The downside of index funds is that investors will never have the opportunity to significantly outperform the market. For more information about index funds, see the following:

- **IndexFunds.com** (www.indexfunds.com), shown in Figure 6-2, is a helpful all-purpose online resource for index mutual funds. You'll find a beginner's message center, ten favorite indexes, and useful articles and links. Use the screener to search for investment candidates using criteria such as expense ratios, net assets, or five-year returns.

- **The Index Investor** (www.indexinvestor.com) is a useful Web site for registered members who are seeking better index fund performance through asset allocation. IndexInvestor.com is divided into free and subscription resource areas. Subscriptions are $25 per year.

- **Vanguard** (flagship2.vanguard.com/VGApp/hnw/FundsStocks Overview) features the Vanguard 500 index fund, which has been around for more than 25 years. You can read all about the benefits of indexes online.

Becoming aware of exchange-traded funds

Exchange-traded funds are passively managed funds that are traded on stock exchanges. A share of an exchange-traded fund is a share of a *unit investment trust*. Unit investment trusts are formed by investment companies with the intention of acquiring a portfolio of shares to be passively managed over a fixed period. The trust is then terminated.

According to *The Wall Street Journal,* as of September 2004, exchange-traded funds had combined assets of $180.8 billion, up 20 percent from $151 billion in December 2003. To create an exchange-traded fund (ETF), investment companies gather stocks or fixed income securities into one basket and then sell shares in the trust on a stock exchange. In other words, ETFs trade like stocks and can't be abused by market timers.

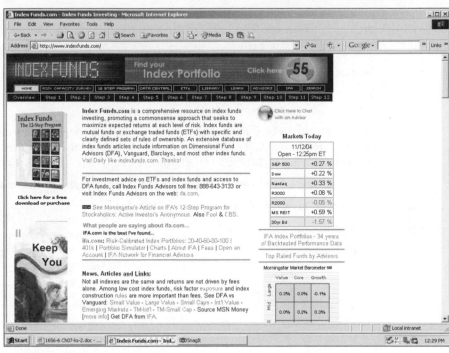

Figure 6-2:
Discover the
12-Step
Program by
IndexFunds.

As of September 2004, there were 143 ETFs. ETFs always include securities that are included in an index. ETFs come in several different types and are based on broad market sector indexes and international indexes. The following are a few examples:

- ✔ **Spiders:** Track the Standard & Poor's Deposit Receipts (SPDR, pronounced "spider").

- ✔ **Cubes:** Track the NASDAQ 100 of big nonfinancial stocks using the ticker symbol QQQ — hence the name *cubes*.

- ✔ **Diamonds:** Track the Dow Industrial Average using the ticker symbol DIA — hence the name *diamonds*.

- ✔ **Vipers:** The Vanguard Group has launched Vanguard Index Participation Equity Receipts, know as *Vipers*. Each Viper is a new class of shares of one of the company's well-known index funds. The underlying portfolios are equal, though fees and other features are different from those of the Vanguard funds.

ETFs are inexpensive to own. Expenses for an ETF are usually 0.4 percent, compared with 1.4 percent for the average equity mutual fund — but you have the expense of the broker. If you follow dollar-cost averaging, your brokerage fees can quickly add up. On the other hand, you don't have to worry about a minimum investment. Other advantages of ETFs include

✔ **The ability to buy and sell at any time during the trading day**

✔ **Instant exposure to stock portfolios of your choice:** You can select an ETF that meets your specific investor objectives.

✔ **The ability to buy on margin:** These purchases are generally subject to the same terms that apply to common stocks. (For more information about buying on margin, see Chapter 16.)

✔ **No sales load:** You still have to pay a brokerage commission.

✔ **No high management or sponsor fees**

✔ **No minimum initial deposits**

✔ **Potential tax efficiencies:** Because ETFs transfer securities between investors, there are no tax consequences to the fund.

For more information on exchange-traded funds (ETFs), see the following Web sites:

✔ **iShares** (www.ishares.com) offers online tools such as the ETF Allocator, which allows you to create a portfolio of ETFs based on the Dow Jones U.S. Sector and Total Market Indexes. This company owns the iShares Russell 2000 Index Fund, which seeks investment results that, before expenses, generally correspond to the price and yield performance of the Russell 2000 Index.

✔ **Investment Company Institute** (www.ici.org/funds/abt/index.html) is a national association for mutual fund companies that provides answers to frequently asked questions (FAQs) about exchange-traded funds. You also find useful industry statistics, investor education, and industry news.

✔ **American Stock Exchange** (www.amex.com) offers a market summary of all ETFs, product information on specific ETFs, new listings of ETFs, an ETF screen and return calculator, and investor education. Additionally, you can download information about all of the American Stock Exchange–traded ETFs and end-of-the-day ETF prices. At the Home Page, click ETFs in the left margin.

Mutual Funds and Your Risk Tolerance Level

Table 6-1 provides a brief overview of the time period and risk-tolerance level of the major mutual fund categories. Please note that this table takes into consideration the different levels of risk for a money market fund and a money market deposit account (MMDA). The primary source of difference between these two securities is the lack of Federal Deposit Insurance Corporation (FDIC) insurance for money market funds. However, this doesn't mean that MMDAs, which are insured by the FDIC, don't have any risk.

Table 6-1	Choosing the Right Type of Mutual Fund	
Investment Time Period	*Risk-Tolerance Level*	*Category of Mutual Fund*
Less than 2 years	Minimum risk to principal	Money market fund (not an MMDA)
	Some risk to principal	Bond fund (short to intermediate bond fund)
Between 2 and 4 years	Minimum risk to principal	Money market fund (not an MMDA)
	Some risk to principal	Bond fund (short- to intermediate-term)
	Moderate risk to principal	Bond fund (intermediate- to long-term)
Between 4 and 6 years	Minimum risk to principal	Money market fund (not an MMDA)
	Some risk to principal	Bond fund (short- to intermediate-term)
	Moderate risk to principal	Growth and income funds
	Greater risk to principal	Growth funds and international funds

Set realistic expectations for your investment choices. The Internet provides many sources of information about the average rates of return for different categories of mutual funds. For example, you can go to RiskGrades at www. riskgrades.com/clients/briefing/rankings.cgi to view the leaders and laggards based on ReturnGrade, average RiskGrade, and so on.

How to Screen Mutual Funds Online

The Internet provides a variety of mutual fund screening tools that sort thousands of mutual funds by criteria that you select. For example, you may want one type of fund for your children's education — something long term because you don't need the money for 10 to 20 years — and a different fund for your retirement to help you reduce your current tax liabilities. With these online screening tools, you can evaluate several funds that meet your financial needs.

Most of the stock-screening sites on the Internet are free. These database searches are an inexpensive way to isolate mutual funds that meet your special criteria. Some databases list funds incorrectly or have outdated information. However, they're useful for pruning a large list of candidates to a manageable short list.

Each screening site uses different criteria to sort mutual funds. You have to decide which criteria you care about and then use the site that offers the criteria you want. Any way you look at it, the selection of the right mutual fund is still up to you.

Here's an overview of the features of two mutual fund screens that are better for beginning online investors:

- **MSN Money** (moneycentral.msn.com/investor/finder/mffinder. asp) offers the Easy Fund Finder, which lets you search a database of more than 8,000 mutual funds for the one fund that meets your needs and investment objectives. MSN Money also offers 11 prebuilt mutual fund screens. Just click Power Searches for screens that include the criteria that you feel are the most important when selecting a mutual fund. Examples of the prebuilt screens include Safety first funds; Do-it-yourself funds (this screen lets you experiment with your own pain threshold); Foreign stock funds; High-yield bond funds; Hot, no-load funds; Large blend funds; NAIC equity screen; NAIC fixed-income screen; Small cap growth funds; Specialty technology funds; and Top-rated funds. You can also design your own mutual fund screens.

- **Morningstar** (www.morningstar.com) offers a free, independent service that evaluates more than 11,000 mutual funds. From Morningstar's home page, click Funds and then Fund Selector. The free screen lets you set the criteria for fund type, cost and purchase options, ratings and risk, returns, and portfolio. You can view five screens developed by Morningstar.com analysts. The advanced search function is comprehensive; expect great performance and historical data. However, you have to be a premium member to use it — $12.95 per month, $115 per year, or $199 for two years (after a 14-day free trial).

The following mutual fund screens are great for more experienced investors:

- **Forbes Mutual Fund Tool** (www.forbes.com/finance/screener/ Screener.jhtml) lets you screen the Lipper database of more than

11,000 mutual funds. You select the criteria that match your investment objectives by using a collection of drop-down lists, radio buttons, and text boxes. Just click the categories you're interested in and then click the Screen link to access the database and see which funds score best. Don't forget to use the glossary to define any terms you're unfamiliar with.

✔ **Smart Money Interactive** (`www.smartmoney.com`) has a do-it-yourself mutual fund finder that searches a database of more than 12,000 mutual funds using more than 60 different financial and valuation benchmarks. View your results in three different formats. Save your favorite screens for repeated use. Further analyze funds using SmartMoney.com's fund snapshots, advanced charting, and technical analysis tools. It also has prebuilt mutual fund screens. There is a 14-day free trial. You'll find three levels of subscriptions: $5.95 per month for SmartMoney Select features powered by 20-minutes-delayed quotes, $10.95 per month for SmartMoney Select real-time quotes and investor tools, and $19.95 per month for the SmartMoney Select real-time with XStream quotes and NASDAQ Level II quotes, which doesn't offer a free trial.

Locating and Reading the Prospectus

EDGAR Mutual Funds Reporting (`www.sec.gov/edgar/searchedgar/prospectus.htm`), shown in Figure 6-3, provides prospectuses for thousands of different types of funds. If you know the name of the fund you're interested in, you can investigate the fund's activities at this site. Target your search by determining the range of dates you want, which filing forms (quarterly, annually, and so on) you want to read, and the name of the specific fund.

If you don't know the exact name of the fund you want, refer to Morningstar (`www.morningstar.com`), which provides a mutual fund search engine. Just enter what you know of the mutual fund's name. The search engine's results provide you with several mutual funds that have similar names. It's likely that the mutual fund you're seeking will be one of the funds listed.

After you find the prospectus you want, download it to your computer so that you can read it at your leisure. Here's how you download a prospectus that you've accessed via the EDGAR Mutual Funds Reporting Web site:

1. **With the prospectus displayed in your Web browser, choose File⇨Save.**

   Your browser displays the Save As dialog box.

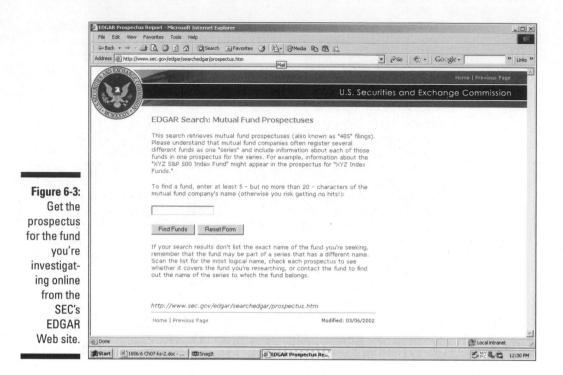

Figure 6-3:
Get the
prospectus
for the fund
you're
investigat-
ing online
from the
SEC's
EDGAR
Web site.

2. **Enter a filename for the prospectus and select the directory in which you want to save the file.**

3. **Click Save.**

   Your browser saves the prospectus on your computer. If you have a dial-up connection to the Internet, you can disconnect from your ISP.

4. **Minimize your Internet browser.**

5. **Open your word-processing program.**

6. **Open the prospectus file.**

   You can now read the prospectus offline and at your leisure.

Checking the facts

When you read the prospectus you've downloaded, look for the following information:

- ✔ **Investment objectives:** The first paragraph of the prospectus describes the fund's investment objectives and lists the types of securities the fund invests in. If the fund doesn't meet your investment objectives, you can stop reading and start evaluating another fund.

- ✔ **Fees:** The SEC requires all mutual funds to list all fees, costs, and expenses in a table at the front of the prospectus.

- ✔ **Additional expenses:** Some funds charge for extra services such as printed shareholder materials, toll-free telephone numbers with 24-hour service, accumulation plans that reinvest your distributions (shareholder profits), and related support and guidance.

- ✔ **Performance:** Year-to-year data for the last ten years (or less if the fund isn't that old) in condensed financial statements indicates the fund's performance. Statistics track the fund's NAV, shareholder distributions, and expenses. For funds that include stocks, the prospectus may also include dividends and price information. Many funds provide graphs that show how a $1,000 investment in the fund increased or decreased over a ten-year period.

- ✔ **Statement of additional information:** This section of the prospectus covers fund details and complex items, such as the biographies of the fund's directors, the fund's objectives, and contracts for professional services. These reports are free to the fund's shareholders that request them.

The SEC requires the prospectus to indicate what fees the fund charges for a $1,000 investment with a 5 percent return redeemed at the end of one year, three years, five years, and ten years. Keep in mind that both load and no-load funds have management fees and operating expenses that are charged to the fund.

Getting it right

Reading a mutual fund prospectus isn't the most exciting thing you could be doing on a Saturday night, but you'll discover many useful facts and disclosures required by federal law. The mutual fund's prospectus may stimulate many questions, but here are a few that you should get answers to before you invest:

- ✔ **Is the fund's performance steady?** Over the last ten years (or life of the fund if it's younger), are one or two good years responsible for the fund's overall performance?

✔ **How does this mutual fund compare to similar funds in terms of performance and expenses?** Keep in mind that higher expenses result in lower investor returns.

✔ **What's the standard deviation or risk level of the fund?** How does it compare to similar funds? (Remember, if the fund has a higher level of risk, it should have a higher level of return. The higher return is your just reward for taking additional risk.)

✔ **What's the fund turnover ratio like?** The *turnover ratio* indicates how actively the fund's managers are trading securities. The higher the fund turnover rate, the higher the brokerage's charges. High transaction costs can take a bite out of investor returns.

✔ **Do any initial sales charges show up in the "how to purchase shares" and "how to redeem shares" sections of the prospectus?** Is there a required minimum investment amount or a minimum amount for subsequent investments? Will you be charged a fee for switching from one fund to another fund in the same fund family? Will you be charged a redemption fee when you sell your shares?

It's unlikely that the prospectus will have an up-to-the-minute listing of the securities currently held by the mutual fund. Check out the fund's current holdings at Morningstar (www.morningstar.com), Smart Money (www.smartmoney.com), or a similar mutual fund super-site.

Analyzing Mutual Funds

As a general rule, the first palce to start analyzing a fund is by by comparing its expense ratio to similar funds. All funds have fees and expenses, but the amounts vary. In addition to sales and redemption fees, the mutual fund's prospectus indicates the fund's management and administration expenses. The fund's investment advisor generally receives 0.5 to 1.0 percent of the fund's average daily net assets. Administrative expenses include legal, auditing, and accounting costs, along with the fees for directors and the costs of preparing the annual report and proxy statements. These administrative expenses are added to the investment advisory fee. The total costs often average between 0.75 percent and 1.25 percent of fund assets. Savvy mutual fund investors are wary of funds with expense ratios that are more than 1.25 percent.

In 1980, the SEC passed Rule 12b-1, which allows mutual fund companies to charge advertising and marketing expenses. These costs typically range from 0.25 percent to 0.30 percent and can be as high as 1.25 percent. Some mutual funds charge these fees and others don't, so read the mutual fund's prospectus carefully.

The Mutual Fund Education Alliance (`www.mfea.com`) is a not-for-profit trade association of the no-load mutual fund industry. The Web site's Mutual Fund Investor's Center is designed to serve investors who want to use mutual funds to reach their financial goals. The site provides links to profiles on performance data for no-load mutual funds, lists of funds with the lowest initial minimum deposit, lists of funds with the lowest expenses, comparative indexes, and other relevant mutual fund information.

Comparing costs and returns

PersonalFund.com (`personalfund.com`) and the premier features of Morningstar (`www.morningstar.com`) allow you to investigate fund alternatives that have similar characteristics but lower costs.

The returns of the mutual fund you select can be radically reduced by hidden costs. When evaluating a mutual fund, consider the following:

✔ **Returns:** Keep in mind the power of compounding, which can be used *against you.* For example, say that you select a fund that has a return of 8 percent when a similar fund has a return of 10 percent. Over your lifetime, that two percent difference can be the difference between retiring in luxury and living in fear that you will outlive your retirement funds.

✔ **Costs:** Predicting the cost of owning your mutual fund is easier than predicting future market activity and the performance of your mutual fund. Keep in mind that mutual funds charge

    • *Management fees:* Shareholders are charged management fees by the company that manages the fund.

    • *Transaction fees:* Shareholders are charged transaction costs when fund managers buy or sell shares of the mutual fund. If the mutual fund has a high rate of turnover, the fund's returns are less than a similar fund with low turnover.

    • *Taxes:* Shareholders are charged taxes on distributions (dividends and capital gains) from the fund. Fund distributions look good to potential shareholders. Unfortunately, current shareholders have to pay taxes at their ordinary tax rate on the short-term gains, which reduces the return of the mutual fund.

At PersonalFund.com, you can personalize your analysis by using Personal Fund.com's questionnaire to indicate how much you're investing, whether the account is taxable or nontaxable, how long you expect to hold the fund, and your required rate of return (before costs). If the fund is in a taxable account, enter your tax bracket for ordinary income and the tax bracket for long-term capital gains. Click the Calculate Costs button to get an analysis of the total cost of ownership.

PersonalFund.com can provide an analysis of your fund and suggestions for three similar funds. All four funds are fully analyzed. Click the Go button to determine whether it makes sense to sell your shares in your fund and replace them with a different fund.

The new analysis looks at the trade-offs (out-of-pocket costs, taxes, commissions, and loads) and future returns, shows you how much better the new fund must do to justify making the switch, and gives you the opportunity to change your assumptions and recalculate. A recent analysis, based on the assumption that the Wilshire 5000 Index Portfolio (WFIVX) has a 0.15 percent higher net return than Matrix Advisors Value (MAVFX), indicates that you wouldn't break even within ten years before taxes, nor would you break even net of taxes. In other words, you wouldn't receive any benefit from replacing the MAVFX fund unless you plan to hold the new WFIVX fund for more than ten years. That's certainly something to think about!

Experienced mutual fund investors typically avoid funds with expense ratios greater than 1.25 percent.

Some mutual fund companies may have low up-front fees but charge high rates for managing fund operations. The prospectus details whether the mutual fund charges these fees. I give you details on prospectuses in the section "Locating and Reading the Prospectus."

Understanding mutual fund risks

Smart investors select opportunities based on their risk return. For example, the promise of a big return may not be worth the level of risk. Conversely, investing in a security with a low guaranteed return (such as a savings bond) may not keep up with inflation. In this situation, you lose money because you didn't take enough risk.

Different investments have different types of risks. You can minimize your risk by investing in different types of securities. RiskGrades (www.risk grades.com) uses scores that are based on statistical analysis of historical price fluctuations of stocks and bonds (and foreign exchange rates and commodity prices). Large price fluctuations are an indication of high uncertainty, or risk. With your free registration, you can measure the risk of a single security or your entire portfolio. For example, imagine two large cap mutual funds that have the same costs and returns. The first fund has a risk grade of 72, and the second fund has a risk grade of 57. All things being equal, you should select the mutual fund that has less risk (or lower risk grade).

Mutual funds provide statements about their objectives and risk posture (which is briefly explained in qualitative terms in the prospectus). Rather than provide precise information to help you evaluate the riskiness of a mutual fund, however, these statements typically offer vague, general explanations of a fund's approach to risk. For more precise, statistical evaluations of a fund's risks, you can turn to independent mutual fund rating services, such as Morningstar (www.morningstar.com).

Morningstar and other independent mutual fund rating services calculate such statistics as the standard deviation of a fund's return. I don't want to turn this chapter into an introductory statistics course, but I can tell you that standard deviation helps you judge how volatile, or risky, a fund is. This statistic shows you how much a fund has deviated from its average return over a period of time. Standard deviation offers a clear indicator of a fund's consistency over time. A fund's standard deviation is a simple measure of a fund's highest and lowest returns over a specific time period. Just remember this point: The higher the standard deviation, the higher the fund's risk.

For example, if the 3-year return on a fund is 33 percent, that statistic may mean that the fund earned 11 percent in the first year, 11 percent in the second year, and 11 percent in the third year. On the other hand, the fund may have earned 28 percent in the first year, 5 percent in the second year, and 0 percent in the third year. If your financial plan requires an 11-percent annual return, this fund isn't for you!

Chapter 7

Online Analysis, Buying, and Selling of Mutual Funds

In This Chapter

▶ Using the Internet to check for overconcentrations of stocks in your mutual funds

▶ Using online rating services to evaluate mutual funds

▶ Predicting your mutual fund's future performance

▶ Buying mutual funds with an online broker

▶ Buying mutual funds online without a broker

▶ Getting Internet advice on when to sell your mutual funds

*W*hen selecting a mutual fund, investors often look at relative performance over the last ten years, five years, and three years to see how the fund reacts to different economic conditions and stock market environments. Other factors in selecting a mutual fund include evaluating the fund manager's experience and record, the fund's level of consistency, and the fund's major investment holdings.

I describe how to use online mutual fund ratings to assist in selecting the very best mutual funds for your personal portfolio. I compare mutual fund rating systems and provide a short list of online mutual funds that you can purchase without a broker. Finally, I provide directions on how to purchase mutual funds with a broker and how to tell when it's time to sell.

Finding the Right Mix of Investments

Asset allocation is the specific amount of money that you spend for each type of investment. In Wall Street–speak, the term describes how you diversify your financial assets (stocks, bonds, and cash) by amounts that you determine.

Asset allocation also means trying to squeeze every bit of return out of each asset type, given the level of risk. Overall, the right asset allocation approach is the one that works best for you. When determining your asset allocation, consider your age, the amount of time you can spend investing your money, your financial goals, your risk-tolerance level, and the impact of taxes on your investment decisions.

Table 7-1 shows all the ingredients for finding the combination of assets that may be just right for you. The source of this guideline is Value Line (www.valueline.com). The table shows Value Line's definitions of nine investor types. The types are categorized as conservative, moderate, and aggressive. The investment time frame fills out the picture. The investment period can be short-term, medium-term, or long-term.

Table 7-1	Mutual Fund Asset Allocations Based on Investor Risk-Tolerance Levels		
Risk	**Time Frame**		
	Short-term (0 to 2 years)	**Medium-term** (3 to 5 years)	**Long-term** (6 years or more)
Conservative Investors	**#1**	**#2**	**#3**
Stocks	0%	30%	50%
Bonds	0%	25%	50%
Cash	100%	45%	0%
Moderate Investors	**#4**	**#5**	**#6**
Stocks	10%	55%	65%
Bonds	30%	35%	35%
Cash	60%	10%	0%
Aggressive Investors	**#7**	**#8**	**#9**
Stocks	30%	70%	100%
Bonds	30%	30%	0%
Cash	40%	0%	0%

Source: Value Line Mutual Fund Survey, How to Invest in Mutual Funds (1995, 2000), Value Line Publishing, Inc., New York, NY.

Many mutual funds match the asset allocation shown in Table 7-1. You can start with one mutual fund, or you can purchase a mutual fund for each allocation. If you purchase several mutual funds, you can diversify your risk even more. For example, to complete your portfolio, you may want to buy a money market fund, a stock mutual fund, and a fixed-asset (bond) mutual fund. It's your money and your choice. See Table 7-2 for a discussion of the investor type numbers #1 through #9 found in Table 7-1.

Table 7-2 shows how you can match mutual fund categories to your financial objectives and risk-tolerance level. Refer to Table 7-1 to decide which of the nine investor types most closely matches your personal financial plan and risk-tolerance profile. For example, Investor Type #1 is a conservative investor who is investing for the short term. Investor Type #9 is an aggressive investor who is investing for the long term. For more detail about the investor types, visit the Value Line site at www.valueline.com. Table 7-2 shows what categories of mutual funds are right for your investor type. The percentages listed in Table 7-2 match the recommended allocations shown in Table 7-1. (For details about fund types, see "A Fund for You, a Fund for Me" in Chapter 6.)

Table 7-2   Suggested Mutual Funds for Nine Types of Investors

Investor Type	Cash	Stocks	Bonds
1	(100%) Money market fund	(0%)	(0%)
2	(45%) Money market fund	(30%) General equity	(25%) Intermediate fixed-income partial equity funds (asset allocation); Tax-free fixed income funds (municipal bonds)
3	(0%)	(50%) General equity funds (income, growth)	(50%) Taxable fixed-income funds (government agency, and income); Fixed-mortgage income, partial equity funds (asset allocation)
4	(10%) Money market fund	(30%) General equity funds (income)	(60%) Short-term fixed-income funds (diversified); Fixed-income partial equity funds (asset allocation and balanced)
5	(10%) Money market fund	(55%) General equity funds (growth, income)	(35%) Intermediate fixed-income funds (diversified); Intermediate fixed-income partial equity funds (balanced); Tax-free fixed-income funds (municipal bonds)

(continued)

Table 7-2 *(continued)*

Investor Type	Cash	Stocks	Bonds
6	(0%)	(65%) General equity funds (growth, growth and equity)	(35%) Fixed-income bonds (diversified, corporate); Fixed-income partial equity funds (balanced); Tax-free fixed-income funds (municipal bonds)
7	(40%) Money market fund	(30%) General equity funds (aggressive growth, small cap)	(30%) Short-term fixed-income funds (corporate high-yield); Short-term fixed-income partial equity funds (convertible)
8	(0%)	(70%) General equity funds (aggressive growth, small cap), Specialty equity (technology, other)	(30%) Intermediate fixed-income (corporate high yield); Intermediate fixed-income partial equity funds (flexible); Tax-free fixed-income funds (municipal bonds)
9	(0%)	(100%) General equity funds (aggressive growth, growth, and growth and income); Small cap equity funds; Specialty equity (technology, other); International equity (European, foreign, global, or Pacific stock)	(0%)

Using the Internet to Help You Choose the Best Funds in Each Class

Past performance doesn't guarantee future performance. However, investors often use annualized returns to compare funds. The Internet offers tables of fund comparisons for each month and for periods ranging from one month to ten years or more. For example, *Business Week* (www.businessweek.com) has a Mutual Funds Scoreboard that provides listings of the returns for the best funds, the bond fund leaders, and the worst funds.

Comparing a fund to similar funds is a good way to examine a fund's performance. Organizations such as Morningstar (`www.morningstar.com`) have mutual fund tables that make comparisons easy by grouping fund classes and including the averages for each category. (See Chapter 6 for details about fund classes.) A fund's ability to consistently outperform similar funds is one sign of good quality. In contrast, you should avoid funds that have consistently underperformed for three years or more.

Make certain that the funds you compare are similar. You'll find a big difference between, for example, an aggressive growth fund and a growth fund. To verify your analyses, check the prospectus of each fund. The fund's investment objectives are listed in the first paragraph. You may discover that the fund that looked so attractive at first is really too risky for you.

Following a mutual fund checklist

As you select your first mutual fund, consider these factors:

- **The fund manager:** Often a fund is only as good as its management. If the fund manager has shown great performance in the past, future performance is likely to be above average. If the fund manager has been replaced, past performance becomes less meaningful and may even be worthless. A poor-performing fund that gets a new fund manager may turn around and become a top performer.

- **The stability of the fund's philosophy:** If the fund seems unclear about its financial goals and is switching investment methods, it may be in trouble.

- **The size of the fund:** Good fund candidates have at least $50 million under management and should be large enough to keep up with institutional investors. At the opposite end of the spectrum, funds with more than $20 billion tend to have problems with being too large.

- **The objectives of the fund:** Some funds focus on specialty or sector funds (gold funds or biotech funds) and often offer great returns. However, they aren't good funds for the online investor who wants to own just one mutual fund. If you own just one specialty fund, you lose the advantage of diversification.

- **Fees:** A debate has raged during the last ten years about which is better: no-load or load mutual funds. All the studies indicate that paying a sales commission doesn't ensure a greater return. However, investing in a fund with high fees and high returns is better than investing in a fund with low fees and poor performance.

✔ **Purchase constraints:** Although some funds require a minimum initial investment of $5,000, many good funds don't have this requirement. If you enroll in a fund's automatic investment program (AIP), the minimum initial investment amount is usually waived. (For more on AIPs, see "Starting Your Mutual Fund Account with as Little as $50," later in this chapter.) Additionally, many fund minimums are waived or substantially reduced for IRA investments.

Reading an online mutual fund listing

As a general rule, mutual fund listings are slightly easier to read than stock listings. (See Chapter 8 to find out about stock listings.) Different online sources and newspapers list mutual funds differently. Mutual fund listings are designed to provide investors with enough information to select, evaluate, and track the performance of a mutual fund. As a general rule mutual fund listings come in five flavors: daily listings, weekly listings, monthly performance tables, and quarterly and year-end reports.

✔ **Daily listings:** Provide a brief description of the fund type (for example, B stands for back-load or N stands for no-load). Other abbreviations include U for a U.S. dollar–denominated fund; NAVPS (net asset value per share) is the current value of one share; NAVPS $Chg (dollar change) and NAVPS %Chg (percent change) are comparisons to yesterday's value of the same fund expressed in dollars or as a percentage. To sum it up, daily listings are good for valuing each share of the fund and for determining how much it was worth yesterday.

✔ **Weekly listings:** Include the same information as the daily listings and then some. You'll find the fund name, a few specifics about the fund, and "Fri $Chg" and "Fri %Chg" columns, showing Friday's change in NAVPS, compared to Thursday for the same fund. The "52W high" and "52W low" columns show the highest and lowest NAVPS reached last year. By looking at the range between the funds' high and low, investors can tell the historical volatility of the fund. Additionally, you can see exactly where the fund stands today in relation to these highest and lowest NAVPS. You also receive a summary of the weekly NAVPS (the highest and lowest NAVPS from the last week, the NAVPS as of last Friday, and how that NAVPS compares to the week previous). Overall, weekly listings are good for determining the high and low value of the fund for the week, the closing value of the fund, and the change in this week's value compared to last week.

✔ **Monthly performance tables:** Include the name of the fund and other specifics, such as the fund's net assets, the rate of return on the fund for the month, the last six months, and the last year, and the average annual rate of return for three, five, and ten years. Some performance tables include the fund's standard deviation (the higher the standard deviation, the higher the level of risk) for the last three years, which indicates the funds long-term volatility. Other data includes the fund's expense ratio. In summary, you can use monthly performance tables to help you in your mutual fund selection process. For example, if you are a conservative investor, you can use a monthly performance table to assist you in finding a stable fund with a low standard deviation.

✓ **Quarterly and year-end reports:** Are useful once you whittle your mutual fund investment candidates down to ten or less. The content and style of these reports varies, but you're able to get a better handle on who is managing the fund, the fund's objectives, and more.

Assessing mutual fund performance

No hard-and-fast rules exist about how to assess a mutual fund. However, the following list provides easy-to-use guidelines to assess the performance of your mutual fund investment candidates. After your assessment, each fund still require additional analysis. Only funds that meet all the following criteria should be selected for further research. They're likely to reduce your chances of losing money without lowering your mutual fund returns.

✓ **Tax liabilities and returns:** All mutual fund performance is shown on a pretax basis because different investors are in different tax brackets. If you invest through taxable accounts (which are different from nontaxable accounts that might include your IRA or other tax-exempt investments), you should compare only the after-tax returns of the funds you're analyzing. This comparison enables you to compare apples to apples instead of apples to oranges.

✓ **The impact of short-term performance:** Ignore short-term performance. Short-term returns are heavily influenced by fluctuations in the market and are valueless.

✓ **Consistent returns:** Avoid funds that have inconsistent returns when compared to unmanaged indexes. In other words, when you compare your fund to the appropriate benchmark, take into consideration the consistency of the two funds. If your fund is more volatile than the benchmark, it may have more risk than you expected. For a quick list of mutual fund benchmarks, see Lipper, Inc. (www.lipperweb.com); with its affiliated companies, Lipper currently tracks the performance of more than 32,000 funds worldwide with assets in excess of $6 trillion.

✓ **Fund ranking when compared to like funds:** Look for a fund whose performance is ranked within the top 20 percent to 50 percent or better of its type. Make certain that your analysis compares growth funds to growth funds and value funds to value funds.

✔ **Fund ranking when compared to unmanaged indexes:** The fund's performance and risk level should be better than an unmanaged index for one-, three-, and five-year time periods. Compare the fund's performance (before mutual fund costs) to a similar index. A broad-based U.S. stock fund should be compared to the S & P 500 (www.stockinfo.standard poor.com) or the Wilshire 5000 Index. Small company funds should be compared to the Russell 2000 Index.

✔ **The fund's price/earnings (P/E) ratios should be 15 to 25:** P/E ratios above 30 tend to be high-risk.

✔ **The fund's standard deviation:** The higher the standard deviation, the higher the risk. The fund's Morningstar standard deviation for 3 years should be 17 or lower. If you use the Value Line–calculated standard deviation (which is different), the standard deviation for 3 years ought to be 12 or lower.

✔ **The fund's risk value:** Value Line rankings range from 1 (low risk) to 5 (high risk). If a fund's Value Line risk rating is 1, it's in the top 10 percent of the safest funds. With the Morningstar rating system, a 5-star rating indicates that the fund is within the top 10 percent of the safest funds.

The evaluation criteria in the preceding list are a good starting point for your analysis. As you become a more sophisticated investor, you're likely to modify, delete, and add criteria. This customization ensures that your mutual fund selections meet your individual risk-tolerance level and financial objectives.

Using Scoreboards and Ratings

In this chapter, I present three different rating systems:

✔ *The Wall Street Journal* (public.wsj.com/home.html) and CBS MarketWatch (cbs.marketwatch.com) use the **Lipper Leaders** system (www.lipperweb.com) and divides each fund into five categories. The Lipper Leader system ranks each category from one to five, with one having the highest rank.

✔ **Morningstar** (www.morningstar.com) rates mutual funds from five to one star, with five stars ranking the top performers. I discuss these rankings in the section "The Morningstar rating system."

✔ **Value Line** (www.valueline.com) scores mutual funds from 1 to 5, with 1 taking top billing. You find a list of these ratings in the preceding section.

In the best of times, the same fund can be ranked a five-star Morningstar winner and a number-one mutual fund by Value Line. Sometimes, a mutual fund's score can indicate a top performer by one mutual fund rating service and a loser by another mutual fund rating service. Why the difference?

Some mutual fund scores are *risk adjusted,* and some are *absolute.* Risk-adjusted scores punish mutual funds for inconsistent returns and reward others for stability. For example, the risk-adjusted mutual funds rating can do the following:

- **Penalize a fund for radically changing from its previous performance.** Additionally, a fund can be penalized for *exceeding* its previous performance. In other words, the fund can receive a lower rating because of unexpected increases in returns. This rating penalty can be just as bad as the penalty for an unexpected decrease in returns.

- **Reward mediocre fund performers:** A fund with consistently mediocre returns can receive a higher rating because of its stability.

With all rating systems, a description of the type of ranking system used is included in the description of how scores are calculated. Conservative investors prefer to use risk-adjusted scores. Other investors prefer to use the absolute numbers. The best approach is to have a clear understanding of the differences in the ranking systems.

The analysis of mutual funds includes more research than selecting a fund by its rating. Remember that the more informed you are, the better your decision-making will be.

Checking for overlaps in your mutual funds

Morningstar (www.morningstar.com) offers Web-based screening tools to assist investors in researching "overlaps" in their portfolios. A *stock overlap* is an overconcentration of a certain equity that can dampen your attempts at diversification and can lead to investing mistakes. Subscribers to Morningstar automatically receive the X-ray screening tools, which indicate whether several mutual funds they hold include the same stocks. The Premium Portfolio X-Ray tool checks your portfolio for unexpected risks caused by an overconcentration of individual stocks. You can view stocks and mutual funds both individually and within mutual funds to determine the portfolio's true asset allocation

and view the portfolio's exposure to turbulence in different regions of the world. You can analyze both stocks and funds together, see your total asset allocation, total expenses, total sector concentrations, and so on. For example, when I used the Portfolio Instant X-Ray, I discovered that about 4 percent of my portfolio is in bonds held by mutual fund companies, but I didn't have any stock overlaps. Subscriptions for this premium service are $12.95 per month, $115 per year, and $199 for two years. See the Web site at www.morningstar.com for details about other products and services included in a premium subscription. A 14-day free trial is available.

The Ratings War

Many Web sites offer information on the ranking of mutual funds. Rankings are useful because they help you digest important performance and risk statistics into one measure. For information on the ranking of mutual funds, check out these Web sites:

- **Barron's** (www.barrons.com)
- **Business Week** (www.businessweek.com)
- **Forbes** (www.forbes.com)
- **The Wall Street Journal** (public.wsj.com/home.html)

Three of the more popular online rating services are Morningstar, Lipper, and Value Line. Morningstar (www.morningstar.com) and Lipper (www.lipper leaders.com) are free services. Value Line (www.valueline.com) is a fee-based service.

The Morningstar rating system

Morningstar is an independent, Chicago-based firm that has been evaluating mutual funds and annuities since 1984. The organization currently evaluates more than 13,000 mutual funds.

Morningstar uses historical data to develop its ratings. The unique feature of the rating system is that it penalizes mutual funds for excess risk that doesn't result in excess returns. Morningstar rates funds for consistently giving the highest returns and adjusts for risk as compared to funds in the same category.

Morningstar's five-star system is as follows:

- **Five Stars:** In the top 10 percent of performance; produces substantially above-average returns
- **Four Stars:** In the next 22.5 percent of performance; produces above-average returns
- **Three Stars:** In the middle 35 percent of performance; produces average returns
- **Two Stars:** In the lower 22.5 percent of performance; produces below-average returns
- **One Star:** In the bottom 10 percent of performance; produces substantially below-average returns

The Lipper Leader system

The Lipper Leader system (www.lipperleaders.com) is a toolkit that uses criteria of a fund's success in meeting certain investor goals, such as preserving capital or building wealth through consistent, strong returns. The strength of the Lipper Leader system is the use of these criteria in conjunction with one another.

The Lipper system uses 1 as the top score. That is, the highest 20 percent of funds in each classification are named Lipper Leaders, the next 20 percent receive a score of 2, the middle 20 percent are scored 3, the next 20 percent are scored 4, and the lowest 20 percent are scored 5.

The Lipper Leader system ranks and divides each fund into five categories, ranked from 1 to 5, with 1 indicating the highest rank. The categories are as follows:

- **Total return:** The fund provides a superior total return when compared to a group of similar funds.

- **Consistency of return:** The fund provides higher consistency and risk-adjusted returns when compared to a group of similar funds. Funds receive high marks for year-to-year consistency relative to others in a particular peer group.

- **Preservation:** The fund has demonstrated an outstanding ability to preserve assets in a variety of markets when compared with its asset class-equity, mixed equity, or fixed-income funds.

- **Tax efficiency:** The fund is successful at postponing taxes over a measurement period relative to similar funds.

- **Expense:** The fund has effectively managed to keep its expenses low relative to its peers and within its load structure.

The Value Line rating system

Value Line uses a dual rating system that includes overall rank and measures various performance criteria, including risk. Funds are ranked from 1 to 5, with 1 as the highest rank (the best risk-adjusted performance) and the best risk ranking (the least risky).

Value Line uses historical data to develop its ratings. The five-number system is as follows:

- **1:** In the top 10 percent; highest overall performance and lowest risk

- **2:** In the next 20 percent; above-average performance and lower risk

    ✔ **3:** In the middle 40 percent; average performance and average risk

    ✔ **4:** In the lower 20 percent; below-average performance and higher risk

    ✔ **5:** In the lowest 10 percent; lowest average performance and highest risk

Value Line's Mutual Fund Survey for Windows (`www.ec-server.value line.com`) is a data/software service that includes extensive capabilities for viewing, sorting, screening, graphing, and preparing reports on more than 11,000 mutual funds. The service has a six-week trial subscription for $50 and an annual subscription for $345 with monthly updates. Users can also access weekly updates online by clicking Data Updates. The software is available on CD-ROM for Windows-based computers. The CD-ROM provides access to reports on mutual funds exactly as published in the Value Line Mutual Fund Survey.

When using mutual fund ratings, you must keep two things in mind. First, past performance doesn't predict future performance. Second, comparing the ranks of two different mutual fund categories is meaningless. For example, you can't compare the rank of a municipal-bond fund against an aggressive-growth fund.

Buying Mutual Funds Online: Using an Online Broker

You have many choices in how you purchase mutual funds. In addition to purchasing directly from the mutual fund company, you can purchase mutual funds through registered representatives of banks, trust companies, stock-brokers, discount brokers, and financial planners. To purchase mutual funds via the Internet, go to an online broker's Web site. (I list a few examples later in this section.)

Register by completing the online application form. You have to provide the same information you normally provide for opening an online brokerage account. (For details, see Chapter 4.)

The Internet is constantly changing, so check out the online brokerage's latest rates, new special mutual fund purchase programs, and brokerage statement download capabilities before sending in your application for a trading account.

To have a fully functioning account, brokerages are required to have your signature on file. After they have your signature on file, you can buy or sell as much as you want.

After you open your account, log on to the Internet, go to your brokerage Web site, and enter orders by completing the online form. Access your account at any time and monitor your investments by using online news or quote services.

Some of the online brokers in the following list are often called mutual fund shopping centers because of the wide variety of mutual funds they carry. For example, you can find funds that have no transaction fees, no-load funds, and front- or back-loaded funds.

- **Charles Schwab** (www.schwab.com) transaction fees vary based on the funds you select. The minimum deposit required to open an account is $10,000.

- **TD Waterhouse** (www.waterhouse.com) requires a $1,000 initial deposit. While selected mutual funds carry no transaction fees, other mutual funds are $24.00 per trade.

- **E*TRADE** (www.etrade.com) offers some no-transaction-fee mutual funds and charges $24.95 commission on other mutual fund trades. E*TRADE has a unique feature — rebates on Rule 12b-1 fees. The minimum deposit to open an account is $1,000.

Commission-Free Mutual Funds

If you purchase a *load fund* (a mutual fund that includes a sales charge), it costs the same amount whether you purchase it through a broker or directly from the mutual fund company. However, you really don't need to pay a load to get a great mutual fund. One of the advantages of no-load mutual funds (which I discuss in Chapter 6) is that you can purchase them directly from the mutual fund company and skip paying a sales commission. In the past, if you purchased a no-load fund through a broker, you were charged a brokerage fee. Now, many discount brokerages and large mutual fund companies offer no-load funds (and even some load funds) with no transaction fees. (Brokers receive a portion of the fund's annual expenses instead.)

The primary advantage of purchasing a mutual fund through your online broker is convenience. You can purchase several mutual funds in the same fund family and thus save time and effort because you don't have to call several mutual fund companies to open accounts and make your purchases. If you're unhappy with one of the mutual funds, you can swap it with another mutual fund in the same family at no cost, subject to certain restrictions. At the end of the month, you receive only one statement that covers all your funds. Your online brokerage provides you with one statement for your taxes, which simplifies the process of calculating the tax you owe on your profits.

Purchasing several mutual funds from one firm can help you with your investment tracking. Many online brokerages allow you to download your brokerage statement to personal finance programs such as MS Money and Quicken. (For more information on downloading your brokerage statement and managing your portfolio, see Chapter 17.) For more information about good one-stop shopping centers for purchasing your mutual funds, check out Table 7-3.

Table 7-3	Commission-Free Mutual Funds		
Broker (URL)	*Number of NTF Funds Available**	*Early Redemption Fees*	*Initial Deposit Requirements***
American Century Investments (www.american century.com)	800	180 days/$50	$2,500 to open a general account
Charles Schwab (www.schwab.com)	1,100	180 days/$25	A 2% redemption fee may apply. Some fund companies may also charge a short-term redemption fee. $10,000 to open a general account.
E*TRADE (www.etrade.com)	800	30 days/$24.95	$1,000 for general individual investor account
Fidelity Funds-Network (www.fidelity.com)	1,100	180 days/$75, except Fidelity funds	$2,500
Siebert Fund Exchange (www.msiebert.com)	1,323	90 days/$14.95	$2,000 for IRA accounts; $5,000 for individual accounts
TD Waterhouse (www.water house.com)	45	90 days/$45 (25% discount if you use Webroker, Talkbroker, or Telemax). Some fund companies may also charge a short-term redemption fee.	$1,000

* Number of No Transaction Fee (NTF) mutual funds available
** Unless the fund specified requires a higher initial deposit amount
Note: *Transaction fees apply to open-end mutual funds only. Some funds may also charge additional sales and redemption fees. Please read the prospectus and check the brokerage Web site for details as the terms and conditions of these transactions are subject to change.*

Starting Your Mutual Fund Account with as Little as $50

The initial minimum deposit for many mutual funds is often in the thousands of dollars. Don't let this stop you from investing in several mutual funds. Many funds have automatic investment plans (AIPs) that can make the most expensive mutual fund affordable. Start by reading prospectuses to find out which mutual funds have AIPs.

In an AIP, a set amount of money is deducted from your checking or savings account each month and invested in the mutual fund. This strategy is also known as *dollar-cost averaging.* In other words, you buy more shares when prices are down and fewer shares when prices are up. Over time, investors usually profit from this approach because they're not chasing the market. (See Chapter 15 for more information about the benefits of dollar-cost averaging.)

A mutual fund with an automatic investment plan often allows you to invest as little as $50 per month, after you meet the minimum investment. The Internet provides information about which mutual funds offer AIPs. For no-loaded mutual funds with AIP plans, see the Mutual Fund Education Alliance located at www.mfea.com. At the Home Page, click Fund Quicklist, then Funds for $50 or less.

After you select several mutual funds with AIPs, ask for the funds' prospectuses and application forms. You can request the forms online, by telephone, or by mail. Fill out the section marked Automatic Investments and complete the form. You're authorizing the mutual fund company to make regular electronic withdrawals from your checking account for the amount you specify.

Some funds have contribution minimums that are a low as $50 and maximums that are as high as $100,000 per month. You decide exactly how much you want to invest each month. For example, Principal provides an online brochure (www.principal.com/funds/mm1117.pdf) that explains how its automatic investment plan works. The minimum initial investment is $50, and monthly minimum subsequent investments are $50. (Minimum subsequent payments for money market funds are $100 per month.) If you reinvest your fund's cash distribution, you enjoy the benefits of compounding, and your capital gains can add up quickly.

Buying Mutual Funds Online: No Broker Needed

Before you invest in a mutual fund, read the fund's prospectus so that you understand exactly what you're investing in. Next, fill out the online account application form for the mutual fund company. At companies like Vanguard (www.vanguard.com), depending on the type of type of account you desire, you can open an account online or print the application and mail it to the mutual fund firm.

For specific details about opening an account, contact the fund company or broker. In general, you need to complete the following steps to open a mutual fund account online or offline:

1. **Provide some basic information (your name, mailing address, e-mail address, and so on — including your Social Security number).**

2. **Mark what type of account you want: individual, joint, or trust.**

3. **Indicate your fund selections and state how much you are investing.**

4. **Indicate the status of your citizenship (U.S. citizen, resident alien, or nonresident alien). If you're not a U.S. citizen, you have to include a W-8BEN form.**

   A W-8 certificate is required of all non–U.S. citizen account holders for nonresident tax reporting purposes in order to claim exemption from backup withholding on interest, dividends, and gross proceeds in the account. To request a W-8BEN, see the IRS Web site at www.irs.gov/pub/irs-pdf/fw8ben.pdf.

5. **Mark whether you want check-writing privileges.**

6. **Indicate whether you want direct or automatic deposits (when you sell or if you receive a dividend) into a checking account or if you want a paper check.**

7. **Print, sign, and send your completed account application if applying by mail.**

   Don't forget to include your check, made payable to the mutual fund.

8. **Provide bank information to make electronic transfers if applying online.**

   When you complete the online application, you're asked to sign the online form using a secure code as your signature.

If everything goes as planned, the mutual fund company sends (to your mailing address) a confirmation number, along with your new account number.

Table 7-4 includes a brief listing of companies that allow you to purchase mutual funds without a broker. All you have to do is contact the company directly. Each company listed in Table 7-4 has account access, allows online transactions, and provides online applications and prospectuses.

Table 7-4	Online Mutual Fund Sources
Company	*Internet Address*
American Century Investments	www.americancentury.com
Baron Funds	www.baronfunds.com
Fidelity Investments	www.fidelity.com
Firsthand Funds	www.firsthandfunds.com
Fremont Mutual Funds	www.fremontfunds.com
Kelmoore Strategy Funds	www.kelmoore.com
Oak Associates	www.oakfunds.com
Royce Funds	www.roycefunds.com
RS Investments	www.rsinvestments.com
T. Rowe Price Associates, Inc.	www.troweprice.com
TIAA-CREF Mutual Funds	www.tiaacref.org
The Vanguard Group	www.vanguard.com
William Blair Funds	www.wmblairfunds.com

The Right Time to Sell Your Mutual Funds

If your fund becomes one of the worst performers, consider selling. However, you need to look at more than just the fund's rating. Consider these guidelines for determining when to sell a fund:

✔ You may want to sell if you have overlapping stocks in your portfolio. (For more about overlapping stocks, see the sidebar "Checking for overlaps in your mutual funds.") You can use the Morningstar Portfolio X-Ray feature (`portfolio.morningstar.com`) to discover whether the two growth mutual funds that you own are holding shares in the same company. To stay diversified, you may want to sell one of the mutual funds and replace it with another mutual fund.

✔ Look at the performance of comparable mutual funds using Personal Fund (`www.personalfund.com`). If a similar fund's overall performance is down 10 percent, your fund is down 16 percent, and your fund's performance consistently trails its peers, your fund may be a loser.

✔ If your fund *drifts* from its original investment objectives, it's not meeting your asset allocation goals. This underperformance can become especially problematic if the drifting fund spoils your efforts of diversification and doesn't meet your asset allocation goals.

✔ Keep track of changes in your fund's management. If the fund hires a new money manager, that person may have a different investment strategy.

✔ You may want to sell if your mutual fund's expenses have been creeping up, if you inherited the fund, or if your broker sold you a fund with a high 12b-1 fee. High fund fees reduce your returns and make the fund less profitable than similar funds with lower expenses.

✔ In a volatile market, you may discover that you're a more conservative investor than you imagined. If you can't sleep at night, sell your fund.

✔ You pay taxes on your capital gains. If one of your mutual funds posts negative returns, consider selling the losing fund to offset your tax liabilities.

✔ If the fund increases by three or four times its original size in a short time period and its performance starts to decline, you may want to sell. As the fund keeps growing and growing, the professional money manager can't invest in the securities he or she knows and loves best, so the fund may start to acquire poor or average-performing assets.

✔ Consider your needs. If you purchased the fund for a specific purpose and your life circumstances change, you should sell the fund and purchase one that meets your needs — even if the fund is doing well.

Figure 7-1 shows FundAlarm (`www.fundalarm.com`), a free, noncommercial Web site. FundAlarm provides objective information to help individual investors decide whether to sell a mutual fund. For details about how you can be automatically notified about when it's time to sell your mutual funds, see the Web site.

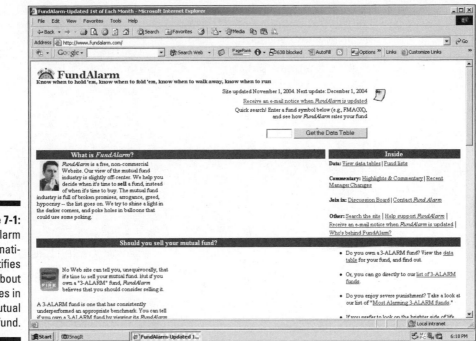

Figure 7-1:
FundAlarm automatically notifies you about changes in your mutual fund.

Chapter 8

The Basics of Stocks and Rates of Return

In This Chapter

▶ Getting your financial house in order to begin wealth building

▶ Matching your investment objectives to the right investments

▶ Understanding different types of stock quotes

▶ Finding online stock quotes

▶ Using robust online valuation tools

*T*he focus of this chapter is stock selection. The savvy online investor prospects all possible stock candidates, looking for companies that are exceptional in some way and positioned to perform well in the future.

In this chapter, I discuss using the Internet to decide which types of securities are right for you. So that you can make wise investment decisions, I also show you how to keep current with online news services, read a stock table, and find the ticker symbols of securities online. I conclude this chapter by showing how you can value bonds, stocks, and cash investments by using robust online valuation tools developed by academics and specialists.

Understanding Stocks

When you buy shares of a company, you purchase part ownership in that company. As a shareholder, you also expect to receive *capital appreciation* — the difference between your purchase price and the market price of your shares — on your investment. If the company prospers, your shares of stock increase in value. If company performance declines, the market value of your shares also decreases.

Shareholders are the owners of corporations. If you buy just one share in a company, you are a shareholder. As a shareholder, you're invited to the company's annual meeting. Additionally, you have the right to vote on the members of the Board of Directors and other company matters.

The dividend a corporation pays is the amount of money, usually a portion of the profits, a board of directors distributes to the ordinary shareholders of the corporation. For example, if a company has one million shares outstanding, and it decides to distribute 3 million dollars to its shareholders, then the dividend per share is $3 (3 million dollars divided by one million shares).

Some successful firms, such a Berkshire Hathaway, don't pay dividends. These companies usually plow dividend payout funds back into the company to finance expansion, which increases the value of the company and the price of shares stockholders own. In other words, if all goes as planned, the stockholders get capital appreciation instead of a dividend check. Some investors in high tax brackets prefer this approach. They don't have to pay taxes on capital appreciation until they sell the stock. With dividends, investors have to pay the taxes right away.

The *annual return* is the percentage difference of the stock price at the beginning of the year from the stock price at the end of the year plus any dividends paid. The price at which you can buy or sell a share of common stock can change radically. As a matter of fact, stock prices are so volatile that accurately predicting annual returns is impossible. (If we had this gift, we would all be rich!)

Common stock returns can vary — for example, from a depressing −43.34 percent in 1931 to a thrilling 53.99 percent in 1933. However, over 73 years, investments in the stock market have consistently outperformed any other type of investment. For example, the return on $1 invested in the S & P Index from the year-end of 1925 through 1998 would be $2,350.89. A dollar invested for the same 73 years in Treasury bonds would be worth $43.93.

For answers to questions like "What is stock?", "What are different types of stocks?", "How do stocks trade?", and "What causes prices to change?", see Investopedia at www.investopedia.com/university/stocks.

Participating in the Market

Just like other investments, several categories of stocks are available to try. Each stock type has characteristics, benefits, and drawbacks that you should be aware of before you invest. The following sections offer a quick summary to help you gain an understanding of these financial instruments.

Common stocks

When people think about investing, they tend to think primarily of common stocks. After all, it's difficult not to be bombarded daily with stock market news and commentary. Additionally, American history is filled with stories about how the Vanderbilts, Rockefellers, Carnegies, and other turn-of-the-century entrepreneurs made their fortunes on Wall Street with common stocks.

Both new and old companies sell common stock to raise capital to fund operations and expand their businesses. Common stocks represent shares of ownership in a corporation. Shareholders have a right to dividends and can vote on mergers, acquisitions, and other major issues affecting the corporation. Additionally, shareholders have a voice in the election of the board of directors. Dividends are paid at the discretion of the board of directors. The liabilities of being a shareholder are limited. Shareholders can't lose any more than the amount of their investments.

Preferred stocks

Preferred stocks are also equity stocks in a corporation. However, preferred stockholders cannot cast their votes on issues regarding company management. For this trade-off, the stockholder gets another benefit: a fixed dividend amount. Preferred stock is sold at *par value* (face value). The par value of preferred stocks is usually $25, $35, or $100. The company assigns a fixed dividend. Preferred stocks (sometimes called hybrids because they include the features of both stocks and bonds) compete with bonds and other interest-bearing financial instruments, which means that the amount of the dividend is affected by the current interest rate at the time that the preferred stock is issued. In other words, to make a preferred stock issue attractive to investors, higher dividends tend to be issued when interest rates are high. Lower dividends are issued when interest rates are low. Preferred stockholders are paid their dividends regularly, and the stock has no maturity date.

Picking the Right Stock for the Right Goal

Selecting your own stocks can be hard work. The exciting thing is that the Internet has much of the information you need, and most of this information is free. With the power of your computer, you can utilize Internet data to gain real insight (as you can see in the next two chapters). As you start to determine which stocks you're interested in, you should be aware of the different types of stocks. Stocks have distinct characteristics, and as general economic conditions change, they behave in special ways.

Write a short list of your financial goals and then investigate how different types of stocks relate to those objectives. Different stocks have different rates of return — some are better for young, aggressive investors; others are better for retirees or for people in high tax brackets. Here are a few examples of the different types of stocks that may match your investor objectives:

- **Blue-chip stocks:** Usually the most prestigious stocks on Wall Street, these high-quality stocks have a long history of earnings and dividend payments. These stocks are often good long-term investments.

- **Cyclical stocks:** The fortunes of these companies rise when business conditions are good. When business conditions deteriorate, their earnings and stock prices decline. These companies are likely to be manufacturers of automobiles, steel, cement, and machine tools.

- **Seasonal stocks:** Similar to cyclical stocks, these companies' fortunes change with the seasons. Good examples of seasonal companies are retail corporations whose sales and profits increase at Christmastime.

- **Defensive stocks:** These stocks tend to be stable and relatively safe in declining markets. Defensive stocks are from companies that provide necessary services, such as electricity and gas, which everyone needs regardless of the economic climate. Companies in this category also provide essentials such as drugs and food, so their sales remain stable when the economy is depressed. (***Note:*** Defensive stocks are *not* related to the military.)

- **Growth stocks:** Growth companies are positioned for future growth and capital appreciation. However, their market price can change rapidly. Rather than pay dividends, growth companies typically spend their profits on research and development to fuel future growth. These stocks are good for aggressive, long-term investors who are willing to bet on the future. If you're in a high tax bracket, these stocks may be for you; low dividends mean fewer taxes. But if expected earnings don't match analyst predictions, expect a big decline in stock price.

- **Income stocks:** Purchased for their regular, high dividends, income stocks usually pay bigger dividends than their peers do. Income stocks are attractive to retirees who depend on their dividends for monthly expenses. Income stocks are often utilities companies and similar firms that pay higher dividends than comparable companies. These companies are often slow to expand because they spend most of their cash on dividend payouts. During times of declining interest rates, bonds are better investments.

- **International stocks:** Investors in these stocks often believe that U.S. domestic stocks are overpriced. These investors are seeking bargains overseas. However, international stocks include some risks that U.S. stocks don't have, such as trading in another currency, operating in a different economy, being subject to a different government, and using accounting standards that don't follow U.S. generally accepted accounting principles. Public information may have to be translated, which causes delays and sometimes miscommunication. All these elements add cost and risk to foreign stocks.

✔ **Speculative stocks and initial public offerings:** Speculative stocks are easy to identify because they have price/earnings (P/E) ratios that are frequently twice as high as other stocks. For example, the S & P 500 Index has a median P/E ratio of 23.2. Speculative companies have a high probability of failure. However, if they succeed, the returns can be very large. A speculative stock could have a P/E ratio of more than 75, in an industry with an average P/E ratio of 50. A second type of speculative stock is an *initial public offering* (IPO). This type of stock often has no track record. A good example of speculative stock is Taser; (TASR) its stock price is relatively high, and its revenues are small.

✔ **Value stocks:** Some Wall Street analysts consider these stocks to be bargains. These stocks have sound financial statements and earning increases, but are priced less than stocks of similar companies in the same industry.

What Does the S & P 500 Have to Do with Anything?

You can measure how good or bad an investment is by comparing it to a market index. For example, the Standard & Poor's (S & P) 500 tracks a broad group of large capitalization stocks that are traded on the New York Stock Exchange and NASDAQ/AMEX. (I define the term *large capitalization stocks,* or *large cap stocks,* later in this section.) You can see the S & P Web site at www2.standardandpoors.com.

Each stock in the S & P 500 Index is weighted by the relative market value of its outstanding shares. Overall, the index represents the performance obtained in the stock market for large capitalization stocks. This index provides performance information so that you can compare the stocks in your portfolio to the market. If your returns are better than the market, you're doing well. If your returns are lower than the market, you need to reevaluate your stock selections.

When you compare the performance of your stock to a market index, you can determine whether the stock outperformed the market, maintained the market rate, or underperformed. As Table 8-1 shows, however, not all market indexes are alike. The Dow Jones Industrial Average is the most well-known index, but it includes only 30 large, mature, consumer-oriented companies. The Wilshire 5000 is the most comprehensive index of common stock prices regularly published in the United States and may be the best indicator of overall market performance. As you can see in Table 8-1, the S & P 500 tracks the performance of large capitalization stocks. In other words, the S & P 500 isn't the appropriate index for evaluating the performance of your small capitalization stock.

Table 8-1	Comparing Apples to Apples with the Right Index
Index	*Type of Security*
Dow Jones Industrial Average	Large cap blue chip
Financial Times World	World stocks
Lehman Bros. Corporate Bonds	Corporate bonds
Lehman Bros. Government Bonds	U.S. Treasury bonds
Morgan Stanley EAFE	International stocks
Russell 2000	Small capitalization stocks
S & P 500	Large capitalization stocks
Wilshire 5000	Entire market

Source: Jim Jubak, The Worth Guide to Electronic Investing (1996, Harper Business, New York, NY).

Table 8-2 helps to explain why the S & P 500 may not be the appropriate index to compare to your small capitalization stock. *Capitalization* (or *cap*) is the total number of shares outstanding multiplied by the current stock price of those shares. For example, a firm with 1 million common shares outstanding at $55 per share has capitalization of $55 million, which makes the company a small cap firm. Table 8-2 shows a quick estimate of how the capitalization of different companies sorts out.

Table 8-2	Defining the Capitalization of Companies
Category	*Capitalization*
Micro cap	Less than $50 million
Small cap	$50 million to $500 million
Mid cap	$500 million to $5 billion
Large cap	More than $5 billion

According to Standard & Poor's, small capitalization stocks have outperformed large capitalization stocks over time. Over certain short-term periods, however, this overperformance may not hold true. From 1983 to 1990, small capitalization stocks, as a group, underperformed larger capitalization firms. From 1991 to 1993, both small and mid-capitalization firms have outperformed large capitalization companies. During times of market volatility, small capitalization stocks tend to fall faster and harder than their bigger siblings. For example, between June 12 and August 23, 1996, NASDAQ was down 7.48 percent. During the same time period, the MicroCap 50 was down 24.52 percent. Following the "bursting of the bubble in 2000," small capitalized stocks have outperformed the market.

Paying the Right Price

You can use several methods to determine the *fair value* of a stock. Throughout the following sections, I discuss three of the more popular methods of determining the right price for a stock:

- Fundamental analysis
- Technical analysis
- Market timing

Valuing securities is important to your financial health. Stocks are more difficult to value than bonds. Bonds have a limited life and a stated payment rate (for more on bonds, turn to Chapter 13). Common stocks don't have a limited life or an upper dollar limit on cash payments. This uncertainty makes stocks harder to value than bonds. Common stock can be valued in a number of different ways, but overall, the value of a stock is the present value of all its future dividends. However, common stockholders aren't promised a certain dividend each year. The dividend is based on the profitability of the company and the board of directors' decision to pay dividends to stockholders.

The second source of return for a stock is the increased market price of the stock. If the company decides not to pay dividends and reinvests profits in the firm, the company's future profits and dividends should grow. This additional value should be reflected in a stock price increase in the future.

Fundamental analysis seeks to determine the intrinsic value of securities based on underlying economic factors. It's the most widely accepted method for determining a stock's true value, which you can then compare to current prices to estimate current levels of mispricing. Fundamental analysts usually forecast future sales growth, expenses, and earnings.

Getting down to fundamentals

Fundamental analysis focuses on the underlying economics of the company being researched. Analysts try to forecast sales, earnings, and expenses, which in turn are used to forecast the company's stock price or returns. All U.S. business schools support this methodology because fundamental analysis seeks to paint the whole economic picture of the company being analyzed.

Fundamental analysis relies on forecasts of the economy, the industry, and the company's commercial prospects. Analysts use fundamental analysis to determine the intrinsic value or fair value of a stock. The fair value is compared to market values to determine whether the stock is underpriced or overpriced. In other words, the objective of fundamental analysis is to locate mispriced stocks or undervalued stocks. Fundamental analysis is the most frequently used approach for common stock valuations.

If the stock has higher risk than usual (because of past volatility, political turmoil, or other factors), investors include a *risk premium* in the required rate of return. This risk premium serves to compensate the investor for the higher than normal risk.

After you crunch all the numbers, do a reality check. The fundamental analysis methodology is limited because it often assumes that the investor holds the stock until termination of the company. If you hold the stock for a short time, you may not get all the expected returns. Additionally, companies, accountants, investors and analysts can make errors in dividend projections or may ignore relevant external factors, which can result in not valuing the stock correctly. Before you log on to your broker, you need to review your analysis and the data you collected. It's your money and your investment decision. What do you think is going to happen to this company in the future?

Using online tools to value stocks

You can visit the following Web sites for more about fundamental analysis and valuing stocks:

- **Global Value Investing with Stock Valuation** (www.numeraire.com/index.html) offers an article that illustrates why stock prices and stock screens are different from stock valuation. You also find an online discount cash flow valuator. The valuator uses models based on intrinsic value for the valuation of common stocks and other investment assets. That is, the model uses the discounted cash flow approach for determining fair market value. Results are shown in text, tabular, and graphical formats.

- **Stockworm** (www.stockworm.com) was developed several years ago by several academics who were interested in investing and the financial markets. It offers stock analysis, customizable technical charts, stock screeners, and portfolio management strategies. Stockworm offers three levels of subscriptions and a free two-week trial. Analyst membership is $7.95 per month for stock valuations, comparisons to industry averages, and technical trading signals. A Manager membership is $14.95 per month for everything in the Analyst level plus advanced stock screeners and portfolio tracking. Autoinvestor is $29.95 per month and includes everything on the previous levels and is geared for investors who want the next level of automating portfolio buy/sell recommendations. Investors configure rule-based strategies for long or short selling (for example, buy a stock if it is in the top 20 results of the screener) and receive daily alerts.

✔ **ValuEngine.com** (www.valuengine.com) was developed by Yale University's Dr. Zhiwu Chen and his team of experts. ValuEngine is a proprietary model for valuing stocks. ValuEngine products include the stock valuation model (which determines the fair value of stocks), the ValuEngine stock forecast model (which forecasts the value of stocks), the ValuEngine portfolio forecast model (which predicts the likely return of a portfolio), and the ValuEngine Portfolio Advisor Model (which suggests ways to maximize the future gains of a portfolio). There are no charges for stock valuations. Premium membership is $24.95 per month with a free seven-day trial. Subscriptions include delayed quotes, portfolio functions, portfolio optimization, advance screening, detailed stock analyses and forecasting, multistock comparisons, research by analysts, and benchmark portfolios.

✔ **ValuePro** (www.valuepro.net) was developed by finance professors to complete stock valuations based on discounted cash flow. The latest improvements include the ability to download data. The financial valuation software, which is $44.95, allows you to download data from the ValuePro Web site to your computer and to use the ValuePro software to analyze your investments.

You can also use the ValuePro Online Stock Valuation Service at no charge. The Online Valuation Service looks up valuation inputs from the SEC EDGAR database and other free sources. The online valuation model uses quarterly and annual income statements, balance sheets, and cash flow statements to calculate the ratios. The calculations are based on observed historical data. (You can see how yearly data is used for the outcome.) The model also attempts to look up data regarding analyst estimates about growth rates. The model then combines these inputs by using the discounted cash flow valuation method to come up with a baseline intrinsic value for a stock. You can alter the 19 variables to update stale data and to fine-tune your long-term fundamentals.

Using the Net to calculate fair value

If you're averse to math, check out the Value Point Analysis Stock Forum at www.eduvest.com. The Value Point Analysis computer model was designed in 1979 to evaluate a stock's worth in terms of its fundamental economic, financial factors and the general condition of the money market. The Value Point Analysis Stock Forum, shown in Figure 8-1, includes a community of investors who share information about their stock picks and their analyses using the Web site's valuation model. To use the model, click Value Point Analysis Model at the home page. Just enter the factors used by the model. For additional insight, you can post your results and get feedback from others. All these features at a price you can't beat — it's free!

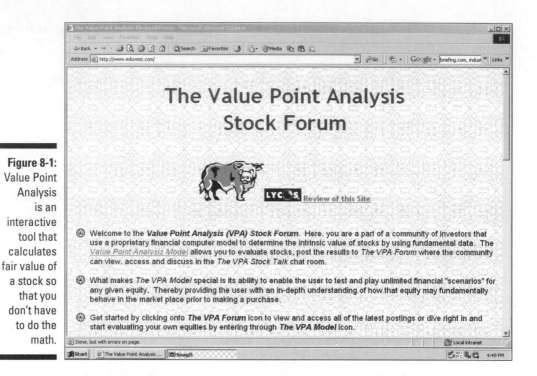

Figure 8-1:
Value Point
Analysis
is an
interactive
tool that
calculates
fair value of
a stock so
that you
don't have
to do the
math.

To determine the intrinsic value (and what some people feel is the real value) of a stock, the Value Point Analysis Model uses 12 factors. Overall, the Value Point Analysis Model, which was designed in 1979, is used to evaluate a stock's worth in terms of its fundamental economic underpinnings and the general money market. The model uses the following factors:

1. **Corporate name, ticker symbol, and exchange of a stock:** This information is used to identify the specific stock you're analyzing.

2. **Number of the corporation's shares outstanding (in millions):** This number represents how many other common shareholders will be paid dividends.

3. **Long-term debt (in millions):** Long-term debt is the amount of any loans or outstanding bonds that mature in five years or more. Debts with terms of one to four years are considered short- or midterm liabilities.

4. **Current dividend payout ($ per share):** This number is the annualized amount of this year's dividend. For example, imagine that you're in the middle of the second quarter. The first quarter dividend is $0.25. The company pays dividends each quarter. The annualized current dividend is $1.00. (In other words, 4 × $0.25 = $1.00.)

5. **Book value or net worth ($ per share):** Many company reports have calculated this number for you. This value is often listed at the bottom of the balance sheet. The formula to calculate net worth is total assets less total liabilities. For example, total assets of $100 million less total liabilities of $75 million equal a net worth of $25 million. Net worth divided by the number of outstanding shares equals the book value per share.

6. **Projected earnings ($ per share):** Many company reports include expert forecasts of expected earnings. For example, if earnings for one year are $1.00, and next year the earnings are $1.10, the growth rate is 10 percent.

   You can use experts' earnings forecasts or the amount you believe is correct for your analyses. Remember that each quarter you may see "earnings surprises," and individual investors have often outsmarted the so-called experts.

7. **Projected average growth in earnings (percent):** Without revenue (sales), you have no profits (earnings), and corporate earnings are what make stocks valuable. At the beginning of each company's annual report is a letter from the CEO. In this letter, the CEO usually states what he or she expects sales to be for the next year. You may or may not agree with this statement. Enter the percentage amount that, in your judgment and based on your research, is correct.

8. **Current earnings ($ per share):** Current earnings are often called *Earnings per Share* and are calculated for you at the bottom of the income statement. In case you have to do your own math, take the net after-tax income and divide it by the number of outstanding shares of common stock. For example, $1.5 million net after-tax income divided by 1 million shares is $1.50 per share.

9. **Current sales price ($ per share):** Check with an online quote server for the current sales price of a share of stock.

10. **Number of years the earning growth rate is expected to be sustained (1, 1.5, 2 years, and so on):** Some companies have variable growth rates, and others have a steady increase that can go on for ten years or more. You need to decide whether the company will sustain its growth rate and for how long. This decision is a judgment call that investors have to make.

11. **Current yield of AAA Bonds (percent):** Luckily, the Value Point Model fills this number in for you.

12. **Projected change of AAA Bonds (percent, 100 basis points = 1%):** The Value Point Analysis Model enters a default amount here. If you agree with the amount, don't change it.

Valuation model input and results

No investor wants to pay more for a stock than it's worth. The following minitable illustrates the input data and results for an online stock valuation using the Value Point Analysis Model, which can help you determine a stock's fair value. An example of user input and results looks like this:

Description	Model Input
1. Stock Name, Ticker Symbol, and Exchange	Example Corporation, EXC, NYSE
2. The number of shares in millions, greater than 0	1,010.00
3. The long-term debt in millions of dollars	28,100.00
4. Current dividend in $/sh (xx.xx), annual	8.00
5. Book value or net worth in $/sh	20.12
6. Projected earnings in $/sh, annual	8.80
7. Projected average growth in earnings (%)	5.00
8. Projected average growth in sales (%)	5.00
9. Current yield of AAA bonds, greater than 0 (%)	5.81
10. Projected change of AAA bonds (%)	0.00
11. Current earnings in $/sh, annual amount	8.17
12. Current price in $/sh, greater than 0	162.00
13. Number of years the earnings growth rate is expected to be sustained (for example, 1, 1.5, 2, and so on)	1.00

Description	Stock Evaluation Results
NAME SYM EXCH	Example name, Example symbol, NYSE
VALUE POINT ($/sh)	150.56
PROJECTED EARNINGS ($/sh)	8.80
PROJECTED P/E	17.11
VALUE POINT/CURRENT PRICE	0.93
CURRENT P/E	19.83
CURRENT YIELD (%)	4.94
CURRENT PRICE ($/sh)	162.00
RELATIVE RISK FACTOR	0.86

The preceding minitable indicates that the Value Point–determined fair value for the stock is $150.56. The model forecasts earnings of $8.80 and a projected P/E ratio of 17.11. The Value Point price is 0.93 times the stock's current price. The stock's current P/E ratio is 19.83. The current yield is 4.94 percent, and the current price is $162. The model assigns a relative risk factor of 0.86 to its estimate of the stock's fair value.

In summary, this chart indicates that the stock's intrinsic value is $150.56. The stock is currently selling for $162.00. This amount is greater than $150.56, which indicates that the stock is overpriced. If I were you, I wouldn't even think about buying this expensive stock. However, if you already own the stock, it might be a good time to sell.

Analysis for value shopping

If you're a bargain shopper, you understand how difficult it is to separate the treasure from the trash. This search for value extends to investors who are seeking securities that seem underpriced relative to the fair value or financial prospects. Experts have a variety of opinions about how to decide whether a stock is undervalued (and unloved) or just a loser.

T. Rowe Price (www.troweprice.com) has developed one approach to spotting stocks that are selling at bargain-basement prices. At the T. Rowe Price home page, click Individual Investors. Then select Investment Planning & Tools⇨Publications. Click the Insights Reports link, then Investment Strategies, and finally the Value Investing link. You see several investment strategies; find Spotting "True" Bargains. Table 8-3 shows a snapshot of this methodology. This approach is one way of separating the winners from the losers. T. Rowe Price suggests that investment candidates meet at least six of the seven factors listed in Table 8-3. (For more about ratios, see Chapter 9).

Table 8-3	Value Investing (Spotting "True" Bargains)
Factor	*Analysis*
Price/book value (1)	Never over 2.0
Price/earnings ratio (2)	Using five-year average earnings, never over 12
Ratio of cash per share to price per share (3)	At least 10%
Dividend yield (the annual dividend divided by the market price)	Never below 3%

(continued)

Table 8-3 *(continued)*

Factor	Analysis
Price to cash flow	80% or less of the S & P 500 cash flow ratio
Ratio of long-term debt (plus unfunded pension liabilities) to total capital	The debt/equity ratio should be under 50% (include unfunded pension liabilities in the debt).
Financial strength	Creditworthiness should be at least equal to the industry average. The S & P rating should be at least B–.

The following list explains the terms used in Table 8-3:

✔ **Price/book value (P/BV) (1):** Expresses the current selling price divided by book value. If the current selling price of the stock is below this amount, the stock is underpriced. Then again, the company may be on the verge of bankruptcy, which may be why the stock price is depressed.

✔ **Price/earnings ratio (P/E ratio) (2):** Reflects how many years of current earnings must be earned to purchase one share of stock. For example, if annual earnings are $2 and the stock is selling at $30, the price/earnings ratio is 15 (30 ÷ 2). Many investors believe that the higher the P/E ratio, the better. If investors expect earnings to decrease, the P/E ratio will decrease to below the industry average.

✔ **Cash flow per share (3):** Expresses the firm's net income plus depreciation and amortization expenses, divided by the number of outstanding shares.

Note: For more information on many of these terms, see Chapter 9.

Getting technical: Technical analysis

Technical analysis is the study of all the factors related to the supply and demand of stocks. Unlike fundamental analysis, technical analysis doesn't look at underlying earnings potential of a company when evaluating a stock. In contrast, technical analysis uses charts and computer programs to study the stock's trading volume and price movements in hopes of spotting a trend. Overall, technical analysts don't care about a company's fair market or intrinsic value. According to Block and Hirt (1999), technical analysis is based on several assumptions:

✔ Market value is based solely by the interaction of supply and demand.

✔ Stock market prices are likely to move in trends that persist for long time periods. However, there may be some minor fluctuations.

✔ Reversals of trends are caused by changes in demand and supply.

✔ Demand and supply shifts can be detected sooner (or later) in charts.

✔ Chart patterns often repeat themselves.

Technical analysis focuses on stock data analyses and stock market statistics. Analysts generally utilize a series of mathematical measurements and calculations designed to monitor market activity. Among other things, actual daily, weekly, and monthly *price fluctuations* are analyzed. Technical analysts are searching for early indicators of pattern changes to capitalize on. Trading decisions are based on signals generated by charts, manual and online calculations, computer programs, or their combinations.

If you're an investor who uses technical analysis, check out these Web sites:

✔ **ClearStation** (www.clearstation.etrade.com) offers customizable charting tools to illustrate the basics of technical analysis. Color-coded trends and standard charts are provided when you type in a ticker symbol. For beginners, explanations of technical analysis methods are illustrated with real-life examples.

✔ **Investtech.com** (www.investtech.com) provides daily updated analyses and recommendations of more than 15,000 stocks in Europe and the U.S.A. This Web site is by subscription only. Analyses include trends, price patterns, and support and resistance levels. A written interpretation of each chart is also provided. You also find a model portfolio and a top 50 list with the most interesting stocks. For examples of reports and subscriptions prices, check the Web site.

✔ **ProphetNet** (www.prophet.net), with your free registration, provides you with basic service. Basic service includes 40 years of interactive charting, 20-days of intraday data for each security, the ability to save two chart styles, 24 technical studies, five custom sets, draw/save trendlines, access to watchlists, flip charts, two portfolios with 100 transactions per portfolio, risk/reward analyses, delayed market data, and 30 results for your chart toppers market scans. You can also create and edit notes. The bronze level is $14.95 per month (or $149.50 per year). The bronze level includes access to everything in the basic level plus quotes, java-charts, snap charts, watchlists, portfolios, delayed streaming intraday charts, Marketmatrix streaming quotes, chart toppers market scans, Prophetscan real-time custom scanning, mini-charts, and notes. The next two levels include more bells and whistles. The silver level of service is $24.95 per month (or $249.50 per year), and the gold level of service is $39.95 (or $399.50 per year.) You can take advantage of a seven-day free trial. See the Web site for details.

Technical analysis uses the Dow Theory to analyze individual stocks. However, Dow developed this methodology to predict changes in the general market. He didn't expect his theory to be applied to individual stocks.

The Tao of investing using the Dow Theory

Although technical analysis consists of many approaches, the most well-known approach is the Dow Theory. The Dow Theory is based on *The Wall Street Journal* founder Charles H. Dow's methodology for identifying signals of bull and bear markets. The theory suggests that as soon as the market heads in one direction, it stays that course until canceled (stopped) by both the Dow Jones Industrial Average (DJIA) and the Dow Jones Transportation Average (DJTA). (It takes both averages to indicate that the market has changed its course.)

The Dow Theory maintains that three major market movements exist. The first is the daily fluctuations that represent normal activity. The second is intermediate or secondary movements that last about two weeks to a month and point out the long-term trends of the market. The third is long primary trends that indicate either a bull or a bear market.

For a more detailed explanation of technical analysis techniques, check out Decision Point at decisionpoint.com/TAcourse/TAcourseMenu.html.

Technical analysis software

Technical analysis requires large amounts of information (usually historical price and volume data) that you can manipulate with technical analysis software programs. Some programs are designed for different types of securities and for specific indicators and markets. Additionally, some programs are designed for beginners, while others are for professionals. Here is a short list of available programs:

- ✔ **Equis MetaStock** (www.equis.com) offers MetaStock Professional, which analysts sometimes refer to as the granddaddy of technical analysis software, for $1,695. (See the Web site for details.) The Web site includes back issues of the Equis newsletter, as well as files of tips, system tests, and custom formulas for use with the software.

- ✔ **Insider TA** (www.stockblocks.com) uses box charting to highlight each trading period's volume and high and low prices. Insider TA costs $129 for the Standard version and $229 for the Pro version. A downloadable demo is available at the Web site.

- ✔ **Stable Technical Graphs** (www.winterra.com) is a Windows-based program that analyzes stocks, bonds, commodities, mutual funds, indexes, and options. Stable Technical Graphs costs $59.95 and offers a downloadable full product version for a 30-day trial.

> ✔ **VectorVest** (www.vectorvest.com) uses fundamental valuation and technical analysis to rank more than 8,000 stocks each day. Stocks are ranked for value, safety, and timing, and VectorVest gives a Buy, Sell, or Hold recommendation on every stock, every day. Go to the Web site to sample the program. Just enter the ticker symbol of the company you're analyzing. The special trial offer is for five weeks and costs $9.95. Subscription prices vary.

Market timing

The underlying theory of market timing is that you purchase stocks when prices are low and sell when prices are high. The market timing strategy is based on reams of historical data that are used to discover patterns and relationships that affect investment returns. Market timing software uses this data to detect or anticipate changes in market patterns. Market timers note that the market can underperform for long periods of time. This low performance can reduce returns for buy-and-hold investors who decide to go ahead and sell before the next upswing. In contrast, market timers attempt to time the purchase and sale of their securities to coincide with ideal market conditions based on their predictions market cycles.

The biggest problem with market timing is the need to predict when to get into the market and when to get out of the market (in addition to ensuring that the timing strategy will make enough increased returns to offset trading costs). A buy-and-hold strategy makes certain that the investor is in the market for the days with the biggest gains. Market timers may be out of the market during these times. For more information about market timing, check out FirstCapital Corporation (www.firstcap.com).

Chapter 9

Internet Stock Screening

In This Chapter

▶ Selecting the criteria to build your first stock screen

▶ Getting familiar with online stock screens

▶ Using prebuilt stock screens

▶ Making use of prebuilt stock screens you can change yourself

▶ Getting online stock recommendations from the experts

▶ Utilizing your online brokerage to screen for stocks and other types of securities

Stock screening boils down to finding the answer to one fundamental question: Which stock (among all stocks) should I buy right now? Of course, finding the answer to this question requires asking many more specific questions about stocks — questions that are difficult to answer without the help of computerized databases.

This chapter shows how you can use the Internet and PC-based stock screening tools to whittle down the universe of stocks to a manageable few candidates. You can then analyze your short list of stocks for gems that may bring you above-average returns. (I provide many online tools and sources for your in-depth analysis in Chapter 11.) Interested in more than stocks? Well, I point what online brokerages have to offer for screening stocks and other types of securities.

Finding the Best Stock Using the Net

Screening is a process that permits investors to discover and distill useful information from a larger set of information. The Internet provides many screening tools that help you prospect stock issues. The goal of stock screens is to point out which stocks are worth your research and analysis time.

Some people believe that using a stock screen is like panning for gold. You use your computer to screen ("pan") for investment "nuggets" from a long list of possibilities. The online investor sets the objectives of any single screen. Different people get different results because no two people have exactly the same selection criteria or investment philosophy.

Overall, the benefit of stock screens is that they enable you to generate your own ideas — ideas that generate profits based on your investor savvy. Stock-screening programs enable you to go beyond finding good stock investments and assist you in finding the very best stocks.

To identify investment candidates, the stock screen uses your preset criteria, such as *growth* (stocks that are expanding faster than the market or their peers), *value* (stocks that have strong financial statements but are selling at prices below their peers), or *income* (stocks that provide higher than average dividends).

Depending upon the criteria you select, you may have to run several iterations of the stock screen. For example, your first screen may result in several hundred possibilities. Because you can't investigate and analyze so many candidates, you have to run a second screen of these results. This fine-tuning should lead to a manageable list of investment candidates that you can research and analyze — perhaps between 10 and 20 candidates. You can quickly pare down this number by using common sense and your investor savvy.

When screening, identifying exactly what types of stocks you seek is important. Consider writing down your investment objectives and the characteristics of your ideal investment. Don't forget to consider your performance expectations and risk-tolerance level. (For more about setting realistic expectations and determining how much risk you can take, see Chapter 3.)

Choosing the criteria for your first stock screen

Typically, you build a stock screen by accessing an online stock-screening tool and filling out an online form. I offer examples of the variables used in these forms later in this chapter, in the section "Important ratios for screening stocks." The first stock screen that you develop may include quantifiable variables that you believe are the most important — for example:

- **Earnings growth:** The percentage of change between current earnings and earnings for the last quarter or last year.

- **Recent earnings surprises:** The difference between predicted and actual earnings.

✔ **Price/earnings (P/E) ratio:** The current price of the stock divided by the earnings per share — that is, net income divided by the total number of common shares outstanding. For example, value stocks have P/E ratios below 10 or 12, and growth stocks have P/Es above 20.

✔ **Dividends:** The annual cash dividend paid by the company.

✔ **Market capitalization:** The number of outstanding shares multiplied by the current stock price of those shares. Market capitalization is sometimes abbreviated as *cap*. This value is a measurement of the company's size. Firms with high market capitalization are called *large cap,* and companies with a low market capitalization are called *small cap.*

Fine-tuning your stock screen

After you select your initial screening criteria, you click Submit, Sort, or a similar command. A list of stock candidates appears. Often, this list includes several hundred stocks. This number is still too large to research, so you should narrow this list by selecting more variables.

You may have some special knowledge about the industry you work in. You may have used certain products over the years and can use your knowledge to your advantage. However, keep in mind that a good product doesn't necessarily mean a good company. You may want to filter out companies that you just don't understand. You might also want to filter out companies about which you lack information. Without at least some basic information, you can't perform a complete analysis.

Using your stock screen results

After you complete your second stock screen and sort the data, you should have a list of 10 to 20 companies. Start a file for each firm and begin to gather data for your analysis. At this point, you might discover that some companies aren't worth additional research — a finding that further reduces your short list. For example, the company may have filed for bankruptcy, or it may be targeted for federal investigation. Maybe the company recently paid a large fine for shady dealings, or the executive management was recently indicted for fraud, misconduct, or some other crime.

Important ratios for screening stocks

Every industry has its own language, and the financial industry is no exception. In the following sections, I define the key terms that the finance industry uses for stock-screening variables.

Figure 9-1 shows MSN Money Central's (`moneycentral.msn.com/investor/ finder/deluxestockscreen.aspx?query=Righteous+Rockets&btnQryFr m=Go`) Power Search for *Righteous Rockets*. Righteous Rockets are defined as companies that appear undervalued, are profitable, and have relatively low debt, thus making them "righteous." Additionally, they're fast growing and have begun to see significant stock price appreciation — making them "rockets." The ticker symbol and name of the company is on the left. The criteria used for this particular stock screen are Market Capitalization, Return on Equity, Price Sales/Ratio, Debt to Equity Ratio, and Revenue Growth This Year Compared to Last Year.

The following are definitions of the criteria most often used in screens. I define these terms so that you can better understand what's included in prebuilt screens. When you get comfortable with using prebuilt screens, you can use these definitions to set parameters to build your own customized screens.

Beta

Beta is the measurement of market risk. The beta is the relationship between investment returns and market returns. Risk-free Treasury securities have a beta of 0.0. If the beta is negative, the company is inversely correlated to the market — that is, if the market goes up, the company's stock tends to go down. If a stock's volatility is equal to the market, the beta is 1.0. In this case, if the stock market increases 10 percent, the stock price increases 10 percent. Betas greater than 1.0 indicate that the company is more volatile than the market. For example, if the stock is 50 percent more volatile than the market, the beta is 1.5.

Book value

Book value is the original cost, less depreciation of the company's assets and outstanding liabilities. (*Depreciation* is the means by which an asset's value is expensed over its useful life for federal income tax purposes.)

Cash flow to share price

The ratio of *cash flow to share price* is the company's net income plus depreciation (expenses not paid in cash) divided by the number of shares outstanding. For companies that are building their infrastructures (such as cable companies or new cellular companies) and therefore don't yet have earnings, this ratio may be a better measure of value than earnings per share (EPS).

Current ratio

Current ratio is current assets divided by current liabilities. A current ratio of 1.00 or greater means that the company can pay all current obligations without using future earnings.

Power Searches

More Stock Searches

Quote, Chart, News
Snapshot
Quotes
Charts
Key Developments
Recent News

Research
Company Report
SEC Filings
Advisor FYI
Stock Rating
Earnings Estimates
Analyst Ratings
Financial Results
Insider Trading
Ownership
Community

Guided Research
Research Wizard

Find Stocks

View: Righteous Rockets   Go

Companies that appear undervalued, are profitable and have relatively low debt -- making them "righteous" -- but that are also fast growing and have begun to see significant stock price appreciation -- making them "rockets".

Customize this screen in our **Deluxe Stock Screener**

Righteous Rockets

Symbol	Company Name	Market Capitalization	Return on Equity	Price/Sales Ratio	Debt to Equity Ratio	Rev Growth Year vs Year
MTLM	Metal Management, Inc.	536.3 Mil	32.90	0.38	0.05	40.70
STTX	Steel Technologies, Inc.	345.1 Mil	17.40	0.44	0.50	53.50
UTIW	UTi Worldwide Inc.	2.054 Bil	13.10	1.11	0.03	28.40
EAGL	EGL, Inc.	1.42 Bil	10.90	0.57	0.26	29.20
HRS	Harris Corporation	4.506 Bil	11.10	1.74	0.30	20.40
ELBO	Electronics Boutique Holdings Corp.	912.7 Mil	17.10	0.57	NA	21.60
MOH	Molina Healthcare, Inc.	1.167 Bil	17.40	1.13	NA	23.20
ZQK	Quiksilver, Inc.	1.69 Bil	13.40	1.47	0.32	38.20
HZO	MarineMax, Inc.	449.2 Mil	14.00	0.59	0.10	25.40
AGP	AMERIGROUP Corporation	1.653 Bil	15.10	0.95	NA	39.80

Page generated 11/19/2004 4:32 PM eastern time

Figure 9-1: Results of MSN Money Central's Power Search for *Righteous Rockets.*

Debt to equity ratio

To determine the *debt to equity ratio,* divide the company's total amount of long-term debt by the total amount of equity. (*Equity* is defined as the residual claim by stockholders of company assets, after creditors and preferred stockholders have been paid.) This ratio measures the percentage of debt the company is carrying. Many firms average a debt level of 50 percent. Debt to equity ratios greater than 50 percent may indicate trouble. That is, if sales decline, the firm may not be able to pay the interest payments due on its debt.

Dividend yield

Dividend yield is the amount of the dividend divided by the most current stock price. You can use dividends as a valuation indicator by comparing them to the company's own historical dividend yield. If a stock is selling at a historically low yield, it may be overvalued. Companies that don't pay a dividend have a dividend yield of zero.

Dividends

Dividends are a portion of a company's net income paid to stockholders as a return on their investment. The company's board of directors can declare or suspend dividends. A primary benefit of dividends is that once paid, they're cash that can be banked and can provide a return (in the form of bank interest) when stocks are weak. A limitation of dividends is that they're taxed as ordinary income. For an individual investor in a high tax bracket, this can increase their usual tax bill.

Earnings per share (EPS)

Earnings are one of the stock's more important features. After all, the price you pay for a stock is based on the future earnings of the company. The consistency and growth of a company's past earnings indicate the likelihood of stock price appreciation and future dividends. *Earnings per share* is often referred to as EPS.

Market capitalization

Market capitalization is the total value of the firm. It's calculated by multiplying the number of outstanding shares times the current stock price of those shares. Market capitalization is sometimes called *market value*.

P/E ratio

You calculate the *price-to-earnings ratio* by dividing the price of the stock by the current earnings per share. A low P/E ratio indicates that the company may be undervalued. A high P/E ratio indicates that the company may be overvalued.

Price-to-book value ratio

Price-to-book value ratio is tangible assets less liabilities, and the price-to-book value is the current price of the stock divided by the book value. If the company has old assets, this ratio may be high. If the company is a new start-up with fixed assets that haven't been depreciated, this ratio may be very low. Therefore, you need to compare this ratio to industry standards and other information about the company.

Return on equity (ROE)

Return on equity (ROE) is usually equity earnings as a proportion of net worth. You divide the most recent year's net income by shareholders' equity (*shareholders' equity* is assets minus liabilities) to calculate ROE.

Shares outstanding

The term *shares outstanding* refers to the total number of shares for a company's stock. To determine the firm's outstanding shares, you need the most recent data. The shares outstanding can be calculated by taking issued shares on the balance sheet and subtracting treasury stock. *Treasury stock* is stock issued but not outstanding by virtue of being held (after it is repurchased) by the firm.

WARNING!

Watching out for investment risks

No one invests in securities to lose money. However, each security has its own fine print. The Securities and Exchange Commission (SEC, at www.sec.gov/investor/pubs.shtml) provides educational materials on how the securities industry works, how you can avoid making investing mistakes, and fraud. To view PDF files, you can download Adobe Acrobat Reader for free. The following are examples of some of the things to watch for:

✔ **The higher the return, the greater the risk.** You may lose some or all of your investment.

✔ **Some investments can't be easily sold or converted to cash.** For example, you may have a hard time selling a municipal bond before it matures.

✔ **If you want to sell an investment quickly, you may have to pay some penalties or transaction charges.**

✔ **Investments in new companies or companies that don't have a long history may involve greater risk.**

✔ **Securities, like mutual funds, aren't insured by the Federal Deposit Insurance Corporation (FDIC).**

✔ **The securities you own may change due to corporate reorganizations, mergers, or third-party actions.** You may be asked to sell your current shares, or you may be offered new shares due to this activity. Make certain that you understand the complexities of this investment decision before you act.

✔ **Past performance of a security is no guarantee of future performance.**

Starting with Quick Online Stock Screens

Web-based stock screens can require between 2 and 80 variables. Computerized stock databases can include anywhere from 1,000 stocks to more than 13,000 stocks. Additionally, computerized stock databases are updated daily, weekly, or monthly. The best stock screen is the one that includes your personal investment criteria.

Some stock screeners are very comprehensive and offer excellent results. Unfortunately, these screens are often the hardest to use. Here are a few examples of bare-bones stock screeners that offer good results for little effort:

✔ **CBS MarketWatch.com** (cbs.marketwatch.com/tools/stock research/screener/) is a free intraday stock screen designed to screen for stocks by using as many or as few parameters as you wish to define. All parameters default to None. From 4:00 to 6:00 p.m. EST, you can complete after-hours stock screening.

✔ **NASDAQ SharpScreen** (`nasdaq.sharpscreen.com`) offers a quick, printable tutorial for its stock screen. SharpScreen screens more than 6,000 stocks. You can select stocks by business sector, type, and exchange. Ten additional criteria are available to whittle down your number of investment candidates.

✔ **Yahoo! Finance** (`screen.yahoo.com/stocks.html`) provides a stock screen that is easy to use. You also find preset screens that indicate high-volume stocks, stocks with the greatest sales revenue, largest market gap, strong forecasted growth, and more.

Using Those Terrific Prebuilt Stock Screens

The Internet provides many prebuilt stock screens that use preselected criteria. Some of these screens are very advanced and can make your research work easier because they already include the investment criteria that you feel are most important. I describe a few examples in the following list:

✔ **BusinessWeek Online** (`prosearch.businessweek.com/business week/general_free_search.html?mode=advanced`) offers a quick-search stock screener and a more advanced stock screener. If you're uncertain about a number, just enter "as high as possible" or "as low as possible."

✔ **MSN Money** (`moneycentral.msn.com/investor/finder/welcome.asp`) offers the Power Search Finder, which identifies stocks that best match your investing strategy. The 30 prebuilt stock screens are divided into technical screens (patterns of price or volume) and fundamental screens (using profits, sales, and other business factors). Screens are based on criteria favored by MSN Money Investor editors and well-known professionals.

✔ **Zacks** (`my.zacks.com`) provides several types of stock-screening tools. At the home page, click Screening to find an overview of the screening tools. You can save up to 13 predefined screens. If you need assistance, just click Screening Help.

Locating Those Prebuilt Screens You Can Change Yourself

Everyone has a different way of setting up his or her stock screen. The following are a few examples of where you can find customized stock screens:

✔ **MSN Money** (`moneycentral.msn.com/investor/controls/finder pro.asp`) offers a free, downloadable *Deluxe Screener*. You can import preset screens and customize them or create your own from the ground floor up by using hundreds of criteria. Results of this customizable screener can be saved and downloaded to an Excel spreadsheet. Click the name of the company that interests you for a corporate snapshot.

✔ **Reuters Investor** (`investor.reuters.com`) requires your free registration. At the home page, click Investing and then click Ideas & Screening. Next, click the *Power Screener* tutorial and discover how to use this valuable online tool. Power Screener offers 13 prebuilt screens. You can add criteria to prebuilt screens and save the screen as a template for later use. It takes awhile to get familiar with how the screen works, but the results are worth it.

✔ **Zacks** (`www.zacks.com/research/screening/custom`) provides a free *custom screener* that includes 96 screening criteria from the Zacks database. You can make the search as broad or a narrow as you like and save the results. It may take awhile to input all your criteria, but you can save the screen as a template for later use.

Advanced Techniques for Building Stock Screens

This section outlines several ways to set up stock screens that may be beneficial for your information mining. I offer a few examples of ways you can build stock screens to discover specific categories of stocks. I use the categories of growth stocks, income stocks, and value stocks for these examples.

Screening for growth stocks

Growth stocks expand at rates faster than their counterparts. They have different degrees of risk and are a way of betting on the future. Your stock screen for growth stocks may consider the following criteria:

✔ **Basic growth:** Any stocks that have an earnings growth of 15 percent or more in one year.

✔ **Long-term growth:** Any stocks that grew 15 percent or more in one year over the past five years. (Companies must have historical EPS records of over five years.)

✔ **Earnings for growth:** Stocks that have a price-to-earnings ratio that is equal to or less than the growth rate of the stock plus its dividend yield.

- **Aggressive growth companies with low P/E ratios:** Stocks with annual earnings growth of more than 24 percent and P/E ratios of less than 15. (P/E ratios of less than 15 are preferable, but rare in the current market.)

Screening for income stocks

Income stocks tend to be stodgy, boring, slow-growth companies that are steady income producers. You may want to include dividend yield in your stock screen for income stocks. For example, you may screen for any stocks with a dividend yield that's at least equal to the S & P 500 and that never falls below 4 percent. (This criterion rules out growth stocks that don't pay dividends.)

Screening for value stocks

Value stocks are companies that have strong financial statements and good earnings but are traded at stock prices that are less than their industry peers. Some criteria that you may want to include in your stock screen for value stocks include the following:

- **Book value:** Stocks for which the book value of the company is less than 80 percent of the average S & P 500 stock.

- **Debt/equity ratio:** Stocks for companies with a debt/equity ratio of 50 percent or less.

- **P/E ratio:** Stocks for which the average of the company's five-year earnings is not less than 70 percent of the average P/E ratio of the S & P 500. Don't include stocks with a P/E ratio greater than 12. (A low P/E ratio may indicate that the stock is selling at a bargain price.)

- **Underpriced stocks:** Three criteria exist for this section of the value stock screen:

  - Small cap stocks with *quick ratios* (current assets less inventory divided by current liabilities) greater than 1.0 and return on assets (ROA) greater than 0.0

  - A price-to-earnings ratio (P/E ratio) that is half of that industry's average

  - A price-to-book value ratio of 80 percent or less, and a price-to-sales ratio of 33 percent or less

Screening for Investment Bargains

Investors are always searching for a *competitive edge* that will enable them to *beat the market*. (Beating the market is usually defined as selecting stocks that *outperform* — that is, provide greater returns than — the S & P 500 Index.) The following sections describe several stock screen variables that you may want to factor into your stock selection strategy. However, keep your risk-tolerance level in mind. After all, you do want to sleep at night.

Stocks selling at below book value

Some stock screens enable you to sort for stocks that have a current selling price below book value. *Book value* is defined as the depreciated value of a company's assets (original cost less accumulated depreciation) less the out-standing liabilities.

Purchasing stocks at below book value may be a bargain-hunter's dream but requires additional research on your part. A company's total assets are often the accounting values of assets purchased over time — in other words, the historical price of an asset less depreciation. For example, the firm may have fully depreciated a 20-year-old building. The sales value of the building may be in the millions, but the value listed on the balance sheet may be zero. (This difference causes the book value to be understated.) Or the building may have environmental problems (because of improper industrial waste disposal, for example) that will cost the owners millions to clean up. In this case, the book value is overstated.

Before purchasing the stock, the prudent investor determines why a company is selling at below book value. Check out the following good online sources for this type of data: The company's annual, quarterly, and other miscellaneous reports are filed with the Securities and Exchange Commission (www.sec.gov), and Reuters Investor (www.investor.reuters.com) offers company profiles and financial highlights.

Try different approaches to your research. For example, you may be able to discover some interesting facts about the company if it was a failed merger or acquisition candidate. If a large corporation or an investment bank didn't want to buy the company, you may want to follow suit.

Securities selling below liquidation value

Your bargain hunting may guide you to screening for stocks that are selling below their liquidation value. *Liquidation value* of a company is defined as the dollar sum that could be realized if an asset were sold independently of the going concern. (Assets are listed in company annual reports. A good Internet source for these reports is Dun & Bradstreet at www.dnb.com.) For example, suppose that no market demand exists for the company's barrel staves and buggy whips, and the company discontinues those product lines. The machinery used to manufacture those products still bears value. The appraised value of the manufacturing equipment is determined as a separate collection. The values of the firm's ongoing or discontinued operations are not factored into this price.

Stocks selling at below liquidation value may be valuable, but you should consider the priority of claims if the company is forced into bankruptcy. Claims against company assets are paid in the following order: (1) secured creditors; (2) expenses incurred for administration and bankruptcy costs; (3) expenses incurred after filing bankruptcy; (4) salaries and commissions (not to exceed a set amount) that were earned within three months of filing bankruptcy; (5) federal, state, and local taxes; (6) unsecured creditors; (7) preferred stock; and finally, (8) you, the common stockholder.

Stocks with low P/E ratios

The price-to-earnings (P/E) ratio is the current price of a stock divided by the earnings for one share of stock and is the value that the investment community places on $1 of the company's earnings. For example, if the current price of the stock is $60 and the earning per share (for the last 12 months) is $3, the P/E ratio is 20 ($60/$3).

Note: In Wall Street–speak, the earnings per share (EPS) for the last 12 months when used in the preceding formula is often called the *trailing P/E ratio*. You're likely to see the trailing P/E ratio listed as a variable in the online stock screens.

P/E ratios vary by industry, so unless you find out the industry average, you can't determine whether a stock has a low P/E ratio. Luckily, Reuters Investor (www.investor.reuters.com) and the Wall Street Journal (www.wsj.com) provide this information for free. At Reuters Investor, enter the ticker symbol or name of the company you're researching. In the left margin, click Ratios. At the public Wall Street Journal, enter the ticker symbol or company name in the quote box at the top of the page. Click Valuations and Ratios in the left margin. When analyzing a P/E ratio, you want to look at the trend of the company's P/E ratio over the last five to seven years. Companies that the investment community expects to grow will have higher P/E ratios than others in the same industry.

Bargain hunters may want to set the variables in their stock screens for low P/E ratios because a company with a P/E ratio of 20 is a more expensive stock than one with a P/E ratio of 10. However, companies with low P/E ratios may be *cheap* for good reason. For example, one way to analyze the P/E ratio is to compare it to the company's growth rate. The company's P/E ratio and growth rate should be equal. The stock price is the present value of all the future earnings. Therefore, if the P/E ratio is low, the company may be plagued by slow growth.

What a low P/E ratio is or what it indicates may be difficult to determine. For example, the company may have a low P/E ratio because investors are bailing out, which can drive the stock price down and make the stock appear inexpensive. Say that a $60 stock drops to $30 per share. The P/E ratio will be reduced to 10 ($30/$3). The stock is now half-priced, but it may not be a good purchase if the company is headed toward bankruptcy or has a major problem.

Companies reporting deficits

You may want to set up your stock screen to determine which companies in a certain cyclical industry are reporting deficits (losses). Cyclical stocks are dependent on external environmental factors, such as the national economy, housing sales, and consumer confidence. You can check out these good online sources of industry information: Lexis-Nexis (www.lexis-nexis.com) and STAT-USA (www.stat-usa.gov). Cyclical stocks have peaks (high points) and valleys (low points) in their revenues, profits, and stock prices. These peaks and valleys can mean that some cyclical companies with strong foundations may be experiencing flat earnings or deficits due to their business cycles.

Be certain that you understand the company's business operations. High fliers can crash and burn. For example, you may want to avoid companies that have no earnings or whose stock prices are based on planned new products, corporate restructuring, or strategic partnering.

The trick with cyclical stocks is to purchase the stock when it's in a valley in the cycle and sell when it's near the peak. A good indicator that the upward part of the cycle may be about to begin is when the P/E ratio is high and the EPS (earnings per share) is low. Other external environmental factors may indicate that the stock is approaching its peak. For example, a sudden drop in housing starts might indicate that your shares in a furniture company are near their peak and it's time to sell.

Prospective turnaround candidates

Using stock screen variables to locate companies that are laggards in sales, earnings, and profits is one way to locate turnaround candidates. The value of investing in turnarounds is that the stock may increase two or three times as the company becomes successful.

Early-stage companies often have ups and downs, but mature companies that have problems frequently don't get a second chance to improve their fundamentals. These fallen angels often have problems with inconsistent product quality, slow response to changing market conditions, high operating costs, low employee involvement, poor customer service, and inadequate methods of allocating resources. Often, management is negative, risk-averse, and bureaucratic. All these factors prevent the company from becoming competitive. The result is that analysts and investors are waiting for a turnaround that never appears.

The preceding situation highlights how timing is everything when investing in troubled companies. The company has to survive long enough to get well. For troubled companies, a larger, more mature company that owns real estate and has cash on hand is superior to a small company with limited resources and rented office space. After all, the company needs to be solvent in order to make a comeback.

Don't be fooled by quick profits when the company starts slashing budgets and implementing a recovery plan. These short-term gains will likely disappear as customers become wary of doing business with the troubled company. The comeback road is bumpy. Many companies get off to false starts and then stumble.

With all these screens, you may think it odd that mutual funds and bonds are forgotten investments. Many online brokerages offer stock, bond, and mutual fund screens to their customers. The more flexible the screener, the better it is. Flexible screeners allow you to set the parameters for the investment candidates that meet your individual investor profile. Table 9-1 illustrates the characteristics of a few screeners offered by several online brokerages.

Table 9-1	Quality of Online Brokerage Screeners
Brokerage (URL)	*Description of Screener*
eTRADE (www. etrade.com)	Screen for mutual and exchange-traded funds. Offers full data customizability and includes many special conditions.
Fidelity (www. fidelity.com)	Uses over 100 different screening criteria, is not fully customizable, and includes extensive bond screening. (Shown in Figure 9-2.)
Harris*direct* (www. harrisdirect.com)	Screen 8,300 stocks with *StockScan*, search 500 fund families, and research bonds. Offers full data customizability and includes many special conditions.
Charles Schwab (www.schwab.com)	Is not fully customizable, but includes solid criteria for stocks and mutual fund screening.

Using a screen provided by your online brokerage can save you time and effort. If you're in the market for several different types of securities, online brokerages are a good place for one-stop shopping. However, if you want to create your own screens (or customize prebuilt screens) and save them for later, you may want to try some of the screens I discussed earlier in this chapter.

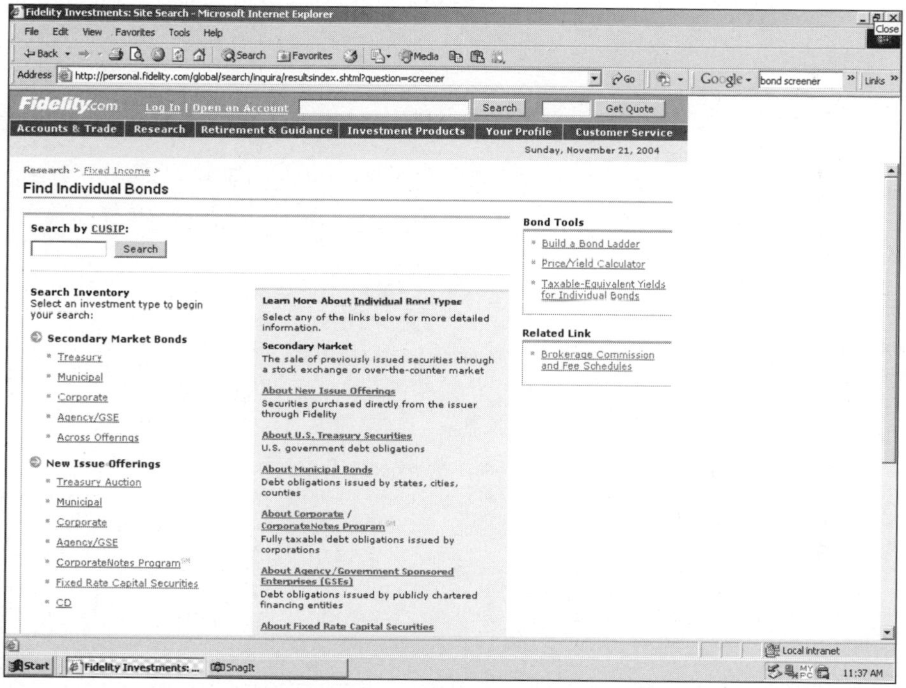

Figure 9-2: You can screen for bonds at Fidelity.

At Bloomberg.com (www.bloomberg.com), you can analyze more than 18,000 funds at its Fund Center. At the home page, click Charts and Analysis and then Fund Center. If you know the ticker symbol for the fund you're researching, you can discover its rank. You can also rank funds by sector and discover the top ten ranking funds. Click a fund for a detailed profile. You can also sort funds by clicking their headings, such as NAV.

Chapter 10

Using Company Information to Make Investment Decisions

In This Chapter

▶ Finding annual reports online

▶ Downloading, printing, and saving annual reports

▶ Analyzing company annual reports

▶ Using prepared company data to make your investment decision

▶ Examining potential bankruptcy candidates

*I*n the past, only large financial institutions had access to high-quality financial data. Clients didn't have anywhere else to go for stock advice, which meant that bankers and stockbrokers charged customers hefty commissions for their research and recommendations. Much of this data is now available on the Internet. Some of the databases are free, and some are fee-based. Databases that charge fees require subscription fees — payment by month, by database, or by document.

Even with free or low-cost information, researching stocks is still hard work. Doing so requires good judgment, the ability to fit all the bits and pieces of information together, and excellent decision-making skills. If you're thinking about investing in stocks, you need to research the following information:

✔ **Companies:** Profiles, management, financial health, insider trading, potential mergers, and acquisitions

✔ **Industries:** Industrial markets, industrial standards, and trends

✔ **Economic indicators:** The national, regional, and local economics

✔ **Other factors:** New legislation, technological breakthroughs, and new stock offerings

Often, the best starting point for researching the stock of a certain company is its annual report. The best place to find annual reports is on the Internet. This chapter shows you how to locate annual reports by using a search engine, special company locator sites, investor super-sites, and EDGAR — the Securities and Exchange Commission's online database.

Publicly traded companies are required to file quarterly reports with the Securities and Exchange Commission (www.sec.gov). These reports provide updates of the company's activities since it filed its annual report. If the company is going through a momentous change (such as a merger or acquisition), it's required to file more often.

You can find important information about a company in its annual report, but annual reports require careful reading. This chapter shows you how to download an annual report and analyze any publicly traded company. After all, reading a company's annual report is a little like kicking the tires of a used car. You want to make certain that you get what you think you're buying.

Finding Financial Statements Online

If you're a stockholder, you automatically receive the company's annual report. Annual reports are also free for the asking to anyone else. All you have to do is call the firm's investor relations department and request a copy.

Accuracy in annual reports

According to a report by the Huron Consulting Group (www.huronconsultinggroup.com) titled the *2003 Annual Review of Financial Reporting Matters*, 206 companies restated their annual filings with the US Securities and Exchange Commission (SEC) in 2003, up from 183 in 2002, 140 in 2001, and 98 in 2000. In most cases, these corrections wiped out the profits that investors relied on when determining the value of the company's stock. Additionally, lax standards and complicated transactions make

understanding annual reports harder than ever before. The company books for American businesses are sometimes so complicated that even experienced forensic accountants find them difficult to understand. As difficult as these reports are, taking the time to understand the nature and economic foundation of a company — before you invest in it — is very important.

For online investors, getting annual reports is even easier. The Internet provides four sources for annual reports:

- **Annual report Web sites:** These Web sites are designed for investors, shareholders, and money managers who want instant access to company annual reports. Many sites include additional company quarterlies, fact books, and press releases.

- **Company Web sites:** Many companies have sites on the Internet that include their annual reports. You can use special corporate linking sites and commercial search engines to find these company sites.

- **Investor compilation sites:** These Internet investor super-sites often include annual reports, company news, earnings forecasts, and other useful information.

- **Securities and Exchange Commission (SEC) filings:** The SEC does a good job of making electronically filed company reports available online to the public.

In the following sections, I show you how to find annual reports by using these sources.

Accessing Web Sites That Specialize in Annual Reports

The Internet features Web sites that focus on the individual investor's need for company information. These sites deliver annual reports in a variety of ways. For example, you can order hard copies of the original reports, immediately access online annual reports, or view annual reports in their original formats using free Internet plug-ins. Here are a few examples of these investor information services:

- **Annual Report Gallery** (www.reportgallery.com) offers over 3,000 annual reports that cover the majority of Fortune 500 companies. The Web site is easy to use. Investors are able to look for a company through five search criteria: alphabetically, by company name, by ticker symbol, by sector, or by industry. Once a company is found, it can be viewed in either HTML (Hypertext Markup Language — the language of the Internet) or PDF (Portable Document Format) format.

- **Investor Relations Information Network** (www.irin.com), shown in Figure 10-1, offers more than 11,600 free company historical and current annual reports in their original formats. Annual reports may include photographs, graphs, and text. You use the Adobe Acrobat Reader program to read the information, which comes to you in the form of PDF files. (With

Acrobat Reader, you can read PDF files on Windows, Macintosh, DOS, and UNIX operating systems. You can download a free copy of Acrobat Reader from the Adobe Web site at `www.adobe.com` or by clicking a link on the IRIN Web site.) To find an annual report, just enter the first few letters of the ticker symbol or company name.

✔ **Public Register's Annual Report Service** (`www.prars.com`) is free and provides hard-copy annual reports from more than 3,600 companies. This service saves investors time by allowing them to order up to eight reports at one time. Search criteria for finding an annual report may include any or all of the following items: industry, ticker symbol, state of business, exchange, or all companies beginning with a certain letter.

✔ **The Wall Street Journal Online** (`wsjie.ar.wilink.com/asp/wsj3_search_eng.asp`) offers a free annual report service provided by World Investor Link and The Wall Street Journal Interactive. The annual report service provides investors with quick access online and hard copies of annual reports from select companies. You have several search options, such as selecting a company by using an alphabetical listing, selecting a company by industry, or selecting a company by its name.

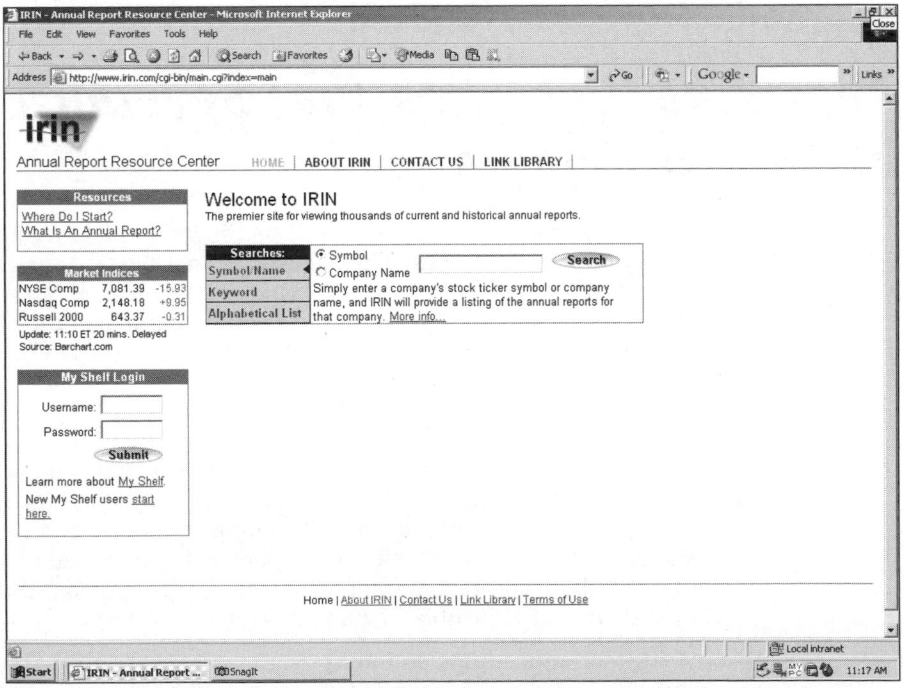

Figure 10-1:
The Investor Relations Information Network offers more than 11,600 free historical and current company annual reports in their original formats online.

IRIN is owned and operated by DST Systems, Inc.

Using Web Sites That Link to Company Home Pages

Numerous publicly traded companies have Web sites on the Internet. Many commercial search engines and special business Web site locators provide links to the home pages of large businesses. These sites often include the company's annual reports as part of the firm's public relations and investor services. For example, the Web100 (`metamoney.com/w100`), shown in Figure 10-2, provides links to the 100 largest U.S. and international businesses on the Internet. You can sort the database by company name or by industry.

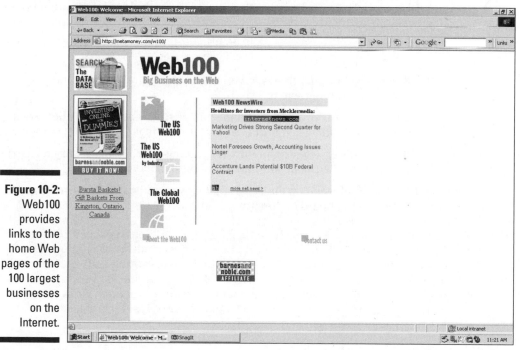

Figure 10-2: Web100 provides links to the home Web pages of the 100 largest businesses on the Internet.

Courtesy of The Web Paving Company, Ltd.

Researching a Company's SEC Filing

In the United States, publicly traded companies are required to file business and financial information with the Securities and Exchange Commission (SEC). These reports are entered into a government-sponsored database called EDGAR (www.sec.gov), which stands for Electronic Data Gathering, Analysis, and Retrieval. The SEC's EDGAR service provides downloadable data that can be accessed by individual investors. You also can save SEC reports on a disk and read them at a later time. One disadvantage of this free service is that financial data can't be downloaded to your spreadsheet program.

When you search the EDGAR database, you're asked for the report number of the document you want. The reports are numbered in the following manner:

- **10-K reports:** Annual reports that include shareholder information covering the firm's fiscal year

- **10-Q reports:** Quarterly reports that include shareholder information for the firm's last quarter

- **8-K reports:** Interim reports covering an odd period due to a merger, acquisition, or other event

- **S-1 registration:** Forms required for businesses that want to offer stock to the public; often used for initial public offerings

- **S-3 registration:** Registration of a secondary offering; necessary form to offer stock to the public after an initial public offering

- **14-A form:** Information about voting matters and candidates seeking election to the board of directors; also called a *proxy*

Annual reports may include more than 50 pages and often exceed 100 pages. For example, the 10-K annual reports include descriptions of the business, business properties, legal proceedings, stockholder voting matters, selected financial data, management's discussion of the firm's financial condition and results of operations, financial statements and supplementary data, changes in accounting procedures and financial disclosures, insider transactions, executive compensation, and leasing agreements.

The Sarbanes-Oxley Act and investors

On July 30, 2002, the Sarbanes-Oxley Act went into effect. Although the Act was adopted in response to accounting and corporate governance scandals at Enron, WorldCom, Tyco, and other large public companies, its ramifications extend to smaller public companies as well.

The Act mandates a number of reforms to enhance corporate responsibility, to improve financial disclosures, and to combat corporate and accounting fraud. It also created a Public Company Accounting Oversight Board (PCAOB) to oversee the activities of auditing professionals. The following are a few highlights of the Act that might interest investors:

- CEO and CFO certifications are required for periodic reports.

- Annual reports must be filed within 60 days of the end of the fiscal year.

- Accelerated filing of insider transaction reports is required.

- Companies are required to adopt codes of ethics for senior financial officers.

- Real-time disclosure of material information is now required.

- Companies must disclose off-balance sheet transactions.

- Companies are prohibited from making loans to directors or executive officers.

- Insider trades are prohibited during pension plan blackouts.

- Stricter conflict-of-interest rules have been put into place.

- New securities fraud offenses are punishable by 25 years of imprisonment and a fine.

- SEC enforcement authority is enhanced.

The full text of the Act is available at `www.law.uc.edu/CCL/SOact/soact.pdf`. You can also find links to all SEC reports issued under the Sarbanes-Oxley Act at `www.sec.gov/spotlight/sarbanes-oxley.htm`.

Downloading SEC filings in just three clicks

When you find the annual report you want, save it to a floppy disk or to your computer's hard drive. After you download the report and save it on your computer, you can read the file at your leisure. You can also use your word processor's snappy text-search features to find the important information you need.

After you find the report you want, you can save the data in just three clicks:

1. **Click the File menu at the top-left corner of your Internet browser screen.**

2. **Click Save.**

Your browser displays a dialog box asking you which drive you want to save the data to and which name you want to file it under.

3. Enter a name for the file and specify where you want to save the file.

Use the company's name, initials, or ticker symbol for the filename and a file extension of .txt or .doc.

4. Click Save.

You're finished downloading an annual report from the Internet!

To read the file, just start your word-processing program and open the file.

If the columns are out of alignment, you may need to adjust the font size for the entire document.

SEC search engines

Many free and fee-based SEC search engines are available online. Free search engines provide users with easy, basic access to SEC EDGAR filings. You can search the databases for the information that you require in a number of ways. For example, you may want to research the most recent SEC filings, or look up documents by company or fund name, filings by industry type or ticker symbol, or some other way. You can then view documents on-screen, clicking a table of contents to move to various sections of a document. Fee-based SEC search engines provide more search tools, such as

- ✔ **10-K Wizard** (www.10kwizard.com) provides fee-based services. The service allows investors unlimited searches of real-time SEC EDGAR filings, insider trading data, and unlimited access to personal alerting. You can download data in Rich Text Format and tables as MS Excel spreadsheets. Prices of subscriptions vary. Call 800-365-4608 (toll free) for specifics.

- ✔ **EDGAR Database** (www.sec.gov/edgar/searchedgar/webusers.htm), shown in Figure 10-3, provides a valuable Quick EDGAR Tutorial that describes the different ways that an investor can search the EDGAR database. EDGAR filings are posted to this site at least 24 hours after the date of filing. Use the EDGAR database for special purpose searches, current events analysis, mutual funds retrieval, prospectus searches, and searches of the EDGAR archives.

- ✔ **EDGAR Online** (www.edgar-online.com) provides fee-based services for individuals, professionals, and corporations. EDGAR Online Access subscriptions are geared for individual investors and offer access to 25 SEC filings monthly, 25 search entries, companies' profiles, top 10 holders, and basic searching for $60 per quarter. EDGAR Online Pro subscriptions are targeted for professional users of business and financial data. It includes unlimited access to SEC filings, Excel downloading, fundamental data, section printing, and e-mail alerts, in addition to institutional holdings, insider trading, IPO information, charts, and quotes. Pro subscriptions are $100 per month with monthly, quarterly, or annual billing options.

✔ **EdgarScan by PriceWaterhouseCoopers' Global Technology Center** (edgarscan.pwcglobal.com/servlets/edgarscan) is an excellent free service that interfaces with the SEC EDGAR filings. EDGARSCAN pulls filings from the SEC's servers and sorts the information to find key financial data. EDGARSCAN can normalize financial and other data across several companies. EDGARSCAN includes *Benchmarking Assistant*, a graphical financial benchmarking interactive program. The resulting tables show company comparisons; you can download these tables as Excel files for future benchmarking. If you want to save your portfolios, you must complete the free registration, and then Benchmarking Assistant keeps your portfolio according to the supplied e-mail address.

✔ **SEC Info** (www.secinfo.com) provides securities information from the SEC EDGAR and CSA (Canadian Securities Administration) SEDAR databases for advanced investors. You can search by name, industry, business, SIC codes, area code, topic, zip code, file number, date, and so on. The standout feature of SEC Info is a plain-language search function that assists investors who are looking for specific names, themes, or events in daily filings. The real-text ability of this Web site saves time and is valuable for alerts about acquisitions, proxy statements, tender offers, and other events. The guest pass includes 45 times of use. Frequent-user subscriptions are $120 per year.

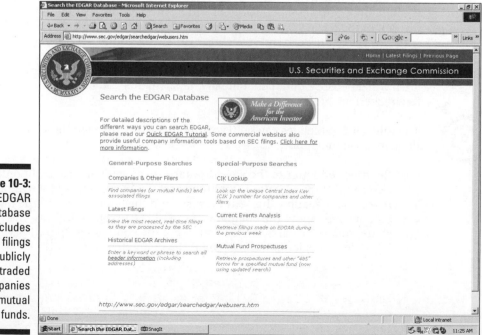

Figure 10-3:
The EDGAR database includes SEC filings for publicly traded companies and mutual funds.

Dissecting the Annual Report

Despite their glossiness, annual reports often present many unglamorous but truthful statements about a company. Sometimes the truth is stretched to hide potential problems. Therefore, annual reports require your careful and unemotional reading. Don't read the small print while you're wearing rose-colored glasses.

In general, annual reports consist of nine sections:

- ✔ Letter to the shareholders
- ✔ Company overview
- ✔ Ten-year summary of financial figures
- ✔ Management discussion and analysis of operations
- ✔ Independent auditor's report
- ✔ Financial statements
- ✔ Subsidiaries, brands, and addresses
- ✔ List of directors and officers
- ✔ Stock price history

As you start analyzing annual reports, you're likely to notice that each company has its own style and approach. Additionally, writing the annual report is often an ongoing company project and not something that happens just at the end of the fiscal year. As you read the annual report, you may notice that some sections are clear and straightforward, while other sections may be almost indecipherable and require your close attention. Several sections may be lengthy, and others provide just a brief overview. These inconsistencies are normal because different company departments and individuals write different sections of the annual report.

The following guidelines can help you find your way through the various sections in an annual report:

- ✔ **Reading the letter to the shareholders:** Although you usually find the letter to the shareholders within the first couple of pages of the annual report, save reading this letter for last and then compare it to the facts you uncover about the company. Is the CEO being truthful with the shareholders? What is the CEO's view of the company's operations? What does this letter tell you about the character of the CEO?

✔ **Viewing the company overview:** After the letter to the shareholders, the annual report usually presents an overview of the company, which includes a description of the company's products and its channels of distribution.

✔ **Figuring out the ten-year summary of financial figures:** Companies often provide selected financial data. The ten-year summary of financial figures should indicate the steady growth of the company, if there was steady growth.

✔ **Analyzing the management discussion and analysis of operations:** The management discussion, which is one of the more significant sections of the annual report, usually focuses on corporate operations. This section addresses such issues as how technology has impacted the company, how the company copes with competition, and what management expects to accomplish in the next year.

✔ **Scrutinizing the independent auditor's report:** Toward the back of the annual report, you generally find an opinion letter with a title like *Report of Independent Auditor* or *The CPA Opinion Letter*. Keep in mind that the company pays the auditor — a fact that may sometimes lead to a biased annual report. (During the savings-and-loan crisis, for example, the annual reports of many thrifts didn't reveal their shaky financial situations.)

The first part of the auditor's opinion is standard. The key words to look for are "In our opinion, the financial position stated in the annual report has been fairly stated in all material aspects and in conformity with generally accepted accounting principles," or something to this effect. If this statement isn't used, a problem may exist.

✔ **Examining financial statements:** Many companies belong to conglomerates that operate in numerous industries and countries. In such cases, it isn't possible to compare company performance to any industry average. The only way you can judge whether the company's performance is improving or declining is by comparing current financial ratios to the firm's previous ratios.

Often, the notes to the financial statements are the most revealing part of a financial statement. Notes define accounting policies and disclose any pending litigation and environmental issues.

✔ **Finding out about subsidiaries, brands, and addresses:** Knowing what the company owns and where the company operates is important. This knowledge can help investors evaluate the political risk of their investments. For example, during the time of South Africa's apartheid, many individuals boycotted Eastman-Kodak. They protested how Kodak products were used in South Africa. In this age of social conscience investing, you might not want to own stock in a company that supports initiatives and products that you disagree with or believe are unsuitable.

✔ **Perusing the list of directors and officers:** The board of directors listing usually appears on the last page of the annual report. Few reports provide details about the experience and professional backgrounds of these individuals. (Director biographies are usually included on the company's proxies to assist you in voting for new or incumbent candidates for the board of directors.) If you feel that this information is intentionally deleted, you can call the company's investor relations department and ask for a background biography of each director.

✔ **Investigating the stock price history:** Evaluating the company's stock price history may provide you with some useful insights. For example, is the current stock price the highest in the history of the company?

When analyzing the financial statements and developing ratios, you should note the following information:

✔ **Growth in sales:** Are sales increasing or decreasing?

✔ **Growth in profits:** Are profits growing as fast as sales? Are high interest payments eating away at profits?

✔ **Profits:** Have earnings per share increased every year? (If not, why not? There may be a logical answer. For example, an aluminum company's profits may not rise every year because the commodity price of aluminum fluctuates.)

✔ **Research and development spending:** Does the company spend the same amount on research and development as similar firms?

✔ **Inventory:** Is a change in accounting procedures causing inventories to go up or down?

✔ **Debt:** Are debts increasing?

✔ **Assets:** Are most of the company's assets leased?

✔ **Litigations:** Are there any pending litigations (lawsuits)?

✔ **Pension plan:** Is the pension plan in bad shape?

✔ **Changes in procedures:** Is the company using accounting changes that may inflate earnings?

The Internet provides many resources that can assist you in reading and understanding company annual reports. Here are a few examples:

✔ **IBM Financial Guide** (www.ibm.com/investor/index_investor resources.phtml) provides information about how to analyze financial statements. According to IBM, financial statements and their accompanying notes attempt to explain a company's financial performance and recent financial history. Financial statements are used to evaluate a company's overall performance, identify strengths and weaknesses, anticipate future successes or problems, and ultimately help decide whether the company is a good investment opportunity.

✔ **Investopedia** (www.investopedia.com/university/fundamental analysis) offers *Intro to Fundamental Analysis*. According to the authors at Investopedia, the massive amount of numbers in a publicly traded company's financial statement can confuse and intimidate investors. On the other hand, if investors know how to read financial statements, they can find valuable information.

✔ **The National Association of Investors Corporation (NAIC)** (www. better-investing.org) is a nonprofit educational organization that supports individual investors and investment clubs. Your online premium membership provides content and tools to assist you in analyzing annual reports. Individual memberships include 12 monthly issues of *Better Investing* magazine, stock selection or mutual fund handbook, a stock or mutual fund kit trial CD-ROM, online premium services or mutual fund resource center, and other membership benefits. Individual stock memberships are $50 per year. Individual mutual fund memberships are $50 per year. Individual stock and mutual fund memberships are $80 per year.

Analyzing a Financial Statement

Companies often use their annual reports to attract new investors; you can guess that these reports contain some marketing fluff and exaggerations. Most of this embellishment is self-evident. Analyzing a company with a calculator, paper, and pencil will take you about an hour, and the results of this examination can help you make sound investment decisions.

Buying stock in a company without reading the annual report is like buying a used car without seeing it. Here's a checklist of the information you need to consider while you review a company's annual report:

✔ **Profitability:** How much money did the company make last year?

✔ **Survivability:** How is the company coping with competition?

✔ **Growth:** Is the company expanding? How fast is this expansion?

✔ **Stability:** Is the company subject to radical changes from year to year?

✔ **Dividends (if any):** Is dividend growth constant? How does it compare to the industry averages?

✔ **Problems:** Does the company have any pending lawsuits? Do any other problems exist?

✔ **Risks:** Is the company subject to any environmental, political, or exchange rate risks?

✔ **Other factors:** Is the management team experienced? Does the company need more executive talent?

You Don't Have to Be a Math Whiz to Calculate Ratios

You may want to calculate several ratios that you can then compare to the company's previous ratios and to industry averages. Industry averages provide a benchmark for your analysis. Here are some of the ratios that provide investor insights:

✔ Last closing stock price (price per share)

✔ P/E ratio (current price per share divided by annualized earnings per share)

✔ Dividend yield (annual dividend divided by price)

✔ Return on equity ratio (net income available to common stockholders divided by common equity)

✔ Debt to equity ratio (total debt divided by common equity)

✔ Percentage change in EPS (earnings per share) from the last quarter (current EPS divided by last quarter's EPS less 1.00)

✔ Earnings growth rate (net income from this year divided by last year's net income less 1.00)

Company solvency ratios include:

✔ Current ratio (current assets divided by current liabilities)

✔ Debt ratio (total debt divided by total assets)

Several software programs can assist you in using the financial data in annual reports to calculate financial ratios — for example,

✔ **Spreadware** (www.spreadware.com) provides Business Financial Analysis for Windows and Macintosh. This easy-to-use software performs financial statement analysis, cash flow forecasting and analysis, and ratio analysis. The financial statement analysis includes cash-flow analysis, easy-to-use standard data entry, and the popular Z-Score model, which helps predict the likelihood of a business going bankrupt. The Business Financial Analysis software costs $99.

✔ **SPREDGAR V4** (www.spredgar.com), shown in Figure 10-4, is a Microsoft Excel add-in that can convert the text of SEC database reports to your Excel spreadsheet. The SPREDGAR V4 software program computes over 70 standard financial ratios in areas of profitability, leverage, and liquidity for 10-K and 10-Q filings. You find Standard Industrial Classification (SIC) comparative data and tabular comparisons of ratios for over 8,000 publicly traded companies. The newly revised program includes "prepackaged software" so that you can compare companies to like companies in a specific SIC category. For example, you can view 370 companies in SIC code 7372, as well as make side-by-side comparisons to see which companies are outperforming their peers. Fundamental data are updated weekly at the Web site. You can also complete free cash-flow analyses and receive newsletters. Just for the fun of it, you can even download a workbook analyzing Enron's financials. You can download a full-featured evaluation copy of SPREDGAR V4 and generate spreadsheets with financial ratios and cash flow for 10-K and 10-Q SEC EDGAR filings. Subscriptions are $19 per month, $59 for six months, and $99 for one year.

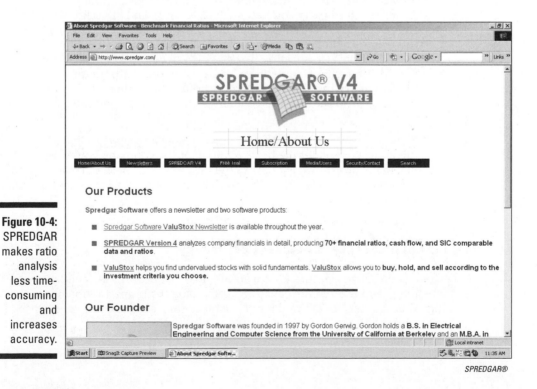

Figure 10-4: SPREDGAR makes ratio analysis less time-consuming and increases accuracy.

SPREDGAR®

Utilizing Prepared Online Ratio Analysis

Many organizations provide online annual reports that include ratio analyses, performance statistics, accounting notes, and other relevant information. You can download, print, and save all these reports. Much of the downloaded data is ready for your spreadsheet program and your analytic skills; however, you may need to reformat some data, and some data just can't be changed into a spreadsheet.

Here are several online sources of prepared ratio analysis and company information:

- ✓ **Reuters Investor** (`investor.reuters.com`) has a database of more than 40,000 companies and is constantly updated with new companies and new corporate information. After your free registration, enter the company name or ticker symbol you want to analyze and then click Go. In the left margin, under Financials, click Ratios for a ratio comparison by company, by industry sector, and against the S & P 500. Click Financial Statements for the Balance Sheet, Income Statement, and so on for analytical information about a company.

- ✓ **Yahoo! Finance** (`finance.yahoo.com`) offers free company analytic data from third-party sources, such as Reuters and EDGAR Online. Enter the company name or ticker symbol of the firm you're researching and then click Go. In the left margin, under Company, click Key Statistics to view the firm's latest ratios. To see how the company stacks up against competitors, click Competitors for a direct competitor comparison. Click Industry to see how the firm is holding up. While on this Web page, click Sector to see how the company is performing compared to its sector.

- ✓ **Zacks** (`www.zacks.com`) offers a quick look at a company's financials. At the home page, enter the ticker symbol for the company you're researching. In the drop-down list next to the ticker symbol, select Financials and then click Go. In a flash, you receive all the company's fundamental ratios.

Understanding Bankruptcy

There is no single measure for corporate financial health. However, overwhelming debt is often the cause of a firm going bankrupt. Companies with a high debt burden are allowed fewer mistakes than similar companies with more net worth.

High debt warning signs

The following are a few warning signs that you should look for when analyzing your investment candidates:

- **Squeezed by short-term debt:** Read the footnotes of the annual report to determine when the company has to repay any short-term debt, discover the interest rate they're paying, and compare this information to its profit margin. Keep in mind that more than one company has failed because it couldn't get an extension on its short-term loan.

- **Debt/equity ratio:** Companies with inflated accounts receivable or inventory need money to support those assets. When the debt to equity ratio is 1.0, the firm is supporting an equal amount of debt and equity. If the debt ratio is less than 0.5, then the firm is considered to be a low debt firm. Therefore, any company with a debt/equity ratio greater than 0.5 can be considered a bankruptcy candidate.

- **Debt/income ratio:** If the firm is borrowing money to produce goods or services at a rate that is lower than their profits, then debt can be a good thing. Here, debt is divided by the earnings before interest, taxes, depreciation, and amortization. (If you can't find this number, you can try dividing the debt by the operating income.) Most analysts believe a ratio of between 7 and 8 is sufficient. Bankruptcy candidates often have double-digit debt to income ratios.

- **Interest coverage ratio:** If the company is borrowing money to make money, that's business. If a company can't make its interest payments, that's bankruptcy. The interest coverage ratio is the operating income divided by that last 12 month's worth of interest payments. A healthy company will have an interest coverage ratio of 4 or more. However, some highly leveraged companies maintain interest coverage ratios of about 1.5. Bankruptcy candidates have interest coverage ratios that are frequently 1.0 or less.

Check out JaxWorks Z-Score Analysis located at www.jaxworks.com/calc2.htm. For a long time, researchers attempted to identify a ratio or set of ratios that provided an early warning of a business going bankrupt. Finally, in the 1960s, Edward Altman combined five ratios into what has become known as the Altman Z-Score, the best-known predictor of bankruptcy. The Altman Z-Score calculates and then combines five financial ratios, assigning each a different weighting. If the total Z-Score is 1.81 or less, the business has a very good chance of going bankrupt in the coming year. If the total Z-Score is 3.00 or better, it has little danger of bankruptcy. Use the free online Z-Score calculator and see whether any of your investment candidates are heading for bankruptcy.

Checking out insider trading

Insider ownership has an affect on a variety of corporate activities and events. Managers can change their holdings just prior to an event and then reverse their trades immediately after the event. The net effect from one year to the next is not reported. Additionally, executives can postpone purchase of shares if a significant stock price decrease is expected (and postpone sales if a significant stock price increase is anticipated).

For example, the SEC claims that Enron chairman Kenneth Lay broke the law by selling $70 million worth of shares in 2001 when he knew that Enron was failing. Because the shares were sold when the company wasn't on the open market, insider trading rules weren't applicable. Lay claims that his long-term stock plan was in effect when he later sold $20 million on the open market. (Stock sales plans are used by executives to insulate them from allegations that a sale or purchase was triggered by insider knowledge.) The SEC contends that Lay amended his sales plan because he knew that Enron was deteriorating due to billions in hidden debt. According to regulators, the use of insider knowledge invalidated Lay's sales plan and exposed him to civil charges.

Scholars are unable to document significant insider sales prior to bankruptcy filings. However, many experts agree that there is an incentive to sell in anticipation of a drop in the firm's stock price even if the firm doesn't file bankruptcy. The 1988 case of insider trading and stock manipulation against investment banker Drexel Burnham Lambert shows the extreme effects of insider trading. In an agreement with prosecutors, Drexel pled guilty to multiple counts of stock manipulation and insider trading and paid $650 million in fines and penalties. Michael Milken, head of Drexel's junk bond department, was sentenced to 10 years in prison and fined $1 billion in 1990 on a wide variety of securities law violations. Milken was released after serving less than two years in prison. Drexel went bankrupt.

The following are some Web sources that can assist you in targeting bankruptcy candidates:

✔ **BankrutcyData.com** (www.bankruptcydata.com) provides access to information on thousands of business bankruptcy filings from federal bankruptcy districts. As of this date, more than 250,000 business bankruptcies are in the database. If you want to understand why a company fails or is being reorganized, this site is the place. Free services include bankruptcy headings from Bankruptcy Week, links to court records of bankruptcies, a directory of bankruptcy courts, and links to bankruptcy publications. You can pay to view bankruptcy filings, docket headers, and bankruptcy news archives. Silver subscriptions are $50 per month or $500 per year for access to Bankruptcy Week, business bankruptcy filings, professional retentions, a news archive, and a public company bankruptcy database. Gold subscriptions are $450 per month or $5,000 per year for all the Silver-level items plus plan summary reports, creditor's committee reports, claims reports, the Bankruptcy DataSource, the Distressed Company Alert, and the Bankruptcy Yearbook & Almanac.

✔ **InsiderScoop** (www.insiderscoop.com) provides real-time publicly traded company information focused on delivering critical insider trading and institutional holdings data. InsiderScoop products allow investors to spend less time gathering and sorting data and more time analyzing it. Investors can set up alerts for 20 companies, discover which companies have insider trades every day, and get summaries of the day's insider trading activity. Basic subscriptions are $20 per month or $200 per year. If you want the e-mail alerts, you need the premium subscription service, which is $60 per month or $600 per year.

✔ **Vickers Stock Research** (www.vickers-stock.com) offers access to SEC information about insider trading, institution holders, and non-U.S. institutional holders. You find portfolio, peer and industry reports, and more. Bronze subscriptions ($19.99 per month) are for limited access and don't include Excel downloads; Silver subscriptions ($99.99 per month, $114.99 with Excel downloads) are for moderate access, and Excel downloads cost extra; and Gold subscriptions ($199.99 per month, and $229.99 with Excel downloads) are for full access, and Excel downloads cost extra. You can access a free three-day trial without the download function.

Chapter 11

Digging Deeper: Advanced Stock Analysis

In This Chapter

▶ Turning your hunches into investment strategies

▶ Getting hard data on the economy

▶ Locating company and industry information online

▶ Researching the background of corporate officers

▶ Uncovering delayed and real-time prices with Level I and Level II stock quotes

*Y*ou may use an online stock screen (see Chapter 9) to whittle down the number of common stock investment candidates you're considering. Or you may select a few companies because you know something about the products they sell. Maybe you work in the industry or have used the company's products or services over a long period of time.

After you find a few investment candidates, you can use online sources to download the annual reports of the companies that you find interesting (see Chapter 10). You read the financial statements, and you calculate the ratios that are important to investors. You might think that you're done, but you need to do a little more research before you contact your online broker.

The next step involves digging deeper to understand the economic environment in which your investment candidate operates. In this chapter, I help you locate the online sources that provide you with further background research into companies that are of interest to you. You can discover where a company stands in its industry and what type of marketing techniques it's using to maintain and increase revenues. I show you where to find out what the experts are saying about your stock pick and where to go online to find analysts' earnings estimates. I also point out where you can get historical stock price information and the latest stock quotes. After you have all these hard facts, you can make your investment decision.

Many investors don't have the confidence to select their own stocks. This chapter shows how you can conduct your own online research to find winning investments. Many of the sources I list in this chapter are the same sources that full-service brokers use in their stock analyses.

In some situations, investors don't have the six to eight hours per week needed to be their own financial advisors. If you're planning to hire a financial advisor, you still need to have a good understanding of what's going on so that you can determine whether you're receiving good or bad advice. After all, no one cares more about your money than you.

Turning Your Hunches into Investment Strategies

Every online investor has his or her own research system for investigating investment candidates. What makes any system work is that it's repeatable, and it ensures that you don't make investment decisions based on emotional factors. The following guidelines can assist you in turning your hunches into investment strategies. You begin by gathering all the facts:

1. **Find the candidates that you want to research.**

   Get familiar with the basics of stocks and their rates of return by reading Chapter 8. Match your hunches about stocks that are positioned to be top performers to your investor profile.

2. **Trim your list of candidates.**

   Use a stock screen or some other method to identify investment candidates. (See Chapter 9 for details.) Locate the online annual reports for your short list of stock candidates by using the techniques I outline in Chapter 10. Conduct your analysis to reduce the list to between six and ten companies.

3. **Find out more about each company.**

   Use the resources in this chapter to delve into the background of the companies on your short list. You may want to use the following outline to organize your advanced analysis of investment candidates. Divide your analysis into the following four sections. The good news is that the Internet has tons of this type of information, and most of it is free.

   Economic Analysis: Take a look at the economic environment of the nation (gross national product [GNP], inflation, interest rates, and other economic variables). Look at the company's current and past profits.

   - **News:** Read the company's press releases and keep current with breaking news. Try to connect isolated news articles to spot trends.

- **Economics:** Note how changes in the national, regional, and local economies affect the company. Will a rising dollar lower corporate returns? What are the Wall Street economists saying?

- **Market:** What's happening in the stock market? Are prices and trading volume increasing? Are insiders purchasing stock?

Industry Analysis: Analyze the company's current ratios and the ratios from the last three years. Compare the company's performance to its industry (see Chapter 10). Note the company's chief competitors and the relative power of suppliers and customers. Determine whether the industry is undergoing any structural changes or is changing due to general economic trends.

- **Industry breaking news:** Read news articles and industry trade journals to spot patterns that may indicate technological break-throughs or new products. Does the industry have problems with oversupply, and if so, how does this situation affect the profits of the company you're researching?

- **Industry research:** Look for any regulatory concerns, international aspects, potential for entry by competitors, and the likelihood of customers using substitute products.

Company Analysis: Using the online resources listed in this chapter, evaluate the demand for the company's products or services. Gauge management's ability to accurately forecast sales and profits. Include analyst's forecasts for future earnings and determine whether the sales forecast is reasonable in relationship to the industry and economic environment.

- **Analysts' evaluations:** Most publicly traded companies have Wall Street analysts who often provide opinions about the firm. Study what the analysts are saying about the company. What they say may provide you with leads for additional research.

- **Management analysis:** Perform background checks of corporate officers by using the resources in this chapter.

Valuation Analysis: Using the resources in this chapter, discover the company's forecast of future earnings. Using the stock valuation tools listed in Chapter 8 and the resources in this chapter, determine the right price for the company's stock.

- **Earnings estimates:** Keep current with the earnings estimates of professionals. Are the estimates going up or down?

- **Historical prices:** Sometimes you can tell where a company is going by seeing where it has been. Evaluating a company's past stock prices may provide you with new insights.

4. **Decide whether the company is a low-priced, high-quality stock or a loser.**

   When you put all the facts together, you gain a good understanding of what causes the company's stock price to rise or fall. Additionally, you know what's normal for the company.

5. **Ask yourself, "What if?"**

   For example, what if sales drop by 10 percent? What if the material the company uses to manufacture its product becomes scarce — would this scarcity cause the cost of goods to increase? Would such a change reduce profits so much that the company couldn't pay its interest expense? Would the company be forced into bankruptcy?

6. **To complete your investment strategy, determine how risky the stock is.**

   Could you lose your entire investment? If so, you need to add a *risk premium* to your required rate of return. This risk premium compensates you for the additional risk of your investment. Should the return be 10 times your investment, or maybe even 50 times your initial investment? Making this decision can be difficult because everyone defines risk differently, and everyone has a different risk-tolerance level.

Conquering Uncertainty with Online Research

You can use the Internet to get background company information by accessing one of the many free and fee-based databases and digging up all kinds of facts and opinions about a company. Some of this information can provide you with new insights, ideas, and leads about additional research. Overall, this information can provide you with an understanding of how a company works within the economy, how it copes with the competition, and how it ranks within its industry. This information is often critical to your investment decision.

With millions of Web pages on the Internet, finding exactly what you're looking for can be a challenge. However, uncovering one small fact can make the difference between purchasing a mediocre stock and buying a stock that can bring you exceptional returns. As you surf the Internet, you may encounter sites that discuss stocks, markets, and online trading. In the following sections, I help you locate the right online sources to assist you in finding the background information you need to complete your company research.

Polson Enterprises (`www.virtualpet.com/industry/howto/search.html#steps`) provides an easy-to-understand program about how to research an industry or specific company. The Web site includes links to related Web sites, answers to frequently asked questions (FAQs), and other guidance.

Gaining new investor insights with breaking news

Daily news and press releases can assist you in keeping current with your investments or investment candidates. These sources often provide the first glimpse of why a stock price is rapidly increasing or falling like a stone. One of the advantages to these online sources is that they have archives that you can search to check past company events that made news.

Here are a few Internet resources for finding press releases and breaking news:

- ✔ **Bloomberg.com** (`www.bloomberg.com`) includes newswire articles, edited columns, audio clips about current market performance, and other information about stocks, bonds, markets, and industry. The site is well organized and provides access to current market statistics, business and financial news, major newspaper stories, Bloomberg columns, and financial analysis tools. (Bloomberg charges a fee for subscribing to its magazines, but you can search its Web site for free.)

- ✔ **PR Newswire** (`www.prnewsire.com`) provides access to breaking news from tens of thousands of organizations from around the world. You can search by company, organization, or keyword. You can even search regional PR Newswire sites like China, France, and Germany. Want an annual report? Just click a link. If you're tracking certain companies, funds, or industries, you can sign up for alerts about Webcasts of corporate events.

- ✔ **VentureWire Alert** (`www.venturewire.com/Product.aspx?fp=NQI`) requires your registration for a free daily e-mail newsletter that provides private company business news. This newsletter is a great source for information about the day's events in venture-backed information technology companies.

- ✔ **The Wall Street Journal Interactive Edition** (`public.wsj.com/home.html`) contains recent news, business, and market columns from *The Wall Street Journal*. Articles contain links to charts, graphs, and tables. Daily news is continually updated. The site includes closing stock prices and a summary of each day's activities.

Business news search engines

To shorten the time you spend on the Internet, consider using a search engine that specializes in business news. Business news search engines provide news stories from hundreds of sources on the Internet. If you really want to target your search, visit a news search engine several times a day. Business news engines are constantly updated with current events that can provide you with focused and timely results.

- ✔ **Google News** (news.google.com) allows you to do a keyword search of thousands of news sources. Advanced news searches allow you to narrow your news sources to certain categories.

- ✔ **Daypop** (www.daypop.com) is a keyword news search engine that searches the content of 59,000 online news sites, Web logs, and RSS (rich site syndication) news feeds for current events and breaking news throughout each day.

- ✔ **KeepMedia** (www.keepmedia.com) isn't exactly a search engine. It's a collection of more than 200 publications and 400,000 articles. Each day, subscribers receive a selection of articles focused on stories that are "In the News." "Suggested Articles" throughout the site are matched against articles you've read. What I like best about this service is the ability to view "similar articles." This feature allows me to skip a step in narrowing my searches. Content is updated every few hours. A free 30-day trial is available. Subscriptions are $4.95 per month or $49.40 per year.

- ✔ **MagPortal.com** (www.magportal.com) allows you to perform keyword searches of magazine articles. You can even narrow your searches by specifying a date or publisher. Browse the directory structure for pertinent articles.

Locating company profiles and related data

In much the same way as the literary world includes biographies of famous people, the world of finance has *company profiles*. Company profiles include all the events that make a company what it is today. You can keep all of a company's pertinent facts handy by obtaining a company profile. Company profiles are often designed for investors and highlight investor-related information.

Here are a few online sources for obtaining company profiles:

- ✔ **CorpWatch** (www.corpwatch.org) takes a critical view of companies. You can look for information on corporations for an activist campaign, investigative article, lawsuit, or socially conscious investment. Corp-Watch allows you to search for news articles from mainstream and alternative sources. Additionally, you can search the press releases from a large number of nonprofit organizations and other enterprises. Don't forget to read its guide about how to develop a research plan.

✔ **CorporateInformation.com** (www.corporateinformation.com) includes 15,000 research reports, 20,000 corporate profiles, 1,700 profiles in French, 600 profiles in Spanish, and other resources. Just enter the company name and search. Subscription prices vary. A free trial subscription includes samples of company profiles from 57 countries.

✔ At **Corptech** (www.corptech.com), with your free registration, you can receive 25 free company snapshots. As a guest member, you receive unlimited searching using more than 30 criteria, including geographic location, size, ownership, and products. You can target individual private and public company snapshots, which include a basic overview of the company. For more information at the Home Page, click on "Be Our Guest." The site has two levels of membership. For pricing information, call (toll free) 866-327-6404.

✔ **U.S. Business Reporter** (www.activemedia-guide.com) is a business research Web site that offers business professionals, managers, entrepreneurs, investors, and others a broad array of research topics that reduces the time it takes to find company profiles, business, industry, and financial data statistics, and forecasts. It offers four levels of subscriptions. Plan 1 gives subscribers full access to the Web site and U.S. Business Reporter (Standard Edition) for $99.95 per year. Plan 2 is a two-year subscription with the same benefits for $179 for two years. Plan 3 is the same as Plan 1, but for $239 for a three-year subscription. Plan 4 is for selected content for unlimited mobile access from various wireless devices, such as personal digital assistants (PDAs) and cellular telephones, for only $4.95 per month.

✔ **Hoover's Online** (www.hoovers.com) includes information on more than 40,000 public, private, U.S., and non-U.S. companies. You can find industry overviews and in-depth industry fact sheets, company and industry news, key people, and executive biographies. A company profile includes the firm's address, phone numbers, executive names, recent sales figures, and company status. This site has links to stock quotes, SEC financial data, Dun & Bradstreet databases, and IPO information. Some information is free, and four levels of subscriptions are available. Call (toll free) 866-720-9410 for pricing information.

Gathering Business Economic and Related Data

Many individuals try to predict economic trends, but few (if any) are successful. However, having a good understanding of current economic conditions and where they're headed is vital to your comprehension of a company in its broader context. After all, many companies are sensitive to changes in the economy. The Internet has many sources for economic information.

The following is a list of the major economic indicators that can affect the value of the shares you own in a certain company. Some investors look at four or five of the major economic indicators to determine whether the market is about to change. If the targeted factors indicate a change, some investors begin a more in-depth analysis. Other investors are concerned about certain industries and look only at the indicators that affect that economic sector or industry. To sum it up, whatever your researching approach, the following list provides a quick and easy way to find the online data you need.

Business economic indicators

- **Chicago Fed National Activity Index** (www.chicagofed.org/economic_ research_and_data/cfnai.cfm) is a weighted average of 85 existing monthly indicators of national economic activity. These indicators are drawn from output and income; employment and unemployment hours; personal consumption; housing starts and sales; manufacturing and trade sales; and inventories and orders. The index is constructed to have an average value of zero and a standard deviation of one. Overall, the index indicates whether the economy is growing above or below the trend.

- **Durable Goods Orders** (www.census.gov/indicator/www/m3), created by the U.S. Census Bureau, provides a preliminary report on manufacturers' shipments, inventories, and orders. The site includes an easy-to-understand summary. The Web site includes highlights from the Durable Orders Report. Click on the appropriate link, and you can view the entire report in Adobe Acrobat Reader.

- **Economic Cycle Research Institute** (www.businesscycle.com/data.php) offers over 100 proprietary indexes for more than a dozen major economies. The Web site includes free and fee-based data. Index data and outlook are available by subscription only.

- **Existing Home Sales** (www.realtor.org) provides free information about the sales of existing single-family homes, apartment condos, and co-ops. At the home page of Realtor.org, click Research. Monthly data and quarterly data can be sorted by volume and price, volume, price, U.S. region, state, and so on. Current volume and price data is in a spreadsheet or in a PDF format.

- **Federal Reserve Statistical Release, Industrial Production and Capacity Utilization** (www.federalreserve.gov/releases/g17) is a monthly report, usually issued midmonth, that measures the industrial production, capacity, capacity utilization, and industrial use of electric power. An annual revision of the report is also published online. You can download reports in text or PDF formats.

- ✔ **Manufacturing and Trade Inventories and Sales** (www.census.gov/ mtis/www/mtis.html) releases manufacturing, trade inventories, and sales information monthly. Refer to the Web site for details on the reliability of estimates, historical press releases, and schedule release dates.

- ✔ **New Home Sales from the National Association of Home Builders** (www.nahb.org) are offered mid-month. Find additional information about the housing market index, homes sales and prices, building materials, and so on.

- ✔ **Producer Price Indexes** (www.bls.gov/ppi/home.htm), shown in Figure 11-1, measures the average change over time in the selling prices received by domestic producers for their output.

- ✔ **U.S. Census Bureau, Construction Spending** (www.census.gov/ftp/ pub/const/www/c30index.html) provides online reports in text or PDF formats about the value of construction spending in the nation. Monthly reports are delayed approximately 30 days. For details and scheduled release dates, see the Web site.

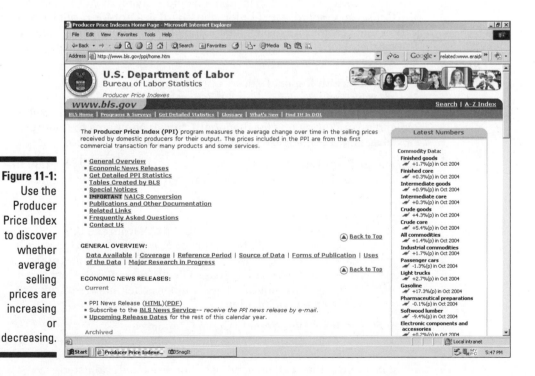

Figure 11-1:
Use the Producer Price Index to discover whether average selling prices are increasing or decreasing.

✔ **U.S. Census Bureau, Current Construction Reports** (`www.census.gov/prod/www/abs/c20.html`) contain monthly statistics for the United States and regions, such as the Puerto Rico Commonwealth, on new privately-owned housing units started, housing units that are issued building permits and that are in the process of being built, and housing units that are authorized but not started. Reports offer both monthly and seasonally adjusted estimates. Comparative data for earlier years is also provided. You can download the report in PDF format.

✔ **GSA Government Information Locator Service** (`www.gsa.gov`) includes many U.S. government agency reports in either full-text or abstract forms. (Government agencies are now required to provide and maintain a database of the information they provide to the public. Most agencies are using the Internet to meet this requirement.) Most information resources are catalogued and searchable. Searches can include more than one agency.

Consumer economic indicators

✔ **Consumer Confidence Index** (`www.conference-board.org/economics/consumerconfidence.cfm`) is an online monthly index published by the Conference Board. The Conference Board is a not-for-profit organization that creates and disseminates knowledge about management and the marketplace to help businesses strengthen their performance and better serve society.

✔ **Consumer Credit Report** (`www.federalreserve.gov/releases/g19`) is a monthly report released by the Federal Reserve Board on the fifth business day of each month. You discover whether consumer credit is expanding or contracting for the month, how it compares to the previous year, and the annualized percentage of change.

✔ **Consumer Price Indexes** (`www.bls.gov/cpi`) is a monthly program that indicates the change in prices paid by urban consumers for a representative basket of goods and services.

✔ **Employment Cost Index** (`stat.bls.gov/news.release/eci.toc.htm`), from the U.S. Department of Labor, is available in text or PDF formats. Information is released quarterly. Among other things, you find out whether total compensation for civilian workers increased or decreased in the last three months and the last six months. This number is helpful when trying to understand the effects of inflation.

✔ **Unemployed Insurance Weekly Claims Report** (`ows.doleta.gov/unemploy/claims_arch.asp`) is a weekly publication of the Department of Labor that indicates an increase or decrease in claims for unemployment insurance. Data can be unadjusted or seasonally adjusted.

Financial market data

✔ **Bureau of Economic Analysis** (`www.bea.doc.gov/bea/dn/home/ gdp.htm`), shown in Figure 11-2, is your source for gross domestic product data. You can download news releases, current period estimates, time series estimates, and supplementary estimates.

✔ **Economic-Indicators.com** (`www.economic-indicators.com`) is a free database with links to financial and economic data and reports. This Web site is valuable for one-stop financial data researching.

✔ **Leading Economic Indicators** (`www.conference-board.org/ economics/indicators.cfm`) are often considered the barometer of economic activity over the next several months. Monthly data are released around the 21st of each month at 10:00 a.m. EST.

✔ **The Beige Book, Current Economic Conditions** (`www.federalreserve. gov/fomc/beigebook/2004`) is published eight times per year. Each Federal Reserve Bank gathers anecdotal information on current economic conditions in its district, which The Beige Book then summarizes by district and sector.

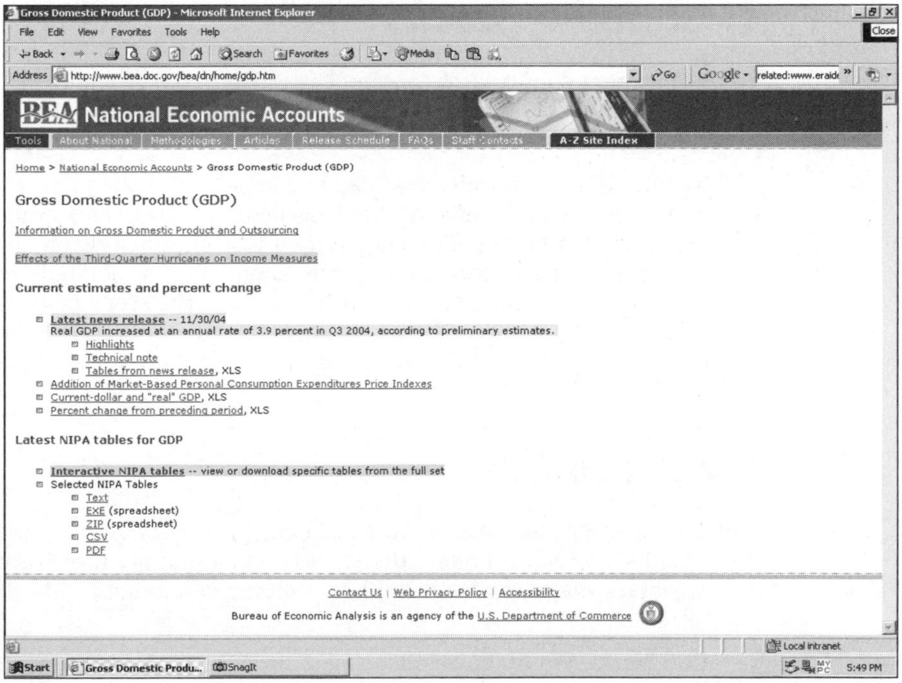

Figure 11-2:
Now you can go online to uncover U.S. gross domestic product data.

✔ **The Economic Statistics Briefing Room** (`www.whitehouse.gov/fsbr/esbr.html`) provides links to federal agencies that maintain up-to-date information on federal economic indicators such as employment, income, international, money, output, prices, production, and transportation. The estimates for economic indicators presented in the Briefing Room are based on the most currently available values.

Collecting Market Information

The valuation process is based on fundamental analysis, which includes looking at the long-term trends and the stock market. Understanding the current market environment can help you select a stock that can provide you your required return and eliminate a potential loser from your portfolio. Overall, collecting market information can give you a better understanding of what drives the company's stock price.

The following sections list some online sources for market information.

Most active stocks

✔ **Bloomberg.com** (`www.bloomberg.com/markets/stocks/movers_index_ibov.html`) offers a listing of current movers on the U.S. markets, historical charts, and a short description of each company.

✔ **NASDAQ-100 Dynamic Heatmap** (`screening.nasdaq.com/heatmaps/heatmap_100.asp`) is a free view of the company prices in the NASDAQ 100 index at a glance. The map of the NASDAQ 100 Index includes the prices of each company in a square. Each colored rectangle represents an individual company. Green or blue means the stock price is up; red means the stock price is down. The deeper the color, the bigger the move. Hold your mouse over the square to see an intraday pop-up chart.

Market indices

✔ **Bloomberg National and World Indices** (`www.bloomberg.com/markets/stocks/wei.html`) offers the World Index (among other features) that measures the performance of U.S. regional economies and other specialized markets.

✔ **CBS MarketWatch.com** (`cbs.marketwatch.com`), with your free registration, provides research about global and regional indices. Index information is updated regularly. After you sign in, at the home page, click Investor Tools and then look for Market Overview. For indices click Market Summary.

Finding Industry and Statistical Information

Annual reports often provide good insights into the forces that drive certain industries. However, this information may not be enough to answer your questions.

Independent research about how a company is doing in its industry is often available from trade associations and periodicals. Market research sites are helpful for determining how the company of your choice stacks up. Here are some online sources for industry and statistical information:

✔ **Bitpipe** (www.bitpipe.com) offers information technology white papers, product literature, Webcasts, and case studies. Additionally, Bitpipe indexes and syndicates information from over 90 top technology analyst firms, including Gartner, IDC, and Forrester, and offers current analyses via its Analyst Direct service and Analyst Views Web site. With your free registration, you can create your personalized Bitpipe service, get free product alerts, and more.

✔ **STAT-USA** (www.stat-usa.gov), shown in Figure 11-3, is sponsored by the U.S. Department of Commerce. This site provides financial information about economic indicators, statistics, and news. The site also includes data about state and local government bond rates, foreign exchange rates, and daily economic news about trade and business issues. Statistics include interest rates, employment, income, price, productivity, new construction, and home sales. Quarterly subscriptions are $75 and annual subscriptions are $175.00.

✔ **DataMonitor** (www.datamonitor.com) is a business information center that provides original industry and company reports based on published research and primary and secondary data sources. This collection includes 2,000 market reports, 10,000 company reports, 500 company SWOT (strategy, weakness, opportunity, and threat) analyses, 50 country profiles, news, and commentary. You can search the database by keyword for full-text reports in PDF format. Company and industry reports are for the most recent 12 months. News and commentary is archived for two years. With your free registration, you can create your own home page, develop a watchlist to track industries or companies, and sign up for free newsletters. You have to contact the company at +44 (0) 20 7675 7000 for the pricing of reports (Note: This company is based in London, United Kingdom).

TIP

✔ **CBS MarketWatch Industry Alerts** (www.marketwatch.com) "don't cost a thing" with your free registration. Get e-mailed news alerts for more than 20 industries. You can even decide when the alert should be sent. At the Home Page, click Free Membership.

✔ **Fuld & Company** (www.fuld.com/i3/index.html) provides a free listing of industry-specific Internet resources. The firm divides industries into 27 categories.

✔ **Harvard Business School, Baker Library, Industry Guides** (www.library.hbs.edu/industries/industry_guides) are generally broad in scope, presenting information and resources that cover the entire industry and its major segments. The guides aren't comprehensive, but the resources are hand-picked and considered the best and most useful for general research.

✔ **Yahoo! Industry News** (biz.yahoo.com/industry) categorizes the business world into ten major industries, each of which has subcategories. Click the appropriate subcategory for industry press releases and current news.

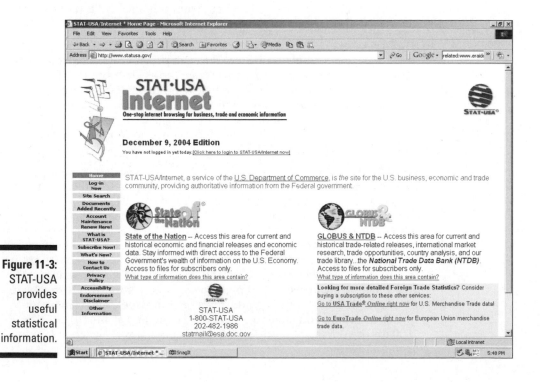

Figure 11-3:
STAT-USA
provides
useful
statistical
information.

Checking out analyst evaluations

Often, stock prices move because analysts recommend or criticize a company. Although these opinions are "informed," they're still opinions and shouldn't overshadow your own good judgment. For example, assume that an analyst suggests buying a stock and forecasts the price to increase to a record high. Over the year, the stock reaches the mark, and then the analyst places a hold on the stock. (A *hold* is a suggestion to investors that they neither sell nor buy the stock.) This hold may look like an unfavorable mark against the stock, but the stock performed just as expected and is currently a good investment.

The Internet now has many analyst reports by individual Wall Street analysts and groups of Wall Street analysts who study a particular stock. However, many of these firms participate in the financing of the companies they analyze. Consequently, you rarely see a "sell" recommendation. Additionally, you may see that analysts' opinions vary. Feel free to disagree with their conclusions, but know what the professionals are saying about a company that interests you.

Here are several examples of sites where you can check out analysts' evaluations:

- **Datamonitor's CommentWire** (www.commentwire.com) offers expert opinions and analysis service. Get intriguing insights about the key stories of the day, written by a global network of more than 200 business experts.

- **MSN Money** (moneycentral.msn.com/investor/home.asp) includes analyst ratings, strategy labs, articles, and more.

- **Standard & Poor's** (www2.standardandpoors.com) offers comprehensive ratings, lists of newly released ratings, ratings news, presale reports, ratings inquiries, and more. Standard & Poor's is one of the few SEC-recognized rating services and provides independent financial analyses on stocks, bonds, mutual funds, and other financial products.

- **BusinessWeek Personal Investing** (www.businessweek.com/investor/index.html) provides its subscribers with *Word on the Street* — coverage of analysts' recommendations for different stocks. Subscriptions are for 51 issues per year at $45.97 or 153 issues over three years at $99.97. *BusinessWeek* mails you your access number for full Web site access within 24 hours. Subscribe to *BusinessWeek* and get four free issues.

- **Zacks Investment Research** (my.zacks.com) provides estimated earnings reports based on analyst opinions. The site includes a listing of current earnings surprises, recommendations, and the company's annual balance sheet and income statement.

Following upgrades and downgrades

Earnings announcements and analysts' upgrades or downgrades are hot news for individual investors. Being the first to act on an upgrade or downgrade can give you the edge you're seeking. For example, many short-term traders see upgrades and downgrades as a way to make a quick profit by *selling short* if there is an unexpected downgrade. (Selling short is when an investor sells borrowed stock in anticipation of a price decline. The investor's expectation is that the stock will be repurchased, to replace the borrowed shares, at a lower price in the future.) Long-term investors couple downgrades and upgrades with historical stock prices to stay one step ahead of the market. These investors are on the lookout for stock splits, acquisitions, takeovers, mergers, and reorganizations. Many investors find it very profitable to get into the action before these activities are made known to the public. The following are two online sources for upgrades and downgrades:

- ✔ **Briefing.com** (www.briefing.com) has three levels of subscriptions. The Silver level of service is free of charge and provides upgrade and downgrade information that is updated three times per day. You can sort this data alphabetically or by broker. Other information includes Briefing.com's view of the overall market, analysis, e-mail services, after-hours updates, weekly wrap, economic calendar, splits calendar, IPO calendar, stock quotes, the ability to track up to 30 stocks, bond analysis, daily columns, and long-term views. For more content, sign up for the Gold subscription ($9.95 per month or $100 per year). For even more content than the Gold subscription, sign up for the Platinum subscription ($24.95 per month or $250 per year). You can receive a free trial for the subscription services.

- ✔ **MSN Money** (moneycentral.msn.com/investor/calendar/ratings/current.asp) provides free upgrade, downgrade, and initial recommendation information from Briefing.com. You can see upgrade and downgrade data from the previous day and back seven days.

Zeroing In on Earnings

Savvy investors often refer to the Investor Relations page of a company's Web site to determine when the company will have corporate events, such as earnings calls and industry presentations. Earnings conference calls or Webcasts have become prime communications events for corporations. These activities are actually telephone conversations between the chief executive officer (CEO), the chief financial officer (CFO), and the director of investor relations.

If your computer has a speaker, you can listen to live conference calls that companies stage for analysts and institutional investors. In the past, these calls were only for the privileged. Today, individual investors can listen to the calls over the Internet (or by telephone) but can't participate. Frequently, RealPlayer (www.real.com) or Windows Media Player (www.microsoft.com/windows/windowsmedia/default.aspx) is used to access the Webcasts. Usually, you can download RealPlayer and Media Player programs at the site of the Webcast conference call for no charge.

Webcast conference calls are used to assist analysts in sorting out current earnings and can assist them in forecasting quarterly earnings. These Webcast conference calls can help individual investors make quicker and better investment decisions. The following are a few examples of where you can find online conference call sources:

✔ **BestCalls** (www.bestcalls.com) helps investors track event schedules for thousands of publicly traded companies and assists investor relations professionals with promoting and disclosing their investor events. BestCalls' CallTracker service allows investors to receive automated and personalized e-mail alerts of conference calls.

✔ **Earnings.com** (www.earnings.com) is designed for investors who are seeking financial information directly from publicly traded companies. With your free registration, you have unlimited access to multimedia research, analysts' recommendations, and earnings calls. Additionally, you can personalize your own earnings calendar to track earnings dates, conference calls, upgrades or downgrades, stock splits, and economic indicators. The free service includes wireless alerts and PDA (personal digital assistant) synchronization so that you can stay connected even if you're away from your computer.

✔ **Yahoo! Finance** (biz.yahoo.com/cc) offers a conference call calendar. Additionally, this free service provides live or archived conferences that Yahoo! hosts.

Tracking down earnings estimates

The price you pay for a stock is based on its future income stream. If earnings estimates indicate that the earnings per share ratio is dropping, the stock price you pay today may be too high for the true value of the stock.

Following are some Internet sources for earnings estimates:

- ✔ **CBS MarketWatch: Analyst Rating Revisions** (`cbs.marketwatch.com/tools/stockresearch/updown/default.asp`) is updated throughout the trading day. The revised analyst reports show the name of the company, the broker, the new and old ratings, and comments. Access requires your free registration.

- ✔ **SmartMoney.com** (`www.smartmoney.com`) offers an Earnings Center that includes the latest results, consensus earnings, and growth estimates of the S & P 500, as well as an earnings archive. At the home page, click on Stocks and then Earnings Center.

- ✔ **The Wall Street Journal Online** (`interactive.wsj.com/public/resources/documents/digest_earnings.htm`) offers a digest of earnings that includes reports prepared over the last five business days. Updates are made continuously throughout the day. For stock quotes, click a company's name. For a Full Report, click an icon.

- ✔ **Yahoo! Finance** (`biz.yahoo.com/research/earncal/today.html`) provides earnings announcements, earnings estimates, and scheduled announcement dates.

Forecasting earnings and the stock market level

An investor who could accurately forecast a company's earnings, general market conditions, national economic activity, or interest rates would make extraordinary returns. Over the years, intrepid investors have studied these factors and determined that the most important factors in separating the winners from the losers are profitability and the general stock market level. However, academics who have studied past earnings have discovered that historical earning trends aren't predictors of future earnings. This information only confirms what investors already know: Past performance doesn't guarantee future returns.

You can forecast the general stock market level with several methods, but not one of them is consistently reliable. For example, the short-term interest ratio theory (the short interest rate for the month divided by the mean daily volume for the same period) theorizes that a very high short-term interest ratio of 2.00 indicates a bull market (up), and a short-term interest ratio of .80 indicates a mildly bearish market (down). When first introduced, this approach was a good way to predict the direction of the market. But over time, this theory hasn't worked well for investors.

Researching the Background of Corporate Officers

Because of the Sarbanes-Oxley Act, corporations are taking more responsibility for the actions of their corporate officers. Consequently, when companies hire individuals for top management positions, they frequently *vet* their candidates in an effort to avoid the potential of fraud and scandal. Vetting in this situation usually means going beyond checking a candidate's educational credentials, work history, and criminal record. A thorough investigation can include

- ✔ Checking the candidate's credit history, history of driving violations, and other violations that indicate a lack of responsibility.

- ✔ Conducting face-to-face interviews with former colleagues, business partners, and spouses.

- ✔ Determining whether a disparity exists between the executive's salary and his or her lifestyle.

Corporate officers should not be unindicted coconspirators of fraud cases, have personal bankruptcies, or show evidence of gambling or drinking problems. If you're suspicious of corporate officers or are a cautious investor, you might want to check out a few things before you invest. The Internet offers many online sources that can assist you in your investigations:

- ✔ **Board Analyst** (www.boardanalyst.com) has free registration. You can search Board Analyst's company and CEO database by using a variety of keywords. You can sort the results by company name, ticker symbol, CEO name, or market capitalization. Free searches are limited to S & P companies only. Higher-level content requires your subscription or is available on a pay-per-view basis.

- ✔ **BoardSeat** (www.boardseat.com/articles.asp) requires your free registration. At this site, you can discover the minimum qualifications for board members, see what the responsibilities of board members are, and find out how an advisory board can assist a company.

- ✔ **Corporate Governance** (www.corpgov.net) aims to enhance the return on capital through increased accountability. Discover research reports on corporate governance. If you're looking for links to corporate governance or related Web sites, this site is the place. Corporate Governance includes an extensive subject-based directory.

- ✔ **Executive PayWatch** (www.paywatch.org), shown in Figure 11-4, is sponsored by the AFL-CIO and geared to assist you in comparing your retirement plan with the average CEO's. Additionally, you can see how CEO pay has been growing while corporate profits and stocks decline. Overall, if you want to investigate corporate excess, this Web site is a good starting place.

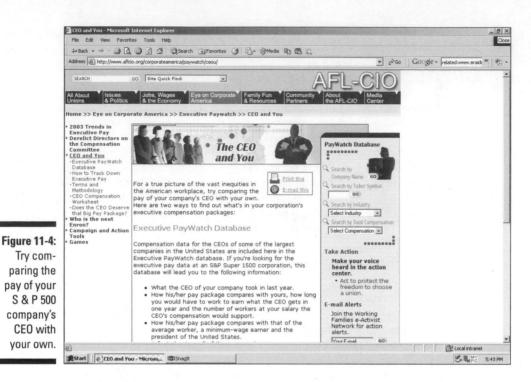

Figure 11-4:
Try comparing the pay of your S & P 500 company's CEO with your own.

Understanding Stock Prices

Determining the correct time to purchase a security can be difficult. Knowing the past sales price of an investment can help you judge today's price. In other words, seeing where a company has been is always important in order to get a feeling about where it's going. Here are a few Internet sources for historical prices:

- ✔ **BigCharts** (`bigcharts.marketwatch.com/historical/`) provides graphs of historical stock prices. The BigCharts tool enables you to look up a security's exact closing price. Type in the ticker symbol and a historical date. The closing price is listed, and a minigraph charts the closing price and the daily closing prices for one full month before and after the date you're researching.

- ✔ **DownloadQuotes** (`www.downloadquotes.com/en/main.phtml`) allows you, with your free registration, to personalize 50,000 quotes to meet your individual needs. Get historical stock quotes for more than 30 stock markets and more than 50,000 stocks worldwide. You can download many of the files to Quicken or Excel for additional analysis.

- ✔ **Historical Stock Data** (`biz.swcp.com/stocks`) offers a year of historical data on the S & P 500 stocks. This Web site can assist you in obtaining a true comparison of the S & P 500 and the stock that you're researching.

Tools of the trade

If you're an active investor and plan to use Level II NASDAQ quotes as part of your trading strategy, you need to take an inventory of your computer hardware and software and possibly make a few upgrades. For example, you need a good quality monitor, Windows 2000 or XP, and Microsoft Internet Explorer Version 6 or higher. Your PC should have a 1 GHz (or higher) Pentium processor with 1024MB (or higher) of RAM, a 100GB hard drive, network card, modem, and video card. Dial-up connections are too slow for active traders, so you need a cable modem or DSL (Direct Service Line) phone line connection for all your trades.

SLS Reference Service assists local libraries in gathering information and educating staff. The organization supports three key functions: reference, consultation, and continuing education. With these goals in mind, SLS provides a great online article titled "Stock Answers: Finding Historical Stock Prices" at www.sls.lib.il.us/reference/por/features/99/stock.html.

Understanding Level 1 stock quotes

Deciding on the proper time to purchase a security is often difficult. Some experts believe that for the first 30 minutes of trading, many investors are buying and selling securities based on yesterday's news. Consequently, it takes nearly an hour of trading before the market starts moving up or down based on today's trading. If the price drops immediately after you purchase, then you may feel that you missed a better buying opportunity. If the price spikes just before you purchase, you may feel that you paid too much for your investment. The bottom line for investors is to purchase a security that is priced below its intrinsic value (see Chapter 8 for details).

The media attention on frequent investors and active traders has created some confusion about what types of stock quotes investors have access to and what type of quotes are needed for successful trading. Most newspapers and many Internet sites, such as The Wall Street Journal Interactive Edition (public.wsj.com/home.html) and Barron's (www.barrons.com), have Level I listings of the day's stock activities. Table 11-1 shows the information in a typical listing from The Wall Street Journal Interactive Edition. (The values in the table are hypothetical.) The stock detailed is for a fictional company called Zoogle (ZGL). Zoogle designs, develops, manufactures, and markets a wide range of computing products, including desktop and portable computers. (Notice that the quote uses decimals and not fractions.)

Table 11-1	Reading the Stock Pages at the Wall Street Journal Interactive Edition
Entry	*Value*
Date	02/08/02
Time	4:01 p.m. EST
Exchange	NYSE
Last	11.59
Change	-0.07
% Change	0.060%
Day Open	11.90
Day High	11.90
Day Low	11.15
Bid	N/A
Ask	N/A
Prior Day's Close	11.66
Volume	14,122,200
Avg. Vol. 10 Day	13,522,000
Avg. Monthly Vol.*	385,024,000
Prior Day's Volume	7,007,800
52-Week High	24.54 (02/15/01)
52-Week Low	7.26 (09/21/01)

* Using the amount of shares traded monthly over the most recent three-month period.

Here's how to interpret all this information about Zoogle's stock:

- ✔ **Date: 02/28/05** — The date of the stock quote.

- ✔ **Time: 4:01 p.m. EST** — The time of the price quote. Some Internet quote services provide real-time quotes; others may be delayed as much as 20 minutes.

- ✔ **Exchange: NYSE** — The exchange that the stock is traded on. Zoogle is traded on the New York Stock Exchange (NYSE).

- ✔ **Last: 11.59** — The dollar amount of the last price for the Zoogle stock. (All stock prices are shown in decimals instead of fractions.)

✔ **Change: –0.07** — The change in the current price to the day's last price. This change compares the current price to the previous day's closing price. It's the monetary amount of today's gain or loss.

✔ **% Change: 0.060%** — The percentage of change in the current price to the day's last price. This percentage of change compares the current price to the previous day's closing price. It's the percentage amount of today's gain or loss.

✔ **Day Open: 11.90** — The price of the stock at the beginning of the day.

✔ **Day High: 11.90** — The highest stock price of the day.

✔ **Day Low: 11.15** — The lowest stock price of the day.

✔ **Bid: N/A —:** Bid is defined as the price a prospective buyer is prepared to pay at a particular time for trading a unit of a given security. It's important to note that the American Stock Exchange (AMEX) and the New York Stock Exchange (NYSE) don't provide Bid information on a delayed basis.

✔ **Ask: N/A** — Ask is defined as the price at which someone who owns a security offers to sell it. It's also sometimes called the "asked price." It's important to notes that the American Stock Exchange (AMEX) and the New York Stock Exchange (NYSE) don't provide Ask information on a delayed basis.

✔ **Prior Day's Close: 11.66** — The previous day's closing price.

✔ **Volume: 14,122,220** — The volume or number of shares traded that day.

✔ **Avg. Monthly Vol.: 385,024,000** — The average number of shares traded monthly over the most recent three-month period.

✔ **Prior Day's Volume: 7,007,800** — The number of shares traded as of this time on the previous day.

✔ **52-Week High: 24.54** — The highest stock price in the last year.

✔ **52-Week Low: 7.26** — The lowest stock price in the last year.

The Wall Street Journal Interactive Edition is continually updated with delayed quotes. For more about how this financial newspaper is structured, see online.wsj.com/public/us.

Discovering Level II stock quotes

Level II NASDAQ stock quotes provide investors with more information than Level I quotes by revealing the best bid and offer prices of every publicly posted market participant for a particular stock. This level is a more complicated way of looking at the market. Mainstream buy-and-hold investors don't need Level II quotes. Active investors may require this data to make informed decisions. Day traders must have Level II NASDAQ quotes to shave a few points and make their profits.

In addition to showing all the Level I data, Level II quotes show the market participants. Level II NASDAQ quotes rank their bids from best to worst, highest to lowest, and number of shares to be traded. Offers are also listed from best to worst and from lowest to highest.

The Level II quotes indicate market makers by using four-letter identification codes. Key market makers are companies like Goldman Sachs (GSCO), Morgan Stanley (MSCO), and Herzog (HRZG), but these are only three of the more than 500 market maker firms. To discover specific market makers, see www.nasdaqtrader.com/trader/symboldirectory/symbol.stm. Click Transaction Services⇨NASDAQ Broker/Dealers. Write down the name of the NASDAQ broker/dealer you're researching.

Return to the Symbol Directory page (at the previously-listed URL), enter the name of the broker/dealer you're researching, search by clicking on name, "starts with" and "market participants". Next click the Execute Search button. You're given the name, symbol, and contact information for the market maker. You have the option of printing or saving this information to a file.

The different types of market participants are color coded, as are the background colors for data. In other words, color changes indicate the best bid and ask quotes. For example, yellow signifies the highest bid or lowest ask quote (Inside Market), green indicates the next best quote (1st Outer), dark blue signifies the second best quote (2nd Outer), and so on.

Finding ticker symbols and stock prices online

A *ticker symbol* is the letter code representing the company's name in the listing for a publicly traded security. For example, if you want to find the current price for a share of Cisco's stock, look for the company's ticker symbol — CSCO. Ticker symbols for companies traded on the NYSE have one to three letters; stocks traded on NASDAQ have four or five letters.

In the past, the average investor had to wait for newspapers to discover stock prices. Today, delayed, real-time, and streaming quotes are available on the Internet. In fact, during the last few years, the number of Web sites offering wireless quotes has proliferated. Here are a few examples of online quote servers:

Free delayed stock quotes

Free delayed stock quotes are often best for buy-and-hold investors. The foremost advantage is that they're free and easy to use. The second advantage is that delayed stock quotes are often the best way to carefully track your investment strategy and to plan your next move.

- ✔ **MSN Money** (`moneycentral.msn.com`) provides free access to 15-minute delayed quotes. MSN Money also provides other investor information so that you can make the most of your Web site visit.

- ✔ **Yahoo!** (`finance.yahoo.com`) offers free delayed quotes, as well as company news and reports. Among other things, you can download company data to an Excel spreadsheet and set up alerts.

- ✔ **CBS MarketWatch** (`cbs.marketwatch.com`) provides free delayed quotes and aftermarket quotes with your free registration. You also receive free alerts, interactive charting, and portfolio tracking.

Free real-time stock quotes

Active traders often use free real-time stock quotes. For these active traders, using old stock quotes that are based on stale prices can be hazardous. The following are a few examples of online sources of free real-time stock quotes:

- ✔ **3DStockCharts** (`www.3Dstockcharts.com`) lets you, with your free registration, view all the bids, asks, and trades on any stock from all the major ECNs (electronic communication networks). These bids and asks are the unexecuted orders, or the "book," for that stock. 3DStockCharts gives you the same information used by the professionals (and at the same time).

- ✔ **FreeRealTime.com** (`quotes.freerealtime.com/dl/frt/S?&`) requires registration for your free access to real-time stock quotes, financial news, and corporate profiles, but doesn't limit the number of quotes you can get per day. You can find Watchlist tracking features, StockTalk message boards, and investment analysis.

Free wireless stock quotes

With wireless Internet connections, you can have stock quotes delivered to wireless devices such as alphanumeric pagers, digital telephones, and PDAs (personal digital assistants). Here are two free services that support wireless connections:

- ✔ **MSN Mobile** (`mobile.msn.com`) has a free service that provides alerts on stock quotes based on dozens of preset options from MSN Money Central.

- ✔ **Yahoo! Mobile** (`mobile.yahoo.com`) provides stock alerts via your mobile device. The service is free for registered Yahoo! members.

Fee-based stock quotes

If you're a frequent or active investor, you probably want to track the stocks you're trading in real time. In the past, individual investors didn't have access to this type of information at any cost. Today, you can access real-time quotes from your wireless hand-held device or at your home or office computer. Here are a few examples of what's available on the Internet:

✔ **DTN Interquote** (www.interquote.com) offers real-time equity, options, and futures quotes; unlimited watchlists; 1,300 symbols; intraday and historical charts; alerts; tickers; and scrolling news for $89 per month (plus exchange fees). The annual fee is $534 (if you buy six months you get six months for free), which includes NASDAQ Level II equity options or free MarketGuide. Expect to pay applicable exchange fees. It has a one-time $95 setup fee and a free seven-day trial.

✔ **eSignal** (www.esignal.com) shown in Figure 11-5, offers continuous, fully streaming, real-time quotes with direct exchange connections for stocks, futures, options data, and Level II NASDAQ market maker information via your Web browser. eSignal offers three levels of service, ranging from the $185 per month Standard Signal level of service to the $395 Platinum level of service that includes lots of bells and whistles. For specifics, go to www.esignal.com/esignal/pricing/default.asp.

Figure 11-5: eSignal offers continuous real-time quotes, Level II NASDAQ quotes, and other financial data.

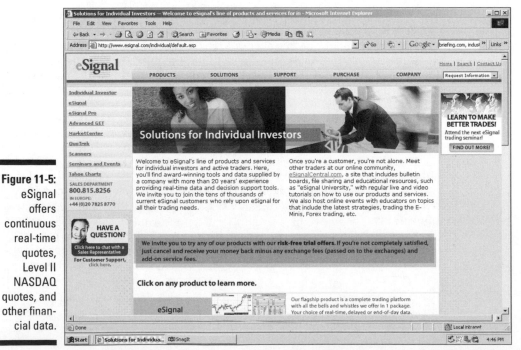

Chapter 12

Going with Fixed-Income Securities: Which Type of Bond Is for You?

In This Chapter

▶ Understanding the basics of bonds

▶ Choosing a money market deposit account

▶ Finding online information about the four general types of bonds

*B*onds are similar to stocks because you make money in two ways. The first way is *capital appreciation;* the bond increases in value if interest rates decline, which means that you can sell the bond at a *premium.* That is, you can sell the bond for more money than you paid for it. (The profit you make is called *capital gains.*) The second way to make money is the periodic interest payment that you receive during the bond term.

Bonds are often called *fixed-income investments*. They represent debts or IOUs from the issuer. The amount of the loan is the *principal;* the compensation given to the investor is called *interest payments*. In this chapter, I show you how the Internet provides information about Treasury, federal agency, municipal, and corporate bond auctions and offerings; historical and current yield rates; education; and tax information.

Bonds can be virtually risk-free and guaranteed by the U.S. government, or they can be speculative high-flyers that can crash and go into default. You may decide that these investments aren't for you, but if you own a mutual fund, you might already be invested in the bond market.

Generic Features of Bonds

Bonds are simply defined as long-term promissory notes from an issuer. Issuers tend to be large organizations, like the federal government and its agencies, and state and local governments. Bonds are contracts that state the interest payment (coupon rate) to be paid to the investor, the *par value* (principal or face value of the bond), and when the par value will be repaid to the investor. Overall, bonds provide the investor with security and a fixed income under a legal contract.

Bondholders want to minimize the business, market, and political risks of investing. From the date of issue, the bond's rate of interest payments (the coupon rate) and maturity date don't change. The price of the bond (the par or face value of the bond when it's issued) can vary during the bond term, depending on changes in interest rates. Generally, if interest rates increase, the bond's value falls. On the other hand, if interest rates decline, the value of the bond increases.

A different type of bond contract is a *variable-rate note* or *floating-rate note*. A few corporate bonds have floating rates. The coupon rate is fixed for a short period of time and then varies with a specific short-term rate (such as a Treasury bill). With floating-rate notes, the investor's interest payments, rather than the price of the bond, go up and down.

Corporate and municipal bonds are usually purchased through a broker. Treasury securities (bills, notes, and bonds) can be purchased directly from the government, without a broker.

The most popular bonds are often long-term debt that matures in ten or more years. A bond is a commitment by a public or private entity to pay the bondholder certain interest payments at specific times and the *principal* (the original investment) at the end of a specified time period.

Bonds have clearly stated terms and maturity dates. These terms can be as short as 13 weeks or as long as 30 years. Sometimes you can't recover your investment until the bond matures. If you have to sell the bond before it matures, you might have a difficult time finding a buyer. The broker's commission takes some of your return, and you lose the sizable return you were going to receive on your original investment.

Bonds have their own terminology that you need to understand:

✔ **Par value:** Refers to the face value of the bond and the amount returned to the bondholder at maturity. Most corporate bonds have a par value of $1,000; many federal, state, and local bonds have par values of $5,000 or $10,000.

✔ **Coupon interest rate:** Indicates what percentage of the par value of the bond is paid out annually in the form of interest.

✔ **Maturity:** Indicates the length of time until the bond issuer returns the face value to the bondholder and terminates the bond.

✔ **Current yield:** Refers to the ratio of the annual interest payment to the bond's current selling price. For example, assume that the bond has an 11 percent coupon rate, a par value of $1,000, and a market value of $700. It has a current yield of 15.71 percent ([0.11 × $1,000] ÷ $700).

✔ **Yield to maturity:** Indicates how much you would pay today for the future benefits of the bond. Yield to maturity is the investor's required rate of return used as the discount rate to arrive at the current value of a bond. (The current value of a bond is determined by the present value of future interest payments and the repayment of the principal at maturity.)

Special benefits and exposures

As evidence that there are no guarantees with bonds, the 1994 bond market experienced worldwide losses of around $1.5 trillion. (Among other things, this loss was attributed to the Peso Crisis in Mexico.) Since that time, the market has radically changed. It's no longer the sleepy market it was before derivatives and similar financial instruments were introduced. However, if you know what you're doing, bonds can provide a fixed cash flow over time. A fixed cash flow from bonds is important if you're planning a comfortable retirement.

The benefit of a fixed cash flow isn't cost-free. Bond returns are usually lower than other investments because of the risk and return trade-off. (High risk brings high returns, and low risk brings low returns.) Bonds are contracts for a certain amount of interest payments along with repayments of the principal at the end of a specified period. The investor can make financial plans based on these contracts. Stocks have no guarantees (or limits) on dividend payments and the sales price. A stock's dividends and value can skyrocket or plummet.

Table 12-1 shows the risk and return trade-offs of different types of bonds compared to different types of stocks over the last 50, 20, 10, and 5 years. For instance, a comparison of the annualized returns of stocks to corporate bonds for the last five years indicates that investing in stocks would have delivered more than twice the returns of bonds (a return of 24.1 percent versus a return of 8.7 percent), and stock investments provided three times the return of Treasury securities (a return of 24.1 percent versus a return of 6.2 percent).

Table 12-1   Historical Returns for Different Types of Investments

| | Annualized returns for periods ended 12/31/98 | | | |
	50 Years (%)	20 Years (%)	10 Years (%)	5 Years (%)
Small company stocks	14.8	16.0	13.2	13.2
Large company stocks	13.6	17.8	19.2	24.1
Corporate bonds	6.2	10.9	10.9	8.7
35-year Treasury bonds	6.2	9.9	8.7	6.2
30-day Treasury bills	5.1	7.2	5.3	5.0
U.S. inflation	3.9	4.5	3.1	2.4

Source: T. Rowe Price (www.troweprice.com/retirement/historical.html)

For more information about investing in bonds, see the following Internet sites:

- ✔ **BondKnowledge.com** (www.bondknowledge.com/introfaq1.html) provides a variety of useful bond investor information, including a valuable easy-to-understand tutorial about investing in bonds.

- ✔ **BondResources.com** (www.bondresources.com) includes news, analysis, charts, rates, and education for Treasuries, municipal, agency, and corporation bonds. At the home page, just click Corporate.

- ✔ **CNN/Money** (money.cnn.com/pf/101/lessons/7/index.html) provides details on how bonds work, has a yield converter, and shows how to evaluate the risk of bonds. Additionally, you discover exactly how and where to buy bonds.

- ✔ **FAQ Bond** (www.bondsonline.com/bpfaq.html) sponsored by BondsOnline, offers answers to all the frequent questions about corporate, municipal, Treasury, savings, and general fixed-income bonds. For additional information, see the Fixed Income Resource Center or post your question to the BondsOnline Discussion Forum.

- ✔ **Investing In Bonds.com** (www.investinginbonds.com), sponsored by the Bond Market Association, features online educational information on a wide range of bonds and other fixed-income securities. This Web site can help you educate yourself about investing in bonds and even has a yield calculator that you can use to compare your returns to other types of investments.

- ✔ **The Investment FAQ** (invest-faq.com/articles/bonds-a-basics.html) provides investors with a good idea of what bonds are all about. If you want to start your bond education with something that doesn't have lots of finance jargon, this site is a good place to begin.

Using the Internet to find new bond offerings

Because bond issuers are anxious to get new bonds sold, new bond issues generally provide a slightly better yield than comparable issues of existing bonds offered on the secondary market.

Here are several useful online sources for information about new bond offerings:

✓ **Smith Barney Municipal Bond Inventory** (www.smithbarney.com/ products_services/fixed_income/municipal_bonds/munical.html) shows the firm's searchable municipal bond inventory. You can discover a free listing of new municipal free issues and bond issues that Smith Barney is involved in or intends to bid on its own, or that are part of a syndicate. (A *syndicate* is a group of investment bankers that jointly share in the underwriting, distribution, selling, and management of a new issue.) The bonds listed at the Web site are updated weekly, but are subject to prior sale (and may not be available). Use of this service requires your free guest registration.

✓ **The Bond Buyer** (www.bondbuyer.com) covers the municipal bond market in minute detail. The online publication provides daily municipal bond news, analysis, and commentary. Five bureaus and 30 reporters cover the bond market geographically and topically. This online edition of *The Bond Buyer* covers new municipal bond offerings, city and state officials involved in issuing debt, underwriters and underwriting, brokerages, and bond lawyers. The online subscription-based service has a free two-week trial. The subscription rate is $1,997 per year. (A printed version of *The Bond Buyer* is also available.)

✓ **Bondpage.com** (www.bondpage.com) allows you to search for new bond issues by CUSIP number (see the following tip), yield, maturity, coupon, and price. Search thousands of new issues for corporate and municipal bonds and certificates of deposit (CDs). You can research current and historical market information, news, economic statistics, and interest rate quotes to make more well-informed decisions. Check out bond quotes and offerings for corporate, municipal, Treasury, agency, and zero-coupon bonds. The online content is free but requires your registration.

CUSIP numbers are unique nine-digit numbers assigned to each series of securities. The Committee on Uniform Security Identification Procedures (CUSIP), established under the auspices of the American Bankers Association, developed this uniform method of identifying securities.

Locating those elusive bond quotes

The primary market of a bond is the price an investor pays for a newly issued bond. Bonds are then traded on the secondary market at rates that are usually different from their initial prices. Bond prices and interest rates are inversely related. For example, if interest rates go down, the value of a bond with a high interest rate increases. If you want to purchase bonds, knowing the price you're paying is wise. The following are several bond-quote Web sites that you might find useful:

- **Bloomberg.com** (www.bloomberg.com/markets/rates/index.html) offers commentary on interest rates, economic news, and bond pricing data. If you want to know the latest rates, this is the place.

- **Briefing.com** (www.briefing.com) offers its Platinum subscribers ($24.95 per month) bond quotes, charts, and key bond market data on the hour. Subscribers receive ongoing analyses of events as they occur in the bond market, in-depth analysis of long-term interest rates and Federal Reserve Policies, and more.

- **Investing in Bonds.com** (www.investinginbonds.com) offers quotes for Treasury, corporate, and municipal bonds. You also find current yield curves and analyses of bond trends.

- **BondsOnline** (www.bondsonline.com) offers clear information about how to search for a bond. Use the bond search and quote center for Treasury, corporate, municipal, and zero bonds. You can also search for CDs. The center includes indexes, global securities, and historical prices.

Finding bond indexes and historical data online

Bond indexes are designed to represent either the average yield to maturity or the average price on a portfolio of bonds that have certain similar characteristics. Historical data can also provide bond performance insights. The Internet offers several sources for these averages and historical data, including these examples:

- **Chicago Board of Trade** (cbotdataexchange.if5.com/Markets.aspx) provides quotes and charts of a wide variety of Treasury, agency, and municipal bonds. Plus, you gain access to the Municipal Bond Index, market commentary, financial product news, and other information.

✔ **The Federal Reserve Board** (www.federalreserve.gov/releases), shown in Figure 12-1, provides statistics about releases of U.S. Treasury securities and historical data. If you have a Palm VII hand-held device, you can download the federalreserve.gov Palm VII Web-clipping application and then use Hotsync technology to transfer the application to your Palm VII hand-held. Download the PKWARE software (www.pkware.com) to get the federalreserve.gov Palm VII application.

✔ **Investor's Guide to Municipal Bonds** (www.investinginbonds.org/info/igmunis/safe.htm) is a 13-page brochure in PDF format that shows how the different classifications of the credit-rating companies compare, the types of yields you can expect from municipal bonds, and the safety of municipal bonds.

✔ **MSN Money** (moneycentral.msn.com/investor/market/leading.asp) provides 20-minute delayed quotes of the leading U.S. indexes, including the U.S. Treasury Indexes. (Standard & Poor's ComStock, Inc. supplies all quotes.)

✔ **Moody's Investors Service** (www.moodys.com) provides long-term corporate bond yield averages based on bonds with maturities of 20 years and more. Corporate bond averages are sorted into average corporate, average industrial, and average public utility groups, and by bond ratings. The content is free but requires your registration.

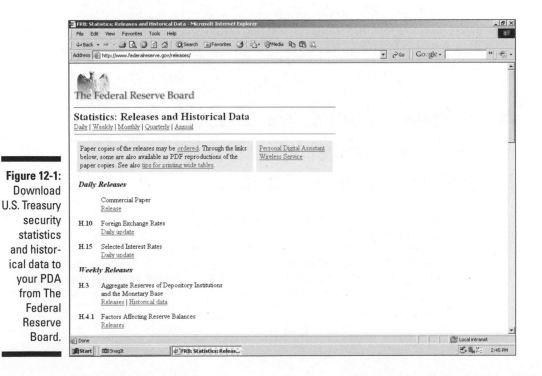

Figure 12-1:
Download U.S. Treasury security statistics and historical data to your PDA from The Federal Reserve Board.

Risks and stability

Moody's Investors Service (www.moodys.com), Standard & Poor's Corporation (www.standardandpoors.com), and Fitch Investor Services, L.P. (www.fitch ibca.com) are generally believed to be the best-known and most prominent credit-rating agencies. These companies assess the risk of bonds by studying all the bond's information and then assigning the bond a rank that reflects the issuer's ability to meet the promised principal and interest payments. This rating might change during the life of the bond, and a change in the rating can dramatically change the value of the bond.

All the credit-rating companies rate bonds in descending alphabetical order from A to C, but each company uses a somewhat different letter scheme. For a comparison of the leading bond rating agencies' alphabetic grading systems, see Bond Markets at www.bondmarkets.com/publications/bondbasics.htm.

Ratings aren't absolute measures of quality. Each rating considers factors such as the issuer's past earnings record and future earnings expectations, the financial condition of the issuer, the nature of the issuer's business, the backing for a particular issue, and the rating agency's appraisals of the issuer's management.

The rating agencies warn investors that a bond's rating isn't a "buy" recommendation. However, because of the risk-reward ratio, bonds with higher ratings offer lower yields, whereas bonds with lower ratings — which represent riskier investments — offer higher yields.

How Small Investors Can Make Money with Fixed-Income Investments and Bonds

In addition to bonds, banks and savings and loan associations have developed new ways of keeping customer assets in their financial institutions. They often offer a variety of investment plans that provide higher returns than traditional fixed-rate savings accounts. For example, many savings and loan associations allow their customers to invest in *commercial paper* (uninsured promissory notes to large business entities) instead of *certificates of deposit* (an insured type of time deposit).

Small investors seeking greater returns may want to consider the following types of fixed-income and bond investments:

- ✔ **Fixed-rate certificates:** In the past, federal regulations required a minimum deposit amount of $1,000 with maturities of at least four years for fixed-rate certificates of deposit (CDs). Financial institutions now set their own minimum amounts (which often range between $100 and $500) for time periods including three months, six months, one year, two years, and five years.

  Banks impose hefty penalties for early withdrawals. These fees can wipe out any gains you may have made.

- ✔ **Small-saver certificates:** Deposits don't require any minimum amount according to federal banking laws, but many banks have established a minimum requirement of deposits of $100 to $500. Maturities are generally 30 months, and the interest paid is slightly below the 30-month Treasury yield. Expect high penalties for early withdrawals.

- ✔ **Six-month money market certificates:** These certificates are for investors with more cash ($10,000 minimum) than time. Yields are higher than those for short-term money market certificates. The interest rate paid is generally slightly higher than the six-month Treasury bill rate. Like the saver certificate, the interest rate ceiling of a six-month money market certificate is a floating interest rate until you purchase the certificate. After you purchase the certificate, the rate is locked until the certificate matures. When the certificate matures, you're free to reinvest (rollover) your investment.

- ✔ **Short-term bond funds:** By purchasing short-term, no-load bond funds, investors can earn higher-than-passbook returns and still have lots of liquidity. Some bond funds even have limited check-writing privileges. (Writing a check is certainly more convenient and inexpensive than placing a sell order.)

  With short-term bond funds, small investors tend to pay more for bonds than professional bond fund managers (who keenly watch every movement of the bond market). Bond funds come in two flavors: tax-free and taxable. If you're in a high-income bracket, tax-free bonds might be to your advantage. However, all these benefits aren't cost-free. Investors will incur an annual fund management fee that averages 0.2 percent. (That is, $200 for every $100,000 invested in the fund.)

Checking out the best online banking deals on the Internet

My favorite place for locating banks that offer online banking is Bankrate.com (www.bank rate.com). At the home page, click Online Finance for information about special online offerings. Click Internet Banking Deals to find an extensive listing of institutions that offer special deals via the Internet. Some institutions even offer more than one deal. Find out whether the bank offers a free trial period for online banking services, the monthly online banking fee, and the availability of any free bill-paying sessions per month. This Web page also shows how you can access the bank via the Internet, an online service such as AOL, or a dial-up network with MS Money, Quicken, or another personal finance program.

You can also search for the best savings rates nationwide, search for the best local annual percentage rate, and check out Today's Averages.

Today's Averages shows the best rates for today, last week, and six months ago for money market accounts (MMAs). You can usually open an MMA account at a financial institution. MMAs usually pay higher returns than regular savings accounts. Your deposit is invested into safe, short-term debt instruments, such as

✔ *General-purpose funds* (certificates of deposit, Treasury securities, and short-term corporate IOUs)

✔ *Government funds* (U.S. Treasury securities)

✔ *Tax-exempt funds* (short-term municipal bonds, which are federally tax-exempt and sometimes state tax-exempt)

Note that MMAs aren't insured by the Federal Deposit Insurance Corporation (FDIC).

The Internet provides more information about fixed investments for small investors. You can discover online what the benchmark rates are and which financial institutions have the best deals. Here are a few examples:

✔ **Federally Insured Savings Network** (www.fisn.com) specializes in insured certificates of deposit (CDs). The firm researches across the nation for the safest and highest CD rates. Discover definitions of fixed-rate jumbo CDs, fixed-rate callable CDs, fixed-rate fixed-term CDs, and stock market CDs.

✔ **money-rates.com** (www.money-rates.com), shown in Figure 12-2, has market updates; information about the economy; consumer interest rates; and investment rates for money market funds, CDs, Treasury securities, and special bank offerings.

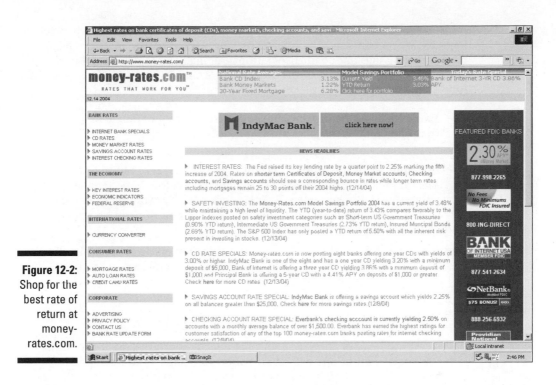

Figure 12-2:
Shop for the best rate of return at money-rates.com.

When to Choose a Money Market Deposit Account (MMDA)

MMAs are different from Money Market Deposit Accounts (MMDAs). Your online bank can provide you with information about a money market deposit account (MMDA) and the specific returns you can expect. An MMDA is a good place to keep your emergency fund and to park funds temporarily. (*Emergency funds,* as I explain in Chapter 3, are generally three to six months of take-home pay that you put in a savings account — or a near-cash account for emergencies. (If you don't have an emergency fund, you need to increase your savings.) An MMDA is a savings account with several unique features.

Your MMDA account is insured by the Federal Deposit Insurance Corporation (FDIC). The minimum balance to open an account might be high. However, as long as you maintain the minimum balance, you earn the money market rate of interest (currently, about 4.5 percent) If the balance falls below the required minimum balance, you earn the current negotiable order of withdrawal (NOW) account interest rate, and you might incur a service charge (usually about $5).

Note: NOW accounts are interest-earning accounts with check writing privileges. NOW accounts may be offered by commercial banks, mutual savings banks, and savings and loan associations. All in all, an MMDA is the perfect place for your emergency fund. For more information about MMDAs, see the following Web sites:

- **Bankrate** (www.bankrate.com) includes a listing of financial institutions that offer special deals on MMDAs. Some of the offers are available only to Internet shoppers, so read the fine print.

- **Instruments of the Money Market** (www.rich.frb.org/pubs/instruments) is the seventh edition of a book that is no longer in print. Due to the importance of this topic, the Federal Reserve Bank of Richmond provides the book online. Each chapter can be read independently.

- **Investopedia** (www.investopedia.com) offers several tutorials. Check out the Money Market Tutorial. After you've completed the tutorial, take the quiz to test your money market knowledge.

- **Money Fund Basics** (www.ibcdata.com/basic.htm) can assist you in discovering all the ins and outs of money market funds with its IBC Financial Data tutorial.

Some financial institutions will let you open your high-yielding deposit account online. Click the hyperlink to the application form and provide some personal information about yourself. The process is similar to opening a mutual fund account online (see Chapter 7 for details) and should take about 10 to 15 minutes.

The Four Basic Types of Bonds

Many organizations issue bonds, but the following types of organizations issue most bonds:

- The federal government (Treasury securities)
- Federal government agencies (agency bonds)
- State and local government agencies (municipal bonds)
- Corporations (corporate bonds)

Uncle Sam's bonds: Treasury securities

Treasury securities are U.S. government securities called Treasury bills, notes, and bonds. These securities are a major source of government funds and a key investment for many consumers. The U.S. government is highly unlikely to default on its Treasury securities, but if it does, your dollar is also probably worthless, so your investment is, essentially, risk-free.

The disadvantage of the risk-free rate of Treasury securities is that it's generally considered the bottom of the yield pile — the lowest yield you can get. As the level of risk gets greater, the reward also increases. You can expect a better yield (but more risk) from corporate bonds with similar maturities.

The Treasury Direct program (www.treasurydirect.com) program enables investors to participate in regularly scheduled auctions. (For details about opening an account, see Chapter 13.) You can search for new issues that meet your investment criteria and manage your Treasury and savings bonds in one account. The minimum investments are $10,000 for bills, $5,000 for notes maturing in less than five years, and $1,000 for securities that mature in five or more years.

Your interest payments are paid into your Treasury Direct account, as is a security's par value at maturity. Treasury bills are sold for less than face value. The discount represents the interest the investor earns. Interest income on Treasuries is usually exempt from state and local taxes, but is subject to federal taxes.

Internet information on Treasury securities

For more information on U.S. Treasury securities, see the following Web sites:

- ✔ **The Investment FAQ** (www.invest-faq.com/articles/bonds-treas. html) has a useful article about the differences among Treasury bills, notes, and bonds. The article also includes a discussion of zero-coupon bonds.

- ✔ **Treasury Direct** (www.treasurydirect.gov/indiv/research/ indepth/auctions/res_auctions_glance.htm) offers information about upcoming auctions, recent auctions of bills, notes, and bonds, and information about how you can receive e-mail reports.

- ✔ **Yahoo! Finance** (biz.yahoo.com/edu/bd/ir_bd2.ir.html) offers clear definitions about U.S. Treasury securities risks and the differences between various types of U.S. Treasury securities.

TIP

If you're uncertain about the fixed-income market and how much you should pay for a bond, the Financial Forecast Center (www.neatideas.com) can assist you. Forecasts are based on data from the last ten years and a forecasting methodology. You may find this information useful for spotting market trends.

Savings bonds: The easiest way to save

At some time in the near future, savings bonds will be available only in a paperless format at Treasury Direct (www.treasurydirect.gov). For many people, not having to deal with paper-based savings bonds will make their lives easier. Investors can purchase savings bonds by deducting funds from their checking accounts or by automatic payroll deduction via the Internet. Managing bonds via the Internet will be easier than it is now.

Income from U.S. savings bonds is exempt from state and local income tax. You can also defer paying federal income tax on the interest until you cash in the bond or until it stops earning interest in 30 years. If you use savings bonds to pay for education, they may provide you with additional tax savings.

Figure 12-3 shows the Web site for the Bureau of the Public Debt at www.publicdebt.treas.gov/sav/sav.htm. This site provides information about the different types of savings bonds that are available.

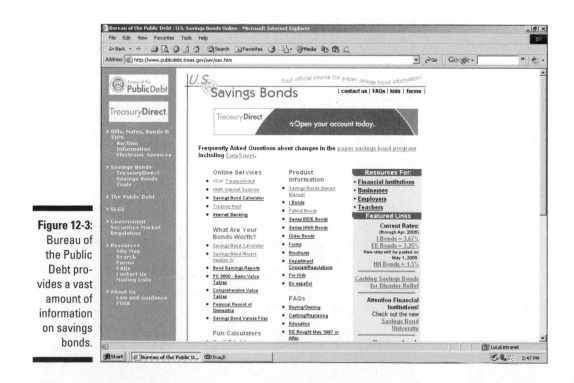

Figure 12-3: Bureau of the Public Debt provides a vast amount of information on savings bonds.

Federal government agency bonds

Agency bonds are similar to Treasury bonds but have marginally higher risk and higher returns. They can be sold for $1,000 to $25,000 and sometimes more. Federal agencies issue bonds to support housing (either with direct loans or the purchase of existing mortgages); export and import activities with loans, credit guarantees, and insurance; the postal service; and the activities of the Tennessee Valley Authority.

Not all government agency bonds are equal. The full faith and credit of the U.S. government guarantees many issues. Although government agency bonds aren't a direct obligation of the U.S. government, they offer little, if any, credit risk. However, some bonds (for example, those of the Tennessee Valley Authority) don't have this guarantee.

The Internet provides additional information on specific types of government agency bonds. The following are some examples:

- **Fannie Mae** (www.fanniemae.com) provides investors with background information about the bonds it issues. At the home page, click Debt Securities. A list of hyperlinked topics appears; check out those that interest you. You might want to start with "Understanding Fannie Mae Debt."

- **Ginnie Mae** (www.ginniemae.gov), shown in Figure 12-4, is a government agency that specializes in nonconforming home loans. Consequently, this agency is always issuing bonds to fund its activities. For investor information, click Guides.

- **Precision Information** (www.precision-info.com/tutorial.htm) provides information about the difference between agency bonds, the types of returns you can expect, and the risks. To get started, go to the Investor Education Center and click the Bond tab.

- **Yahoo! Finance** (bonds.yahoo.com/ir_bd4.html) provides clear definitions of agency bonds and lists the types of government agencies that offer bonds.

The beauty of tax-free municipal bonds

Towns, cities, and regional and local agencies issue municipal bonds. Municipal bonds usually have lower interest rates than comparably rated corporate bonds and Treasury securities. The minimum amount required for investment in municipal bonds is $5,000, and municipal bonds are sometimes issued at a discount. This discount compensates investors for the additional risk that these bonds may have due to the financial difficulties of some local governments.

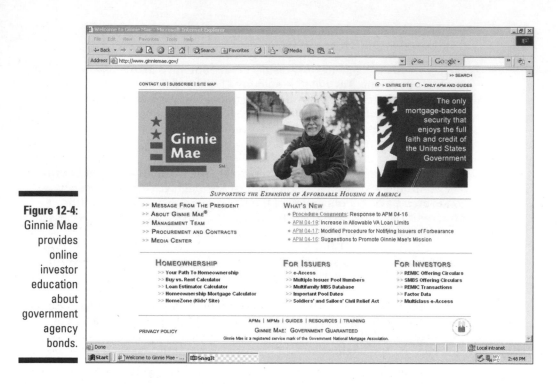

Figure 12-4:
Ginnie Mae
provides
online
investor
education
about
government
agency
bonds.

The most important feature of municipal bonds is their tax-exempt feature. In subsequent judgments based on the 1819 *McCullough v. Maryland* ruling, the federal, state, and local governments don't possess the power to tax each other. Consequently, municipal bonds can't be subject to federal tax. Additionally, income from state and local municipal bonds can't be taxed if purchased within the geographic area. For example, Virginia residents don't pay state taxes on Virginia bonds. However, residents of California are subject to state income taxes on their Virginia bonds. This tax-exempt feature makes municipal bonds very attractive to investors in high tax brackets. You treat capital gains on such bonds as normal income.

Three primary types of municipal bonds exist, each with its own special features:

- ✔ **General obligation bonds** are backed by the full faith and credit of the issuing agency. For municipal bonds, *full faith and credit* also means the taxing power of the issuing municipality.

- ✔ **Revenue bonds** are backed by the funds from a designated tax or the revenues from a specific project, authority, or agency. These bonds aren't backed by the full faith and credit (or the taxing power) of the issuing agency. In other words, revenue bonds are only as good (and as credit-worthy) as the ventures they support.

✔ **Industrial development bonds** (IDBs) are used to finance the purchase or construction of industrial facilities that are to be leased to businesses. Leasing fees of the facilities are used to meet construction expenses and the repayment requirements of the bonds. Often, these bonds provide inexpensive financing to firms choosing to locate in the geographical area of the issuer. Examples of IDBs are bonds for the construction of piers and wharves. Municipalities can also issue short-term securities called *tax-exempt commercial paper* and *variable-rate demand obligations*.

The following brokerages provide a variety of bond information, such as frequently updated offerings for individual investors, informative articles, and starter kits. The securities listed by these firms are subject to changes in price and availability.

✔ **BondsOnline FAQs** (www.bondsonline.com/asp/research/faqmuni.asp) provides answers to the most frequently asked questions about municipal bonds.

✔ **Stone & Youngberg** (www.buybonds.com), shown in Figure 12-5, offers weekly listings of mortgage-backed securities, corporate bonds, and municipal bonds. For the listing of the municipal bond type you're researching, click Research on the home page and then click the Weekly Municipal Market Reports link.

✔ **eMuni** (www.emuni.com) offers, with your free registration, documents, news, and financial information relating to the U.S. municipal bond market. In addition to viewing a calendar of official statements, you can search for municipal bonds by issuer name, state, date, principal amount, and so on.

✔ **First Miami Securities** (www.firstmiami.com/yields.html) is a financial institution that provides tables and charts of investment-grade municipal bond yields, among other things.

✔ **Lebenthal.com** (www.lebenthal.com) offers investor education and case studies of the risks of municipal bonds. Complete the Muni-Profiler survey to determine which types of municipal bonds are best for your investor needs.

✔ **Smith Barney Access** (www.salomonsmithbarney.com/prod_svc/bonds) offers an interactive learning center with your free registration. Guests can use the interactive calculators and other features to assist investors in learning the basics of investing in municipal bonds.

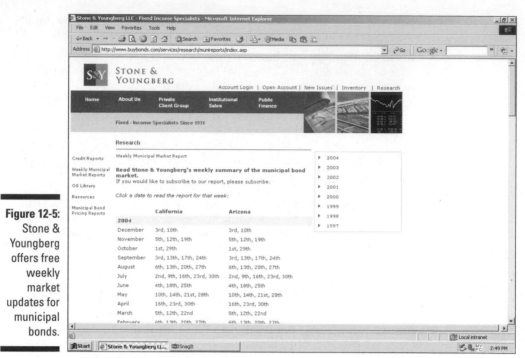

Figure 12-5:
Stone &
Youngberg
offers free
weekly
market
updates for
municipal
bonds.

Floating with corporate bonds

Corporate bonds are a major source of corporate borrowing. When corporations make corporate bonds, they "float a bond issue." Such bond issues take the form of either *debentures* (which are unsecured corporate bonds backed by the general credit of the corporation) or *asset-backed bonds* (which are backed by specific corporate assets like property or equipment). Income from these bonds is taxable. However, top-rated corporate bonds are often almost risk-free and have a higher return than Treasury securities. Corporate bonds are generally considered safer than stocks because

✔ **The bonds state exactly how much the corporation will pay the bond-holder.** Shareholders are entitled to cash dividends, but payment and the amount of the dividend is at the discretion of the corporation.

✔ **Bondholders are creditors.** Bondholders receive payment before the corporation can distribute any cash dividends to shareholders, which means that bondholders have greater protection in getting at least some return on their investment. (In bankruptcy, bondholders are paid from corporate assets before common stockholders.)

Some risk of default always exists. In the 1980s, many companies used junk bonds to finance highly leveraged takeovers of rival companies. Their bonds were rated non-investment grade and speculative by the bond-rating agencies. Because of the additional risk, these bonds paid above-average interest rates. For some bondholders, these bonds were a windfall. For bondholders who invested in the corporate bonds of companies that failed, their bonds went into default and became worthless junk.

Some professional money managers are required by law to purchase investment-grade securities so that they can't purchase junk bonds. These organizations generally limit their corporate bond purchases to issues rated B or higher by Moody's Investors.

Using the Internet to screen bonds

The Internet provides many online tools to help you make bond selections. Some Web sites include search engines that sort through thousands of bond offerings looking for bonds that meet your criteria. These services are free but are often accompanied by a sales pitch. The Internet provides many tools and resources for analyzing bonds.

- ✔ **BondVillage** (`www.bondvillage.com`) offers *bvPerspectives,* which shows a bird's-eye view of the bond market by providing a graphical overview of the retail bond market. The graphics and underlying tabulated data show how the yields of typical bonds vary with credit rating, issue maturity, and the investor's time frame. Bond Village also provides *bvBondSelector,* a proprietary bond analytical engine. This bond screener analyzes thousands of bond issues to identify the best bond investment ideas, as measured by superior prices and yields in comparison to typical bonds of the same maturity and with comparable or even lower credit ratings. Bond Village includes quotes and investor education. With your registration, you receive use of bvPerspectives and bvBondSelector at no charge. You have the choice of two levels of subscriptions. bvInvestor is $30 per month (or $330 per year) for the membership access and premium features. bvProfessional is $150 per month (or $1,650 per year) for full access and premium features. Each subscription level has a free two-week trial.

- ✔ **Yahoo! Finance** (`bonds.yahoo.com`) offers bond rates, historical yields, commentary, and market news. Investor tools include a bond calculator for computing a bond's price and yield. The bond screener allows you to search for corporate, municipal, Treasury, and zero bonds. (Bond screener data is provided by ValuBond.) The advantage of the Yahoo! bond screener is that you select the bond criteria that match your investment profile.

Two Alternate Types of Bonds

Two other types of bonds might be of interest to online investors: zero-coupon bonds and Eurobonds. I describe these alternative bond types in the following sections.

Zero-coupon bonds

Zero-coupon bonds offer no interest payments but are put on the market at prices substantially below their face values. The return to the investor is the difference between the investor's cost and the face value received at the end of the life of the bond.

If you don't rely on interest payment income, zero-coupon bonds may be the way to go for your nontaxable retirement plan (such as an individual retirement account, Keogh plan, or other nontaxable pension fund). The Internal Revenue Service taxes zero-coupon bonds as if investors received regular interest payments. This tax is based on amortizing the built-in gain over the life of the bond. In other words, for taxable accounts, investors have to pay taxes on income they haven't received, but for nontaxable accounts, they're a great investment choice.

Some brokerages offer *Treasury strips.* Large companies purchase 30-year Treasury securities and clip the interest-bearing coupons. The brokers then sell these Treasury coupons like zero-coupon bonds. You purchase the Treasury strip at a discount (say $4,300) and redeem the coupon at face value ($5,000). Treasury strips are like zero-coupon bonds because no interest is paid during the maturity term.

If you're looking for more information about zero-coupon bonds, the Internet provides many educational articles — for example:

- **The Federal Reserve Bank of New York** (www.newyorkfed.org/about thefed/fedpoint/fed42.html) has an overview of zero-coupon bonds and strips, as well as a short history of Treasury zero-coupon bonds.

- **The Bond Market Association** (www.investinginbonds.com/info/ zeroes.htm) provides useful examples of how zero-coupon bonds can increase returns and eliminate reinvestment risk.

- **Kiplinger.com** (www.kiplinger.com/basics/investing/bonds/ zeros.html) offers an overview of zero-coupon bonds. Kiplinger.com points out innovative ways to purchase zero-coupon bonds and shows how to lessen your tax burden when you cash out.

Eurobonds

Investments in foreign securities typically involve many government restrictions. *Eurobonds* are bonds offered outside the country of the borrower and usually outside the country in whose currency the securities are denominated. For example, a Eurobond may be issued by an American corporation, denominated in German deutsche marks, and sold in Japan and Switzerland.

For additional information about Eurobonds, try BradyNet Pro (`www.brady net.com`). BradyNet Pro offers "Live" Brady bond prices and spreads updated throughout the trading day. This feature assists you in "breaking the chains to the trading desk." You can leave the office while still being able to keep an eye on the market at home, in hotels, at airports, and so on. The BradyNet CyberExchange allows you to find the best prices and yields from many data contributors. The CyberExchange also includes descriptions, charts, data downloads, and links for a comprehensive number of Eurobonds, Brady bonds, and other emerging market's debt issues. You can communicate with fellow bondholders, issuers, and underwriters through asset-specific discussion forums.

BradyNet Pro subscriptions include the Toolbox (custom charting software to analyze and chart bond statistics) and BradyNet Rolodex (an online directory of emerging market participants). Portfolio services automatically update and analyze an emerging market's debt portfolio's vital statistics (such as yield, duration, profit, and loss), and a new issues analyzer details issues that fall within your search parameters. Basic service is $99.95 per month. Premium service is $199.95 per month. There is a 14-day free trial.

Chapter 13

Valuing, Buying, and Selling Bonds Online

In This Chapter

▶ Making sense of why bond values change

▶ Determining the value of any type of bond

▶ Discovering the easiest way to determine your bond returns

▶ Buying savings bonds online and setting up your own Treasury Direct account

▶ Purchasing U.S. Treasury securities without a broker

▶ Using a hot strategy for reducing bond risk

*I*n this chapter, I show you how to analyze, buy, and sell a variety of fixed-income investments. I explain where to buy bonds online. For you online investors who are interested in paying the right price for a bond, I show you how to value all types of bonds and determine bond yields (returns). Doing so may sound complicated, but with a little practice, you'll be calculating your returns in no time, and you'll have the Internet to help you with the math.

I explore the benefits of savings bonds, detail new regulations, and explain the limitations of this type of investment. I also show you where to find the Savings Bond Wizard, which you can use to determine the exact value of your savings bonds.

I also explain how to purchase Treasury securities without a broker. You can now purchase Treasury securities online or over the phone with *Buy Direct,* a U.S. Treasury Department–sponsored program. In addition, you can access your account online to see your online statement. Other online services include helpful information — for example, dates of government auctions, Treasury yields, auction results, and instructions about how to open your investor's account at Treasury Direct (the master record of the securities you own that is maintained by the federal government). Finally, I offer a hot strategy that can protect you from interest rate risk.

The Math of Bonds

The bond market is dominated by institutional investors (insurance companies, pension funds, and mutual funds) that account for 80 to 85 percent of all trading. Individual investors tend to purchase municipal and corporate bonds because of their lower denominations (around $1,000) and tax-exempt features. However, the impact of individual investors can also be felt through the purchases of mutual funds that specialize in bonds.

The following section shows the valuation process of bonds and the relationship of interest rate changes to the value of bonds. I provide several easy-to-use approaches that take the mystery out of determining your bond yield.

Calculating bond values

A bond issued by a corporation is called a *debt instrument*. The bond states how the debt holder (investor) is repaid. Generally, these terms are normal debt arrangements. The borrower makes interest payments and then pays the principal at a predetermined date. Several issues make bonds complicated, such as provisions to convert the bonds to common stocks at a predetermined stock value, or terms that allow the bond issuer to retire the bond before maturity.

Treasury securities and government agency and municipal bonds are valued in the same way as corporate bonds. However, this valuation doesn't show the entire picture. Treasury securities are subject to federal taxes but are exempt from state and local taxes. Government agency securities are generally taxable for federal, state, and local purposes, but some exceptions exist. Municipal bonds are generally tax-free (from federal, state, and local taxes). Therefore, when you value corporate bonds, the calculated rate of return is somewhat overstated because it doesn't consider the impact of taxes.

The value of the bond is based on the investor's assessment of the bond's value. The receipt of future interest payments, the repayment of principal, and the credit rating or riskiness of the bond usually temper these assessments. You aren't obligated to hold a bond until maturity, and bonds are traded freely in the marketplace.

Calculating the value of a bond involves determining the present value of the interest payments and the eventual recovery of the principal. *Present value* means discounting the future cash flow to calculate how much you're willing to pay today for these future receipts.

At times, calculating the yield on bonds can seem more complicated than it really is. For example, if you purchase a one-year Treasury bill for $9,500, and redeem it in 12 months at full face value ($10,000), your gain is $500 (subject to federal income tax but exempt from state and local taxes). To determine your yield if your holding period is one year, use the following formula:

(Face Value – Price) ÷ Price = Annual Return

($10,000 – $9,500) ÷ $9,500 = 0.0526, or 5.26%

See the section "The easy way to value your bond returns," later in this chapter, where I show you how to calculate the yield for a bond that has a maturity term greater than one year.

Creating yield curves

A *yield curve* is a diagram that illustrates the relationship of bond yields to maturities on a specific day. You can use yield curves to decide which type of bond is best for your financial objectives. Bond yields and maturities are posted daily at the Bloomberg.com Web site (`www.bloomberg.com/markets/rates/index.html`), shown in Figure 13-1.

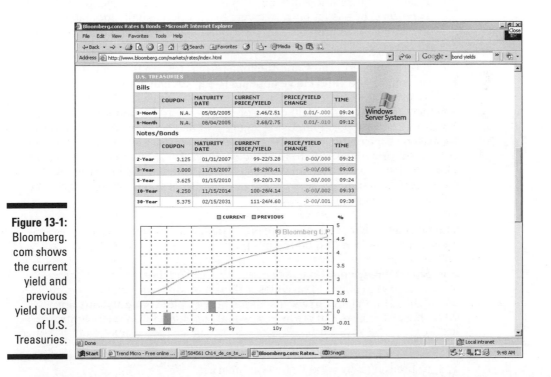

Figure 13-1: Bloomberg.com shows the current yield and previous yield curve of U.S. Treasuries.

Figure 13-1 indicates the current and previous yields for U.S. Treasury bills, notes and bonds. The horizontal axis plots the maturities of Treasury securities from left to right starting with the maturity of 3-months to 30 years. The yield of each security is plotted on the vertical axis. The dots are connects to make a current and a previous yield curve.

When analyzing the yield curve in Figure 13-1, keep in mind that short-term yields are controlled by the Federal Reserve. Long-term yields of Treasuries are controlled by the market. Figure 13-1 illustrates that there is very little difference between the current and previous yield curves. Look at the bar chart below the yield curve in Figure 13-1. This chart indicates that the yield on 6-month Treasury bills has decreased and the yield on 3-year Treasury notes slightly increased. See the curve descriptions in the following list to find out what yield curves can indicate:

✔ If the short-term rates are higher than the long-term rates, the yield curve becomes *inverted,* or has a downward swing to it, which tells you that this situation tends to be *bearish* for the market. In this situation, monetary policy is likely to be tight, and the Federal Reserve is pushing up short-term rates.

✔ If the short-term rates are lower than the long-term rates, the yield curve is *positive,* or has an upward swing to it, which usually indicates that investors are willing to tie up their money in long-term commitments to reap higher rewards.

✔ If the short-term rates and the long-term rates are the same (or nearly the same), the yield curve appears to be flat, like a line.

You can create you own yield curve on a piece of graph paper or with your MS Excel software program. Using Figure 13-1 as you example, on the horizontal axis, plot the maturities of Treasury securities from left to right starting with the shortest maturity to the longest maturity. Then, on the vertical axis, plot the yield of each Treasury security. Next, connect the dots to make a yield curve. Creating your own yield curves allows you to analyze the data that interests you the most.

The Internet provides many sources for yield curves. Here are a few examples of what you can find on the Internet:

✔ **SmartMoney.com** (www.smartmoney.com/onebond/index.cfm?story=yieldcurve) provides a 12-part guide to purchasing bonds. "The Living Yield Curve" discusses how to plot today's yields and chart the curve. Curves are then analyzed for additional insights.

✔ **CNN Money** (money.cnn.com/markets/bondcenter) offers bonds and rates. You find easy to read yield curves, prices, and yields, in addition to breaking news about the bond market.

> ✔ **The Federal Reserve Board** (www.federalreserve.gov/rnd.htm) pro-
> vides all the statistics and historical data you need to plot yield curves.
> Dataset include daily, weekly, monthly, quarterly, and annual statistics.

The yield curve approach also works for other types of bonds, such as government agency, municipal, or corporate bonds. Remember that you only
need to include bonds with the same level of risk, such as all AA-rated corporate bonds. *Note:* A strong feature for a bond issue is the rating received by
Standard & Poor's or Moody's Ratings. The ratings generally range from AAA
to D, with AAA being the highest quality. Corporations may have to pay an
additional ¼ point if a bond issue is rated A and not AA. For more information
about bond ratings, see Chapter 12.

The easy way to value your bond returns

Bonds are often quoted at prices that differ from their stated (or *par*) values,
a situation that can be troublesome for investors who want to determine the
yield of the bond. You can calculate the yield value of a bond in many ways.
In my opinion, the *approximate yield to maturity* method provides the easiest
way to determine a bond's current yield.

To calculate the approximate yield to maturity (YTM), you need the following
information:

> ✔ Annual interest payment (I)
>
> ✔ Principal payment, or par value (P)
>
> ✔ Price of the bond (B)
>
> ✔ Number of years to maturity (M)

Using these values, calculate the approximate YTM by using the following
formula:

$$YTM = [I + ((P - B) \div M)] \div [(0.6 \times B) + (0.4 \times P)]$$

For example, what is the yield to maturity on a 12-year, 7 percent annual
coupon, $1,000 par value bond that sells at a discount for $942.21? Here are
the calculations:

$$YTM = [70 + (($1,000 - $942.21) \div 12)] \div [(0.6 \times $942.21) + (0.4 \times $1,000)]$$

$$YTM = [70 + (57.79 \div 12)] \div [565.33 + 400]$$

$$YTM = [70 + 4.82] \div 965.33$$

$$YTM = 74.82 \div 965.33$$

$$YTM = 0.0775$$

$$YTM = 7.75\%$$

If your required rate of return is 8 percent, you should *not* purchase the bond because the approximate yield to maturity (7.75 percent) doesn't meet your financial requirements (an 8 percent return). Conversely, if the bond has a return that is equal to or *greater* than 8 percent, the bond meets your objectives and is a "buy" candidate.

Note: If the value of the bond is discounted (that is, sells below its par value — in this case, below $1,000), the yield to maturity (YTM) is greater than the 7 percent coupon rate.

Let the Internet do the math

When you invest in bonds, calculating the worth of the bond today, in the past, or in the near future is often helpful. Additionally, you might want to use a bond calculator to determine whether investing in a tax-free municipal bond provides a better return than investing in a taxable investment. The following are a few examples of online calculators that can assist you with the math:

- ✔ **FICALC** (www.ficalc.com) is a free, online, fixed-income calculator. At the home page, just click Use Calculator. Select the security market by choosing from a list (U.S. Treasury Securities, U.S. Agency Securities, U.S. Municipal Securities, U.S. Corporate Securities, and so on). Click Select Market and then select the security type. For example, if you selected U.S. Treasuries, you then select from Bills, Notes — Fixed Coupon, and Bonds — Fixed Coupon. Make your selection and click Select Structure. Enter bond-specific data such as the price of the security, issue date, maturity, and settlement dates. (If you plan to sell before maturity, enter your personal sell date also.) To determine the yield on your proposed investment, click Calculate.

- ✔ **Key Bank** (www.key.com/templates/t-ca3.jhtml?nodeID=H-3.32) offers 11 online bond calculators so that you can analyze your bonds in any way you desire.

- ✔ **Smith Barney Access: Taxable Equivalent Yield Calculators** (www.smithbarney.com/cgi-bin/bonds/teymey.cgi) shows how tax-free municipal bonds can benefit you by calculating your taxable equivalent yield and your municipal equivalent yield.

✔ **SmartMoney.com Bond Calculator** (`www.smartmoney.com/onebond/`
`index.cfm?story=bondcalculator`) can assist you in determining
whether your bonds are making the returns you desire. Begin by entering the bond's coupon rate and maturity. The calculator displays the
bond's yield to maturity. If you enter **yield,** the calculator indicates the
corresponding price. You can also see how changes in price affect your
yield.

Trading Bonds Online

All of the big five online brokerages — Ameritrade (`www.ameritrade.com`),
Charles Schwab (`www.schwab.com`), E*TRADE (`www.etrade.com`), Fidelity
(`www.fidelity.com`), and TD Waterhouse (`www.waterhouse.com`) — trade
bonds online. Many online bond brokerages are designed for professional
bond traders. However, a few are beginning to cater to the needs of individual
investors.

Often, investors can increase the performance of their bonds by purchasing
the right securities at the lowest price by viewing a wider selection of the
fixed-income investment candidates. Some online bond brokerages specialize
in certain types of fixed-income products. Other online bond brokerages provide access to thousands of securities in all the major fixed product areas,
such as bank certificates of deposit, Treasury securities, government agency,
municipal, and corporate bonds, and mortgage-backed securities.

Examples of online bond brokerages include the following:

✔ **Bondpage.com** (`www.bondpage.com`) trades thousands of different types
of fixed-rate securities. Although you pay no initial minimum deposit
amount, you must have the amount of your purchase in your account
before the firm will execute your trade. A flat $50 transaction fee applies
to trades of fewer than 100 bonds. No transaction fee applies to trades of
100 bonds or more, but the firm may act as principal in the transaction.

✔ **FMSBonds.com** (`www.fmsbonds.com`) is an all-in-one site for municipal
bond investors. You can discover investor education about bonds,
market yields, and analyzing your portfolio. You can view its bond offerings and check out its daily featured bonds. If you don't find anything to
your liking, let the company know exactly what you're looking for, and
it can e-mail you information about bonds that meet your investment
needs at no charge. You can also sign up for a free e-mailed newsletter.

✔ **Muni Direct** (`www.munidirect.com`) is an online brokerage that specializes in municipal bonds. Muni Direct offers detail search capabilities,

access to new issues, and a large selection of municipal bond offerings. A Muni Wizard can guide you in finding municipal bonds that meet your investment needs. This firm has no initial minimum deposit. Commissions or markups are no more than $5 per bond ($1,000 face value).

✔ **TradeBonds.com** (www.tradebonds.com) offers an abundance of bond research and tools that are geared for mid-sized institutional investors. There is no charge for the Web site's bond search capabilities and 20-minute delayed quotes. A key feature is the online portfolio function that allows you to sort by bond type, maturity, and coupon. Additionally, you can find the best bid and offer prices in the market for your bond holdings. You can open a trading account online and start trading as soon as your account is funded.

REMEMBER

You can open a Treasury Direct account (www.treasurydirect.gov) and trade Treasuries online without a broker.

Nice and Simple: Savings Bonds

The only way many people can save money is by purchasing savings bonds. The United States Treasury Department offers three main types of savings bonds:

✔ **Series EE:** Series EE savings bonds (now called Patriot Bonds) are backed by the full faith and credit of the United States. Series EE savings bonds that you buy today earn market-based rates for 30 years. However, you can cash in the bonds at any time after six months from the purchase date. At this time, newly issued EE bonds pay 3.25 percent.

You pay half the face value of a Series EE bond at the time of purchase, and you receive the face value when the bond matures. The interest rate isn't fixed so the maturity term is variable. The minimum denomination is $50 and the maximum denomination is $10,000. Interest rates for Series EE bonds are 90 percent the average rate on five-year Treasury securities.

✔ **Series HH:** Series HH bonds pay interest directly to your account at a financial institution every six months. These bonds have fixed interest rates for ten years and earn interest for up to 20 years. Series HH bonds are available in denominations of $500, $1,000, $5,000, and $10,000.

As of August 31, 2004, the U.S. government pulled the plug on Series H and Series HH bonds. As of September 1, 2004, investors were no longer able to reinvest HH bonds and Series H bonds or exchange Series EE or E bonds. Not being able to reinvest can create an enormous tax bill for investors. Go to www.savingsbond.gov to determine your tax bill and discover what you can do to lessen your tax liability.

✔ **Series I:** Series I bonds are inflation-indexed savings bonds. The U.S. government adjusts the amount of the I bond semiannually to keep up with inflation and to protect the purchasing power of the bondholder. The first part is the 1.1 percent that applies to the 30-year life of the bond. The second component is a variable that is annually set and is currently at 2.57 percent. The variable component is designed to reflect the Consumer Price Index and the buying power of investors who own the bond. It's interesting to note that the current yield on T-bills is significantly less than that of I bonds. As of this date, newly issued I bonds pay 3.67 percent.

Check for old bonds in your safe-deposit box or among the papers of elderly relatives. More than $2.3 billion in savings bonds have never been redeemed.

Hanging on to your old bonds may seem like a good idea, but they no longer pay interest after specified periods.

You can get additional information about savings bonds from the following Internet sources:

✔ **The Bureau of the Public Debt** (www.publicdebt.Treas.gov/sav/savbene.htm) provides information on the benefits of savings bonds and covers interest rates and maturity periods.

✔ **SavingsBonds.com** (www.savingsbonds.com/infocenter.cfm) offers free, easy-to-understand information about buying, redeeming, and valuing your savings bonds. You can even create an online savings bond portfolio.

The good and the bad about savings bonds

The returns on savings bonds are so low that they'll never make you rich. In fact, returns are so low that large pension funds and other big investors don't purchase savings bonds. However, for many individuals, savings bonds are the best approach for saving money. Savings bonds offer the following advantages:

✔ **You can save automatically:** Employers who sponsor savings bond programs can automatically deduct an amount that you designate from your paychecks. For many people, this program is a painless way to save money.

✔ **You can diversify your risk:** If you already have investments in stocks and bonds, you may want to invest in savings bonds, which add a no-risk element to your portfolio.

✔ **Your investment is safe:** In exchange for a low return, savings bonds offer absolute safety of principal — they're no-risk investments because they are as safe as the money in your pocket.

✔ **You don't pay any sales commissions:** Savings bonds don't require the services of a broker to help you purchase them, thus you pay no sales commissions.

✔ **Your minimum investment is low:** The minimum investment in savings bonds is $25, and employer-sponsored plans can make the per week minimum even lower.

✔ **You pay low taxes, if any:** The difference between the purchase price and the redemption value of EE bonds, and the payments made on HH bonds, comes in the form of interest. This interest income is subject to federal income tax, but not state or local income taxes. You can defer paying federal income tax on the interest until you cash in the bonds.

✔ **You gain education tax benefits:** For EE bonds purchased after 1989 and cashed to pay tuition and post-secondary education fees, the interest earned isn't subject to federal income taxes.

Calculating the value of your savings bonds

Savings bonds have always been easy to purchase and are popular gifts for new parents and grandchildren. But as easy as these financial instruments are to buy, they're equally difficult to value. This difficulty can be especially troublesome if you need to cash in a bond before it matures. Additionally, bondholders may have problems keeping an accurate inventory of the savings bonds they have on hand.

Recognizing this problem, the federal government developed two nifty approaches to the problem. The first is an online *Savings Bond Redemption Calculator* at `www.publicdebt.treas.gov/sav/savcalc.htm`. This online calculator, provided by the U.S. government, can assist you in quickly understanding the value of your savings bonds.

The second approach is a downloadable software program called the *Savings Bond Wizard,* located at the Bureau of the Public Debt at `www.publicdebt.treas.gov/sav/savwizar.htm`. The easy-to-use software program, shown in Figure 13-2, is free. All you have to do is click the appropriate link. The Savings Bond Wizard's features enable you to calculate interest amounts, import and export files created in Excel spreadsheets, track cash or exchanged bonds, and display the rate each bond is earning, and it provides specialized reports and includes an easy inventory builder feature. Beginning with Wizard IV, you receive all available update values. With Savings Bond Wizard, bondholders can print copies of their bond inventories. (After a flood or fire, this inventory is an invaluable record of the bondholder's investment.)

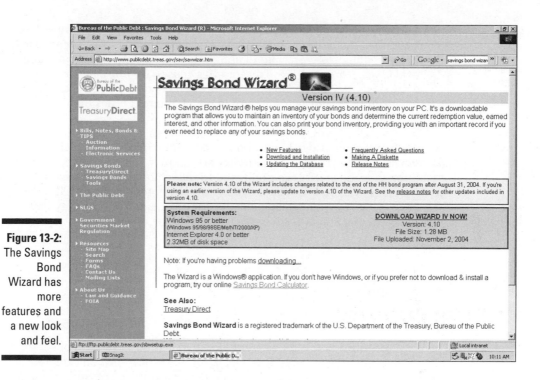

Figure 13-2:
The Savings
Bond
Wizard has
more
features and
a new look
and feel.

Just Uncle Sam, Treasury Securities, and You

The federal government sells Treasury securities to the public to pay off maturing debt and to raise the cash needed to operate the federal government. These securities are sold at 150 auctions throughout the year. There are three types of Treasury securities. All Treasury securities have a minimum purchase price of $1,000, and additional purchase increments of $1,000. The chief difference between Treasury securities is the life of the obligation:

- **Treasury bills (T-bills)** mature in three months, six months, or one year. Treasury bills are purchased at a discount, so interest is actually paid. You write a check for $10,000, and the government refunds the discount (which equals the interest rate determined at auction). In other words, your return is the difference between the purchase price and the maturity value.

- **Treasury notes** are considered intermediate-term securities and mature in two to ten years. They provide state and local tax-exempt interest payments to note holders.

✔ **Treasury bonds** are long-term securities that mature in more than ten years from the issue date. You can usually buy bonds for a price close to their par value. Interest paid to bondholders is exempt from state and local taxes. *Note:* The U.S. Treasury has ceased issuing 30-year bonds. In the past, the 30-year bond rate was often used as a benchmark for long-term rates and as a standard in many different types of financial calculations.

The U.S. Treasury sells two kinds of notes and bonds, *fixed-principal* and *inflation-indexed*. Both pay interest every six months, but the principal value of inflation-indexed securities is adjusted to reflect inflation as measured by the Consumer Price Index. With inflation-indexed notes and bonds, the U.S. Treasury calculates your semiannual interest payments and maturity payment based on the inflation-adjusted principal value of your security.

Buying Treasury Securities via the Internet

Treasury securities may not look very lucrative if you're used to double-digit returns, but they're excellent investments for investors who can't tolerate risk. In other words, if you're a conservative investor, U.S. Treasury securities may be your type of investment. You can buy and sell U.S. Treasuries through investment professionals, commercial banks, or online brokerages. If you purchase Treasury securities using a broker, they're issued in a commercial book-entry form, which means that the securities are held in the name of your broker or dealer. The broker then maintains records of each individual investor's Treasury securities.

Do-it-yourself investors can now purchase Treasury securities over the Internet or by telephone. The Internet purchase program is called *Buy Direct*. You simply submit a noncompetitive bid (which I explain later in this chapter) via the Internet (or by calling 800-722-2678). The price of the security is debited from the account you previously designated to receive Treasury Direct payments. (This is called a Treasury Direct account. I show you how to open your own account later in this chapter.) Tender forms and payments may also be submitted electronically through your financial institution or government securities broker or dealer.

Opening Treasury Direct accounts

Treasury Direct is a book-entry system that is managed by the federal government. You can open two types of Treasury Direct accounts. The first Treasury Direct account is for savings bonds. To open a savings bond Treasury Direct account, you must be 18 years of age or older, provide your Social Security number, driver's license or state ID number and expiration date, birth date, bank routing and account number, e-mail address, postal address, and telephone number. A U.S. mailing address is required. If you don't have a driver's license, just enter **none** in the online form. Keep in mind that there are no fees for opening a Treasury Direct account.

As of this date, two types of Treasury Direct accounts exist. The first account is a Treasury Direct account for Treasury securities. The second account is a Treasury Direct account for savings bonds. With a Treasury Direct account, you can purchase Treasury bills, notes, and TIPS (Treasury Inflation-Protection Securities). To open an account, download, complete, and mail in an application form. Don't worry about money when opening an account; there is no minimum initial deposit. Once you open your account, the minimum purchase amount for Treasury bills, notes, and TIPS is $1,000.

Opening your savings bond Treasury Direct account for as little as $25

You use the second type of Treasury Direct account to purchase savings bonds. You can open a Savings Bond Treasury Direct account without mailing in a printed and signed form. The minimum purchase amount for a Savings Bond Treasury Direct account is $25. To open an account, follow these steps:

1. **Go to Treasury Direct at** www.treasurydirect.gov.
2. **Click Individual/Personal.**
3. **Click My Accounts.**
4. **Click Open an Account.**

It takes about one minute to verify your Savings Bond Treasury Direct account information. Once you complete your Treasury Direct application, you're asked to create a password. After you create your password, you're asked to provide three reminder security questions in case you forget your password. You can change your answers to your authentication questions or even change the authentication questions.

Within five minutes after you submit your password and authentication questions, you receive your savings bond Treasury Direct account number via e-mail. At this point, if you have money in the account you designated on your application form, you can immediately log in to your Treasury Direct account and start purchasing savings bonds.

Buying your first savings bond online

Using *Buy Direct,* you can purchase a savings bond for $25. If you want to, you can purchase savings bonds one at a time or schedule purchase dates that you determine are best for you. If you want a regular savings plan, you may want to schedule weekly or monthly purchases with a designated start date and end date.

Once you enter your buying information, Buy Direct provides a Purchase Review. Check for any errors or mistakes. By clicking the Submit button, you authorize the Bureau of the Public Debt to debit your account at the financial institution you specified. You certify that all the information on the form is correct and that you're authorized to make the transaction. Click Submit, and you purchase your first electronic savings bond online.

Redeeming your savings bonds online

Series EE and I bonds mature in 30 years. At that time, the bond will automatically be redeemed and the proceeds used to purchase a zero percent certificate of indebtedness (called a zero percent C of I) in your Primary Treasury Direct account. Proceeds of gifts that have matured will be held in the Gift Box as gift proceeds.

If you want to redeem your Series EE or I bonds after five years, no penalties apply. There is a three-month penalty (that is, you don't receive interest for a three-month period) if you cash an EE or I bond within the first five years from its issue date.

Redeeming EE, and I bonds by using Treasury Direct is very simple. In Current Holdings, select the savings bonds you want to redeem and click Submit at the bottom of the screen. The Current Holding Detail screen for the security selected appears. Click Redeem at the bottom of the screen. At the redemption request screen, indicate whether you want full or partial redemption and where you want the redemption proceeds to be deposited. Treasury Direct makes payments using the direct deposit method to any U.S. financial institution account or to your zero percent C of I, whichever account you designate.

Treasury bills, notes, and TIPS Treasury Direct accounts

To open a Treasury Bills, Notes, and TIPS (Treasury Inflation-Protection Securities) Treasury Direct account, you must complete a paper form. The New Account Request form (PD F 5182) is available at `wwws.publicdebt.treas.gov/NC/FoRMSHome?FormType=TDF`.

Download the application form, fill it out online or print it and fill in the blanks, and then mail the completed form to your local Federal Reserve Bank. (You need Adobe Acrobat Reader to display and print the form. You can download the free Acrobat Reader program from `www.adobe.com`.)

You can open a Treasury Direct account without submitting a minimum deposit. When you mail the application form to open an account, don't send any cash; it's free. For the address of the nearest Federal Reserve Bank, go to `www.publicdebt.treas.gov/sav/savfrb.htm`, type your zip code, and then press the Locate button.

Treasury Direct sets up an account, and you can purchase securities later, when you choose. After you've established an account (and Treasury Direct has confirmed your deposit arrangements), you can purchase securities and maintain your account either by the traditional paper-and-mail method or online.

If you purchase Treasury securities directly from the federal government, they're issued in a book-entry form that is held in the Bureau of the Public Debt's Treasury Direct system (`www.publicdebt.treas.gov/sec/sectrdir.htm`). The securities are issued to your individual account.

You can see your account balance online at `www.publicdebt.treas.gov/sec/sectdes.htm`. Just go to the Virtual Lobby by clicking Continue, typing your Treasury Direct account number, and then clicking Enter the Lobby.

Your Treasury Direct Account can be less than $100,000, but expect maintenance charges of $25 per year for each $100,000 in your account. Treasury Direct provides information about how to open and maintain a Treasury Direct Investor Account at `www.publicdebt.treas.gov/sec/secacct.htm`.

You may want to consider accumulating cash in a money market account (for any purpose other than education). The interest rate paid is often as good as or better than an investment in Treasuries, and you have much more liquidity. (You don't have to wait three months to five years to get your money back.)

How to buy Treasuries online

To discover when you can buy Treasuries, refer to the calendar of upcoming auction dates at the Bureau of the Public Debt (`www.publicdebt.treas.gov/of/ofannpr.htm`), which provides a constantly updated three-month calendar of tentative auction dates so that you can plan ahead. Official auction dates are announced about seven days before the securities are offered.

Treasury bills, notes, and bonds are sold through competitive and noncompetitive bidding:

✔ **Noncompetitive bid:** You agree to accept a rate determined by the auction, and in return you're guaranteed that your bid successfully results in purchasing the security you desire. Most individual investors submit noncompetitive bids. Noncompetitive bids from individual investors can't exceed $5 million for the same offering of Treasury notes or bonds.

✔ **Competitive bid:** For a bill auction, the investor submits an offer — or *tender* — specifying a discount rate to two decimal places (for example 5.12 percent). For a note or bond auction, the investor submits a tender specifying a yield to three decimal places (for example, 5.123 percent). Common fractions may not be used. If the bid falls within the range accepted at the auction, the investor is awarded the security. If the bid is at the high rate or yield, the investor may not be awarded the full amount bid. Most financial institutions (banks, insurance companies, brokerages, and so on) submit competitive bids.

Don't let the jargon of Treasury securities make purchasing seem more complex than it really is. A noncompetitive bid is similar to a market order (you definitely get the security, but you don't know what price you receive), whereas a competitive bid is similar to a limit order (you know what price you get, but you don't know whether you definitely get the security).

With *Buy Direct,* you can make a noncompetitive purchase of Treasuries during the hours of 8:00 am to 12 midnight EST, Monday through Friday, excluding Federal holidays. Most investors submit their bids prior to noon EST on the day the security is auctioned. Most individual investors purchase Treasuries by making noncompetitive bids. Buy Direct only allows you to make noncompetitive bids for Treasuries via the telephone or the Internet by completing the following steps:

1. **If you use a telephone, dial 800-722-2678 and wait for the prompt.**

   Press I to indicate that you want to invest or reinvest.

2. **If you use the Web, indicate that you want to invest and enter your Treasury Direct account number and your Social Security number (or employer identification number).**

3. **Choose the security you want to purchase.**

4. **Choose the amount of money you want to invest.**

   The minimum is $1,000, and the maximum is $5 million for any one bill, note, or TIPS. Bids must be made in multiples of $1,000.

5. **On the Internet, select the security's issue date.**

   Telephone users don't have this option; you'll automatically receive your chosen security at the next available issue date.

6. **If you purchase a Treasury bill, choose the number of times you want to reinvest the security.**

   You can reinvest between zero and eight times for a 13-week Treasury bill and zero to four times for a 26-week Treasury bill.

7. **When the transaction is complete, the system automatically provides you with a confirmation number. Keep this number for your records.**

When the U.S. government issues your Treasuries to you, Buy Direct will deduct the purchase price from the bank account you specified when you opened your Treasury Direct account.

By mail Treasuries can be purchased by noncompetitive and competitive bids using Form PD F 5381, which is available at `wwws.publicdebt.treas. gov/NC/FoRMSHome?FormType=TDF`. Just fill it out and send it in. On the PD F 5381 Form, you must decide whether you want to send in a competitive or a noncompetitive bid, both of which are explained previously in this section. If you submit this form and don't already have an account, Treasury Direct establishes an account for you and then processes your bid for securities.

Selling your Treasury securities

The good news is that you can sell your Treasury securities before they mature, with or without a broker. The bad news is that both approaches cost you extra money.

- ✓ **Let the federal government sell your Treasury securities.** If you want to sell one or many Treasuries that you're holding in your Treasury Direct account before they mature, complete the Sell Direct Request form (PD F 5179-1). Send the completed, signed, and certified form to Federal Reserve Bank of Chicago, Investment Division for Sell Direct, 230 LaSalle Street, Chicago, IL 60604.

  Sell Direct, shown in Figure 13-3, gets quotes from different dealers, and you get the best price offered. The fee is $34 for each security sold. The proceeds from the sale of the Treasury security are deposited directly to your savings or checking account, less the transaction fee. You receive a sale confirmation, the appropriate IRS 1099 form, and a Statement of Account showing your new balance. For more information, see `www. publicdebt.treas.gov/sec/secselld.htm`.

- ✓ **Sell your Treasury securities through a broker.** In a secondary market for Treasury securities, investors can sell Treasury securities before they mature through a brokerage. For instance, assume that you purchased a six-month Treasury bill. Three months later, you decide to sell. Other investors will purchase the Treasury bill at a slightly higher price than what you paid because it's closer to maturity. Brokerage fees vary for these services, so shop around for the best price.

You can also _purchase_ Treasury securities in the secondary market — that is, through your full-service or online brokerage — if you want to have securities (money) come due on a specific date to meet a financial objective.

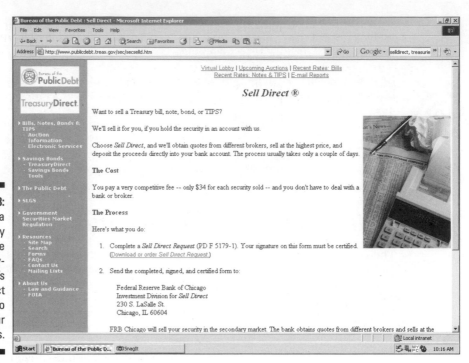

Figure 13-3:
Avoid a broker by using the federal government's Sell Direct program to sell your Treasuries.

Online sources for more information

Information provided by the government is written in a way that makes purchasing Treasuries seem more difficult and complex than it really is, but don't get discouraged. For more information about understanding and purchasing Treasury securities, refer to the following online resources:

- **Investing In Bonds.com** (www.investinginbonds.com), sponsored by the Bond Market Association, offers tutorials about purchasing Treasury securities and explains how to read bond tables.

- **PC Trader** (www.pctrader.com) offers a GovPX full feed package that includes U.S. Treasury and government markets. Subscribers ($250 per month) have full access to GovPX quotes that many professional traders use. All PC Trader products start with a $40 data delivery and software fee. There is a free 15-day trial.

- **SmartMoney.com** (www.smartmoney.com/bondmarketup/?nav=Drop Tabs) provides the latest information about the bond market and what's happening with key interest rates.

- **The Educated Investor** (www.theeducatedinvestor.com/online tutorial/tut243883497-1.html) provides a short tutorial about a wide variety of bonds.

Fraud alert! Some fraudsters employ scams that involve the renting or leasing of U.S. Treasury securities. Usually, the securities offered don't exist (the offer is for bearer securities in an amount that exceeds the amount that remains outstanding on the bearer form for a particular security) or are not owned by the party making the offer (the securities don't exist or are owned by someone else who isn't aware of this transaction). If someone approaches you with one of these offers, ask the individual to produce the securities or otherwise prove ownership. He or she will be unable to do so, offering excuses like, "They're frozen at my bank," "A wealthy philanthropist has assigned them to me to assign to others for infrastructure or humanitarian purposes in third-world countries and wishes to remain anonymous," or "Bank secrecy laws of this country (often Great Britain, Greece, or South Africa) prevent such a verification." In an effort to fool you, the scam artist might additionally misuse Public Debt forms or CUSIP numbers as evidence of ownership and/or claim that the scam has been certified by a well-known or official organization.

Increasing Your Profits with a Treasuries Ladder

One way to lessen your risk to changes in interest rates and to manage your cash flow is to create a Treasuries ladder. Each rung of the Treasuries ladder consists of a different bond maturity. For example, the first rung of the ladder may include Treasuries that mature in one year. The second rung can include Treasuries that mature in two years, and so on for ten years.

Bond ladders are the fixed-income equivalents to dollar-cost averaging with stocks or mutual funds. With a bond ladder, a part of your portfolio matures each year, and you reinvest it regardless of what happens to yields. This approach reduces exposure to interest rate fluctuations and requires low maintenance on your part.

Here's how it works. Imagine that you have $20,000 to invest in Treasuries:

Year Zero: You buy at auction the following combination of securities: eight 1-year bills, eight 2-year notes, two 5-year notes, and two 10-year notes, each with a face value of $1,000.

Year One: You let a year go by, and your bills mature. You use the proceeds at the next auction to buy two 10-year notes, two 5-year notes, two 2-year notes, and two 1-year bills.

Year Two: You let another year go by. Your bill and the 2-year notes you bought in Year Zero mature. You use the proceeds at the next auction to buy two 10-year notes, two 5-year notes, four 2-year notes, and two 1-year bills.

Year Three: Can you see how your bond ladder is shaping up? Another year goes by, four securities mature, and you use the proceeds to buy two 5-year notes and two 10-year notes.

Year Four: As the fourth year closes, four securities mature, and you use the proceeds to buy two 5-year notes and two 10-year notes. Your bond ladder is now complete. From this point on, only two bonds will mature per year. When these bonds mature, you can use the proceeds to buy two new 10-year notes.

For more online information about bond ladders, check out the following Web sites:

- **Investopedia** (www.investopedia.com/articles/02/120202.asp) offers an article about the basics of bond ladders.

- **PIMCO** (singapore.pimco.com/LeftNav/Latest+Publications/ 2004/The+Limitations+of+Bond+Maturity+Ladders.htm) supplies an interesting article about the limitations of bond ladders.

Part III
Expanding Your Investment Opportunities

The 5th Wave   By Rich Tennant

"Oh, that's Jack's area for his paper crafts.
He's made some wonderful US Treasury
Bonds, Certificates of Deposit, $20's, $50's,
$100's, that sort of thing."

In this part . . .

In this part, you find out how you can invest in foreign securities without leaving your computer. You also discover how to reduce the purchase costs of buying your favorite stocks by using direct purchase and dividend reinvestment plans. You see the benefits and hazards of online investing in initial public offerings (IPOs), and you find out how you can increase your profits and reduce your portfolio's risk by making online international investments. You also discover how stock options work and how you can determine the value of your employee stock options. You discover online asset allocation tools that can help you balance your holdings and ensure that you're adequately compensated for your investment risk. You become aware of the latest online portfolio management tools and how you can aggregate your checking, investment, and credit card accounts online so that you'll always know your financial position.

Chapter 14

Going International Online

In This Chapter

▶ Understanding the benefits of investing in foreign equities

▶ Tracking down online sources of information about international investments

▶ Trading online while you're overseas

▶ Identifying the unique risks of international investing

▶ Purchasing American Depository Receipts (ADRs) online

▶ Spotting indirect international investments that can increase your returns

*1*n this chapter, I explain how international investing can assist you in diversifying your portfolio beyond the usual alternatives. You discover how you can find indexes that indicate those economies that aren't moving in the same direction as the United States' and how you can use this information to reduce the risk of your personal portfolio. When you decide which market meets your investment criteria, check out the country's political, market, and inflation risks at the Web sites that I suggest in this chapter.

I also describe the many ways in which you can make foreign investments. You may be surprised to discover that, even though you should be a specialist in foreign securities to invest directly in an international company in its foreign market, even beginning investors can invest in foreign markets by purchasing American Depository Receipts (ADRs). This chapter explains how ADRs, which represent foreign equities, have the look of domestic stocks and can be purchased online through your electronic brokerage. You can even purchase ADRs online without a broker.

This chapter also explores how you can make indirect purchases of international equities by buying international mutual funds or by purchasing shares of multinational corporations. Keep in mind that international investments are subject to their own unique kinds of risk. This chapter explains how political risk, currency risk, and other types of risks can quickly reduce your profits or even wipe out your initial investment.

Taking Advantage of International Opportunities

According to JPMorgan's *U.S. Investors: Equity Capital Flows Abroad, 4Q03 and CY03* report, in the fourth quarter of 2003, U.S. investors owned $1.944 trillion in foreign shares and ADRs. During this time period, the total amount of U.S. investor holdings in domestic and foreign shares was valued at $15.5 trillion. The average foreign component of U.S. equity portfolios was about 12.5 percent. According to the Federal Reserve, this number was a record high for U.S. investors.

Non-U.S. equity performance versus the S & P 500 drove investors to invest overseas. Additionally, the hope of a global economic recovery spurred investors to go bargain hunting abroad. Coupling these factors to the recent decline in the U.S. dollar has made foreign markets more attractive. I've heard some U.S. investors complain that if they didn't invest overseas, they wouldn't have any profits at all.

One of the benefits of international investing is that it offers an opportunity to diversify your portfolio. *Diversification* is defined as the lack of concentration in any one item. In other words, a portfolio composed of many different securities is *diversified.* Diversification can mean spreading your personal assets among different types of investments (such as stocks, bonds, and mutual funds) so that returns don't depend on the performance of any one type of investment. Diversification can also include diversifying your assets among different sectors, such as technology and consumer products. In addition, you can diversify your portfolio by investing in international companies, either directly or indirectly, as I explain in this chapter.

The advantage of international diversification is that foreign markets often don't move in the same direction as U.S. markets at any point in time. Consequently, a portfolio containing stocks from many countries may have less volatility than a portfolio of just domestic stocks. Additionally, the returns on your foreign securities could be higher than those of your domestic investments.

However, investing in foreign securities isn't a surefire way to avoid investment risk. In the market crash of 1987, about 19 of 23 foreign markets declined more than 20 percent. (A *crash* is usually defined as a decline of 33 percent.) This decline was considered unusual because of the low degree of correlation between the historical returns of different countries.

In general, the benefits of international investing are

- ✔ **More investment opportunities:** Studying the market indexes of foreign markets may provide you with insight about new investment opportunities.

- **Greater diversification safety:** Not investing all your personal assets in one type of security or industry sector may *bulletproof* your portfolio, insulating you from domestic market volatility.

- **Uncovering new world-class companies:** The emergence of high-quality foreign companies is one of the many drivers of the demand for international investing. In many cases, these companies can provide higher-than-usual investor returns.

- **Higher overall returns:** Global markets frequently don't move in the same direction as the U.S. market. If the U.S. market is down, a foreign market may be up.

 You might want to consider investing 10 percent of your portfolio in foreign securities. Then use dollar-cost averaging (see Chapter 15 for details) to increase your international holdings to a risk level that allows you to sleep at night. Keep in mind that international investing has its own unique risks.

Getting Started with Online International Quotes and Indexes

Stock indexes or *averages* are sets of stocks that are grouped to make a composite index. Stocks are selected and given a weighting relative to the other stocks in the group. Comparing stock indexes from different countries around the world is a good place to start your search for international investment candidates. By looking at the price and percentage change of an index, you can gain a good idea of which markets are moving in which direction. You can use this information to compare markets and spot investment opportunities.

Keep in mind how stocks are ranked in the different indexes. For example, the Dow Jones Industrial Average is a *price-weighted average.* The higher the sales price of a particular stock, the greater the impact on the average. In contrast, the Standard & Poor's 500 Index is a *value-weighted index.* Each company is weighted in the index by its own total market value as a percentage of the total market value of all the firms in the index. In this case, the higher the number of shares outstanding, the bigger the impact on the index. For example, if two companies have stock selling at the same price but one company has more outstanding shares, the company with the most outstanding shares has a bigger impact on the index when the price of its stock changes.

For online international quotes and indexes, visit the following Web sites:

- **CBS MarketWatch** (cbs.marketwatch.com) offers information about international indices and European and Asian ADRs. (I discuss ADRs in the section "Buying ADRs Is an Easy Solution," later in this chapter.) Global market information includes Asia, Europe, Latin America, and Canada. At the home page, click Global Markets.

✔ **Morgan Stanley** (www.msci.com) offers data and comparisons of different indexes. Index coverage is by sectors, industries, regions, and countries. This site also offers alternative index calculations, news about sectors and industries, real-time indexes, and style and asset class indexes.

✔ **MSN Money** (moneycentral.msn.com/investor/market/foreign. asp) offers brief, easy-to-read international indexes as part of its market news.

✔ **Standard and Poor's Index Services** (www.spglobal.com) provides a wealth of information free of charge. Discover S & P Global Indices in addition to country indices, non-equity indices, and a wide range of other indices that can be used for benchmarking purposes. The Web site also has links to press releases, stock exchanges, and FAQs for each index. You can download up-to-date news and analyses of various global indexes in PDF format.

✔ **Yahoo!** (finance.yahoo.com/m2?u) offers delayed quotes for the major world indices. Many indexes include related information, such as a summary of the index, charts, information about the components of the index, historical prices, and news headlines.

Gathering International News and Research

The political environment of your international investment is important. The Internet can assist you in monitoring and researching your current investments and investment candidates. For example, you can track breaking international news stories through all the online major news organizations, including Google News (news.google.com), ABC News (abcnews.go.com), CNN/Money (money.cnn.com), MSN Money (moneycentral.msn.com/investor/home.asp), and CBS MarketWatch (cbs.marketwatch.com/news/default.asp). Online magazines and newspapers, such as *Business-Week* (www.businessweek.com/globalbiz/index.html), the *International Herald Tribune* (www.iht.com/frontpage.html), and *The Economist* (www.economist.com), provide timely analysis of the latest international news.

The Internet even provides international investor Web sites for specific geographic locations and hard-to-locate information that can assist you in your research. Here are a few examples:

✔ **EIN News** (www.einnews.com/centraleurope) includes general and business news, stocks and currencies updates, news from Central Europe Review and BBC Monitoring, country information, discussion boards, chats, and classifieds. Get information about the Czech Republic, Hungary, Poland, Romania, Slovakia, Slovenia, and the

Balkans. A subscription costs you $29.95 per month, and a free seven-day trial subscription is available.

✔ **Economist Intelligence Unit ViewsWire** (`www.viewswire.com`) provides daily country analyses for decision makers. Just click the name of the country you're researching. For each country, get the following information: basic data; quarterly economic indicators; briefings on the economy, industry, and politics; and country forecasts. You can subscribe to the Web site (there is a free two-week trial) or purchase reports. For information about pricing, call 212-554-0600.

✔ **The International Economics Study Center** (`www.international econ.com`), shown in Figure 14-1, requires your free registration for reports on international trade theory and policy analysis, international finance theory and policy analysis, and news from the International Center for Trade and Sustainable Development. All the Web content is free, but the center does accept donations via PayPal.

✔ **LatinFocus** (`www.latin-focus.com`) is a reliable source for Latin American economic information, offering news, market indicators, economic briefings, economic forecasts, commentaries, and more.

✔ **LatInvestor** (`www.latinvestor.com`) provides country, industry, and company research reports, stock recommendations, and an extensive link directory. Report samples and some short reports are free. Prices for other reports range from $10 (for 1 to 5 pages) up to $150 (for 60-plus pages).

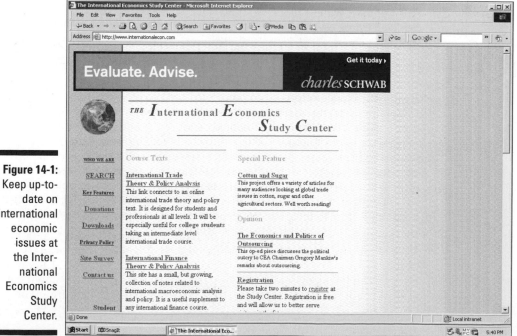

Figure 14-1:
Keep up-to-date on international economic issues at the International Economics Study Center.

- ✔ **Morgan Stanley: Global Economic Forum** (www.morganstanley.com/GEFdata/digests/latest-digest.html) provides the latest views of Morgan Stanley economists and includes weekly Webcasts and archives. Insights are categorized by country.

- ✔ **WorldNews Network** (www.worldnews.com) offers breaking news from around the world. With one click, you can access the latest happenings in North America, Asia, South America, Australia, Europe, the Middle East, Africa, and the Caribbean. News is also classified into business, industry, science, society, and sports categories. You find video broadcasts, photos, editorials, and a useful archive.

Acquiring International Company Information

One of the problems with investing in international companies is getting accurate information about the company you're researching. One approach to gathering this information is to use several online resources to examine your investment candidate. The following are a few examples of online sources for international company information:

- ✔ **ADR.com** (www.adr.com), sponsored by JPMorgan, offers regional, industry, and company-specific data, an economic calendar, commentary, and timely analyses. Discover today's top-performing ADRs, today's top world markets, ADR market commentary, and ADR top stories.

  For more information about what American Depository Receipts (ADRs) are and how they work, see the section "Buying ADRs Is an Easy Solution," later in this chapter.

- ✔ **Business Times Online — Singapore** (business-times.asia1.com.sg) is a southeast Asia business online daily. Here, you can find comprehensive and concise corporate, financial, economic, and political news, analysis, and commentary. The emphasis is on Singapore and Asian news and trends, but developments elsewhere in the world are also covered in considerable depth because Singapore's business interests are global. Read from 4 a.m. Singapore time (8 p.m. GMT) when you subscribe to the print or online editions of *The Business Times*. Online subscriptions are $48 per year. Access is free after 6 p.m. (10 a.m. GMT).

- ✔ **FT.com** (news.ft.com/business) includes Company Briefings, a database of "as reported" company fundamentals, financials, and primary activities for more than 18,000 companies in over 55 countries. FT.com offers three levels of content. International business news, commentary, company information, analyses, stock prices, and indices are free. The second level of content costs $110 per year for industry and country reports and e-mail news about company and business trends. The third level of service costs $300 per year and includes all the previous levels of content plus company balance sheets and analyses of 18,000 listed companies. Additionally, you can search the World Press Monitor's 12 million articles.

✔ **Fortune** (www.fortune.com) provides the Global 500, a list of the world's largest corporations. Discover the top-performing companies, biggest money losers, top 25 companies in Asia or Europe, and so on. To search the list, enter the name of a company, CEO, or industry.

✔ **ShibuiMarkets.com** (www.shibuimarkets.com) offers both free and fee-based content. Free content includes a corporate database screener, industry overviews, and corporate and country discussion forums. You can view your credit risk profile or company financial ratios and "dossier" on a pay-per-view basis. Information available on both a pay-per-view and a subscription basis includes emerging markets sovereign and corporate bond prices, stock prices, company profiles with SWOT (strengths, weaknesses, opportunities, and threats) analysis, industry profiles and guides, as well as MarketWatch and PharmaWatch newsletters for industries ranging from automotive to food to oncology. Subscribers also have a comprehensive data feed from the leading news agencies in Asia at their fingertips. Live emerging market quotes are $65 per month. Subscriptions to closing prices are $19 per month.

✔ **Wright Investors' Service** (www.wisi.com) includes a research center with company analyses of more than 20,000 companies from around the world, market commentary, and recent economic news. A market commentary reviews current financial events and explains how they could impact the near future. You can research industry, country, and company profiles.

Online Trading Abroad

If you're traveling internationally, don't stop monitoring your online investment accounts. Additionally, you may be able to trade stocks online with your current online brokerage while you're traveling abroad. (If you haven't selected an online brokerage, see Chapter 4.) Before you hit the road, however, you have to do some preparation. You need to do three things:

1. **Make certain that your Internet service provider (ISP) has an international connection or counterpart.**

   Recently, when I traveled to Europe, the "international" part of my ISP was in a dispute with its U.S. partner, and I had to sign up with another ISP.

2. **Purchase and install an international modem card for your laptop computer.**

3. **Get telephone adapters (just like the electrical adapters you'll bring along) for each country you plan to visit.**

Test each foreign city's local dialup number from your home. Using your travel itinerary as a guide, write down the names of the cities and countries you plan to visit. Refer to your ISP for the local dialup telephone number for each city. Dial the number and make certain the connection to your laptop computer works. If anything doesn't work, fixing the problem is easier done before you leave home.

If, for some reason, you can't get your online connection to work, you may want to consider opening an account while abroad. For example, consider the European counterpart to a U.S. online brokerage, such as E*TRADE and TD Waterhouse.

E*TRADE UK is a different operation than E*TRADE. E*TRADE UK (uk. etrade.com), which specializes in U.K. and other European securities, trades in pounds sterling instead of in American dollars.

Investing in Emerging Markets

A foreign country with an emerging market is making an effort to improve its national economy and productive capacity. However, emerging markets might be neither poor nor small. For example, China is defined as an emerging market. Other examples include Chile, Jordan, Korea, Thailand, and Zimbabwe. These emerging countries may have the potential of risk reduction for U.S. investors because the factors that affect the economic welfare of the emerging market are often different from key factors in the United States.

In you're interested in researching foreign emerging markets, check out the following sites:

✔ **ISI Emerging Markets** (www.securities.com) offers hard-to-get information on more than 55 emerging markets. You find news articles, financial statements, company information, industry analyses, equity quotes, macroeconomic statistics, and market-specific information that are derived from more than 8,500 local and global information providers.

✔ **Emerging Markets Online** (www.emerging-markets.com) offers in-depth management studies, consulting, and an industry database. Emerging Markets Online specializes in global energy and utilities intelligence. Industry reports can be parsed by region. Research reports average 200 pages in length and include detailed charts, graphics, figures, and tables. Prices vary from around $1,095 for a print version to almost $1,200 for a PDF version.

✔ **FDI Xchange** (www.fdixchange.com) is a free service sponsored by the World Bank's Multilateral Investment Guarantee Agency. This Web- and e-mail-based information service provides corporate investors, advisors, and financial institutions with periodic updates containing timely and specific information about new investment opportunities and business environment information from developing countries and economies in transition around the world. You can customize content (by region, industry, category, and size of investment) so that your trash-to-treasure ratio is better than average. You also find useful links to additional information.

Problems with Investing Directly in Foreign Companies

The most obvious, but least likely, approach to participating in foreign investments is by directly purchasing shares of a firm in its own foreign market through a foreign online broker or overseas branch of an American online brokerage. This approach may be the source of numerous problems for an inexperienced online international investor. These problems can be summarized into three areas: administrative, tax, and information gathering.

Administration troubles

Administration rules in foreign countries sometimes differ from the rules in the United States. For example, in the Swiss and Mexican stock markets, investors must settle their accounts one day after a transaction. London has a two-week settlement procedure. And in France, you may have several different settlement dates depending upon the securities you purchase. Additionally, transaction costs (fees and commissions) may be higher than in the United States. For example, mutual funds with foreign equities usually have higher fees and expenses, in addition to difficulties with stock delivery and capital transfers, than funds that invest in stocks of U.S. companies.

Tax problems

Some foreign countries levy withholding taxes of 15 to 30 percent on dividends or interest paid to nonresidents. You may need to hire a tax accountant to secure an exemption or rebate on part of the foreign withholding tax. This time-consuming, costly paper shuffling may reduce your net returns.

Information difficulties

The SEC closely regulates U.S. equities. For example, American companies have to send the SEC reports of their activities every 90 days. If something extraordinary happens during this 90-day period, the publicly traded firm has to send in a report explaining what's happening. Additionally, all financial reports have to meet established accounting standards, and publicly traded companies must provide investors with audited annual reports.

Foreign investment standards may not be this rigorous. Additionally, you may encounter language problems. Even with English-speaking countries, you may be in for a few surprises. For example, British financial statements are upside-down when compared to U.S. statements. Fixed assets are listed first, and current assets are listed last; U.S. financial statements list current assets first and fixed assets last.

Buying ADRs Is an Easy Solution

Only the most sophisticated money managers tackle the problems associated with investing directly in a firm in its own foreign market. (However, with the consolidation of many of the world's exchanges, this pattern may change in the near future.) The solution for individual investors is to purchase shares in foreign firms in the United States through American Depository Receipts (ADRs). ADRs enable American investors to acquire and trade foreign securities denominated in U.S. dollars without concern for the differing administration procedures, such as settlement time, that usually accompany trading in foreign markets.

ADRs were first introduced in 1927 in response to a law passed in Britain. Two banks are generally involved in maintaining and listing ADRs on a U.S. exchange:

- ✔ An investment bank establishes an ADR by arranging to buy the shares on a foreign market and issuing the ADRs on the U.S. markets.

- ✔ A depository bank, such as the Bank of New York (www.bankofny.com), handles the issuance and cancellation of ADR certificates backed by shares based on investor orders, as well as other services provided to an issuer of ADRs, but isn't involved in the selling of ADRs.

ADRs are U.S. dollar–denominated, negotiable instruments issued in the United States by a depository bank representing ownership in foreign securities. ADRs are generally listed with the letter *a* after the firm's name. You can find ADRs on the New York Stock Exchange (www.nyse.com) and NASDAQ (www.nasdaq.com). You can trade ADRs online just like any other type of security. Dividends are paid in dollars, and annual company reports are in English. Online brokerage commission rates are usually the same as for any other type of security.

You can purchase ADRs without a broker. For details, see NetstockDirect at www.netstockdirect.com. At the home page, click Stock Plans, select International Company for the type of company you want to invest in, and click Find Plans. The next page shows almost 400 ADRs you can purchase without paying a brokerage commission.

The risks of international investments

For the most part, ADRs look and feel pretty much like any other stock. However, although investing in ADRs may be convenient, it isn't risk-free. Keep in mind the risk/return trade-off. Generally, the higher risks associated with ADRs include country or political risk, as well as changes in currency valuations.

Country and political risk

Many foreign governments operate in unstable environments. Some countries may be subject to civil wars or revolutions. The danger of *nationalization* (when the government takes control of a company you've invested in) can limit the capital flows to foreign investors. Countries that can't meet their foreign debt obligations are subject to political problems. Other questions to consider: Is inflation under control? Are there any trade barriers? Do rulers succeed one another without civil war or revolution?

Exchange rate risk

If the currency exchange rate changes for your investments, you may earn less or more than you expect. If the value of the U.S. dollar weakens relative to the foreign currency, the foreign currency increases in value. If the U.S. dollar gets stronger, the foreign investment decreases in value. One way to avoid this situation is to purchase financial futures that guarantee you a return if the value of the foreign currency decreases relative to the U.S. dollar.

Currency devaluation may be the biggest risk for international investing. Investing in a foreign equity from a country that has a strong currency is better than investing in a foreign equity that has promises of big gains but an unstable economy or a high likelihood of political upheaval.

Online ADR resources and research

The Internet can assist you in researching the company profiles of foreign companies and provide lists of companies that offer ADRs. Here are several examples of what you can find online:

- **ADR.com** (www.adr.com) shows investors the benefits, definitions, and mechanics of ADRs and offers market commentary, information about top-performing ADRs, and what's new in ADRs. Receive market commentary, news, and analyses by Thomas Financial, as well as weekly publications covering international investing news and trends. Discover JPMorgan white papers on issues impacting the ADR market. For in-depth company information, order annual reports of selected companies at no charge. The site even offers a handy portfolio tool to track and build your ADR portfolio.

- **Citibank ADR Services** (wwss.citissb.com/adr/www) is a wonderful source for ADRs listed in the United States. You find investor and broker information, FAQs, and a short tutorial about purchasing ADRs and how you can purchase ADRs at Citibank. You can view the directory online or download the directory as an Excel spreadsheet.

- **Investor Relations Asia Pacific** (www.irasia.com) has a search engine that makes finding Asian ADRs for Australia, Hong Kong, Malaysia, Singapore, and Thailand easy. More than 2,500 companies are listed in this geographic area, searchable by symbol, name, country, and industry. Listed companies provide company profiles, links to corporate home pages, contact information, and so on. You find earnings releases and important announcements, and don't forget to sign up for free e-mail alerts for earnings reports, important announcements, and more.

- **The Bank of New York** (www.adrbny.com) provides a complete listing of all ADRs, including issuer name, exchange, ticker symbol, ratio, and effective date of issue. The list is available alphabetically, geographically, and by industry classification. You can view the directory online or download the directory as an Excel spreadsheet. You can search ADRs by industry, country, and region, and you can set up an ADR watchlist. Discover ADR analytics of performance, corporate actions, dividends, and distributions, as well as ADR publications, education, utilities, and references to brokers. To keep informed, sign up for the free ADR e-newsletter.

Indirect Foreign Investing Is a Great Approach

ADRs are a great approach to directly purchasing foreign investments, but they have one drawback: Many ADRs aren't available for the majority of foreign corporations. If you're like many individual investors who want to participate in foreign markets, check out international mutual funds. The advantage of mutual funds is the ability to vary your foreign investments and professional management so that you don't have to hassle with the many administrative and legal barriers to online international investing.

As with all investments, you want to look beyond this quarter's earnings. Check the company's profits relative to competitors and to industry standards. Find out whether the company's market share is dominant and growing.

Diversification through foreign funds

You can choose from many types of foreign funds to achieve the type of diversification, as well as professional management, that you want. Foreign fund managers are veterans in investing overseas and are prepared to handle the administrative problems that you, as an individual investor, don't have the time or expertise to deal with. Keep in mind that these managers can't guarantee you supernormal returns, but they can assist you in avoiding investing blunders or costly mistakes.

Foreign mutual funds, like domestic mutual funds, can be either closed-end or open-end funds, as well as load or no-load. For information about the limitations and regulations surrounding the different types of funds, see Chapter 6. Keep in mind that like open-end funds, the portfolios of international closed-end mutual funds can be equities, bonds, convertibles, or any combination of these securities. The holdings of the closed-end mutual funds can be geared toward income, capital gains, or a combination of these goals. For example, Korea Fund specializes in the stocks of Korean companies. In contrast, ASA Limited, another international closed-end mutual fund, specializes in the stocks of South African companies involved in gold mining.

Over the years, the mutual fund industry has made investing in foreign funds easy for American investors by establishing funds whose policies mandate investing in the five specific areas that are listed below. Additionally, mutual fund companies may select foreign companies that are growing quickly or are value stocks, which money managers hope will rebound.

- ✔ **Regional funds** focus on a certain geographic area. Frequently, these areas are Europe, Latin America, and the Pacific Basin. The prices of these funds tend to be more volatile than funds that cover a broader area and are more diversified.

- ✔ **Single-country funds** are limited to just one country. The fund may include stocks, bonds, and other types of investments. Because of their narrow focus, these funds tend to be risky.

- **Emerging-market funds** invest in countries that are moving from an agricultural to an industrial economy or from a government-controlled economy to a free enterprise economy. These funds frequently offer more risk than funds from developed countries.

- **Global funds** are often a mix of U.S. and foreign equities and are usually geared toward long-term growth.

- **International funds** concentrate on equities that are outside the United States and don't include any domestic securities.

Global funds invest in companies wherever they're located, including the United States. International funds focus solely on companies outside the United States. If you don't have lots of U.S. investments, a global fund may be the way to go. On the other hand, if you already have many U.S. stocks or mutual funds, you may discover that an international fund better meets your requirements for diversification.

Buying shares in multinational companies

Many large U.S. corporations are multinational companies with assets and operations spread throughout the world. Purchasing shares in these companies is an easy way to indirectly participate in the international marketplace. However, some analysts warn that investing in multinationals doesn't provide the investment benefits that individual investors are seeking because the stock prices of multinational companies tend to move in the same direction as their own country's financial markets.

Investing in international securities is a long-term commitment. Plan on at least a five-year time horizon for your investment. International markets can be more volatile than U.S. markets. Therefore, a long-term commitment and the self-discipline to stay the course are essential to your financial well-being.

Finding International Mutual Funds Online

Investments in international mutual funds enable investors to diversify their portfolios beyond the usual choices. Foreign markets are often influenced by different factors from those that affect domestic markets. Investing in international mutual funds is one way investors can take advantage of international opportunities without having to become specialists in international securities.

Here are a few examples of online sources for international mutual fund information:

- **EmergingPortfolio.com** (`www.emergingportfolio.com`) tracks equity and bond fund flows, cross-border capital flows, country and sector allocations, and company holdings data from its universe of 7,000 international, emerging markets, and U.S. funds. You can subscribe to a wide variety of products and services. Check out product and service samples online. Call 1-617-864-4999 ext. 26 for details about prices.

- **ETF Connect** (`www.etfconnect.com/select/cef/global.asp`) covers daily pricing, includes a fund search engine, and offers fund sponsor information, a portfolio tracker tool, and industry links and news for more than 600 funds — including ETFs (exchange-traded funds), country, municipal, fixed-income, and preferred funds. The education center is very helpful.

- **Morningstar.com** (`www.morningstar.com`) provides an easy way to select international stock funds. At the home page, click Funds and then click International Investing in the left margin. The International Fund Center appears and includes feature articles, investment ideas, fund comparison tools, fund analyst picks, and more.

- **Site-By-Site!** (`www.site-by-site.com`) provides closed-end fund profiles and articles, key decision-making performance information on the entire universe of closed-end funds, comparisons of this week's current data to historical averages, and potential buy and sell opportunities. This site also offers information on open-ended mutual funds, divided into regions and countries.

- **Standard & Poor's Fund Services** (`www.funds-sp.com/win/en/Index.jsp`) monitors more than 38,000 international funds on a daily, weekly, and monthly basis. The database is intuitive, and the search results are easy to understand. When you go to its Web site, the S & P registration page appears. Without registering, you can view the latest fund news, up-to-date fund management ratings, and fund databases showing the latest performance figures. With your free registration, you have access to in-depth fund management ratings analysis, fund news, free access to one of S & P's 23 databases for all sectors, and fund and management group fact sheets. S & P offers both pay-per-view tools and annual subscriptions to gold, silver, and bronze databases, which offer still more useful investment tools.

Chapter 15

Looking for the Next Big Thing: IPOs, DPOs, and DRIPs

In This Chapter

▶ Evaluating initial public offerings (IPOs)

▶ Getting in early with direct public offerings (DPOs)

▶ Bypassing broker fees to buy shares directly from the company (DPPs)

▶ Using dividend reinvestment plans (DRIPs) to increase your personal wealth

*E*veryone has heard stories about someone who got rich by purchasing the right stock at the right time. Looking back at these stories, the type of stock these individuals usually purchased was an initial public offering — called an IPO for short. In this chapter, I show how you can evaluate these types of stocks, determine what their limitations are, locate online sources of IPO news and research, and know which brokers specialize in IPOs or the mutual funds that include this type of financial asset.

An even grander opportunity is a direct public offering, or DPO. Even more speculative than IPOs, shares in these companies are comparable to investments by venture capitalists. In this chapter, I explain the limitations of DPOs, how to purchase DPOs, and where to find online DPO research and information. For frugal investors that don't want to pay brokerage commissions, I show you how you can use direct purchase plans (DPPs) to purchase shares directly from the companies that interest you, in addition to how you can participate in dividend reinvestment plans (DRIPs).

Looking for Investment Opportunities: IPOs

The much-anticipated IPO of Google, likely the most popular search engine on the Internet, celebrated the return of individual investors to the IPO market. Moreover, the excitement surrounding the Google IPO topped off a five-year recovery of the IPO market. For example, IPOs increased in 2004 by 30 percent and raised over $43 billion. To the surprise of many experts and individual investors, IPOs for the Internet, energy, and cyclical products and services had the strongest returns. Overall, the 2004 IPO market commemorated four consecutive years of positive IPO returns. This is a real feat because none of the major indices, such as the S & P 500 or the Dow Jones Industrial Averages, can claim the same success.

When a company sells stock that trades publicly for the first time, that event is called an *initial public offering* (IPO). The United States market averages between 250 and 275 IPOs per year. These IPO company issuers sell shares to an underwriter. The underwriter, in turn, resells shares to investors at a prearranged offering price. Underwriters often underprice issues by 5 to 10 percent to ensure adequate demand. Generally, shares begin trading immediately on a stock exchange or *over the counter* through the NASDAQ stock market. About one week after issue, due to market efficiency, the excess returns due to the initial discount disappearing. This scenario indicates that the best time to purchase an IPO is on initial distribution from the underwriting syndicate (which includes investment bankers, dealers, and brokers).

Every year, development companies and companies just starting to generate revenues seek additional capital for business expansions. Investors purchase shares so that they can reap the short-term rewards of price swings or share in the long-term prosperity of getting in early on a new investment opportunity.

The investment in an IPO is speculative. These companies often have no proven strategies for success and no track record of marketing success or corporate earnings. Many of these companies crash and burn, and only a few endure to become big-time financial success stories. Keep in mind that for every Intel or Microsoft, 50 companies go bankrupt. (Studies show that about 50 percent of IPO firms are in business five years after their initial offerings.) In other words, the success rate of IPOs is one out of every two.

Understanding the basics of IPOs, performing fundamental research, and knowing how to be an early shareholder can increase your chances of success. Ameritrade (www.ameritrade.com/education/html/encyclopedia/tutorial1/t1_s10.html) provides education about the basics of IPOs. Click the hyperlinks for a short investor tutorial about IPO offerings and investing strategies.

Getting the scoop on IPOs

The following guidelines may help you select a winner out of the thousands of companies that have initial public offerings each year:

- **Read the prospectus.**

  Read the preliminary prospectus to find out about the company's expected growth. The *red herring* (a preliminary prospectus that provides information but isn't an offer to sell the security and doesn't include any offering prices) includes a description of the issuer's business, the names and addresses of key corporate officers, the ownership amounts of the key officers, any litigation problems, the company's current capitalization, and how the company plans to use the new funds from the offering.

- **Perform fundamental analysis.**

  Evaluate the company's financial performance by using fundamental analysis, just like you would for any other stock.

  Fundamental analysis is a form of security valuation that seeks to determine the intrinsic value of a stock based on the stock's underlying economics. You then compare the intrinsic value and the asking price. For more details about how to perform a fundamental analysis, see Chapter 11.

- **Check out the company's management.**

  Examine the backgrounds of the firm's senior managers. What is their executive management experience and education? Do they have work experience in their current jobs?

- **Read the mission statement.**

  Investigate the firm's strategy. Is it realistic? How large is the company's market? Who is the competition? If the company plans to gain less than 25 percent of the total market, the firm may not be a long-term success.

- **Investigate the planned use of funds.**

  Determine why raising a certain amount of capital is so critical to the company's success. If the money is used to pay debt, the company might be headed for problems; using the money for expansion is a positive sign.

- **Compare IPO prices.**

  Compare expected IPO prices in the red herring with the final prospectus. If the price is higher in the later prospectus, the underwriters are enthusiastic about the offering. Lower prices indicate a lack of interest by the investment community.

✔ **Determine whether it's your kind of company.**

Decide whether you want to own stock in the company you're researching. Maybe it's a great financial opportunity, but you have reservations about the product or service. (For example, do you really want to be part owner in a company that kills frogs?)

✔ **Estimate your planned holding period.**

Decide how long you plan to keep the shares. If the IPO is going to be successful, it will be a better long-term investment than short-term investment because IPO stock prices tend to move up or down with the stock market.

For more information on IPOs, see `www.invest-faq.com/articles/ stock-ipo.html` for an article that includes educational materials about IPOs, the mechanics of IPO offerings, the underwriting process, and IPOs in the real world.

Understanding the limitations of IPOs

If your goal is to create massive wealth or to enjoy a comfortable lifestyle, making the most of your money takes time and vigilance. You always need to be on the lookout for new opportunities and new ways to invest your savings. To many online investors, an IPO may seem like the perfect way to get in on the ground floor of a great opportunity for high-flying returns. If the IPO you select is going to be a good investment, then with luck, it could pay off over the long term. Your investment will grow as the company expands and becomes profitable. But a high level of risk exists. IPOs are speculative investments. Many promising firms go bust. You need to consider the limitations of IPOs. For example:

✔ **Many IPOs lose much of their value after the first day of trading.**

✔ **Many positive-looking IPOs are offered only to the "best" clients of large brokerage firms, pension plans, and institutions.** However, you can always gain access to an IPO when it starts trading on the secondary market. (The stock begins trading on the secondary market when an investor purchases it from the investment-banking firm in the primary market and begins to sell it on a stock exchange.) The performances of these stocks are similar to the performances of small cap stocks and are very volatile.

✔ **After three to six months, IPOs may underperform some small cap stocks.** The source of this problem may be employees selling their shares and forcing the stock price to decline.

✔ **After three to six months, the popularity of a strong IPO often fades.**

A sure-fire way of owning IPOs

Most IPOs go to large institutional buyers, such as banks, pension funds, and mutual funds. Frequently, traditional brokerages receive a few shares for affluent or active investors. To get on the preferred customer list, an IPO investor might need more than $100,000 invested in his or her trading account. Some brokerages require balances as high as $1 million. One way for the do-it-yourself online investor to catch a potential IPO winner is to tap into the up-to-the-minute IPO information that's available on the Internet. A fail-safe approach to getting in on the IPO of your choice is to purchase shares in a mutual fund that has already purchased shares of the IPO. Several large mutual funds include IPOs. However, participation in IPOs shouldn't be the only reason you purchase a mutual fund. Before making your investment decision, you still need to carefully read the fund's prospectus and compare it with other mutual funds and your overall financial objectives.

Locating IPO online super-sites

Over the last several years, the number of IPO super-sites has decreased. Many of the remaining Web sites now charge for access to content. Some of the content on one Web site may be identical to another IPO super-site. However, the subscription rate for one Web site may be three to four times higher than for another. Therefore, it's important to shop for the IPO super-site that provides the content that best matches your interests and your pocketbook.

The following IPO super-sites are good examples of what you can find on the Internet. Each IPO super-site offers online investors convenient one-stop shopping and is loaded with a wide variety of amenities. Investors frequently discover that much of the cutting-edge IPO information they find is geared toward their unique investor strategies. Therefore, checking out and subscribing to an IPO super-site, such as one of the following, may well be worth your time and money.

- **EDGAR Online's IPO Express** (ipoportal.edgar-online.com/ipo/home.asp) offers *Edgar Online Access* for $58.95 per quarter. This subscription includes 25 SEC EDGAR filings per month, IPO data, 25 portfolio-based watchlist tools with real-time e-mail notifications of new filings, and 25 saved searches. Tools include financial statement downloads that you can export to Excel, document formatting, section printing, company profiles, full text search, quick search, and people search.

- **Edgar Online Pro** (www.edgar-online.com/products/edgarpro.aspx) is $100 per month (billable monthly, quarterly, or annually). Discover real-time and historical SEC filings and take advantage of search tools and alert options using more than 15 criteria, as well as standardized financial data with five years of history and 75 data elements, institutional and insider trading, and position history, representing 2,200 institutional holders. In addition to company profiles displaying performance, liquidity, profitability, financials and more, this site has carried new and supplemental public offerings since 1997. There's also Word and Excel downloading.

✔ **Hoover's IPO Central** (`www.hoovers.com/global/ipoc/index.xhtml`) gives you all the important facts about a new issue on one Web page. IPO Central has the latest filings, pricings, views of IPOs, IPO scorecards and statistics, and a handy beginner's guide. Call (toll free) 866-328-2397 for subscription prices.

✔ **IPOhome** (`www.ipohome.com`), with your free registration, offers Hot and Cold IPO rankings, past IPO picks, chats, polls, and learning tools for new IPO investors. Market content includes calendars, news and views, pricings, rankings, IPO data, and information about underwriters. Reports by IPOhome analysts are $60 each. IPOhome also promotes its IPO Plus aftermarket mutual fund, a mutual fund that invests at least 80 percent of its assets into IPOs. The minimum initial investment is $5,000 for investing accounts and $2,500 for IRA accounts.

✔ **IPO Monitor** (`www.ipomonitor.com`) offers free information on recent IPO events. Subscribers have access to IPO news delivered through e-mail, a searchable IPO database, company profiles, information about the IPO market, special reports, and tools. Information is available online or via e-mail to subscribers. Subscriptions are $29 per month or $290 per year.

Mining the Internet for valuable IPO information

You can access various Internet sources for IPO-related news and information. A few of these sources follow companies from the initial filing to their performances after the issues become public. Many of these sites provide news, commentary, and quotes. Other information includes recent Securities and Exchange Commission (SEC) filings, scheduled pricing, and registration information. Additionally, some sites include statistics on aftermarket performance, IPO ratings, and company performance data.

The following Web sites provide IPO news:

✔ **CNN/Money** (`money.cnn.com/news/deals`) offers a useful mergers and acquisitions databank.

✔ **IPO Daily Report** (`cbs.marketwatch.com/news/ipo`) offers daily IPO news and tools from CBS MarketWatch. You can find listings of new filings, a calendar, aftermarket reports, IPO performance news, and more.

✔ **Yahoo! IPO News** (`biz.yahoo.com/reports/ipo.html`) offers IPO news from Yahoo!, the topic-specific search engine that has expanded into different areas.

The following Web sites provide IPO filings:

- **IPO Data Systems** (www.ipodata.com) is a subscription service that includes an IPO calendar, company profiles, listings of top performers, IPOs by underwriter, and online information about IPOs. At the time of this writing, fees are $15 per month, $30 per quarter, or $100 per year.

- **NASDAQ** (www.nasdaq.com/reference/IPOs.stm) lists recent IPO filings with ticker symbols, pricings, share information, a listing of IPO ceremony events, and IPO summaries. At the NASDAQ home page, click IPOs.

The following Web sites provide online IPO pricing and IPO newsletters:

- **123Jump IPO Center** (www.123jump.com) supplies a large collection of summary IPO profiles and performance statistics. Discover issue data, delayed quotes, news, and an earnings archive. For $99 per year, you can subscribe to John Fitzgibbon's weekly e-mail IPO newsletter, which includes IPO comparisons, statistics, and commentary.

- **IPO Data Systems** (www.ipodata.com) offers free daily headlines and an IPO Pipeline that's linked to the EDGAR database. Subscriptions for full access to the Web site are $15 per month, $30 per quarter, or $100 per year. Content includes IPO underwriter listings, top 25 and bottom 25 weekly IPO price performers, top 25 IPO offerings by first trade, IPO industry reports, all IPO offerings and filings reports, and so on.

- **TechWeb News: High-Tech IPO News** (www.techweb.com) offers a free e-mail newsletter that focuses on the high-tech sector and tracks IPO news, technologies, and industry.

Finding online brokers that offer IPOs

After researching IPOs, you might decide that you want a broker who specializes in this type of security. The Internet can assist you in locating the right broker. Here are a few examples:

- **Charles Schwab** (www.schwab.com) provides its best customers (those with substantial assets in their trading accounts — usually $100,000 or more) with offerings underwritten by Credit Suisse, First Boston, Hambrecht & Ouist, and J.P. Morgan Securities, Inc.

- **Harris***direct* (www.harrisdirect.com) offers IPO shares to online Preferred customers ($100,000 or more in assets in Harris*direct* accounts) and Select customers ($1 million or more in assets in Harris*direct* accounts).

   ✔ **E*TRADE Financial** (www.etrade.com) offers a listing of current IPO offerings and filings. You can easily check all the IPOs the brokerage has participated in. E*TRADE offers express links to bid history, current offerings, recent filings, and so on. Minimum initial deposit to open an account is $1,000.

   ✔ **WR Hambrecht + Co** (www.wrhambrecht.com/ind/index.html) is a brokerage firm that provides high-quality IPO research, analysis, and market data. One of the unique features of WR Hambrecht + Co is its OpenIPO auction, which allows individuals and institutional investors to bid online for shares of an IPO. Additionally, investors can also bid on IPOs in mutual funds. Minimum initial deposit is $2,000 for an individual investor account.

The Internet and your IPO timetable

When it comes to purchasing an IPO, it's important to do the right thing at the right time. In other words, you need to finish all your homework before you make your move. Table 15-1 shows some of the activities investors engage in before purchasing shares in an IPO. The first column of Table 15-1 illustrates the steps of purchasing IPO shares. The second column shows the timing of your IPO purchase. The third column of Table 15-1 illustrates the types of actions you have to take to ensure that you get the IPO shares you desire. I include examples of Web sites that can provide you with the resources and tools you need to complete the necessary actions to make your ownership of an IPO a reality.

Google auctions its IPO

In 2004, search engine behemoth Google completed its highly anticipated IPO. Traditionally, when companies go public, only large financial institutions and affluent investors have access to new shares. Google wanted to give everyone a chance to purchase shares and decided to auction shares to individual investors. Unfortunately, due to individual investors being wary of the IPO market and the complex auction process, the Google shares didn't sell well. In the end, the IPO was done more or less the old-fashioned way:

That is, pricing shares at a 30-percent discount to their original price range as demanded by several large institutional investors such as Fidelity. During this time period, media attention about the IPO, discounted pricing, and positive analyst reports resulted in Google shares being bid up to 100 percent of their initial price. For Google, auctioning the IPO meant not receiving the full amount of capitalization it expected and more shares going to big institutional investors than it intended.

Table 15-1	Your Checklist for Participating in an IPO	
Activity	*Timing*	*Action*
Review online brokerages	ASAP	Open one or two online brokerage accounts that handle IPOs. Example: WR Hambrecht + Co (www.wrhambrecht.com)
Review online underwriter directories	ASAP	Bookmark several underwriter directories or set up e-mail alerts for new IPOs that meet your investment criteria. Example: IPOhome (www.ipohome.com)
Search online for pending IPOs managed by a broker	Weekly	Check the latest IPO filings and IPO calendars. Example: IPO Monitor (www.ipo monitor.com)
Create an IPO investment candidate list	Once a month before IPO	Examine the IPO profiles of your broker's upcoming IPOs. Screen IPOs to create a short list. Analyze and track potential investment candidates. Example: NASDAQ (www.nasdaq.com/reference/ipos.stm)
Complete your research	Two weeks before IPO	Analyze prospectus. Example: SEC EDGAR (www.sec.gov/edgar/searchedgar/webusers.htm)
Check calendars for deal timing.		Example: IPO Daily Report (cbs.marketwatch.com/news/ipo)
Contact your broker	When IPO starts trading	Check for pricing by referring to breaking news. Example: Yahoo! IPO News (biz.yahoo.com/reports/ipo.html) Confirm you received your shares. Example: E*TRADE Financial (www.etrade.com)

Be Your Own Broker with Direct Public Offerings (DPOs)

Historically, small companies have had a difficult time finding capital to expand their businesses. Traditional lenders are frequently unwilling to take risks with untried companies. Venture capitalists negotiate tough deals that often force company founders out of key management roles. And traditional IPOs require a minimum of $15 million in annual revenue.

If you take an initial public offering (IPO) and cut out the underwriter, what you have left is a *direct public offering* (DPO). Direct public offerings (DPOs) are defined as the direct sale of shares in a company to individual investors. DPOs have been around for more than 20 years. For example, Ben & Jerry's used a DPO to raise capital for the ice cream company. However, the offering was limited to investors from its home state of Vermont.

In October 1995, the SEC fueled DPOs with a ruling that makes electronic delivery of a prospectus acceptable. Consequently, companies can raise needed capital by selling their shares directly to the public via the Internet. These DPOs have the following advantages for small companies:

- **Cost and time savings:** The company saves thousands of dollars in underwriting expenses.

- **Regulation of Internet IPOs:** Issuers can file faster, turnaround times are quicker, filing is less expensive, the sales process carries fewer restrictions, and issuers can announce planned offerings.

- **Management remains focused:** Management isn't drawn away from the company's day-to-day business needs and customers.

- **Investors can get in really early:** Investors have access to venture capital types of investments.

- **No broker commissions:** Investors don't have to pay high broker commissions.

Recognizing the limitations of DPOs

Many companies are offering DPOs instead of initial public offerings (IPOs). For many online investors, a DPO is the best way to get in on the ground floor and share in a company's success. Investors can purchase shares directly from the companies that they want to be part owners of. However, DPOs have some limitations:

✔ **Blue sky laws:** Issuing companies must be registered with the SEC and in the states in which they offer securities, but new legislation allows companies to use the Internet to present direct public offerings. This new legislation is inconsistent with regulations passed in 1911. The 1911 rule requires issuers to register in the states in which they offer stocks, but the Internet has no boundaries and thus offers worldwide distribution of stock offerings. Does this mean that issuers have to register in each state that uses the Internet? Some issuers register in all 50 states before offering shares. However, one state, Pennsylvania, only requires companies to clearly indicate where they're registered and who may purchase securities.

✔ **Fraud and abuse:** Stock issues are highly regulated, but the Internet is an unregulated environment. The enforcement of registration issues on the Internet is keeping the SEC more than busy. The result may be fraudulent solicitations on the Internet.

Buying DPOs

DPO issues often open in a blaze of glory due to strong public interest. Then the share prices settle down to a consistent trading range. During the stock's initial period of volatility, the stock price may double or triple. Cashing in at this point can be very profitable and may compensate you for earlier investment mistakes.

DPOs are speculative and definitely for aggressive investors. In other words, if you can't afford to lose all your investment, you shouldn't be in this market. That said, even the most aggressive investors should invest only between 5 and 10 percent of their total portfolio in this type of financial asset.

To purchase shares, obtain a subscription agreement for the DPO. The subscription agreements are usually included in the last page of the prospectus. If you can't find the form, request one by e-mail or through the U.S. mail. Send the completed agreement and a check for the appropriate amount to the company. The company sends a confirmation letter within five days and the stock certificate within 30 days. (I suggest making a duplicate copy of your check and subscription agreement for your records and sending the originals by registered mail.)

The following list offers some additional sources of DPO information:

✔ **SCOR Report** (www.scor-report.com) offers answers for small-business managers; for individuals who are considering starting businesses, SCOR Report asks the questions they should answer before quitting their day jobs. Investors can use this information to determine whether a DPO has covered all the bases and is a viable investment candidate.

✔ **Direct Public Offering** (www.gopublictoday.com/financing/financing-types-dpo.php) is a Web site sponsored by registered investment advisors. You can find a short but informative tutorial about DPOs here.

✔ **Mellon Investor Services** (www.chasemellon.com) offers InvestDirect Search, an easy-to-use search engine that allows you to search through a list of several thousand plans. With InvestDirect, you can search for and compare DPOs or DRIPs (direct reinvestment plans) and link to company Web sites. You can review plan brochures, prospectuses, and link to research Web sites. The best part of InvestDirect is that you can use InvestDirect Wizard and immediately enroll in a plan. The minimum initial price per plan varies. At the home page, click For Investors and then click Investment Plans.

Small, unproven firms carry very high risks. You should do lots of homework before you invest in companies that big banks avoid.

Buying Stock in a Direct Purchase Plan (DPP)

In the past, utilities were the main companies with direct purchase plans (DPPs). In 1996, 150 companies sold their stock directly to the public. In 1997, more than 300 companies offered DPPs. At this time, more than 3,500 companies sell their stock directly to the public.

About one million individuals purchase stocks directly. Minimum investments can be as small as $50 a month. Some of the DPPs include dividend reinvestment plans (DRIPs), tax-deferred IRA investments, and loans against stock holdings. A few companies even sell shares below market price.

DPPs are different from DPOs because the stock being offered is from established publicly traded companies with long track records of performance. Where most people get confused is in defining the difference between DPPs and dividend reinvestment plans (DRIPs). DRIPs allow existing shareholders to purchase additional shares without a broker. Direct Stock Purchase Plans (DPPs) differ from DRIPs because you don't already have to be a shareholder to purchase shares.

Sometimes, direct purchase plans (DPPs) are called *no-load* stock plans. These plans allow you to join direct purchase plans (which include dividend reinvestment features) without first purchasing shares through a broker. Some corporations with DPPs sell shares only to corporate customers, and others are open to all investors. The Internet provides many sources for DPP information and education:

- ✔ **American Stock Transfer & Trust Company** (www.investpower.com) allows you to search over 3,500 DPP plans by entering the ticker symbol or company name. You can search an alphabetical listing of direct purchase plans and employee stock purchase plans, check out plans ranked by investment amount, and research a company's financial and market performance. You can purchase fractional shares to determine the dollar amount you want to invest. To purchase shares, you determine the dollar amount of funds you want deducted from your checking account as a lump sum or automatic monthly deduction. The site offers online retrieval of your account information 24 hours a day, 7 days a week. Fees for purchasing DPPs through American Stock Transfer & Trust Company start at $2.60.

- ✔ **MyStockFund** (www.mystockfund.com) integrates dollar-cost averaging (see the sidebar "The benefits of dollar-cost averaging," later in this chapter, for more information) and dividend reinvestment programs (DRIPs) into an easy-to-use online plan that encourages individual investors to build wealth over time. Three cost-effective plans are available. The basic plan is $5.98 per month and includes two purchases. The Flex plan is $59.99 per year and offers unlimited purchases for $1.99 per purchase. The Diversified plan is $39.99 per year and offers unlimited purchased for 99 cents each.

- ✔ **NetstockDirect** (www.netstockdirect.com), shown in Figure 15-1, allows investors to purchase common stock without a broker. You can research nearly 1,400 companies, buy fractions of stocks by investing a specified dollar amount, invest as often you want, and enroll online. Search stock plans by company name or symbol. Find stock plans for Forbes 500 and Fortune 500 companies, stocks that are available for an initial investment of $100 or less, and plans with no purchase fees. Invest directly in mutual funds as a single investment amount, or set up an automatic monthly investment plan. Learn about different mutual funds by reading the online prospectus, linking to market information, or ordering materials for U.S. mail delivery. Each plan has its own requirements, such as a minimum purchase amount or initial minimum deposit, in addition to possible enrollment fees, automatic investment fees, optional cash purchase fees, commissions on sales, and so on.

The benefits of dollar-cost averaging

Like many mutual funds, DDPs and DRIPs offer automatic investment plans (AIPs) that allow you to take advantage of *dollar-cost averaging*. Dollar-cost averaging is a method of putting equal dollar amounts into an investment at regular intervals, regardless of that investment's performance. Dollar-cost averaging buys more shares when prices are low and less shares when prices are high. The result is that you purchase more shares at low prices than shares at high prices. In other words, dollar-cost averaging guarantees that you follow the investor's maxim of "buy low and sell high."

Let's say, for example, that you regularly invest $100 a month in your DPP plan. In January, the price is $10 per share, including any miscellaneous fees, so you buy 10 shares. By February, the price has increased to $12 a share, so your $100 buys 8.33 shares. In March, the price rises to 15 per share, and your $100 buys 6.67 shares. You now own 25 shares, and your $300 investment is now worth $375.

Of course, if you had invested all your $300 in January when the shares were at their lowest, your investment would be worth $450 when shares hit their highest price of $15 in March. What would have happen if the market declined? Let's say that you purchased 20 shares at $15 in January for a total of $300. If prices slide to $10 in March, your investment would be worth $200, a loss of $100. What if the share prices were reversed, and you used dollar-cost averaging? Your investment would be worth $250 in March. This $50 loss is much less than the $100 loss you would have experienced if you invested your $300 in January.

To sum it up, dollar-cost averaging doesn't guarantee that you'll make more money, and it's not a guarantee that you won't lose money, but it does ensure that you don't buy only at the top or only at the bottom of the market.

Ford, IBM, British Telecommunications, and many other companies have direct purchase plans (DPPs). All you have to do is contact the firm via the Internet, telephone, or U.S. mail. Direct your request to the Investor Relations Department and ask whether the company has a direct purchase plan and, if so, ask for an application. Complete the application form and include a check for your initial investment. Make a copy of these items for your records. Send the signed application and check to the company by registered mail.

In more than half of the DPPs, the minimum investment is $250 or less and as little as $10 thereafter. The plans are designed for long-term investors who plan to hold their shares for at least three to five years. Processing your order is slower than going through a broker; it usually takes about a week. You can make subsequent stock purchases with cash payments and reinvested dividends.

Purchasing DPPs is proof that there's no such thing as a free lunch; these so-called no-load stocks aren't cost-free. You still have to pay a few fees. You often pay a one-time enrollment fee of $5 to $15, a per-transaction fee of up to $10 plus $0.01 to $0.10 per share, and higher fees when you sell. Some plans charge an annual account management fee. To reinvest your dividend, you may have to pay up to $5 per quarter.

When comparing the fees of some DPPs with the low rates that online brokers charge (between $10 and $30 per transaction), you don't appear to be saving much by buying shares directly from the company. However, the SEC is continuing to relax its regulations about DPPs. Soon, companies will be able to advertise their programs at their Web sites. As the market for DPPs heats up, fees are likely to decrease, and you may be able to charge your DPP purchase to your credit card via the Internet.

A great place to start is with ShareBuilder (www.sharebuilder.com), shown in Figure 15-2. ShareBuilder specializes in dollar-based automatic investment accounts for small investors who want to avoid high brokerage fees. For example, popular investments such as Microsoft and Cisco don't have direct stock purchase plans, so ShareBuilder creates its own direct stock plans for these companies and similar companies. For automatic purchases, costs are $4 per recurring transaction, or you can pay $12 per month and purchase as many stocks as you like for a diversified portfolio. Additionally, ShareBuilder offers real-time trades for $15.95 per transaction.

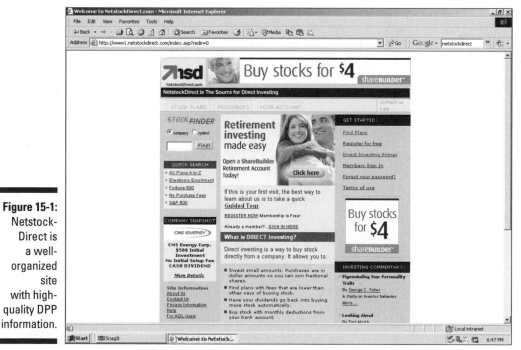

Figure 15-1:
Netstock-Direct is a well-organized site with high-quality DPP information.

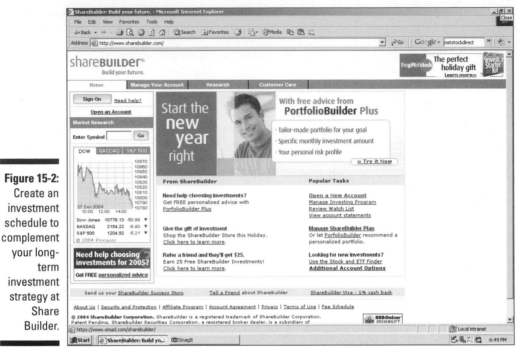

Figure 15-2:
Create an investment schedule to complement your long-term investment strategy at Share Builder.

Copyright ©2002 Netstock Corporation, ShareBuilder is a registered trademark of Netstock Corporation. Patent Pending.

Profiting with Dividend Reinvestment Plans (DRIPs)

Dividend reinvestment plans (DRIPs) are sometimes called *shareholder investment programs* (SIPs). These plans are an easy, low-cost way to purchase stocks and reinvest your dividend income. About 1,000 companies and closed-end mutual funds sponsor DRIPs.

Most plans require you to purchase your first share through a broker, the National Association of Investors Corporation (NAIC) buying club, or some other method. A share purchased in a DRIP is like any other stock share. You have voting rights and stock splits, and your uninvested dividends are taxed when you sell your shares.

Shares must be registered in your name. You can purchase subsequent shares directly from the company, often at discounted prices and with no broker commissions. Most plans allow investors to make voluntary payments to the DRIP to purchase more shares. In other words, the advantages of DRIPs include the following:

- ✔ No brokerage commissions and few fees for purchasing stock through the DRIP.

- ✔ Frequent discounts of 3 to 5 percent off the current stock price.

- ✔ Optional cash payment plans (OCPs). Usually after the first dividend has been reinvested, the investor can send voluntary cash payments directly to the company to purchase more shares. Amounts can be as small as $10 to $25. (This option enables investors to own fractions of stocks.) For example, General Electric allows OCPs of $10 to $10,000 every month.

Many of the nation's premier corporations have DRIPs, including most of the companies in the Dow Jones Industrial Average. The InvestorGuide page on DRIPs and DPPs (www.investorguide.com/dripslist.html) has a public directory with links to the corporate home pages of many companies that have dividend reinvestment plans. For more information, contact each company you're interested in and ask for a DRIP prospectus. At the corporate home page, you can e-mail your request. If the company doesn't have a Web site, use the IRIN Annual Report Resource Center (www.irin.com) to locate the corporation's address and telephone number.

Additional features of DRIPs

One of the benefits of DRIPs is their (often free) certificate safekeeping service. This service eliminates the need to pay for a safe-deposit box and the possibility of your stock certificates becoming lost or stolen.

DRIPs often have gift-giving programs. For example, Texaco lets you open an investor services plan in another person's name, and the company provides you with a gift certificate to give to the recipient.

Not all DRIPs are alike

Each company has its own plan. With some firms, you can pay for additional shares with cash; some allow partial redemption of shares, and some have termination fees. However, the plan may purchase shares only once a month, and if you want to sell your shares, completing the transaction may take five to ten days.

Some plans allow you to buy shares one at a time. However, some companies have a minimum purchase amount. For example, Bristol-Myers Squibb requires a minimum purchase of 50 shares. Bristol-Myers Squibb also charges a fee of 4 percent of the dollar amount of dividends being reinvested (a maximum of $5 per share). In general, plans differ from one another in the following ways:

✔ Some companies allow (and some companies don't) the reinvestment of preferred dividends for common shares.

✔ Some companies allow partial reinvestment of dividends.

✔ The amount of optional cash payments (OCPs) varies from company to company.

✔ Fees for participating in the DRIP vary from company to company.

How to get your first DRIP share

Sometimes, getting started is the hardest part of investing. You have many ways of getting your first share for a DRIP. Here are some different approaches — one of these methods may be right for you:

✔ **Join a special investment club.** First Share Buying Club can assist you in getting your first share so that you can participate in a DRIP. Annual membership in First Share is $30 per year. Referral requests for current Portfolio Builder Companies (www.firstshare.com/Portfolio_ Builder_Companies.htm) are $5 per request; referral requests for all other companies in the First Share program are $10 per request. Selling members are usually charged a handling fee to cover their expenses (a typical fee is $7.50) in addition to the price of the share.

For individuals who don't want to join the club, you can buy one share in one company for a flat fee of $20. If you want to purchase more than one share, becoming a member is more cost-effective. You can request any number of shares in any number of companies. For more information, call 800-683-0743.

✔ **Share the cost with a friend.** You can use a buddy system to reduce the cost of purchasing your first share. You and a friend pay the brokerage to purchase two shares. Have both shares registered to one person and join the company's DRIP. After you've joined, transfer one share to your friend and split the cost of the fees.

✔ **Join the NAIC.** The National Association of Investors Corporation (NAIC) enrolls people in any of more than 100 DRIPs via its Low Cost Investment Plan. The NAIC enrolls its members in a company for a $7 per company fee. Membership in the NAIC is $50 for individuals. See the NAIC Web site at www.better-investing.org or telephone 801-583-6242 for details.

✔ **Use a deep-discount online broker:** Sometimes, the simplest way to purchase your first share is to go through a deep-discount broker. Online brokerage costs vary from $7 to $40. To participate in the DRIP, the stock must be registered in your name.

Selecting the right DRIP

DRIPs have many advantages, but you shouldn't let one characteristic be your sole criterion for purchasing a stock. Regardless of how attractive the DRIP is, you still need to make certain that the stock fits in with your overall investment strategy. In other words, don't select a stock just because it has a DRIP. Check out these sites for more information about dividend reinvestment plans:

✔ **DRIP Central** (www.dripcentral.com) offers DRIP information for beginning investors. The Web site provides links to useful online articles, newsletters, directories, and other DRIP Web sites.

✔ **DRIP Investor** (www.dripinvestor.com) offers suggested books, an investor glossary, and DRIP information. Subscriptions for the monthly Internet newsletter are $42 for six months and $69 for one year with a free one-month trial period.

✔ **NAIC Low Cost Plan Overview** (www.better-investing.org/about/lowcost/faq.html) offers a terrific plan to get your first share without going through a broker. For a one-time setup charge of $7 plus the price of one share of stock in any of the participating companies listed, you can get started with a new holding in your personal portfolio. However, transactions take between 8 to 12 weeks for investing in monthly companies. Companies investing quarterly require even more time.

Chapter 16

Taking the Option: Alternative Investing

In This Chapter

▶ Increasing your stock profits with options

▶ Recognizing the characteristics of calls and puts

▶ Locating online option quotes, news, calculators, and screens

▶ Avoiding mistakes by testing your strategies online

▶ Selecting the best option analysis software

*I*n this chapter, I explain how purchasing stock options can assist online investors to make money in a bear or bull market. Here, you find the basics of online investing in stock options, as well as discover which Internet sites provide guidance, news, quotes, online tools, and software to help you leverage your investment dollar. You can uncover which exchanges list stock options and also gain an understanding of the online brokerages that specialize in these types of transactions as well as the commissions that they charged.

Trading Stock Options

Suppose that a well-known novelist decides to let Hollywood make a movie based on one of her books. The novelist receives a payment from a Hollywood producer for the option of deciding within a specified time to make the movie. If the Hollywood producer decides to go ahead and make the movie, the novelist sells him the screen rights. If the Hollywood producer changes his mind, the novelist keeps the option payment and her novel.

Trading stock options is a similar transaction. Options are contracts between a buyer and a seller. These contracts represent the right of the investor to buy or sell shares of the stock that the shares represent, called the *underlying stock*. Contracts are usually for 100 shares and don't oblige the investor to purchase or sell shares of the underlying stock.

Types of option contracts

An *option* is a contract between a buyer and a seller. An option contract that gives the owner (holder) the right, if exercised, to buy or sell a security or index at a specific price, called the *strike price,* within a specific time period. Option contracts are generally available for one to nine months, although some longer-term options are available on selected securities. Each contract usually equals 100 shares of stock. Calls and puts are two types of options, and I explain them in the following sections.

Why buy stock options? Stock options enable investors to position them-selves for a big market move even when they don't know which way stock prices will move. For example, the cost of the *premium* (the amount paid for the option contract) is often less than what the investors would lose if they purchased shares that later suffered a steep price decrease.

Stock options enable large and small investors to *leverage* (the wherewithal to control large amounts of a financial asset with a somewhat small amount of capital.) their investment dollars. For example, a stock might increase by only 25 percent, but the investor receives a 100-percent return on his or her cash investment in the stock option contract. However, if the stock experi-ences a decrease or remains at the same price, the investor suffers a 100-percent loss of the premium paid for the stock option contract.

 Short rallies exist even in a down market. With options, investors can exer-cise an option during one of these peaks to gain short-term profits. If the rally doesn't materialize, the only loss the investor suffers is the cost of the pre-mium paid for the options contract.

Some large corporations, such as insurance companies, want to reduce their exposure to the market. They sell their options to offset losses incurred by their current stock holdings. Individual investors can limit the exposure of their personal portfolios (especially in a volatile market) in the same way.

Exercising your stock option

All stock options have exercising dates that are stated upon the option's introduction to the market. During this time, the same stock option can be bought and sold many times. To exercise the stock option, you can do one of three things:

- **Buy or sell the underlying shares of stock (exercise the option).** Shares purchased can be held for long-term gains. Shares sold realize an immediate capital gain.

- **Sell the option on the open market.** Profits from the sale of your option are automatically credited to your trading account and are taxable.

- **Let the option expire.** If the option expires, it loses all value.

Call options

A *call* is defined as the right to buy a specific number of shares at a specified price by a fixed date. If the stock is above the agreed-upon price by the fixed date, the investor wins — he bought the stock for less than what it's worth that day on the market. For example, you believe that IBM is underpriced. You purchase a 3-month call at $100 when the stock is selling at $90. The call options selling price is $3 per share, which is the premium. You purchase ten contracts (of 100 shares). You now control 1,000 shares. The total amount of the premium is $3,000 — that is

$3 (the option selling price) × 10 (contracts) × 100 (shares) = $3,000

One month later, IBM's shares are selling for $110. You can now either

- Exercise your option by purchasing 1,000 shares at $100 and then sell the shares at $110 for a profit of $10,000 less commission (the premium). Before taxes, you would net $7,000.

- Sell your call option, which is worth approximately $10,000.

Using call options has two advantages. First, you need less cash to control a large number of shares. As you can see in the preceding example, the purchase of the option was $3,000, and the cost of purchase of the shares is $90,000. Second, if the IBM stock price severely drops, an investor who owns the shares loses more than an investor who owns only the option.

Put options

A *put* option contract gives the holder the right, but not the obligation, to sell 100 shares of common stock at the strike price on or before the date of expiration. For example, thinking that IBM is way overpriced, you buy 10 IBM

February puts at $2 per contract. That is, you buy 10 contracts, and each contract represents 100 shares of stock, so you control 1,000 shares. Here is the game plan:

- ✔ **IBM is the stock.**
- ✔ **February is the month when your option expires.**

   Options always expire the third Friday of the month.

- ✔ **$100 is the strike price.**
- ✔ **$2 is the price you paid per contract.**

   Well, actually, $2 is the price per share that you control — so buying 10 of these puts (1,000 shares total) costs you $2,000 plus commission.

As the owner of this put, you have the right (but not the obligation) to sell up to 1,000 shares of IBM at a price of $100 per share anytime between the February day when you buy and the third Friday of February. Most people wouldn't do this because it's complicated. Selling the contracts that you've bought is easier (just as you would sell stock) and often just as profitable. Suppose that you pegged IBM correctly, and its price drops sharply. Say the value of your put increases from $2 to $10. You sell at $10 and make a huge profit.

In the event that you're wrong and IBM keeps going up, your option expires worthless. All you lose, however, is the $2,000 that you initially invested (and any brokerage fees). The appeal of options is that you have unlimited upside potential. You can make five or ten times your initial investment, but you can never lose more than what you initially invested.

Education and Data Sources

Many helpful Web sites can assist you in getting a grip on buying and selling options. Some of the better sites are sponsored by option brokerages and exchanges. Here are a few examples of what you can find online:

- ✔ **Chicago Board Options Exchange** (www.cboe.com) offers many educational resources. The Trading Tools section includes delayed quotes, charts, news, market data, company research from Zacks (www.my.zacks.com), and an options calendar.
- ✔ **Optionetics** (www.optionetics.com/education/trading.asp) offers help on topics such as understanding basic and advanced option concepts, option strategies, understanding investment proofs, and suggestions for selecting a broker.

✔ **Options Industry Council** (www.888options.com) is an industry trade group that supplies access to educational material and free educational seminars across the country. It offers 12 online training courses. The Options Industry Council (OIC) invites you to expand your options knowledge by attending one of its three free educational equity option seminars (LEAPS Seminar, Practical Applications Workshop, and Basic/Intermediate Seminar). Exchange professionals teach the OIC seminars, which take place from 6 to 9 p.m. Check the Web site to find out when a seminar will be held in your area.

Online sources for option quotes

To make intelligent investment decisions about your stock options, you need the latest stock quotes. (It's the only way to tell whether you're making money or you're out of the game.) The following Internet sites provide real-time and delayed option quotes:

✔ **INO.com** (quotes.ino.com) features information on stocks, options, futures, and currency, as well as intraday (delayed) daily and weekly charts.

✔ **Chicago Board Options Exchange** (www.cboe.com/delayedquote/quoteqable.aspx) offers delayed quotes. Just enter the stock or index symbol; for most searches, click List Near Term At-The-Money Options. For *volume leaders* (the most active options), go to www.cboe.com/mktdata/mostactives.asp.

✔ **Philadelphia Stock Exchange** (www.phlx.com) offers quick links to New Options Listings and 15-minute-delayed options quotes. Click Marketplace and then Quotes for easy-to-read information.

✔ **U.S. Futures & Options** (www.site-by-site.com/usa/optfut.htm) offers quotes and charts, news, commentaries, book and software suggestions, and much more.

Online sources for options news and data

Option prices are affected by many variables including time, market expectations, market volatility, stock price, dividend yields, and other factors. The Internet provides many sources of information about these variables, including the following:

✔ **Covered Calls** (www.coveredcalls.com) offers tools, data, and resources to options traders. Discover how to write a covered call and follow an ongoing case study. Don't forget to check the list of covered calls that pay 10 percent or more.

✔ **OptionSmart** (www.optionsmart.com), shown in Figure 16-1, provides stock quotes, news, broker reports, charges, analysts' reports, and research based on technical and fundamental analysis. The Web site has free and fee-based content. Several types and levels of subscription services are available with a free ten-day trial.

✔ **Options Industry Council** (oic.theocc.com/default.jsp) offers FAQs of the Week, strategy information, and 20-minute-delayed options quotes. Check out the useful glossary, as well as a basic and advanced option-pricing calculator.

✔ **PitNews.com** (www.pitnews.com) provides daily derivative market news and commentary. You find a futures forum, commodity prices, an education center, and information about futures seminars.

✔ **SchaeffersResearch.com** (www.schaeffersresearch.com) offers a well organized but somewhat busy Web site loaded with tools, data, and educational features. Type a ticker symbol for detailed quotes. Features include best trades, year-to-date returns, and more. SchaeffersResearch. com offers a variety of fee-based products and services. Two examples are *The Option Investor* newsletter for $149 per year and online access to Schaeffer's *Gold* section that includes commentary, tools, data, and filters for $9.95 per month. The Gold section has a free 30-day trial.

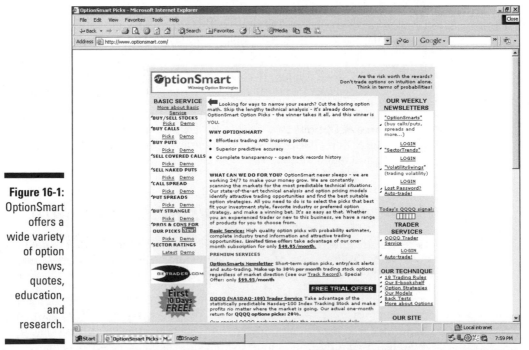

Figure 16-1:
OptionSmart offers a wide variety of option news, quotes, education, and research.

Option Screeners and Calculators

Just like mutual funds and stocks, options have online screeners and calculators to assist you in valuing and screening investment candidates.

- ✔ **optionsXpress** (www.optionsxpress.com) offers the Trade & Margin Calculator, which graphically illustrates the buying power required and potential profit or loss of a trade. In other words, you can easily calculate the investment risk or reward of your potential trading order without losing a dime. To sum it up, the Trade & Margin Calculator lets you test your knowledge and grow your experience on paper.

- ✔ **PowerOptions** (www.poweropt.com) offer four levels of content and services. Limited access is free with your registration. PowerOptions Essentials, at $9.95 per month, includes limited access to the Web site, 20-minute-delayed quote position reports, full access to the help section, and lots of research. PowerOptions Plus is $59.95 per month for unlimited access to the Web site, 20-minute-delayed searches, and option chains to find high return option positions. Subscribers have access to more than 150 pages of tools and articles. PowerOptions RT is $79.90 per month and includes everything you get in the PowerOptions Plus subscription but with real-time prices, investment opportunity search, calculations, and option chains.

- ✔ **Chicago Board Options Exchange** (www.cboe.com) offers both free and fee-based trading tools. The CBOE and IVolatility have partnered to bring you a suite of option analysis and strategy tools. Free services include IV Index, which offers basic end-of-day information. The Option Calculator brings you features that were previously available only to professionals. You can customize all the input parameters (option style, price of the underlying instrument, strike, expiration, implied volatility, interest rate, and dividends data) or use the IVolatility database to populate all those fields for you. Both services are free. Fee-based services include Strategies Scanners & Worksheets, Advanced Volatility Ranker, Advanced Options, and Spread Scanner. Each premium service offers a free trial.

- ✔ **Options Industry Council** (www.optionscentral.com/desk/options_calc.jsp) offers a basic calculator and an advanced calculator. The basic calculator walks novices through the process of setting the variables that affect the price of an option. This calculator provides an explanation of all input variables and the output generated (theoretical prices and risk parameters). The advanced calculator provides those users who are familiar with option trading with a fast interface. The advanced online calculator has an additional feature that allows users to calculator theoretical option prices and risk parameters over a range of strike prices.

✔ **SchaeffersResearch.com** (`www.schaeffersresearch.com/streetools/market_tools/hedge_calculator.aspx`) provides a Portfolio Protection Analyzer. This hedging calculator estimates the value of your portfolio if it declines 5, 10, 15, or 20 percent. Then it suggests the amount of puts that you should purchase to protect your portfolio.

Determining Stock Option Values

The value of the stock option is derived from an actual stock or equity. The price movement of the underlying stock makes the value of the option increase or decrease. This price movement is the *intrinsic value,* or *fair value,* of the stock. (See Chapter 8 for more information on determining the fair value of stocks.)

In addition to their intrinsic values, options also have *time values,* which reflect what the holder is willing to pay for an option in anticipation of a stock price increase before the expiration date. Most options are for nine months, and the option can be bought or sold many times during this time period. As an option gets closer to the expiration date, the value of the option can decrease, increase, or remain unchanged, depending upon the current value of the underlying stock. Just before the expiration date, the time value becomes zero.

The Chicago Board Options Exchange (CBOE; `www.cboe.com`) provides many materials for novices to check out, including an excellent introduction to options, profitable trading strategies, answers to frequently asked questions, a glossary of option terms, and a schedule of educational events and seminars for beginning investors. To access these materials, go to the CBOE home page and click Learning Center.

Investors often use stock options to hedge their bets or to gamble on the future. Investors need to know four things to make a good investment decision:

✔ **Name of the underlying stock:** The name of the underlying stock or equity. The name could be a company that your analysis shows might soon rapidly increase — a company stock that you want to purchase but can't afford. You might want to select stock options for a company in which you already own stock to protect your portfolio from a market-driven decline in price.

✔ **Strike or exercise price:** The stated price per share for which the underlying security can be purchased (in the case of a call) or sold (in the case of a put) when you exercise the option contract. Option contracts are usually for 100 shares. The higher the exercise price, the lower the value of the call option. (See the section "Types of option contracts" for more on calls and puts.)

✔ **Expiration date:** Option contracts are for three, six, or nine months (or remaining fractions thereof) on three calendar cycles. Cycle 1 is January/April/July/October; Cycle 2 is February/May/August/November; and Cycle 3 is March/June/September/December. As the option approaches the expiration date, the value of the option decreases. Options usually expire at midnight EST on the third Friday of the expiration month.

✔ **The premium paid for the option, plus the broker's commission:** The price of the option contract is the *premium.* All things being equal, the longer the time period of the option, the higher the premium. The commission is the amount that you, as the investor, pay the brokerage for executing the transaction of purchasing the option contract.

optionsXpress (www.optionsxpress.com/paper_trading.asp) offers *virtual trading,* which is a practical method of gaining experience with options trading without risking any of your precious capital. All your trades are tracked on paper only. Virtual trading is useful because you make decisions and experience the results of those decisions in real time. Virtual trading is available to individuals who open an optionsXpress trading account. No minimum amount is required to open a cash account; there is a $2,000 minimum to maintain a margin account.

Taking a closer look at options

Using the business school approved intrinsic value method, a stock option's value is equal to the difference between the option strike price and the fair market value of the stock. For example, suppose that you're granted an option to purchase 100 shares of the company's stock for $10 each. The stock sells for $54. The *intrinsic value* of the option is $44 because $54 – $10 = $44. The intrinsic value is a positive number, so the option is in-the-money. However, this formula doesn't consider brokerage fees or interest fees on a margin loan from your broker, which can reduce the actual gain you realize.

Keep in mind that the intrinsic value method also doesn't consider that option holders have the right to use their options at some time in the future, which can result in a greater profit or loss if the trading price of the underlying stock falls.

myStockOptions.com (www.mystockoptions.com), with your free registration, provides step-by-step instructions that help you to determine exactly how much money you'll take home (after taxes) if you exercise your stock option today. Use the Quick Take Calculator by entering the number of shares in your stock option grant, the exercise price, and the company's current stock price and then click Calculate. What makes this calculator unique is that it applies taxes to your transaction. You can even use the myStockOptions modeling tool to perform a what-if analysis. For example, enter a percentage increase or decrease under the What If Company Stock Price to determine an ideal selling price.

Discovering what your options are worth

The first step in understanding what your options are worth is to be able to understand an option premium table. *Premiums* (prices) for options that are traded on stock exchanges are published daily in newspapers and online. Table 16-1 shows what a typical listing looks like.

Table 16-1		Sample Option Premium Table Listing					
Closing Stock Price	**Strike Price[3]**	**Calls- Last**			**Puts- Last**		
		May[5]	June[5]	July[5]	May[5]	June[5]	July[5]
XYX[1]	105	7½	9¼	10⅛	¼	⅝	1⅛
112⅜[2]	110	3	4¾	6¼	1³⁄₁₆	1⅞	2⅝
112⅜	115	¹³⁄₁₆	2⅛	3½	4	4⅝	5
112⅜	120	³⁄₁₆	⅞	1¾	8⅛	8⅜	8¾
112⅜	125	¹⁄₁₆	S**	¹³⁄₁₆	R*	S	R
112⅜	130	S					
	S	⅜	S	S	18¾		

*R = Not Rated
**S = No Option Listed

Use this guide to help you understand some of the key elements in Table 16-1:

1. **Identification of stock:** This is the ticker symbol for the underlying stock.

2. **Stock closing price:** This is the closing value of the stock on the New York Stock Exchange.

3. **Option strike price:** The *strike price* is the stated price per share that the underlying stock can be purchased for (called) or sold (for a put) if the option contract is exercised. Option strike prices usually move by increments of $2.50 or $5. In this example, the strike price moves in $5 increments.

4. **Option closing prices:** This is the closing value of the option contract.

5. **Option expiration months:** This shows the termination date of an option contract. Remember that U.S. listed option contracts expire on the third Friday of the expiration month.

In Table 16-1, XYZ July $115 *calls* closed at 3½ ($350) per contract. XYZ stock closed at $112bf3/8. Therefore these options were *out-of-the-money* because the closing price didn't reach the $115 or greater.

Puts are the opposite of calls. Table 16-1 shows how a put must be greater than $112⅜ to be in-the-money. The July $120 puts closed at 8¾ ($875) per contract. Therefore, in this example, these puts are in-the-money because $120 is greater than the closing price of $112⅜.

Online brokerages and options

Not all electronic brokerages trade stock options. The sales commissions for option transactions vary from broker to broker. Some online brokerages charge a flat rate plus $1.50 to $2.50 per contract. Others just charge a flat fee. See Table 16-2 for a few examples of online brokerage commissions for options transactions.

Table 16-2	Online Brokerage Commission Rates for Options Contracts	
Online Brokerage	**Internet Address**	**Commission Rates**
Harris*direct*	www.harrisdirect.com	$1.75 per contract, plus $25
E*TRADE	www.etrade.com	1–8: $19.99 + $1.75 per contract
		9–26: $12.99 + $1.50 per contract under 50, $1.25 per contract 50+ More than 27: $9.99 + $1.50 per contract under 50, $1.25 per contract 50+

(continued)

Table 16-2 *(continued)*		
Online Brokerage	*Internet Address*	*Commission Rates*
Charles Schwab	www.schwab.com	Up to 30 contracts: $29.95 + $42 per contract
		30+ contracts: $1.75 per contract
Fidelity	www.fidelity.com	1–71: $25 + $2.25 per contract 72+; $20 + $1.75 per contract
		OR, with $30,000 1–35: $25 + $2.25 per contract 36–119: $20 + $1.75 per contract 120+: $8 + $1.50 per contract

Online brokerages that specialize in options trading frequently offer investors unique tools for research and analyses. For example, optionsXpress is an online brokerage that doesn't require a minimum initial deposit for opening a trading account. The commission fees are $1.50 per contract. The minimum number of contracts you can trade at one time is ten — or if you trade less than ten contracts, you'll pay $14.95.

The CBOE offers a listing of options brokerages at www.cboe.com/resources/ brokercontacts.aspx. The brokerages aren't endorsed by the CBOE and will require your investigation. Many of the listed option brokerages don't have Web sites, so you'll have to contact some brokerages by phone.

Optionetics (www.optionetics.com/broker/review.asp) provides useful reviews of top options brokers. You can compare brokers by site design, user friendliness, options usefulness, option trading cost, and so on. You can also find useful information about what you need to know about your broker, such as questions you should ask your broker.

Software Tools for Options Trading

Option analysis software tools measure the probability of profit and identify profit goals and stop-loss points while often providing prebuilt strategies or allowing simulations of investor strategies. As an investor, you'll find all this information valuable. Each year, software developers spend hundreds of thousands of dollars developing these software tools and often sell the product for a few dollars.

Investors can frequently get their favorite tools enhanced and upgraded on a regular basis. With all these great programs available, selecting the one that meets an individual investor's specific needs can be difficult. Table 16-3 lists some of the analysis software that can help you maximize your returns with stock options.

Table 16-3	Stock Option Analysis Software Tools		
Name of Software Product	**Price**	**Operating System**	**Markets Followed**
Option Master, Option Master Deluxe (www.option connection.com/online_ store.php#software)	$89.95–$359	Win, Mac, DOS, Palm Pilot	Options
Option Wizard (MS Excel add-in) (option-wizard.com)	$599.95	Any	Stocks, options
Options Laboratory (www.manticsoft.com)	$149.95	Windows 95/98 and 2000	Stocks, indices, options
OptionVue 5 (www. optionvue.com)	$995	Windows 95/98, NT, and 2000	Options

Options software can assist you with

✔ Creating computer-generated strategies

✔ Taking risk measurements

✔ Experimenting with multiple pricing models

✔ Graphing your option analyses

✔ Forecasting or making projections using what-if analysis

If you can't determine whether investing in options is for you, and you don't want to spend a lot of money on a software program, I suggest trying one of the demos that I list in Table 16-3. Or you can download one of the more limited software programs at Shareware.com (www.shareware.com). Just select your operating system — Windows, Mac, Linux, and so on — and enter **Stock Options** in the search box. Click the Search button. The options software at Shareware.com comes from several third-party sources. The shareware includes *freeware* (no cost), *shareware* (try it for free), and company-sponsored no-cost demos.

Checking Out the Latest Strategies

More experienced options investors are likely to be interested in the latest strategies for different types of markets. Often discovering a new strategy can help you increase the amount of your profits (or decrease the amount of your losses).

- ✔ **Chicago Board of Trade** (www.cbot.com) offers many regularly scheduled Webinars, tutorials, and trading strategies that can assist you in becoming an educated options investor. *Note:* Don't forget to check out the strategies archive.

- ✔ **optionsXpress** (www.optionsxpress.com) offers *Strategy Scan,* which is a valuable tool that allows you to develop an investment approach based on your option of the market. Through a series of drop-down menus, you enter your bullish or bearish opinion of a stock, your investment time frame, your experience, and investment (risk) amount. After you enter Strategy Scan, it shows you up to three opportunities with potential profit and loss amounts for each action, and a ready-made link to preview each trade. To get started, you need a trading account, but opening an account online takes only about ten minutes, and no minimum initial amounts are required to open an account.

- ✔ **Options Industry Council** (www.888options.com/learning/strategy_index.jsp) provides nine preset trading strategies that are explained so that beginners and more sophisticated options traders can easily understand the results of their decision-making. At the home page, enter the Learning Center and choose Strategies. Then click Strategy Index.

- ✔ **SchaeffersResearch.com** (www.schaeffersresearch.com) offers a top-notch primer on basic option strategies, such as straddles, spreads, and hedges. This Web site is designed for beginning and experienced investors who are serious about investing in options. Click the Education tab for an online tutorial.

Chapter 17

The Internet and Managing Your Portfolio

In This Chapter

▶ Tracking investment information

▶ Taking the work out of calculating your investment returns

▶ Selecting the portfolio tracking program that works best for you

▶ Keeping up with online news

▶ Using proven strategies for improving your investment performance

*P*ortfolio management is not busywork: Knowing how much you own in cash, stocks, bonds, and other investments is important. Without portfolio management, how can you determine whether your returns are meeting your financial requirements? Are you missing opportunities by not buying or selling securities at the right time?

In this chapter, I cover three Internet-based approaches to managing your portfolio:

✔ **Purchase prebuilt portfolios.** This strategy allows you to diversify your portfolio and avoid high brokerage and administration fees.

✔ **Use free and fee-based Web portfolio tracking tools.** You can customize these tools, which often provide e-mail alerts on price changes and end-of-the-day quotes. Over the last two years, these tools have become more sophisticated, and they can now even track all your credit cards, bank accounts, and investments at one Web site.

✔ **Take advantage of PC-based tools that are free, offer free trials, or cost only a few dollars.** These programs use your Internet connection to automatically update portfolio quotes. (If you already have MS Money or Quicken, you can use the portfolio feature and update price quotes in just a few clicks, as I explain in this chapter.)

Also in this chapter, I describe the difficulties of measuring portfolio performance and risk.

Why Manage Your Investments?

The gyrations of the market over the last five years have dampened many investors' hopes of easy riches. According to *The New York Times,* investing isn't the popular hobby it once was; personal finance magazine subscriptions are down; and the number of investment clubs has declined from a peak of 37,000 clubs in 1998 to 21,000 as of June 2004. In a recent survey of 1,100 people who own stocks and mutual funds, the National Association of Investors Corporation (www.better-investing.org) discovered that investors believe that stocks are worth buying but are uneasy over the volatility of stock ownership. This apprehension is not unfounded. Stocks slumped for most of 2004, falling by as much as 4 percent. However, by the end of October 2004, stocks rebounded, and the S & P 500 completed the year with an increase of 8.99 percent.

Monitoring your portfolio in a volatile market is very important. You can select the best investments, but if you don't have a way to track your gains and losses, you can lose time and money. Good record keeping is invaluable for calculating your taxes, preparing for retirement, estate planning, and taking advantage of opportunities to increase your personal wealth.

Sources on the Internet can assist you in keeping careful records of every stock, mutual fund, bond, and money market security that you own. Setup time can be as little as ten minutes. You can update and monitor your portfolio once a week or once a month. Your investments can be in one portfolio (for example, your retirement fund) or many (say, your retirement fund, an emergency fund, and your children's college fund). You can also track investments that you wish you owned or that you're considering for investment.

The Internet offers programs that automatically update your portfolio with daily price changes and then re-tally your portfolio's value to reflect those changes. Many portfolio management programs can

- Help you determine how much you own in cash, stocks, and bonds
- Show you how these investments line up with your asset allocation targets
- Indicate what returns (capital gains or losses) you're receiving
- Compare returns with your financial requirements
- Alert you that securities are at the prices at which you want to buy (or sell)

Tracking the Right Information

If you own more than one investment, you probably want to compare the performances of your investments. The more investments you have, the harder this task is. Many novice investors find it difficult to determine whether they're making money, losing money, or just breaking even. To determine how your investments are performing, you need to look at the following data:

- ✔ **52-week high and low:** The highest and lowest selling prices in the previous 365 days
- ✔ **Dividend:** The annual per-share amount of cash payments made to stockholders of the corporations
- ✔ **Dividend yield percent:** The total amount of the dividend paid in the last 12 months divided by the closing price (the price at which the last trade of the day was made)
- ✔ **Growth rate:** How much the dividend increases from one fiscal year to the next
- ✔ **P/E ratio:** The price/earnings ratio of the closing price to the last 12 months' earnings per share
- ✔ **Volume:** The number of shares traded in one day
- ✔ **High, low, close:** Highest selling price of the day, lowest selling price of the day, and closing selling price
- ✔ **Net change:** The difference between the day's closing price and the previous day's closing price

You can compare these amounts and ratios with the performance of your other investments, the firm's previous performance, the industry, and the market indexes (for example, the S & P 500).

If you own several securities, how do you keep track of all this data? Once again, the Internet provides an answer. The Internet has hundreds of Web- and PC-based portfolio management programs that are just waiting to assist you. Some of them are free, others are fee-based, and some are automatically set up for you by your online broker.

Mobile portfolio management is a reality at CBS MarketWatch (cbs.market watch.com/mobile/default.asp?siteID=mktw) for registered users. You can receive price and volume alerts, or news alerts for your Portfolio on your mobile phone, Palm VII, or Pocket PC. At the CBS MarketWatch Web site, you can customize alerts by indicating exactly what you want and when you want it delivered.

Balancing Your Portfolio with Web-Based Asset Allocation Tools

When building your portfolio, remember that diversification is the key to ensuring that the volatility of the market doesn't affect your returns. In other words, you want to make certain that your portfolio is not overwhelmed if the price of one asset plummets. When seeking to diversify your portfolio, I suggest that you try one or several of the following approaches:

✔ **Invest in different asset types.** Asset types include mutual funds, stocks, bonds, CDs, money market funds, and other types of financial instruments.

✔ **Invest in diverse sectors and industries.** Investing in different stock sectors and industries can protect your portfolio from economic changes, unanticipated technological innovations that can make your investment obsolete, and unfavorable regulatory changes.

✔ **Invest in numerous geographic locations.** If the value of the U.S. dollar weakens, international investment can be a new source of profitability. Companies located on one geographic area can be devastated because of natural disasters.

✔ **Invest in assorted company sizes.** It's often difficult to diversify by investing only in large companies. Investing in medium-size companies can provide consistent returns. Small companies can rapidly expand, but then just as quickly go bankrupt.

Many Web sites can assist you in determining how you should allocate your assets. Some of these Web sites include questionnaires that can help you determine how much risk you can take — and still sleep at night.

Fidelity (www.fidelity.com) offers an online worksheet to assist you in diversifying your annuity assets. The Annuity Asset Allocation Worksheet is geared to help you determine what the optimum asset allocation is for you based on your tolerance for risk. The worksheet takes about ten minutes to complete. At the home page, click the Retirement & Guidance tab and then click the Guidance Tools link. Click the Go To Fidelity Portfolio Analysis link and then click Additional Resources. Click the Calculators, Planners, and Worksheets link; then scroll down to the Annuity Asset Allocation Worksheet. Other portfolio tools, such as Portfolio Review, are available only for Fidelity clients.

NETirement.com (www.netirement.com/calcs/pnaapie.htm#TableTop) offers an online calculator that indicates the asset allocation you should use based on the level of risk that you can tolerate. The calculator starts a portfolio that has the highest minimum return over 30 years with a 5 percent comfort level. (Ninety-five percent of the time, its average returns will be higher.)

Click More Risk or Less Risk to see how different asset allocations affect the amount of your returns. This online calculator is useful for assessing how much risk you'll have to take to receive a predetermined amount of return.

Using the Internet to Uncover the Risk in Your Portfolio

Over time and without your intervention, the characteristics of your portfolio will change. Ignoring these changes can be dangerous to your financial health. There are no set guidelines for how often you should review, analyze, and rebalance your portfolio. Some individuals check the risk of their portfolio on a weekly or even a daily basis. I suggest that the more volatile the market, the more often you should analyze your portfolio's risk exposure.

As part of your portfolio management, you'll need to watch for unexpected changes that can affect your portfolio's long-term objectives and plan for short-term volatility. If your portfolio is not performing to your expectations, don't panic or ignore the problem. Find out what's driving your portfolio's performance. It may be that you're taking on more risk than you originally anticipated.

Online portfolio risk analysis measures the risk exposure of your assets to market risk. For individual investors, this analysis is often the first time they can determine whether their investment return is equal or better than their risk exposure. In the past, only financial institution had access to this type of analysis. The following are a few examples of the online financial institutional strength tools that can make certain that you don't take on more risk than is necessary.

RiskGrades

RiskGrades (www.riskgrades.com) offers free tools to determine your risk tolerance and to measure the risk of your assets. Assets are assigned a risk score from 0 for cash to 10,000 for highly risky stocks. The My Portfolio screen allows you to view the risk statistics of your portfolio. You can view your results as a table or graph. You can also print your results. RiskGrades provides definitions at the bottom of the page so that you don't get confused. Click the statistic or story icon within each asset class.

RiskGrades allows you to analyze your investment style against benchmark indices, perform a risk ranking of your portfolio, and create a risk versus return chart to determine whether you're being fairly compensated for the amount of risk you're taking.

RiskGrades offers What If analyses so that you can try out different strategies to your portfolio. For example, if you buy or sell assets, what are the tax consequences? RiskGrades offers risk event analyses, price acceptability testing, a helpful risk map of the market, and an asset selector function. You can also find online tutorials about understanding risk and a risk profile quiz.

FinPortfolio

FinPortfolio (www.finportfolio.com) is the Cadillac of online portfolio analysis tools. You find information about how to plan a portfolio that matches your investment goal and discover how to use online portfolio analyses to optimize your portfolio's returns and minimize risk. Two levels of service are available for individual investors. Basic service is a set of easy-to-use planning and analysis modules that provide interactive guidance and support through the financial planning and investment decision-making process. You can track up to 50 stocks or funds in one portfolio and perform analysis on up to 5 stocks or funds at no charge. You can import portfolio data from other financial Web sites and screen investment candidates, research assets based on risk and return, and perform risk analysis. The premium service extends the basic service by offering additional online portfolio management related services, including the ability to track up to 100 stocks or funds in up to 5 portfolios, perform analyses of 30 stocks or funds across multiple portfolios, and create up to 5 multiple-goal financial plans. Premium subscriptions are $100 per quarter or $300 per year.

Morningstar

Morningstar (www.morningstar.com) has one of the better online portfolio management programs for mutual funds. First, set up the free portfolio at the Web site.

If you want Premium Portfolio X-Rays, you have to become a member. Membership is $12.95 per month (or $115 per year). X-Ray Reports includes information on fees and expenses for each of your mutual funds, indicates how all your assets (cash, stocks, bonds, and others) are allocated in your personal portfolio, and shows the fundamental statistics for each of your holdings (P/E ratio, price-to-book ratio, and earnings growth). With Premium Portfolio X-Rays, you can check for your Stock Stats. This feature of the portfolio management program looks into the equities you own individually and those held by your mutual funds, and then tallies the total percentage that is invested in each company. For example, assume that 10 percent of your portfolio is invested in individual shares of Cisco, and you have two mutual funds that recently invested in Cisco. The total percentage of Cisco holding in your portfolio is now 17 percent. That's *stock overlap.* Stock overlap can defeat your attempt at reducing investing risk with diversification. In this situation, you might consider replacing the number of shares you own in Cisco with an equal amount of shares (that meet your investor requirements) in a different industry.

To determine your portfolio's asset allocations, Premium Portfolio X-Rays looks into the holdings of your mutual funds and then analyzes the total of all your portfolio's assets. For example, assume that your entire portfolio is invested in equities and mutual funds. Using this X-Ray feature, you might discover that about 4 percent of your portfolio is in bonds held by mutual fund companies. Overall, Premium Portfolio X-Rays enable you to gain better control of your personal finances.

Keeping the Winners and Selling the Losers: Measuring Performance

Measuring portfolio performance is often difficult. For example, suppose that you invest $2,000 in a mutual fund that returns 15 percent in the first quarter of the year. In each of the next three quarters, you invest $2,000, but the fund doesn't provide any returns during those months. Your return on the first $2,000 is 15 percent. Your return on $6,000 for following nine months is zero. The fund reports an annual gain of 15 percent, not counting dividends and gains distributions. However, these percentages don't mean that you should measure performance on a short-term basis. Market prices vary and returns fluctuate for many reasons. What really counts is the true rate of return, which can't be measured from quarter to quarter.

Another problem in measuring portfolio performance is risk. *Risk* is defined as the variability of returns. In other words, the more the returns vary, the greater the risk. One of the disadvantages of using *standard deviation* (a measurement of the variability of historical returns around the average return) is that it considers *good variability.* Good variability means that returns are exceeding expectations — an event that increases the stock's volatility and standard deviation. The stock is now considered more *risky* because returns are higher than expected. What this shows is that standard deviation isn't always a good way to judge risk. In other words, standard deviation is just a measurement of volatility. Risk enters the picture only if volatility is below the investor's return target.

You have many ways to measure the performance of your portfolio. One way to measure performance is to use *benchmarks* — that is, compare the performance of your various investments with top performances and indices. For example, you can rank them by

✔ **P/E ratio:** Divide your stocks into capitalization groups (small-cap, mid-cap, and large-cap) and rank each group by P/E ratio. Compare your investments with top-performing stocks in each capitalization group daily and weekly. (For more information about capitalization groups, see Chapter 7.)

✔ **Yield:** Divide your fixed-income investments (bonds and Treasury securities) by quality rating and then rank each group by yield. Compare your investments with the top-performing bonds in each asset allocation class.

Your Portfolio Management Options

Managing the performance of your investment portfolio is as important as selecting the right investments. Market conditions can change at a moment's notice. Your continuous monitoring of your portfolio can ensure that you reach your investment objectives by staying on track. You can use a variety of tools to assist you in analyzing your portfolio and the market environment. The following is a list of several of the portfolio management options that you can use to evaluate your portfolio:

✔ **Online purchasing of prepackaged portfolios:** Called *portfolio investment programs,* these investments allow investors to own *basket* of securities that are tailored to meet their individual requirements.

✔ **Web-based portfolio management programs:** Investor super-sites, Internet portals, and large news organizations generally sponsor online portfolio management programs for free (or free with your subscription). These programs usually don't require any software downloading, and they constantly update your portfolio. However, these programs don't offer many features, such as customized graphs or charts, fundamental analysis, or tax-planning tools.

✔ **PC-based portfolio management programs:** These programs present portfolio tracking as a feature of a personal software program, such as Quicken (www.intuit.com) or MS Money (www.microsoft.com/money). PC-based portfolio management involves tracking with a software program downloaded from the Internet. These programs can be very inexpensive or even free. PC-based portfolio tracking programs usually have more choices and functions than Web-based portfolio management programs. However, you must download the proprietary software, and you might have to *import* (transfer data from one source to another) stock quotes.

✔ **Portfolio management with your online broker:** Portfolio management with your online broker is automatic. Your online broker knows what you traded, so the brokerage can automatically update your portfolio. This choice is a terrific way to track distributions from mutual funds and stock splits. Overall, the advantages of using your broker's portfolio management system are that you don't have to manually add transactions, and your portfolio always reflects the current value of your investments.

You don't have to limit your portfolio tracking to just one approach. For example, you might use an online tool to determine your percentage rate of return for the current year and use your PC portfolio software to track your annualized returns. When traveling, you may want to use your online brokerage's portfolio services to verify the completion of investment transactions, dividend reinvestments, or stock splits.

In the following sections, I offer examples that detail the features and functions of various types of portfolio management programs.

Purchasing Portfolio Investment Programs

Online do-it-yourselfers can now purchase prepackaged portfolios and baskets of securities that are geared for their unique needs. Both beginning and advanced investors can easily understand the portfolio investment programs, which tend to be a low-cost way for you to own hundreds of stocks. The primary difference between prebuilt portfolios and mutual funds is that with prebuilt portfolios, you know exactly what you own because you're the manager.

In other words, there's no lag time between purchasing the shares and receiving the information from the fund managers. If you're an advanced investor with unique investing needs, prepackaged portfolios can be more desirable to you than a mutual fund because you can custom tailor the prepackaged portfolio to meet your particular requirements. For new investors, a prepackaged portfolio can be a way to control a number of individual shares and avoid errors of investing in just a few individual stocks.

Here are two sites that offer prebuilt portfolios:

✔ **FOLIO*fn*.com** (www.foliofn.com) offers more than 120 prebuilt portfolios. Each prebuilt portfolio averages 50 securities; 2,500 stocks are available. Additionally, trades are free with some limitations. For example, trades are executed twice a day at the market price. You can rebalance a prebuilt portfolio at no charge, but individual trades cost $14.95. If you're not sure where to start, use the FOLIO Wizard to identify your investor profile and which Ready-to-Go Folio might be right for you. FOLIO*fn*.com hasn't set a minimum investment requirement.

There are three folio plans. The 1-Folio Plan includes up to 200 commission-free trades every month, 50 (1 folio of up to 50 securities), one-click diversification, and automatic rebalancing for $19.95 per month or $199 per year. The 2-Folio Plan includes up to 400 commission-free trades every month, 100 (2 folios of up to 50 securities each) one-click diversification, and automatic rebalancing for $29.95 per month or $299 per year.

The 3-Folio Plan includes up to 600 commission-free trades every month, 150 (3 folios of up to 50 securities each) one-click diversification, and automatic rebalancing for $39.95 per month or $399 per year. You pay an annual $25 IRA fee. You can also take advantage of a free 30-day trial.

FOLIO*fn*.com has partnered with Reuters (www.reuters.com) to offer members a way to purchase portfolio derived from the Reuters Select screens. After you subscribe to FOLIO*fn*.com, add the Reuters Select Folio service for an additional $99 per year to get started. You can select eight Reuters Select Folios, including Consensus Choices, Favorite Value Plays, and Growth.

✔ **Merrill Lynch HOLDRs** (www.holdrs.com) — Holding Company Depositary Receipts — are baskets of securities that can be broken into their component stocks. You buy HOLDRS just like a stock. With each HOLDR, you get ownership in 20 or more stocks, but you pay only a single commission. And the annual fees on HOLDRS are inexpensive — only eight cents per HOLDR. Assuming that you bought 100 shares of a HOLDR with a market price of $100, the annual fee on your $10,000 investment would be $8 (or 0.08, expressed as a percentage). And it can get even better: The annual fee is waived to the extent that dividends and cash distributions on the underlying stocks are not enough to cover the fee.

To cancel your HOLDRs, just instruct your broker to deliver your HOLDRs to the HOLDRs trustee and pay a cancellation fee of $10 per round-lot of 100 HOLDRs. This converts your HOLDRs to individual stocks. Canceling your HOLDRs isn't a capital gains event, so you don't have to pay taxes.

Overall, HOLDRs allow you to diversify your investments and give you personal control of your investments. HOLDRs offer you tax benefits, liquidity, and flexibility — and no management fee. However, you do pay a small annual custody fee that's taken against dividends and distributions when HOLDRs are issued.

Using Web-Based Portfolio Management Programs

Many Web sites provide online portfolio tracking services. Some of these services are free, and others are fee-based. The aim of Web-based portfolio management tools is to help you make better investment decisions and thus increase your capital gains. Each Web-based portfolio management program offers something different. In the following sections, I describe just a few examples.

Don't let the fascination of having your portfolio online tempt you into overtrading (buying or selling) your investments.

Investor compilation or super-sites provide, among other things, free and fee-based portfolio tracking. Some investor supersites require your free registration and are supported by advertisers. Other compilation sites provide different levels of services, costing up to $8 to $10 per month.

The benefit of tracking your portfolio at one of these sites is access to the vast repositories of investor information, data, and tools that they offer. If you want to research or analyze something in connection with your portfolio, you don't have to go to several investor sites to get the job done, which can save you time and money if you need to make a quick investment decision. In the following sections, I profile several of these investor compilation sites.

B4Utrade.com (`b4utrade.com`) offers (among other things) a real-time streaming portfolio tracker that gives you the ability to view your portfolio in the same way as the professionals. All the quotes are updated live without you having to refresh your screen. You can create up to 10 portfolios of 50 stocks each and either watch the expanded quotes or track your gains and losses, all streaming in real time. Monthly subscriptions are $25 (or $250 per year). There is a free 30-day trial.

MSN Money (`moneycentral.msn.com/investor/home.asp`) offers two types of portfolio management programs. The basic program doesn't require a download to get a quick view of your investments. The MSN Money Deluxe program, however, requires you to download a program that includes customizable portfolio management, instant analyses, charts, stock and fund screens, and more. This flexible portfolio tracker can bring together all your personal accounts on one page under one security key. The MSN Money Deluxe Portfolio Manager allows you to

- ✓ **Customize your portfolio view.** Choose and arrange columns, sorting the information so that the information that is the most important to you is listed first. Your Deluxe Portfolio Manager page provides quotes, information about insider trading, a current valuation of your portfolio, today's events, portfolio tracker alerts, valuation ratios, analysts' ratings, and technical rankings.

- ✓ **Conduct research and analyses.** For example, the portfolio and each stock are rated on a scale of Strong Sell to Strong Buy, based on the recommendations of analysts who follow the company. Over- and undervaluation are based on the price/sales ratio, with individual statistics on different fundamental factors.

- ✓ **Access your credit card, bank, and investment accounts.** You can view the history of your transactions for up to 90 days. Assign categories to your transactions and then use the MSN Financial Tools to look at how you're spending your money. If you want, you can even create a budget. In the Investment Accounts section of the program, you find the following: current quotes, dollar and percentage changes on your account values, alerts, and news on your holdings.

The MSN Money Web site also provides a listing of financial institutions that can provide MSN Money with your account balances and other account details. To sign up for this expanded service, go to the My Accounts section of MSN Money and follow the easy-to-understand instructions. The process takes about 10 minutes, requires a Microsoft password account (you can get one while signing up), and the information you use to sign in to your financial institution's Web site. (In the later section "Personal finance software programs," you see how you can combine this feature with your MS Money personal finance software program.)

Reuters (www.reuters.com) offers a reliable portfolio tracker and Watchlist tool with your free registration. Enter your portfolio data (ticker symbol, price, number of shares purchased, and commissions). Analyze your portfolio by selecting from the viewpoint of performance, valuation, fundamentals, and today's action. The color-coded performance view is an immediate eye-opener about the health of your portfolio. One of the great advantages of the Reuters Portfolio Tracker is the ability to click a stock's ticker symbol and view the financial institution quality company research, stock information, news, and charts. At the home page, click Investing, then look in the left margin.

StockSelector (www.stockselector.com), in my opinion, lets you view your portfolio "every which way for Sunday." You can look at today's change, portfolio value, today's news, today's discussion, earnings summary, analyst summary, valuation summary, technical summary, fundamentals, and so on. Additionally, you can see how capital gains can impact your profits. The portfolio tracker is free with your online registration.

The Wall Street Journal (online.wsj.com/public/us) offers easy access to your portfolio. Click the top-right corner of almost any page of the Interactive Edition to access the portfolio program. You can establish five portfolios with as many as 30 securities in each one. Delayed stock prices constantly update the portfolio, which also shows percentage change and gain/loss information.

✔ The grid displays an issue-by-issue breakdown of your investments. Total value (along with your portfolio's current gain/loss and percentage of change) is included at the top of the grid, along with the current value of the Dow Jones Industrial Average. You can download investment information to your favorite spreadsheet program.

✔ If news is available for any company in your portfolio, a flag appears next to the company's name. To access the news, click the flag. Links to detailed quotes and mutual fund snapshots are also available. These links provide additional performance and background information. Annual subscriptions cost $59.

Following Online News with Portfolio Tracking

With online portfolio tracking tools, investors can see exactly how their investments are prospering. Many large news organizations provide portfolio-tracking services that can make your portfolio tracking very convenient if you already use one or more of these news sources. The portfolio tracking functions of online news organizations generally require the security's ticker symbol, quantity you purchased, purchase price, and date of purchase. In return, your portfolio tracker shows today's delayed market price, today's change, market value of your shares, the value of your investment, your gain or loss, and the percentage of the return. The following sections profile a few examples of online news organizations' portfolio trackers.

Business news

Many online business news organizations provide portfolio tracking. Getting your investment news and tracking your investments at the same site is like one-stop shopping and can be a real timesaver. You can read the news and check on your securities at the same time. Check out the following sites:

- ✔ **CBS MarketWatch** (`cbs.marketwatch.com`) offers (with your free registration) a program that enables you to create an unlimited number of portfolios and to track up to 200 ticker symbols for options, mutual funds, and stocks on all the major exchanges in each portfolio. You can also customize price and value views to display the data you want to see first. Prices are automatically updated every five minutes.

- ✔ **FT.com** (`www.ft.com`) is a handy online portfolio tracker if you're trading in a variety of currencies. You can track 24 currencies on a number of exchanges. The *Financial Times* allows you to analyze your allocations, as well as link to financial data and news. A convenient online currency converter tallies up your international gains or losses. The portfolio tracker is free with your registration.

- ✔ **New York Times** (`www.nytimes.com/pages/business/index.html`) lets you set up or see the status of your portfolio (with your free registration). Go to the Business Section and click Stock Portfolio. To set up your portfolio, just enter the securities that you own or want to own by inputting the ticker symbol, amount of shares, commission paid, and date of purchase. The portfolio program does the rest. PC Quote (`www.pcquote.com`) provides the quotes, and *The New York Times* provides the free service.

Portal portfolio management

Portals are Web sites that are designed to be the Internet user's first window onto the Web — the first page that comes up when the user accesses the Web. Often, you can personalize portals so that you can access news, sports, current portfolio data, or interest rate information before moving on to other sites. In the following sections, I profile two examples of portals with free portfolio tracking.

Yahoo! portfolio management

Yahoo! features a personalized portfolio program (finance.yahoo.com). To use the free portfolio, you need to set up an account with My Yahoo!. Click the Log In link that appears on the Portfolio line and then click Create an Account. Click the Edit link that appears and enter a portfolio name. Add the ticker symbols of your investments, separated by commas where indicated. You can also enter indexes like the S & P 500 (SPX) for comparison purposes. You can use the same ticker symbol to record separate purchases. Enter or edit the number of shares or purchase prices by clicking the Enter More Info button at the bottom of the page.

Quotes are delayed by 15 minutes for NASDAQ and 20 minutes for other exchanges. Portfolio management information includes company ticker symbol, price at the last trade, amount of price change at last trade, trading volume, number of shares held, the total value of the issue, dollar and percentage of change between the purchase price and the current value, amount paid per share, dollar capital gain or loss, and percentage of capital gain or loss.

The program provides charts, news, research, SEC (Securities and Exchange Commission) filings data, and related information. Recent headlines that link to news stories about your portfolio investments appear at the bottom of the page. You can get your information by signing in on any computer (and use the sign-out feature to make certain that others can't pry).

You can select a nontable version of the portfolio's data, choose to have all portfolio data downloaded to a spreadsheet, and retrieve detailed quotes for each investment. You can customize the portfolio by deciding to sort information alphabetically, use a small font, or display the portfolio by using detailed quote information rather than basic quote data.

Detailed quote information includes last trade (date and time), change (dollars and percent), previous closing price, volume, the day's price range, 52-week range, and bid, ask, and open prices. Also included are ex-dividend dates, earnings per share, P/E ratio, last dividend per share amount, and yield. Charts of the security's price for the last three months, year, two years, five years, and maximum number of years are available.

You can view your portfolio in a floating window, which lets you track your portfolio even when you leave My Yahoo!. Just click the stacked pages icon in the top-right corner of the portfolio module. If you get tired of seeing your portfolio, click the X to close the floating window.

Excite

Excite (`my.excite.com/myexcite/my.jsp`) is a portal that lets you customize more than any other portal Web site (after you enter your zip code and e-mail address). You can choose your favorite links, decide how the page looks, pick which news stories will be listed first, set select reminders, and more. You can select stocks to track and create multiple portfolios.

The first portfolio view shows only the ticker symbol, current price, and percentage of change since the last closing price. The portfolio tracker provides alerts, information on the most active stocks, and a market update. The full portfolio screen shows the ticker symbol, current price, today's change, percentage of change, volume, shares you own, gains or losses, and links to company news and chats. If you need to look up a company's ticker symbol or find a delayed quote, Excite includes the service.

Portfolio management alerts

Many Web-based portfolio management programs offer registered users free daily updates on their portfolios. Investors can receive news, alerts, and closing prices on all the securities listed in their online portfolios. Investors usually enter their preferred e-mail address and complete a confirmation process. Many programs allow investors to set the criteria for specified alerts. For example, if the price change of a certain security changes by more than 5 percent in a day, an *alert* is automatically launched to notify the investor of the change. The following are a few examples of portfolio alerts:

- **Marketocracy** (`www.marketocracy.com`) believes there is no one solitary path to success in the stock market. The common destination is to learn about the strengths and weaknesses of the market environment. To that end, Marketocacy offers Marketscope Newsletter, stock alerts, weekly insights, and daily stock information. There is a free 30-day trial. The subscription price for this premium level research is $60 for three months or $180 for one year.

- **MSN Money Deluxe** (`moneycentral.msn.com/investor/home.asp`) is a free downloadable program that takes a few minutes to download with a 56 Kbps modem. At the Investor home page, click on Portfolio in the header. You can save personalized views of your portfolio, use the MSN Stock List to track symbols, import stock screener results to a watch account in your portfolio, see an analysis of your portfolio and easily add new symbols to your account. Among other things, the MS Money Deluxe launches e-mail alerts delivered to MSN Messenger, Windows Messenger, e-mail, or your mobile device. Alerts can be based on stock or mutual fund ticker symbols to notify you of changes in price, volume, and more.

✔ **SmartMoney.com** (`www.smartmoney.com`) offers intraday stock alerts. Get notified as soon as your stock hits your specified price target, volume target net change, and more. You can add, edit, and remove alerts for immediate use. You can even set up multiple alerts each. For example, you can be notified when your stock goes up or down 10 percent and when it hits a 52-week high. There is a free two-week trial. Subscriptions start at $5.95 per month for delayed quotes ($59.95 per year) and $10.95 per month for real-time quotes ($109.00 per year).

✔ **Stock Alerts** (`www.stockalerts.com`) offers custom alters for a variety of events and periodic reports on stocks and portfolios. Delivery is to desktop e-mail, pagers, cell phones, and any other e-mail capable Short Message Service (SMS) device. Messages are in HTML (HyperText Markup Language) or plain-text formats. There are three subscription levels. The free subscription is one report or watch, one portfolio, a maximum of ten lots per portfolio, total of two deliveries per day, a total of three destinations for messages per day, and ten messages archived to the Web. The mini-subscription is $29.95 per year and includes five watches or reports, one portfolio, 25 maximum delivers per day, 50 delivers per day, three destinations, and 15 recent messages archived on the Web. The full subscription is $84 per year and includes 20 watches or reports, three portfolios, 50 lots per portfolio, a maximum of 50 deliveries per day, five destinations for messages, and 50 recent messages archived on the Web.

Using PC-Based Portfolio Management Software

If you want more analysis, including graphs of your investments' performance, tax data, and price and volume alerts, consider a PC-based *portfolio manager* (a software program that operates on your PC). For example, you can select MS Money or Quicken (which you perhaps already use for your online banking), shareware, or free Internet programs. In the following sections, I describe a few examples of PC-based portfolio management programs.

Personal finance software programs

Personal finance software programs often offer much more than what you pay for. These programs provide a way to access online banking, organize your personal finances, understand what you have and what you owe, and organize your financial accounts for the tax collector. Additionally, portfolio management programs track and analyze your portfolio's performance. Most personal finance software programs automatically use your portfolio's gains and losses for your net-worth calculations. With many personal finance programs, if you're connected to the Internet, you can automatically update securities prices. In the following sections, I describe the two most popular personal finance software programs: MS Money and Quicken.

The National Association of Investors Corporation (NAIC) portfolio management program and other portfolio management programs enable investors to sort investments by type of industry or company size and then print the reports. In this way, investors can make comparisons within their own portfolios. In other words, it's a convenient way to sort out the winners and losers. A limitation of some personal finance software programs is that they don't include this feature. Additionally, personal finance software programs often have trouble with dividend reinvestment plans.

MS Money

MS Money (www.microsoft.com/money/default.mspx) is a personal finance software program that can help you stay organized by tracking activities in your savings and checking accounts, and doing your banking and bill paying online. You can use Money to manage your investments by downloading quotes and brokerage statements from the Internet, plan your retirement, and more. Four types of MS Money products are available, but only two of the products include the full menu of portfolio management tools: MS Money Premium ($79.95) and MS Money Small Business ($89.95).

MS Money tracks your portfolio's investment positions, updating the price or quantity held without entering all purchase and sales data. You get a detailed analysis of your investments by risk, performance, and asset allocation. The portfolio management program tracks stocks, CDs, and bond capital gains throughout the year. The asset allocation feature analyzes the allocation of the assets in your current portfolio and suggests ways to improve it, based on the historic returns for the investment classes that you hold. Portfolio management features include

✔ **Portfolio manager:** You can directly download account information from banks and brokerages nationwide. You can access your account information 24/7.

- **Portfolio tracking:** MS Money includes features that many online free portfolio trackers lack. For example, you can track stock splits in the transaction list, as well as in the portfolio and transaction report. Additionally, there is a 401(k) manager and automatic Internal Revenue Service (IRS) Schedule D reporting (of capital gains and losses).

- **Capital gains estimator and capital gains tracking:** The capital gains estimator calculates your capital gains taxes and alerts you of taxes owed if a specific investment is sold. You also discover capital gains tracking and optimization features.

- **Asset allocation and investing alerts:** MS Money provides timely market information, as well as an Investing Advisor FYI module featuring recent alerts. These alerts can give you a quick snapshot of what's happening with your stocks and can notify you of any significant news so that you can stay on top of your portfolio.

Quicken

Quicken (`quicken.intuit.com`) is similar to MS Money in that both personal financial programs offer you the option of downloading your checking, savings, and investment data directly from your bank or brokerages. Additionally, when it comes to managing your portfolio and tracking your investments, both MS Money and Quicken provide high quality, personalized tools. The Quicken Premier ($79.95) personal finance software program

- Can help you track tricky financial transactions, such as stock splits and corporate takeovers

- Offers a portfolio analyzer, a capital gains estimator, and the ability to customize your portfolio data

- Lets you download up to five years of stock quotes for trend analysis and recordkeeping

---

Have portfolio, will travel

In the past, if you were traveling, you couldn't access your desktop MS Money program to determine your exact financial position. Now you can get anywhere, anytime access to your MS Money data via CNBC on MSN Money (`www.moneycentral.com`). After you organize your finances on MS Money, use MSN Money to extend the power of your software — access your data from any computer with an Internet connection. In other words, you can now synchronize with MSN Money to access your MS Money data on the Internet while you're away from home.

Quicken offers tax-preparation and planning tools. Quicken can help you calculate your capital gains taxes (not an easy task with today's tax laws), and it easily integrates with Intuit's TurboTax software programs, a feature that users truly appreciate at tax time. Quicken also features Online Investment Tracking, which connects individuals to financial institutions for online banking, online bill paying, and online investment tracking.

Portfolio management software programs

Several hundred portfolio management programs are available for your investment tracking. The programs vary in price from free to $800. Many of the freeware and shareware portfolio management programs include an amazing amount of features, but are somewhat cumbersome to use.

Some brokers give free portfolio management programs to customers who open an account. Financial data providers frequently give free portfolio management programs with a subscription to their services. Other portfolio management programs are components of larger investment analysis applications.

To discover what works for you, try some of the free demonstrations or trials that vendors offer. They require no obligations, and after sampling several programs, you can get a good idea of which features you need. Here are some examples of PC-based portfolio management programs:

✔ **Portfolio Systems Inc.** (www.scscompany.com) comes in three flavors:

- *Portfolio Gains* ($145) is geared for individual investors and allows data export to TurboTax, provides unlimited quotes and portfolio updates, has complete privacy, allows an unlimited number of accounts, tracks stock and options trades, and provides an account summary view.

- *Option Money* ($345) is designed for active stock and option traders. Investors can track their option strategies, check out account statistics, and view their option and stock positions. Additionally, Option Money supports an interface between investors and their brokerages.

- *Portfolio Director* ($795) includes all the previous features and consolidates reports, easily manages multiple accounts, and offers an aggregate portfolio view. A free 30-day trial period is available. To use real-time quotes with Option Money or Portfolio Director, you have to subscribe to either the Chicago Board Options Exchange (www.cboe.com) for $19.95 per month for unlimited quotes plus exchange fees, or PCQuote.com (www.pcquote.com) for $19.95 per month for unlimited real-time equity and option quotes plus exchange fees.

✔ **Captool Individual Investor for Windows** (www.captools.com/
individual.html) includes a portfolio management tool for all types
of securities and transactions. One of the benefits of this portfolio program is that it accounts for reinvestments, short sales, splits, mergers,
and return on capital. The program contains over 70 transaction codes
to facilitate modeling all situations and calculates returns on investments (ROIs), estimates your tax liabilities, and performs batch valuations (for multiple portfolios). Captool Individual Investor automatically
updates security prices with your Internet access. You can also make
manual entries as well as customized reports and graphical reports to
include valuation versus time, ROI versus time, and portfolio growth
versus indices. The program runs under Windows 95/98/NT/2000/Me/XP,
and it costs $249 plus shipping and handling.

✔ **Fund Manager Version 7.1** (www.beiley.com/fundman/index.htm) is
a top-rated portfolio management program for stocks and mutual funds
for the average individual investor. You might experience a learning
curve, but samples will help you get the hang of it. Fund Manager provides many easy-to-read graphs, charts, and reports that you can print.
Update prices by clicking Internet. Retrieve the latest quotes from AOL,
CompuServe, or many international Internet sites. Fund Manager
imports from Prodigy, MSN, Quicken, and other sources, tracking your
investment performance quickly and easily. The program runs under
Windows 95/98/NT/2000/Me/XP. There are three versions of the program. You can try all three for free. The Personal version is $59, the
Professional version is $195, and the Advisor version is $395.

✔ **NAIC Personal Record Keeper 3.0** (www.quantixsoftware.com) is
the official software offered by the National Association of Investors
Corporation (www.better-investing.org) for personal portfolio
management. The program tracks investment transactions (buy, sell,
income, and reinvestment) for a variety of investments. It also automatically updates prices from online services. You can print reports that
record the full history of your portfolio or for a specified time period,
including industry and company size breakdowns and return calculations. The program generates more than 35 reports and graphs, keeps
tax records, indicates diversification, compares portfolio performance
to the market, and automatically notifies you if a price alert has been
reached. The program runs on PCs with Windows 95/98/2000/Me/XP. A
free 30-day demo is available for download. The program costs $89.

✔ *Personal* **StockMonitor** (www.personalstockmonitor.com), shown in
Figure 17-1, is an investment tool that uses the Internet to assist you in
making better financial decisions by providing continuously updated
quotes and charts on your desktop computer for free. *Personal* Stock
Monitor collects quotes from 15 markets worldwide and includes a portfolio manager that works in the background, recalculating the value of

your holdings. You get links to news, research, and charts. You also get configurable intraday, end of day, and asset allocation charts, as well as import and export capabilities from Quicken, MS Money, MetaStock (www.equis.com), and similar software programs, giving you a consolidated view of your accounts. In other words, *Personal* StockMonitor retrieves raw data from the Internet and organizes it according to your preferences. Your portfolio information is stored on your hard drive instead of the Internet.

Overall, *Personal* StockMonitor combines online finance Web sites with the convenience, automation, and privacy of a desktop application. The program runs on PC Windows 95/98/2000/Me/XP. *Personal* StockMonitor Gold is $49.95, and *Personal* StockMonitor is $29.95. A free 30-day trial is available.

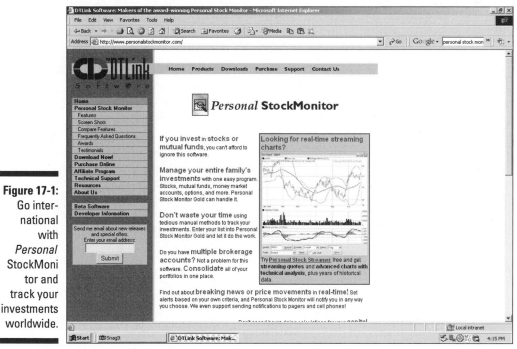

Figure 17-1:
Go inter-national with *Personal* StockMonitor and track your investments worldwide.

Part IV
The Part of Tens

The 5th Wave   By Rich Tennant

Mr. Grady had a way of getting more out of an online project than other teachers.

Ms. Stubb's 7th Grade Class
CLOGGING 'n Squash Carving

Mr Grady's 6th Grade Class
GLOBAL ECONOMIC STABILITY

In this part . . .

In The Part of Tens, I offer some timely advice about how you can tell a good deal from a scam, some guidelines about determining the time to sell, and information on how to spot the green flags for buying.

Chapter 18

Ten Warnings About Cyberfraud

In This Chapter

▶ Recognizing potential online investment scams

▶ Requiring real financial disclosures

▶ Unmasking dishonest brokers by asking the right questions

▶ Knowing where to complain online if you receive an unscrupulous investment offer

*T*he Securities and Exchange Commission receives hundreds of complaints of online investment fraud every day despite many consumer warnings and a federal crackdown. Don't get taken for a ride on the Information Superhighway. In the past, swindlers used the U.S. mail and telemarketing boiler rooms to exploit unsuspecting investors. Cyber scam artists have now taken online investor fraud to a more sophisticated level with look-alike portals of legitimate brokerages complete with hyperlinks to fabricated press releases and fake news stories that look almost like the real thing.

Investigating investments is difficult. The terms of the deal might be hard to understand, and the investment literature and salespeople might omit key facts. However, you can observe warning signs of potential scams, schemes, and deceptions. Doing so involves a little effort, homework, and investigating, but isn't that what investing is all about?

In this chapter, I provide ten warnings (and then some) about online investment information and offers that may be too good to be true. I provide guidelines for checking out brokers and investments, as well as tips for identifying a pyramid scheme. I show you how to read financial disclosures to get the facts, and I explain how to complain online.

Don't Believe Everything You Read

Every investor dreams of being an early stockowner in a Microsoft or Intel Corp. Dishonest brokers and stock promoters prey upon this greed and offer unsuspecting investors low-priced stocks in companies with new products or technologies (like the self-chilling soda can). Many fraudulent Internet messages are about general stock-picking advice or mention other investment possibilities. However, some messages tout specific stocks, moneymaking ventures, and service providers. Just remember one simple rule: Don't believe anything you read until you've done some of your own research first.

The following are ten examples of online investment scams that you should be wary of.

Multilevel marketing plans and pyramid schemes

Pyramid schemes, sometimes called *multilevel marketing plans,* are sure ways to lose money. Individuals are often contacted via e-mail messages and encouraged to recruit six friends; those six people recruit six more friends — and so on, in a relentless search for new recruits. New recruits are expected to purchase a minimum amount of the pyramid's products. If everyone cooperates, then by level 15, the scheme needs 7.6 billion participants — more than the Earth's population.

Profits from these schemes don't come from selling products or distributorships but from recruiting new participants. The endless recruiting of more participants eventually leads to an oversupply of sellers. Investors are left with garages full of products and the loss of their investment.

Three elements characterize pyramid schemes:

- A reliance on funds from new investors (recruits) to pay returns, commissions, or bonuses to old investors.
- The need for an inexhaustible supply of new recruits.
- The promise of earning profits without providing goods or services.

A good example of a pyramid scheme is located in the United Kingdom and online. The enterprise is called a "gifting scheme" and was still available online as of February 2005. Unfortunately, because it doesn't' appear to breach any current U.K. legislation on pyramid schemes or multilevel marketing and doesn't involve any trading of products for services, it has wriggled through a legal loophole and (at this time) can't be shut down by U.K. authorities.

Here's how the scam specifically works: If eight individuals invest £3,000 and then progress through the levels of the network, they can each expect to receive £24,000 when they reach the top level. However, to reach that top level, 64 people have to each invest £3,000. Each of those 64 investors also expects to collect her £24,000. However, that means that another 512 investors need to participate. The next level requires 4,096 participants, then 32,768 participants, and then 262,144 participants.

To sum it up, each investor needs eight investors in the scheme in order to get her money back and to make a return. In most cases, the supply of potential investors dries up, leaving the majority of investors with nothing to show for their investment.

Financial chain letters and Ponzi schemes

Financial chain letters can sneak around your spam-blocking software because they're usually sent by people you know. Generally, the e-mail message states that you're missing out on a big investment opportunity. If you forward the message to a dozen of your friends, you'll be allowed to see the details of this once-in-a-lifetime investment opportunity and reap big returns.

Most financial chain letter promoters claim that if you participate, your name will eventually be at the top of millions of lists and you'll receive millions of dollars. You may be asked to send ten dollars to each of the first ten people whose names are at the top of the list. Next you're instructed to delete the name at the top of the list and add your name to the bottom of the list. Money is made solely by getting other new recruits to join the chain. Most people receive nothing for their "investment." Anyone can break the chain and deprive you of your possible "gains." Even if the financial chain isn't broken, about 95 percent of financial chain letter participants don't ever receive anything in return for their "investment."

According to the U.S. Postal Service, financial chain letters are a form of Ponzi scheme and are illegal. Ponzi schemes are named after a 19th-century clerk, Charles Ponzi, who conned investors out of $10 million by promising returns as high as 40 percent. Ponzi schemes are a close cousin to pyramid schemes because they rely on new recruits. What makes the two approaches different is that with a Ponzi scheme, any profits go to one person. In contrast, in a pyramid scheme, any profits go to early investors that have reached a certain level.

If you've been targeted to receive a financial chain letter or if you believe you have been solicited for a Ponzi scheme, notify your Internet service provider or the Federal Trade Commission at spam@uce.gov.

Cons based on bogus research reports and newsletters

The Wall Street Journal (www.wsj.com) has a circulation of 1.8 million, and *USA TODAY* (www.usatoday.com) has a circulation of 1.6 million. In contrast, more than 70 million adults log on to the Internet each day. By using mass e-mailing programs, fraudsters can quickly and inexpensively reach more people than these publications can. In other words, with one keystroke, fraudsters can reach thousands, even millions, of potential online investors. This type of e-mailing strategy is called *spam*. Spam is junk e-mail, and creating it is easy. Often, you may receive unsolicited e-mail newsletters that tout stocks expected to double or triple in value over a very short time. If you look closely enough, you might find a disclaimer, usually included in the very small print at the bottom of the newsletter. The following are several examples of potential disclaimers:

- The publisher of the report isn't a registered investment advisor or broker dealer. The report isn't an offer to buy or sell securities.

- The owners of the report may already own shares of the stock described in the publication and may immediately sell all or a portion of these shares into the open market at or about the time that the report is published.

- Investing in the profiled company is high-risk and use of the report is for reading purposes only. If the reader decides to act as an investor, it's at that investor's sole risk.

- Statements in the report are forward-looking statements within the meaning of The Private Securities Litigation Reform Act of 1995. These terms may include such words as *expect, believe, may, will, intend,* or similar terms.

Some so-called research reports are nothing more than paid advertisements for certain stocks. The authors of these supposedly legitimate newsletters don't disclose conflicts of interest or biases in their reporting. For example, in December 2000, a stock guru misled prospective investors in companies highlighted on his Web site by failing to disclose that the companies had paid his firm a fee to publish favorable research analyses of their firms.

In October 1999, the SEC conducted their first nationwide sweep against these so-called research reports that touted stocks on the Internet but didn't disclose that they were being paid to make the promotions. The SEC filed fraud charges against 44 people and firms, following up in February 2000 with charges against another nine people and four companies.

Spammers can purchase your e-mail address from a variety of sources. Sometimes, you may unwittingly provide the information yourself. For example, when you complete a free registration form at a Web site, you may overlook a little box that states Uncheck This Box if You DO NOT Want a Newsletter. Unwanted e-mail newsletters are often marked Urgent or Recommended Strong Buy. You should ignore e-mail messages like this and delete them immediately. Unsubscribe as soon as possible because this type of junk mail is a waste of your precious time. For more on how to protect yourself from unwanted e-mail of this nature, check out *Fighting Spam For Dummies* by John R. Levine, Margaret Levine Young, and Ray Everett-Church (Wiley).

Phishing for your personal information

Phishing (pronounced "fishing") is a type of brand spoofing. That is, the Web page of a legitimate Web site — such as your bank, PayPal, Best Buy, and so on — is recreated by a fraudster. An e-mail message is sent to you in an attempt to fool you into revealing your personal financial information or password data. Sometimes, to gain your personal financial information, "Phishers" will use

- **Social engineering:** Phishing sometimes uses social engineering to gain your confidence. Social engineering is when unscrupulous individuals exploit the weaknesses in people to gain confidential information, such as passwords that will compromise information system security. Social engineering is as a low-tech way that Internet users can have their identities stolen.

- **High-tech lures:** The term *phishing* is used to describe how fraudsters use sophisticated lures to deceive everyday Internet users. Experts note that about 5 percent of all recipients respond to phishing exploits.

Industry experts state that about 95 percent of all phishing exploits originate from a spoofed (forged) Internet address. About five new phishing exploits are reported each month. This is how it works:

- **The bait:** You receive an e-mail message from your bank stating that, due to a security break-in, they need to verify your password and ID number.

- **The hook:** You follow the link to the phisher's Web page. The spoofed Web page has a similar URL and looks just like the page you usually use.

- **Reeling you in:** A pop-up appears, requesting that you sign on using your personal password and user ID.

The pop-up is often a dead giveaway that something is wrong. It's important to report suspicious activity to the FTC. Another way to check whether something is wrong, in case a pop-up doesn't appear, is to compare the current URL to the URL you usually use. If the URLs are different, you're being scammed. If you get spam that is phishing for information and you want to help stop this type of activity, forward it to spam@uce.gov.

Nigerian e-mail letter investment scam

Over the last 18 months, I have received 147 variations (that's almost three e-mail messages a month) of the Nigerian investment scam. I call these e-mail messages *Nigerian,* but recently many of these bogus business opportunities or advanced fee scams have originated from Iraq, Zimbabwe, London, Hong Kong, and South Africa. Often, these e-mail messages promise that I'll receive millions in return for helping a VIP collect money trapped in a Central Bank. The plea for help assures me that the investment is 100-percent safe. Each version of the e-mail appeal is slightly different, but the scam remains the same: I'm guaranteed 20 percent of all recovered funds. In some instances, the fraudster will ask for enormous amounts of money for fees, taxes, traveling expenses, and so on. I'm then asked to provide the name, address, and account number of my bank. For those investors who fall for the scam, the con artist uses this information to rob the investors' accounts. See the Federal Trade Commission's Consumer Web site located at www.ftc.gov/bcp/conline/pubs/alerts/nigeralrt.htm, which offers a short history and details about this scam.

If you're interested in more information about these scams, including copies of some of the initial letters and the extensive official documents that are sent to victims, download the Nigerian Advance Fee Fraud report from the U.S. State Department (www.state.gov/www/regions/africa/naffpub.pdf). You need to download Acrobat Reader from www.adobe.com to view the PDF file (if you haven't already downloaded and installed the free program).

Investment hoaxes designed to get your cash

Many individuals have used the Internet as a medium for investment hoaxes. The following are two real-life examples of how a bogus press release allowed unscrupulous individuals to make thousands of dollars in illegal profits:

- ✔ A bogus press release stated that Uniprime Capital claimed to have documentation from the government of Spain indicating that the Plasma Plus was a breakthrough treatment for the virus that causes AIDS. The stock was touted online in several investment chat rooms as undervalued. In a few days, more than 5 million shares were traded, and the stock skyrocketed by 800 percent. The investment hoax cost investors about $20 million.

- ✔ In a similar story, an individual issued a negative press release about Emulex, a fiber-optic company. In the press release, the fraudster claimed that the CEO had quit and that the company was restating its quarterly earnings. In an effort to cover his tracks, the fraudster — who lived in El Segundo, California — went to a hotel room in Las Vegas to make his online stock trades on the day of the hoax. The stock dropped by 62 percent, and the con artist made $241,000 by *short-selling* the stock.

Bogus IRA-approved investment schemes

Many Americans are seeking ways to profitably invest their retirement nest eggs. Fraudsters are aware of this demand and have devised online schemes that may scramble the dreams of many investors with so-called IRA-approved or otherwise endorsed Internal Revenue Service (IRS) investments. Fraudsters frequently contact investors through bogus e-mail newsletters or Web sites to offer huge returns that will ensure investors an easy retirement. Investments include high tech (including wireless cable television and specialized mobile radio) to exotic livestock (ostrich farming, anyone?) to real estate investment pools.

Con artists use the "IRS approved" statement to evade the consumer protection requirements of state and federal securities laws by claiming the investments are unregulated *general partnerships* and *limited liability companies*. Keep in mind, there is no such thing as an "IRA-approved" or "IRA-sanctioned" investment. These investments are designed to fly below the regulatory agencies' radars and are a guaranteed way to lose most or all of the money that you invest.

Guaranteed high returns frauds

Many fraudsters provide online ads that guarantee "the potential to make a six- or seven-figure annual income." The Securities and Exchange Commission (www.sec.gov) has started a campaign to warn online investors about this type of stock market scam by creating a *sting* Web site — that is, a Web site that's designed to shock online investors into being more cautious with their hard-earned cash. In the first two days, the SEC's sting Web site drew 125,000 hits by advertising fake offers, drawing interest in March 2002 with a press release that praises the biological defense firm McWhortle Enterprises (www.mcwhortle. com). The site features bogus testimonials and analysis reports regarding McWhortle. Clicking an Invest Now tab transports potential victims to a Web page, which states, "If you responded to an investment idea like this . . . You could get scammed!" The text goes on to explain how the Web site incorporates the telltale signs of online investment fraud, including information about how to tell that the corporation is a fake. Look for these signs:

- **Promises little or no risk with the reward of fast, high profits:** Believing extravagant claims of quick wealth is a dangerous practice. Often, returns are based on *pro formas* (the hypothetical performance) of the company — not on actual returns.

- **Doesn't offer any track record and has no legitimate products (being a fictitious company, it has neither):** Before you consider spending any money, do some homework. For example, you can — and should — ensure that a company is a registered corporation and find its location and the names of its corporate officers.

✓ **Offers a lucky few investors an opportunity to get in on the ground floor of "pre-IPO investing":** Pre-IPO investing is the investment stage that carries the most risk for any venture. Consequently, this investment *cannot* be risk-free.

✓ **Requests that each investor supplies a credit-card number and a Social Security number online for identification purposes:** With these two numbers, the fraudsters can steal a potential investor's identity and ruin his or her credit rating.

Get rich quick with investment seminars

One of the newer online scams is the fake investment seminar. Investors are encouraged via e-mail messages to enroll in expensive seminars to become day traders or to learn how to trade options, commodities, or futures. Often, unlicensed practitioners teach the seminars. These unlicensed practitioners are unlikely to disclose conflicts of interest. For example, attendees may be required to open a trading account at a specific brokerage (usually a firm that isn't as inexpensive or reliable as a top-rated brokerage). Attendees must also pay hidden costs, such as buying a particular brand of software from the investment seminar company and using an expensive interface for real-time data. (Software for these courses can be in the thousands of dollars.) Unfortunately, naive investors often believe that if they follow the recommendations they learn in the course, they can earn 250 percent (or more) back on the money they spent for the course. Seminar leaders foster this belief by touting false testimonials about how past attendees are now using the fail-safe trading system and making hundreds of dollars per day.

Pump-and-dump schemes

Pump-and-dump schemes are swindles in which greedy people manipulate the stock prices so that they can make illegal gains. Frequently, pump-and-dump schemes target elderly investors. For example, fraudsters purchase shares in small companies with low stock prices and then use high-pressure telemarketers to hype the stock to unsuspecting would-be investors. The fraudsters pocket the money as the stock's price rises, leaving investors with virtually worthless shares.

Fraudsters are using the Internet to perpetuate pump-and-dump schemes. Pairgain, a California company, was touted by scam artists on Internet message boards as being poised for a takeover by an Israeli company. The "takeover" announcement was hyperlinked to a bogus news release made to look like a legitimate financial reporting service had written it. This scenario is a classic pump-and-dump scam; fraudsters artificially drive up the stock price and unload it on unsuspecting investors who believe the stock is on the rise.

Cyber smears are also common. For example, a fraudster borrows 100 shares of a certain company's stock from a broker and immediately sells them at $10 a share. Then the fraudster starts an illegal negative message board campaign with fabricated news stories. The stock price drops to $8 a share. The fraudster purchases 100 shares at $8 a share and returns them to the broker. He then pockets the $2 a share difference, less interest. The Investing Simulator Center, located at www.investingonline.org/isc/index.html, offers an interactive "Don't Get Burned" simulator to assist you in test-driving what can happen when you take phony research reports seriously.

If you believe you've been scammed, file your complaint at www.ftc.gov and then visit the FTC's Identity Theft Web site at www.consumer.gov/idtheft to learn how to minimize your risk of damage from ID theft. Visit www.ftc.gov/spam to learn other ways to avoid e-mail scams and deal with deceptive spam.

If an Offer Seems Too Good to Be True, It Usually Is

As the popularity of the Internet grows, millions of people flock to the new Global Village. Inevitably, individuals with criminal intent follow the crowd.

Online investor fraud often starts when you receive an e-mail message describing an appealing offer. Remember that offers that seem too good to be true usually are. Here are a few of the warning signs to help you identify potential scams:

- **Exceptional profits:** Usually, the profits are large enough to get your interest but not large enough to make you suspicious.

- **Low risk, high return:** All investments involve some risk. If a fraudster advertises a no-risk investment, a red flag should immediately go up that something is wrong. Don't invest if you don't know exactly what the risks are. (Remember, fraudsters don't honor money-back guarantees.)

- **Urgency:** Fraudsters usually offer a reason why you must invest as quickly as possible. They may tell you that delays mean losses of big profits or that they're limiting the offer to just a few individuals. Fraudsters often play on new technological advances that create a brief market that you must get into right away. However, if you feel that the posting is valid, wait before you respond. Others won't be shy about posting their opinions.

- **High-pressure tactics:** Fraudsters often act like they're doing you a favor by letting you get in on the investment opportunity. Don't be afraid to ask questions publicly. Post a follow-up message. If the original post is valid, the person who sent it will be happy to post a public response.

Although you can find plenty of helpful investment-related postings online (after all, that's what this book is all about), the Internet, like other places, has its share of fraudsters. The National Association of Securities Dealers Web site is at www.nasd.com. At the home page, click Investor Alerts on the left side of the page. Next you find alerts that can give you the timely information you need to protect your money and to avoid scams and investment problems.

Checking It Out Before You Put Your Money Down

If you're an online investment victim, the chances of getting your money back are slim. Even in cases in which government agencies recover money, the consumer usually gets back less than 10 cents on the dollar. The best defense is to thoroughly investigate an online investment *before* you put your money down.

The Federal Trade Commission (FTC) inspects investment swindles and provides summaries that document recent allegations of corporate fraud and misconduct in relation to securities investors. Here are some suggestions about how to investigate that "once-in-a-lifetime offer":

- ✔ **Check with your city or state consumer protection agency for information about a firm you're considering for investment:** Additionally, a consumer protection agency can direct you to other organizations that might have information about the investment.

- ✔ **Contact regulators:** Regulatory organizations include the Federal Trade Commission (www.ftc.gov), the Securities and Exchange Commission (www.sec.gov), and the National Association of Securities Dealers (www.nasdr.com).

  For the name and contact information of your securities regulator, go to the North American Securities Administrators Association (NASAA) Web site at www.nasaa.org/QuickLinks/ContactYourRegulator.cfm.

- ✔ **Write or telephone law enforcement agencies:** Fraud is illegal in all 50 states. You can contact your local public prosecutor, your state's attorney general, or your state's securities administrator (or all three).

The Better Business Bureau Web site (www.bbb.org) provides helpful reliability reports on firms. You need to read reliability reports before you purchase the firm's securities. Each report indicates how long the firm has been in business, how long the Better Business Bureau has known about the company, complaint patterns (if any), and whether any government agencies — for example, the FTC or the state attorney general — have taken any enforcement actions against the company in the last three years.

Understanding What Real Financial Disclosures Include

If you're considering investing in a company, you may want to download and print a copy of the investment offer. If the sales literature doesn't include a prospectus with financial statements, ask for one. If you're told that the company doesn't have a prospectus, request a written financial disclosure about the company. All in all, you should have the following information:

- ✔ **Offering circular:** Sales literature that presents the investment.

- ✔ **Prospectus:** A formal written statement that discloses the terms of a public offering of a security or a mutual fund. The prospectus is required to divulge both positive and negative information to investors about the proposed offering.

- ✔ **Annual report:** A written report that includes a statement by the chief executive officer, a narrative about last year's performance, and a forecast for next year's performance. Financial statements include a balance sheet, income statement, a statement of cash flows, and retained earnings.

- ✔ **Audited financial statements:** Financial statements audited by a certified public accounting firm.

The SEC, located at www.sec.gov, doesn't require companies seeking less than $1 million to be registered, but it does require these firms to file a *Form D*. Form D doesn't include an audited financial statement, but it does state the names and addresses of the owners and promoters of the firm. Other information is limited. If a Form D isn't available, the SEC suggests that you call its Investor Education and Assistance Department at 202-942-7040.

Telltale Signs of Dishonest Brokers

Dishonest brokers often ask their victims a steady stream of questions designed to derail honest investors from asking the right questions. In contrast, honest brokers encourage you to ask questions, provide you with additional educational materials, and make certain that you understand the risks involved in your investment decision. And if you decide not to spend your money, they're untroubled by your investment decision.

The National Futures Association has collected 16 questions that are turn-offs for dishonest brokers (www.pueblo.gsa.gov/cic_text/money/swindles/swindles.txt). In the following list, I've tailored those questions to meet the needs of online investors:

- **Where did you get my name?** The dishonest broker may answer, "from a select list of investors," but your name was probably obtained from a Usenet newsgroup question that you asked, from a bulk e-mail response, or from a mailing list subscription.

- **What risks are involved in the investment?** All investments except U.S. Treasury securities have some default risk. (U.S. Treasury securities are considered *risk-free.* The Federal government backs these securities just as it does the *legal tender* — that is, the money in your pocket. The government isn't likely to fail, so the securities — and your money — are risk-free.) Some investments have more risk than others do. A salesperson who really has a sure thing won't be on the telephone talking with you.

- **Can you send me a written explanation of the investment, so I can consider it at my leisure?** This question provides two turn-offs to dishonest brokers. First, swindlers are reluctant to put in writing anything that may become evidence in a fraud trial. Second, swindlers are impatient; they want your money right now.

- **Would you explain your investment proposal to my attorney, financial planner, investment advisor, or banker?** You know the investment is a scam if the salesperson says something like, "Normally, I would be glad to, but . . ." or "Unfortunately, we don't have enough time," or "Can't you make your own decisions?"

- **Can you give me references and the names of your principal investors and officers?** Swindlers often change their names so that you can't check their histories. Make certain that the reference list contains the names of well-known banks and reputable brokerage firms that you can easily contact. The Investor Protection Trust page (www.investorprotection.org) includes links to various resources that you can use to check out a broker or other financial professional.

- ✔ **Which exchanges are the securities traded on? Can I have copies of the prospectus, the risk disclosure statement, or the audited financial statements?** For legitimate, registered investments, these documents are normal. A legitimate investment may or may not be traded on an exchange. However, fraudulent investments never are.

- ✔ **What regulatory agency is the investment subject to?** Tell the broker that you want to check the investment's good standing with its regulatory agency before going forward. The possibility of having to talk to a representative of a regulatory agency is a real turn-off to a swindler.

- ✔ **How long has your company been in business, and what is your track record? Can I meet another representative of your firm?** If the broker or the investment doesn't seem to have a past, the deal may be a scam. Many swindlers have been running scams for years and aren't anxious to talk about it.

- ✔ **When and where can I meet you to further discuss this investment?** As you might imagine, dishonest brokers often won't take the time to meet with you, and they don't want you in their places of business. Legitimate registered brokers are happy to sit down and discuss your financial goals.

- ✔ **Where will my money be? What type of accounting can I expect?** Often, funds for certain investments are required to stay in separate accounts at all times. Find out which accounting firm does the firm's auditing and what type of external audits the firm is subject to. (Make certain that the well-known accounting firm is actually the auditor.)

- ✔ **How much of my money will go to management fees, commissions, and similar expenses?** Legitimate investments often have restrictions on the amount of management fees the firm can charge. Getting what the firm charges in writing is important. Compare the firm's fees with charges for similar investments.

- ✔ **How can I get my money if I want to liquidate my investment?** You might discover that your potential investment can't be sold or that selling your investment involves substantial costs. If you're unable to get a solid answer in writing, the investment might be a scam.

- ✔ **If a dispute arises, how will it be resolved?** No one wants to go to court and sue. The investment should be subject to a regulatory agency's guidelines so that disputes are resolved inexpensively through arbitration, mediation, or a reparation procedure.

 Is your broker dishonest or just incompetent? The state of Massachusetts provides a list of investment watchdog agencies at www.sec.state.ma.us/sct/sctlink/linkidx.htm. You can also find the names, telephone numbers, and, when possible, the Web link to each state's securities commission.

Where to Complain Online

The Internet provides many ways to complain about online investor fraud. Here are four good resources:

- ✔ **Better Business Bureau** (www.bbb.org) has an online complaint form and promises to follow up within two weeks of your complaint.

- ✔ **Federal Trade Commission** (www.ftc.gov) provides an easy-to-use complaint form. Click File A Complaint Online at the home page.

- ✔ **Securities and Exchange Commission** (www.sec.gov) has an excellent online complaint process.

- ✔ **National Fraud Information Center** (www.fraud.org) forwards your complaint to the appropriate organizations and includes it in the center's Internet fraud statistics (which might not help you get your money back but might be helpful to other online investors).

Chapter 19

Ten Important Selling Points

In This Chapter

▶ Getting a grip on selling principles

▶ Setting profit goals and maintaining them

▶ Facing your disappointments

▶ Moving out mediocre performers

▶ Keeping an eye on the right economic indicators

▶ Watching what the insiders are doing

*K*nowing which stocks to sell and when to sell them is the hallmark of a savvy investor. Selling decisions are difficult because no single solution fits all investors. In this chapter, I present some general rules and insights. You discover that individual investors routinely sell winners too early and ride losers too long. From the time that you purchase a stock, you want to start considering the right time to sell and reap your rewards.

If you're pondering a sale, don't focus on only the sales price. Take the time to ask several questions and to research the Internet for answers about the security's future. Use this chapter to develop your personal selling system checklist. Compare your selling candidates with your personal selling system checklist. If your investment choice is a loser, face up to your disappointment and take your losses. If your investment is a winner, you can laugh all the way from cyberspace to the bank.

Determining Your Personal Selling Rules

When you purchase a security, you anticipate a certain rate of return. To examine your investment selection's performance, calculate what you have gained by holding the security:

✔ **For bonds,** measure the current yield by taking the annual interest payment and dividing it by the current price of the bond. (For details, see Chapter 13.)

✔ **For stocks and mutual funds,** calculate the investment's total return (ending value less beginning value plus income divided by beginning value). See Chapter 3 for more information.

Visit the several credit-quality Web sites to check the quality rating of all bonds. Read the appropriate annual reports and fund statements for your stocks and mutual funds. Remember that no scientific formulas exist to guide you in your selling decisions. Knowing some wide-ranging rules and the kinds of questions to ask, however, can help you become a more successful investor. I describe some general examples of selling rules that beginning investors might find valuable. Veteran investors can have the same selling rules or quite different ones. Regardless of which category you fall into, both new and experienced investors need to choose a personal system and stick to it.

When it's time to sell, consider using a *stop-loss order* — also called a *stop market order* (see Chapter 5). You can place a stop-loss order to sell when a certain price is reached. Its purpose is to limit your loss on a particular security. For example, you can set a stop-loss order for 10 percent below what you bought the stock for to limit your loss to 10 percent. For investors who are unable to watch their portfolios for an extended period of time because of holidays, vacations, and so on, this order can be a tremendously useful tool.

A sure way to lose big money is to hang on to an investment that's losing money. Try not to involve yourself emotionally with your investment selections. One way to lower the likelihood of holding on to an investment for too long is to develop a few personal selling rules. Write your personal selling rules in your investment plan and store the plan on your computer's hard drive. If you're thinking about selling an investment, use these rules to compare your current state of mind with what has worked for you in the past. Your personal selling rules may state, for example, that you should sell the stock if any of the conditions in the following sections occur.

The stock drops below your predetermined trading range

This selling technique is called *scaling out.* In other words, it is a structured selling method based on your predetermined trading range. For example, you can sell stock at predetermined levels as it goes up, say 20 to 25 percent of your investment at a time, securing profits along the way. Each time you sell 20 to 25 percent, the average cost of the stock remaining decreases, protecting you from the effects of a sudden possible decrease in the price of the stock. Some industry experts suggest selling any stock that increases by 30 percent above the original purchase price. In contrast, sell the stock if it drops below 10 percent of the purchase price.

Before you sell it, however, remember why you purchased the stock in the first place; then find out what changed and how it affects your portfolio. In the past, maybe the company was a market leader or the company had a new technology. Perform a post-sale analysis of the stocks that plan you sell. Determine the best time for selling by examining the tax consequences of your actions. For more about how you can avoid profit wipes-outs due to capital gains taxes, see the last section of this chapter.

You discover that the company's relative strength is flat or trending downward

Relative strength is how the company compares with the market or operates in the current market environment. (When researching, you often discover the relative strength number calculated for you.) Check out the relative strength of the stock's performance over the latest 12-month period. Compare this number with other stocks' numbers to determine whether your stock is a loser. Low relative strength ratings are often the first red flags for sell candidates. The rating scale is between 1 (lowest) and 99 (highest). Stocks rating 70 or lower may be laggards and potential sell candidates.

You recognize that the industry is in a serious downturn

To recognize a downturn, you must watch the company, the industry, and the sector rather than just the stock price. Management changes can also adversely affect stock prices. Sell the stock if the company shows signs that it may not produce the earnings or sales growth you originally expected when you purchased the stock.

You determine that the company is in decline

Even great companies are cyclical — that is, they have up periods and down periods. Sometimes you can purchase shares at bargain prices, and other times you buy shares that are overpriced. In general, all companies are affected by the economy and have selling cycles. Some stocks trade with a low P/E ratio even if the company is earning money. These low P/E ratios indicate that investors fear the company's earnings will decline. These fears, which may be based on new competition in the marketplace, can also adversely affect earnings growth and long-term prosperity. For example, does the company rely on one single product whose life cycle or patent may be running out? If so, consider selling this stock and replacing it with a similar stock that has more promise.

You discover that the company's profitability or financial health is in trouble

If profit margins and the financial structure of the company seem to be weakening, you should consider selling. That is, sell if the stock shows below-average profitability compared with the industry standard or other selling standards based on the firm's financial statement. For example, determine whether the stock has three years of earnings that are up 25 percent or more and a return on equity ratio (ROE) of 17 percent or more. Use a selling standard that meets your required rate of return. If the stock doesn't meet your standards, sell it.

Market experts call the company "steady" or dividend increases are behind the general market

Some investors seek earnings growth (net income for a company during a specific period, usually after-tax income) of at least 10 percent per year. Determine the amount of returns you can expect over the next five-year period. Make your best estimate of earnings and discount them heavily if you expect the market to be depressed. (See Chapter 8 for details.) Keep in mind that, because of market volatility, your estimates may be subject to big errors. Compare your results with your own required rate of return (which is different for each investor). Is the stock worth holding if that's your potential gain? If not, it's time to sell.

Company insiders are selling in the public marketplace

Insiders are individuals who own 10 percent or more of the company and are required to report all their company stock trades. If insiders are selling their shares in the company or if the company is purchasing its own shares — both activities that may indicate future financial problems — you might want to sell.

Rebalancing Your Portfolio: Which Winners Should You Sell?

Over time, your portfolio will go out of alignment if it's not actively managed. Rebalancing and allocating your assets can assist you in reaching your financial goals. Selling securities to rebalance your portfolio can be difficult because you have to "prune" some of your winners. In other words, to keep your portfolio in balance, you might have to replace some of the investments you have grown to count on. You can use online portfolio trackers to unemotionally determine which investments need to be pruned. Most online brokerages include portfolio tracking; however, what's offered by your brokerage may not meet your specific needs. Here are a few examples of what you can find online:

- ✔ **GainsKeeper** (www.gainskeeper.com) provides accurate cost basis, capital gains tax data, and trade decision tools that can maximize after-tax returns. GainsKeeper allows you to import your portfolio from your broker, MS Money, Quicken, or Excel files. You can export results to Excel files, TurboTax, TaxCut, and other tax software programs. Expect to pay $49 to track 100 stocks and $140 to track 1,000 stocks.

- ✔ **Morningstar.com** (www.morningstar.com) offers Premium Membership, which includes analyzers that can help you understand the tax and cost consequences of replacing a security within your portfolio. Additionally, you can discover a plethora of online asset allocation tools that can help balance your holdings, determine your optimum asset allocation, and uncover the risk in your portfolio. A free 14-day trial is available, and subscriptions are $12.95 per month, $115 per year, or $199 for two years.

- ✔ **Reuters** (www.reuters.com/finance.jhtml) requires your free registration to take advantage of the portfolio tracker. The Reuters portfolio tracker is easy to use and allows you to set up multiple portfolios with on-demand research for domestic and international stocks, U.S. funds, and cash. You can edit your portfolios by adding or deleting companies and changing investment amounts or shares. You can view your portfolios by performance (How is the portfolio doing?), fundamentals (How do my investments compare?), valuation (Am I making any gains or losses?), and daily action (Do I need to make a trade?). Help icons provide additional information about portfolio functionality.

- ✔ **Risk Grades** (www.riskgrades.com) is based on a complicated scientific formula for calculating the risk of your investments. With your free registration, you receive five portfolios, graphing features, risk versus return analyses, risk alerts, "what-if" analyses, and historical event simulations. Using these tools, you can determine which investments are beyond your risk-tolerance level. Additionally, you can determine whether you're being properly compensated for the investment risk you're taking.

Setting Profit-Taking Goals

Realizing your profit is what investing is all about. Paper profits may look good, but money in the bank is what pays for your child's education or enables you to retire early. If your stock is selling for a high price and is now a large part of your portfolio, you might want to sell.

What's more, if you're contemplating selling the stock, you don't want to sell before the stock reaches its peak. In other words, you want to sell at the best price, before the stock starts to decline. What should you do? The following list gives you some ideas:

- Suppose that you purchased your shares in 1996 and, despite market downturns, your stock is currently selling for 50 percent more than your purchase price. If the stock isn't likely to go any higher, you may want to take the money and run.

- Set a target price that might not be your sell price but will be a benchmark. If your stock reaches the benchmark price, reevaluate your investment plan. Make certain that you check similar companies to see whether they're selling at the same level or higher. If so, you might want to raise your target price.

- If a winner now represents more than 10 percent of your portfolio, you might want to sell *part* of your holdings. That way, you lock in part of the profit and still benefit if the stock keeps rising.

- Don't try to sell at the stock's top price. You didn't buy at the bottom, so don't expect to sell at the very top. Even after all your analyses, you still need to rely on your gut feelings about the right time to sell.

You Can't Be Right All the Time

Selling a loser is often harder than selling a winner. If you purchase a stock with a certain expectation, but the company *never* lives up to your expectations, you should sell. The following list provides a few examples of such situations:

- You may want to consider selling a stock if it declines 20 percent in a down market and 10 percent in an up market. If a stock drops 15 percent in a flat market, reevaluate.

- The company's growth rate and earnings trends peak and then fall.

- The company cuts its dividend or stops dividend payments entirely.

If you sell a loser, note exactly why it didn't turn out as expected and include these notes in your investment plan. Such documentation helps you avoid making similar mistakes in the future.

Everyone expects strong performers to keep up the pace. Past performance, however, doesn't guarantee future performance. For more information, see the article "Do Past Winners Repeat?" at the Investor Home Web site (www. investorhome.com/mutual.htm#do).

If the Stock Is Going Nowhere, Get Going

If the stock or fund in which you invested is a mediocre performer, you need to replace it. You may not want to rush to judgment, however. Give the company about a year to make any needed changes to bring its performance up to speed. If you don't see any improvement at all, sell it.

You can tell whether you have a nowhere stock by comparing it with the appropriate index; see Chapter 8. If the index consistently matches your nowhere stock, consider selling. Doing so frees up funds for you to purchase better performers. If you don't have any great investment candidates, think about spreading the proceeds among your portfolio's best existing ideas. Or, better yet, just hang in there — a good investment opportunity is likely to appear sooner or later.

To beat the crowd, get some help from The Online Investor at www.invest help.com.

Don't Be Fooled by P/E Spurts

Be suspicious of sudden jumps in the P/E (price/earnings) ratio, which may indicate that the stock is headed for a fall. Soaring P/E ratios and depressed dividend yields can be signs that market prices are unstable. Consider selling if the P/E ratio rises more than 30 percent higher than its annual average for the last ten years. Suppose that the P/E ratio for the last ten years is 20, for example, and then it suddenly climbs to 26. Consider selling the stock. (On the other hand, don't sell stocks that are in a temporary sinking spell.)

Watch Interest Rates

Bond investors must anticipate the turns and directions of interest rates. If interest rates increase, bonds and bond fund prices decrease because buyers are less willing to purchase investments with lower rates than those stated on new bond issues. Bonds with longer maturity terms lose more value if interest rates continue to climb. Bonds are subject to inflationary expectations, monetary demand, and changes in short-term interest rate expectations. Thirty-year bonds purchased in the '70s, for example, lost approximately 45 percent of their value after interest rates increased in the '80s; for details, see Chapter 13. Keep in mind the following principles for a personal selling system:

✔ Rising interest rates tend to divert money from the stock market and depress stock prices.

✔ Low interest rates usually indicate a good time to own stocks because the economy grows as a result, and stock prices are sure to increase.

✔ Declining interest rates indicate less fear of inflation.

✔ Income stocks are often more sensitive to changes in interest rates than are other types of stocks.

Keep an Eye on Economic Indicators

From December 31, 1948 to December 31, 1998, U.S. inflation has averaged 3.9 percent a year. Investments such as certificates of deposit (CDs), Treasury securities, agency bonds, and corporate bonds are fixed-income investments; their yields don't vary regardless of the inflation rate. Over the long term, therefore, low-yielding fixed-income securities can lose out to inflation.

Stock market declines often precede economic recessions. Indications of an economic slump may suggest to you that you want to get out of the market. Stock prices often rebound at the end of a recession, however, which argues against selling during a recession.

For more information about what to look for in economic data, see the CBS MarketWatch Web site (cbs.marketwatch.com/news/economy/default. asp?siteid=mktw).

Sell When the Insiders Sell

Do you want an inside tip? Watch what insiders do with the stocks for their own companies. The SEC requires that officers, directors, and shareholders owning 10 percent or more of the company's stock report their trades. These reports are readily accessible on the Internet.

Insiders trade shares so that they can purchase shares by using the options that they receive as part of their employment contracts. Additionally, if the stock's value is significantly different from its selling price (either higher or lower), you see lots of insider trading activity. High sales activity by insiders may foreshadow a financial debacle. Consider selling your own shares if such trading occurs (especially if the sale price is decreasing).

For a daily report of insider trading, see Yahoo! Finance (`finance.yahoo.com`). Look up a quote for the company you're researching and click Insider Transaction in the left margin for a list of the most recent insider trades. Keep in mind that some of this data may be delayed.

Get Out if the Company or Fund Changes

The company in which you own stock may have changed its core business since your purchase, or the fund may have changed its objectives or increased fees. You need to think about the original reasons you purchased a company's stock or a mutual fund. If the investments no longer meet these criteria, your best bet is to move on.

Similarly, if your own financial situation changes, you might want to sell some or all of your investments. A good reason to do so is if your risk-tolerance level changes; for example, you're getting close to retirement or your child is about to start college.

Have you witnessed a material change in the company? For the latest news, see MSNBC (`www.msnbc.com/news/COM_Front.asp?0dm=C---B&ta=y`) or Yahoo! Finance (`quote.yahoo.com`).

A Final Word about Stopping Profit Wipe-Outs

Selling your investments at the wrong time can result in Uncle Sam receiving a big chunk of your gains. When deciding which investments to sell, you should take into consideration the tax consequences of your decision-making. However, don't forget the elements listed earlier in this chapter. After all, the best strategy is to make good investments, hold on to them, and maximize your returns.

In December of each year, look at your portfolio and determine whether it still fits your long-term financial objectives. Over the last year, some of your investments may have shifted. The shifting of these investments and your long-term financial objectives can result in a mismatch. Calculating the tax consequences of selling these particular securities might help you decide whether now is the right time to sell or to hold.

Capital assets are defined as any property you can buy and sell. A *capital gain* occurs when you sell an asset for more than what you paid for it. Conversely, a *capital loss* happens when you sell an asset for less than what you paid for it. Table 19-1 shows a simplified view of how you calculate the basis for your capital gains. The first row gives the sales price of the securities. The second row shows how the original cost of the asset is deducted from the sales price. The third row lists the brokerage fees for buying and selling the securities that was deducted from the proceeds. The fourth row shows the net gain.

Table 19-1	Calculating the Basis of Capital Gains/Losses
Description	**Selling the Asset**
Proceeds: The amount you get when you sell the asset	$52,000
Basis: The original cost of the asset	$50,000
Basis: The cost of buying holding, and selling. In other words, the broker's commission and fees on the sale.	$400
Capital gain or loss	$1,600

You can hold your capital assets until the cows come home and not have to pay any taxes. However, the minute you sell, all your deferred capital gains (or losses) are taxed at your personal capital gains rate. There are two types of capital gains rates:

- **Short-term capital gains:** Capital assets owned for less than a year and sold for a capital gain (that is, more than their purchase price) result in a short-term capital gain. Short-term capital gains are taxed as ordinary income (at your regular tax rate).

- **Long-term capital gains:** Capital assets held for more than a year and sold for a capital gain are taxed at a maximum rate of 15 percent (if your marginal tax rate is 25 percent or higher). If your marginal tax rate is 10 or 15 percent, your long-term capital gains are taxed at 5 percent. (*Note:* These capital gains rates are scheduled to remain in effect until 2009).

Table 19-2 shows the impact of the capital gains tax on an investor in the 35-percent tax bracket. Table 19-2 illustrates how the investor sells $30,000 worth of securities. The investor's personal tax rate is 35 percent. The next row shows how the securities are taxed at the appropriate capital gains tax rate. The last row illustrates the tax liability for the sale of the securities. To sum it up, Table 19-2 shows how the investor saves $6,000 if he has a long-term gain.

Table 19-2	Comparing the Tax Consequences of Selling	
Description	*Sell On or Before One Year*	*Sell After One or More Years*
Capital gain	$30,000	$30,000
Capital gains tax rate	35 percent	15 percent
Tax liability	$10,500	$4,500

For more information about the tax consequences of selling your securities, see these Web sites:

- **InvestorGuide** (www.investorguide.com/igutaxinv.html) offers a quick tutorial about taxes and your investments. Discover the ins and outs of how to calculate the cost basis of your securities.

- **IRS Tax Tips for Capital Gains and Losses** (www.irs.gov/newsroom/article/0,,id=106799,00.html) offers a brief account of how exemptions from capital gains are calculated and when you should pay taxes on capital gains. Additionally, find links to in-depth coverage of the capital gains rules for mutual fund distributions, investment income and expenses, and the sale of investments.

- **SmartMoney.com** (www.smartmoney.com/tax/capital/index.cfm?story=capitalgains), as part of its Personal Finance section, offers a guide to assist you in estimating your capital gains liability. The guide also includes a Capital Gains Tax Estimator. Just plug in your gains and losses for the investments you sold last year to figure out the taxes you owe.

Chapter 20

Ten Green Flags for Buying

In This Chapter

▶ Buying low so that you can sell high

▶ Checking out earnings forecasts

▶ Watching for bargain stocks that are trading under book value

▶ Selecting a P/E ratio strategy that works for you

*M*ore Americans own equities than ever before. According to the Securities Industry Association (www.sia.com/press/FAQs/html/question11.html), a total of 84.3 million individuals owned equities (stocks) in early 2002 — about 49.5 percent of all American households, a total of 52.7 million households. This number is a big change from 1983, when only 42.4 million individuals owned equities. Despite all this popularity, equities have a serious drawback: They don't offer the security of interest-bearing investments (market funds, CDs, and fixed-income securities).

Interest-bearing securities offer consistent returns. In contrast, stock price fluctuations just "happen." Every stock investor can count on market increases and decreases. These fluctuations aren't company-specific, but that fact doesn't offer much comfort. Over time, stock investments tend to reward patient investors with good, inflation-beating returns that are greater than those of any other type of investment. For many individuals, investing is the only way to reach their financial goals.

Over the years, avid investors have developed many methods to help others decide which stocks to buy and when to purchase them. No hard-and-fast rules exist. The approach that's best is the one that works for you. The following sections offer a collection of investor wisdom that can assist you in maximizing your personal wealth.

Digging Out of a Recession with Dollar-Cost Averaging

Many investors have learned that markets can decline as fast as they can increase. Frequently, a recession causes these market turnarounds. The National Bureau of Economic Research (NBER), located at www.nber.org, defines a recession as two or more quarters of negative gross domestic product (GDP) growth. The NBER documents the beginning and ending of recessions. Many companies (such as automobile manufacturers) have business cycles that are closely related to the GDP. For companies that are linked to the GDP, a recession means a reduction in sales and earnings, which in turn affects the profits of individuals who have invested in these companies.

Understanding that the economy may be affecting the future performance of an investment candidate and factoring this information into your buying decision can be difficult. Ideally, you want to buy low and sell high. Some economic reports can assist you in predicting upturns. In other words, referring to these reports can help you get ready to buy. For example, if the consumer confidence survey (www.conference-board.org) shows an increase, the market may be improving; employment increases for two consecutive months (www.bls.gov/home.htm) may indicate an upturn; and the Census Bureau (www.census.gov/ftp/pub/indicator/www/m3/index.htm) showing a consistent rise in capital-goods orders may be a predictor of a stronger market.

What if there are no clear indicators of the market moving upward or downward? In this situation, the dollar-cost averaging approach is the best way to get back into the game. The dollar-cost averaging approach is used when you regularly invest a fixed sum. When stocks are down, you buy more. When stocks are up, you buy less. Use your online broker, a direct purchase plan, a low-fee direct purchase plan (such as ShareBuilder), or buy no-load mutual funds (for example, from Charles Schwab), which may let you invest as little as $50 per month.

- ✔ For a $4 monthly brokerage fee, ShareBuilder (www.sharebuilder.com) allows you to purchase the stocks you want and to automatically deduct the amount you select (it can be as little as $25) from your checking account.

- ✔ For the more affluent, Charles Schwab (www.schwab.com) has a similar plan; if you invest $500 per month in a no-load mutual fund, you pay no quarterly maintenance fees. Maintenance fees are $45 for accounts under $5,000 and $30 for accounts under $50,000.

Buy If the Stock Is at Its Lowest Price

"Buy low" is easier said than done. Excellent investment candidates are stocks that are selling at their lowest price in three to five years (assuming that the company's financial position hasn't deteriorated). Wait for the price to stop declining and the company to show some strength, however, before you put your money down.

You must condition yourself to work against the crowd. For free, delayed quotes and online company reports, see Reuters at www.reuters.com. At the home page, click Investing and then click the appropriate link in the left margin for the data you seek.

Invest in Companies with Beautiful Balance Sheets

Carefully analyze a firm's financial statements before investing. The only way to determine a company's true financial situation and to evaluate the potential risk of investing in the firm is to do your homework and look behind the numbers:

- **The statement of cash flows:** Does the company generate more cash than necessary to sustain the business? Does it look like this situation will not change for several years? If so, you may have found a winner.

- **A change of auditors:** Some firms use aggressive accounting standards that may require them to restate their earnings. If a firm has to restate earnings, the value of the stock usually decreases.

- **The financial statement:** If you don't understand the financial reports, don't buy the stock.

To find the latest financial news on publicly traded companies, see the following:

- ***The Wall Street Journal*** (www.wsj.com): An annual subscription costs $79 for the online edition, with two weeks free.

- **CNN/Money** (money.cnn.com): Gives free information.

- **CBS MarketWatch** (cbs.marketwatch.com): This site requires your free registration for more in-depth content.

- **Investor's Business Daily** (www.investors.com): This site requires your free registration for most of its content.

Check Out the Earnings Forecast

People use *earnings forecasts* in fundamental analyses to determine the fair value of a stock. If this fair value is less than the stock's current price, the stock is overpriced. If the fair value is more than the current price, the stock might be underpriced and therefore a bargain.

Financial software developers and most brokerages have analysts that develop earnings forecast for companies. Prices for these reports vary from free to several hundred dollars. The Internet provides many sources for earnings forecast reports:

- **123Jump (Investing Newsletters)** (`www.123jump.com/letters/letters.htm`) provides free earnings upgrade and downgrade information in addition to other related information.

- **MSN Money** (`news.moneycentral.msn.com/category/topics.asp?iSub=1&Topic=TOPIC_EARNINGS_FORECASTS`) provides earnings reports, earnings forecasts, and earnings surprises of publicly traded companies.

- **Stock Wiz Links** (`www.i-soft.com`) provides a links page for company information. Just enter the ticker symbol of the company you're researching, and you have your choice of hyperlinks to quotes, news, broker recommendations, research analysts' earnings estimates (and actuals), company profiles and fundamentals, SEC filings, and intraday charts.

Watch for Stocks That Are Trading under Book Value

Book value is the company's net asset value — that is, assets minus liabilities divided by the number of outstanding shares. This amount appears in the company's annual report. See the Reuters (`investor.reuters.com`) and use its high-powered stock screen to find companies that are trading below book value. Then go to the Securities and Exchange Commission (`www.sec.gov`) and read the annual reports of likely investment candidates. Companies that sell below book value (if they don't have serious problems) are often bargains.

Look for Strong Dividend Pay-Out Records

Income stocks tend to hold their value in volatile markets because investors are confident that they're going to continue to receive sizable dividends.

To find companies that investors categorize as income stocks, see Reuters Ideas & Screening at `www.investor.reuters.com/ReadHTML.aspx?target=about&html=IncomeStocks`. Reuters has developed a screen for income stocks. The screen seeks yield and companies that have realistic expectations of how much they can grow, how much capital they can productively reinvest into the company, and how much they can pay out to shareholders. Scroll down to the bottom and click the Daily Results of This Screen link to see the daily results. The 50 income stock candidates can be downloaded to your Excel application program for further research, or you can use the results for additional sorts using Reuters *Power Screener*.

Seek Out Firms with Low Debt Ratios

Usually, the lower the debt ratio, the safer the company. Compare the company you're researching to similar firms. Get an industry report from BigCharts (`bigcharts.marketwatch.com/industry/bigcharts-com`) and discover the average debt ratio for the industry. Compare this average to the debt ratio of the firm you're researching. To discover which firms have low debt ratios, use the online stock screens at MSN Money (`moneycentral.msn.com/investor/research/welcome.asp`). Use the Basic or Deluxe stock screeners to find companies with low debt equity ratios. Remember that companies that have paid down their debt over the last two or three years may be up-and-comers — and well worth your serious consideration.

Invest in Industry Leaders

If you investigate a company in a specific industry, determine which companies are growing the fastest in that industry and which ones are the industry leaders. By focusing on just these two elements, you're likely to reduce the number of investment candidates for your consideration in this industry by 80 percent. You also discover that

- Many companies in the industry have no growth or display lackluster growth.

- Older companies have slower growth rates than do younger companies.

Remember that investing in industry laggards seldom pays, even if they're amazingly cheap. Look for the market leader and make certain that you have a good reason to invest in the industry in the first place. Additionally, be aware that all industries have cycles of growth; you want to invest in an industry that's in an upswing. For industry surveys and reports, see Value Line Investment Surveys (www.valueline.com).

Buy Good Performers

Try to buy for value and not for price. Select companies that regularly outperformed their competition in the last three to five years and that have consistent rather than flashy returns. Also consider the following guidelines:

- Check the company's stability and examine its five-year earnings record.

- Keep in mind that an annual percentage increase is desirable, but so is stability and consistency over the past five years' earnings.

- You may want to consider not including a company's one-time extraordinary gains in your calculations.

- Determine whether the company's annual growth rate is between 25 percent and 50 percent for the last four or five years. If so, it may be a winner.

Don't try to chase after last year's high performer; it could be this year's loser. Double-check what you want. For company reports, see CAROL (www.carolworld.com), which provides Company Annual Reports On-Line from companies in the United States, Asia, and Europe. Your free registration is required.

Select Your P/E Ratio Strategy

Any analysis of investment candidates includes P/E (price/earnings) ratios. The importance of these ratios varies from analyst to analyst. The following sections describe two strategies that are worthwhile to consider. Select the one that works best for you. (See Chapters 8 and 9 for additional information about P/E ratios.)

Low P/E and high dividend approach

Long-term investors often employ the *7 and 7* approach — that is, they purchase stock in companies with a P/E ratio of 7 or less and a dividend yield greater than 7. Additionally, if the company's P/E ratio is lower than 10, and the earnings are rising, you may have found a winner. Make certain by investigating the security, however, that no major long-term problems exist that can drive the P/E to 4 or lower. (See Chapters 8 and 9 for details.)

High P/E ratios are worth the price

You often get what you pay for; consider the following example: From 1953 to 1985, the average P/E ratio for the best-performing emerging stocks was 20. The Dow Jones Industrial's P/E at the same time averaged 15. If you weren't willing to pay for the stocks that were trading over the average, you eliminated most of the best investments available. In other words, sometimes it doesn't pay to be frugal. Investors who bit the bullet and bought the best-performing emerging stocks were overwhelmingly rewarded for it in the next several years for their timely purchases.

For more information about how to use P/E ratios in your stock buying analyses, visit the Investorguide Web site (www.investorguide.com/igustock choose.html).

Index

• Numerics •

3DStockCharts (Web site), 219
7 and 7 approach, 371
10-K Wizard (Web site), 182
123Jump (Web site), 287, 368

• A •

AARP Webplace (Web site), interest
    calculators, 49, 50
A.B. Watley (brokerage), 70, 90
ABC News (Web site), 41, 268
About Investing for Beginners (Web site), 33
ADR.com (Web site), 270, 276
ADRs (American Depository Receipts),
    274–276
A.G. Edwards (broker), 65
agency bonds, 235
aggressive growth funds, 105
AIPs (automatic investment plans), 14, 126,
    135, 294
alerts, portfolio management, 329–330
Altman Z-Score, 191
American Century Investments (mutual
    fund company), 134, 137
American Depository Receipts (ADRs),
    274–276
American Stock Exchange (Web site), 110
American Stock Transfer & Trust Company
    (Web site), 293
Ameritrade (brokerage)
    for active investors, 70
    for beginning investors, 68
    commission structure, 73
    extended-hours trading, 89–90
    initial account minimum, 75
    IPO information, 282
    for mainstream investors, 69
    wireless trading, 95

analyst
    conflicts, 58
    evaluations, 209
    reports, content of, 56
    stock-picking communities, 57–58
    types, 56–57
    upgrades and downgrades, 210
    Web sites for, 58–59
Annual Report Gallery (Web site), 177
annual reports
    accuracy in, 176
    analyzing, 184–187
    sections, 184
    sources for, 176–177
    Web sites for, 177–178
annual return, 142
ask price, 87, 217
asset allocation
    mutual fund, 121–124
    tools, Web-based, 318–319
asset-backed bonds, 238
auditor's report, 185
automatic investment plans (AIPs),
    14, 126, 135, 294

• B •

Backflip (Web site), 36
balanced funds, 105
Bank of Hawaii (Web site), 55
Bank of New York (Web site), 274, 276
bankerages, 77–78
Bankrate.com (Web site), 230, 232
bankruptcy, 190–193
BankruptcyData.com (Web site), 192–193
Baron Funds (mutual fund company), 137
Baroudi, Carol (*The Internet For Dummies*),
    4, 32
Barron's (Web site), 130, 215
basis, 83

The Beige Book (Web site), 205
benchmarks, 60, 127, 321
BestCalls (Web site), 58–59, 211
beta, 162
Better Business Bureau (Web site), 349, 352
B4Utrade.com (Web site), 325
bid price, 87, 217
Big Money Adventure (Web site), 27
BigCharts (Web site), 214, 369
Bitpipe (Web site), 207
Bloomberg.com (Web site)
  active stocks, 206
  bond quotes, 226
  multimedia news, 41
  National and World Indices, 206
  as news source, 38, 41, 199
  stock screen, 173
  yield curves, 245
blue sky laws, 291
blue-chip stocks, 144
Board Analyst (Web site), 213
board of directors, 186
BoardSeat (Web site), 213
The Bond Buyer (Web site), 225
Bond Market Association (Web site), 240
Bond Markets (Web site), 228
BondKnowledge.com (Web site), 224
Bondpage.com (Web site), 225, 249
BondResources.com (Web site), 224
bonds
  agency bonds, 235
  benefits and exposures, 223–224
  corporate bonds, 238–239
  description, 221–222
  Eurobonds, 241
  floating-rate note, 222
  funds, 101, 229
  indexes and historical data, 226–227
  information sources, 224–228
  interest rates effect on, 359–360
  ladders, 262
  municipal bonds, 235–238
  online calculators, 248–249, 252
  quotes, 226
  ratings, 228, 247
  risk and stability, 228
  savings, 234, 250–253, 255–256

  screening, 239
  selling rules, 353–354
  tax-free, 235–238
  terminology, 222–223
  trading online, 249–250
  Treasury securities, 233–234, 253–262
  value, calculating, 244–245
  yield curve, 245–247
  yield to maturity, 247–248
  zero-coupon, 240
BondsOnline (Web site), 226, 237
BondVillage (Web site), 239
book value, 151, 162, 168, 169, 368
bookmark managers, 36–37
bookmarks, 32, 36–37
BradyNet Pro (Web site), 241
Briefing.com (Web site), 210, 226
Brill's Mutual Funds Interactive, 106
brokerages
  for active investors, 70, 90–91
  for affluent investors, 70–71
  bankerage, 77–78
  for beginners, 68
  bond trading, 249–250
  comparing, 71, 72–76
  extended-hours trading, 89–90
  fees, 72–73
  incentives, new account, 80
  investigating, 67
  for mainstream investors, 68–69
  minimums, initial account, 74–75
  mutual fund purchases, 132–135
  opening an account, 77–78, 79–80
  options trading, 311–312
  rating, 76–77
  selecting discount, 66
  selecting premium, 65–66
  stock screens, 172–173
  trade costs, 73–74
  wireless trading, 94–96
brokers
  deep-discount, 299
  DRIP investing and, 299
  portfolio management and, 322
  signs of dishonest, 350–351
  traditional, 64

BrownCo (brokerage), 70, 73
budgeting, 55
Bureau of Economic Analysis (Web site), 205
Bureau of the Public Debt (Web site), 234, 251, 252, 257
business news organizations, portfolio tracking and, 327
Business TalkRadio Network (Web site), 41
Business Times (Web site), 270
Business Week (Web site)
  analyst evaluations, 209
  content, 39
  international news, 268
  mutual fund rankings, 130
  Mutual Funds Scoreboard, 124
  stock screen, 166
Buy Direct program, 254, 255, 258–259
buying, green flags for, 365–371

• *C* •

Calcbuilder (Web site), 54
calculators
  bond value, 248–249
  compound interest, 49
  IRA comparison, 54
  option, 307–308
  savings bond value, 252
call option, 303, 311
capital
  accumulation, 50
  appreciation, 141–142
capital gains
  description, 81–82
  long-term, 82–83, 362
  measuring, 83
  offsetting with losses, 83–84
  taxes and, 362–363
capital losses, 83–84, 362
capitalization, 146, 161
Captool Individual Investor for Windows (software), 334
CAROL (Company Annual Reports On-Line) (Web site), 370
cash flow to share price, 162

CataList (Web site), 23
CBS MarketWatch (Web site)
  Analyst Rating Revisions, 212
  economic data, 360
  extended-hours stock information, 89
  Industry Alerts, 208
  international indexes, 267
  market indices, 206
  mutual fund ratings, 128
  as news source, 38, 367
  as portal, 19
  portfolio management, 317, 327
  stock quotes, 219
  stock screen, 165
Census Bureau (Web site), 366
Central Registration Depository (CRD), 67
certificates of deposit, 229
Charles Schwab (brokerage)
  for active investors, 91
  for affluent investors, 71
  commission structure, 73
  CyberTrader, 94
  dollar-cost averaging, 366
  extended-hours trading, 89–90
  fees, 72–73
  financial planning, 51
  initial account minimum, 75
  IPOs, 287
  for mainstream investors, 69
  mutual fund purchases, 133, 134
  option commission rates, 312
  services, 65
  stock screen, 172
  Street Smart Pro trading platform, 91
  wireless trading, 95
Chicago Board of Trade (Web site), 226, 314
Chicago Board Options Exchange (Web site), 304, 305, 307, 308, 312
Chicks Laying Nest Eggs (Web site), 44
children, investor Web sites for, 27
Citibank ADR Services (Web site), 276
Citibank (bankerage), 78
ClearStation (Web site), 57, 155
Closed-End Fund Center (Web site), 102
closed-end mutual fund, 102
club, investment, 43–44

CNN/Money (Web site)
  bond information, 224
  international news, 268
  IPO news, 286
  mutual fund information, 100
  news, 268, 286, 367
  online tutorial, 33
  yield curves, 246
commercial paper, 228
commissions, option, 311–312
common stocks, 142–143
Company Annual Reports On-Line (CAROL)
    (Web site), 370
company information
  annual reports, 176–178, 184–187
  bankruptcy, 190–193
  company home pages, 179
  financial disclosure, 349
  financial statement, analyzing, 187–188
  insider trading, 192–193
  international, 270–271
  ratio analysis, online, 190
  ratio calculation, 188–189
  Sarbanes-Oxley Act and, 180–181
  SEC filings, 180–183
  selling rules and, 355–356
company profiles, 200–201
compound interest, 48–50
Conference Board (Web site), 204
conference calls, 210–211
Consumer Confidence Index (Web site), 204
Consumer Credit Report (Web site), 204
Consumer Price Indexes (Web site), 204
Consumer Search (Web site), 77
corporate bonds, 238–239
Corporate Governance (Web site), 213
corporate officers, 213
CorporateInformation.com (Web site), 201
Corptech (Web site), 201
CorpWatch (Web site), 200–201
coupon rate, bond, 222, 223
Covered Calls (Web site), 305
crawlers, search engine, 17
CRD (Central Registration Depository), 67
Cubes, 109
current ratio, 162, 188
CUSIP number, 225, 261

cyberfraud
  bogus IRA-approved schemes, 345
  bogus research reports and newsletters,
    342–343
  brokers, dishonest, 350–351
  complaints, 352
  financial chain letters, 341
  guaranteed high returns, 345–346
  investigating, 348–349
  investment hoaxes, 344
  Nigerian investment scam, 344
  phishing, 343
  Ponzi schemes, 341
  pump-and-dump schemes, 346–347
  pyramid schemes, 340–341
  seminars, investment, 346
  warning signs of, 347
cyclical stocks, 144, 171

• D •

databases
  fee-based, 25–26
  free, 24–25
DataMonitor (Web site), 207, 209
day order, 84
day traders, 86, 87, 91–94
Daypop (Web site), 200
debentures, 238
debt instrument, 244
debt ratio, 188, 369
debt/equity ratio, 163, 168, 191
debt/income ratio, 191
Decision Point (Web site), 156
defensive stocks, 144
depreciation, 162, 169
Diamonds, 109
Dinkytown.net (Web site), Compound
    Interest Calculator, 49
direct public offering (DPO)
  buying, 291–292
  description, 290
  limitations, 290–291
direct purchase plan (DPP)
  description, 292
  dollar cost averaging, 294
  fees, 294–295

information on, 293
purchasing, 294–296
diversification, 99, 266–267, 277–278
dividend funds, 105
dividend reinvestment plan (DRIP)
  advantages, 297
  description, 296
  differences among, 297–298
  direct purchase plans and, 292
  dollar-cost averaging, 294
  purchasing first share, 298–299
  selecting, 299
dividend yield, 163, 168
dividends
  buying high dividend stocks, 371
  description, 142, 163–164
  income stocks, 369
  stock screening and, 161
  tax liability and, 81, 82
DJIA (Dow Jones Industrial Average),
  145, 156, 267
DJTA (Dow Jones Transportation
  Average), 156
Dogpile (metasearch engine), 16
dollar-cost averaging, 135, 294, 366
Dow Jones Industrial Average (DJIA),
  145, 156, 267
Dow Jones Transportation Average
  (DJTA), 156
Dow Theory, 155–156
DownloadQuotes (Web site), 214
downturn, industry, 355
DPO. *See* direct public offering
DPP. *See* direct purchase plan
DRIP. *See* dividend reinvestment plan
DRIP Central (Web site), 299
DRIP Investor (Web site), 299
DTN Interquote (Web site), 220
Dun & Bradstreet (Web site), 170

• *E* •

earnings
  conference calls, 210–211
  estimates, 211–212
  forecasting, 151, 212, 368
  stock screening and, 160–161, 164, 167

earnings per share (EPS), 164, 170
Earnings.com (Web site), 211
ECN (electronic communications network),
  86–87
Economic Cycle Research Institute (Web
  site), 202
economic indicators
  business, 202–204
  consumer, 204
  watching, 360
Economic Statistics Briefing Room (Web
  site), 206
Economic-Indicators.com (Web site), 205
Economist Intelligence Unit ViewsWire
  (Web site), 269
The Economist (Web site), 40, 268
EDGAR Online (Web site), 182–183, 285–286
EDGAR (Web site)
  database, 182
  Mutual Funds Reporting, 113–114
  report numbers, 180
EDGARSCAN (search engine), 183
The Educated Investor (Web site), 260
Edustock (Web site), 27
EIN News (Web site), 268–269
electronic communications network (ECN),
  86–87
Electronic Data Gathering, Analysis, and
  Retrieval. *See* EDGAR
e-mail
  mailing lists, 23–24
  newsletters, 41–43
  spam, 342–343
emergency fund, 51, 231
emerging markets, 272–273
Emerging Markets Online (Web site), 272
EmergingPortfolio.com (Web site), 279
Employee Benefit Research Institute (Web
  site), 53
Employment Cost Index (Web site), 204
eMuni (Web site), 237
Enron, 192
EPS (earnings per share), 164
Equis MetaStock (Web site), 156
equity, 163
equity funds, 101
eSignal (Web site), 220

ETF Connect (Web site), 279
ETF (exchange-traded funds), 108–110
E*TRADE (brokerage)
  for active investors, 92
  for beginning investors, 68
  chat window, 76
  commission structure, 73
  extended-hours trading, 89–90
  fees, 72–73
  initial account minimum, 74
  IPOs, 288
  mutual fund purchases, 133, 134
  option commission rates, 311
  Power E*Trade trading platforms, 92
  stock screen, 172
  UK, 272
  wireless trading, 95
Eurobonds, 241
Everett-Church, Ray (*Fighting Spam For Dummies*), 343
Excel software program, 246
exchange rate risk, 275
exchange-traded funds (ETF), 108–110
Excite (Web site), 18, 329
Executive PayWatch (Web site), 213
expiration, option, 303, 308, 309, 311
extended-hours trading, 88–90

• F •

fair value, 147–148, 149–151, 368
Fannie Mae (Web site), 235
Fantasy Stock Market (Web site), 45
FAQ Bond (Web site), 224
FDI Xchange (Web site), 273
Federal Deposit Insurance Corporation (FDIC), 67, 77, 231
Federal Reserve Bank of Chicago (Web site), 49
Federal Reserve Bank of New York (Web site), 240
Federal Reserve Bank of St. Louis (Web site), 24
Federal Reserve Board (Web site)
  The Beige Book, 205
  bond information, 227

economic indicators information, 202–203, 204
  yield curves, 247
Federal Trade Commission (FTC)
  complaining to, 352
  Consumer Web site, 344
  cyberfraud and, 341, 343–344, 348
  Identity Theft Web site, 347
Federal Web Locator (Web site), 24
Federally Insured Savings Network (Web site), 230
FICALC (Web site), bond calculator, 248
Fidelity (brokerage)
  for affluent investors, 71
  Annuity Asset Allocation Worksheet, 318
  bankerage, 78
  commission structure, 74
  extended-hours trading, 89–90
  initial account minimum, 75
  for mainstream investors, 69
  mutual funds, 134, 137
  option commission rates, 312
  services, 65
  stock screen, 172, 173
  trading platforms, 92
  wireless trading, 95
Fighting Spam For Dummies (John R. Levine, Margaret Levine Young, and Ray Everett-Church), 343
financial chain letters, 341
financial disclosure, 349
Financial Economics Network (Web site), 40
Financial Forecast Center (Web site), 234
Financial Services Modernization Act of 1999, 77
financial statements, 187–188, 367
Financial Times (Web site)
  international company information, 270–271
  as news source, 39
  portfolio management, 327
FinPortfolio (Web site), 320
First Miami Securities (Web site), 237
First Share Buying Club (Web site), 298
FirstCapital Corporation (Web site), 157
Firsthand Funds (Web site), 137

Firstrade.com (brokerage), 74
Fitch Investor Services, L.P. (Web site), 228
fixed-income investments. *See also* bonds
 information on, 230–231
  MMDA (Money Market Deposit Account),
   231–232
  types, 229
fixed-rate certificates of deposit, 229
floating-rate note, 222
FMSBonds.com (Web site), 249
FOLIO*fn*.com (Web site), 323–324
Forbes (Web site), 40, 112–113, 130
Fortune (Web site), 271
FreeLink (Web site), 36, 37
FreeRealTime.com (Web site), 219
Fremont Mutual Funds (Web site), 137
FTC. *See* Federal Trade Commission
Fuld & Company (Web site), 208
Fund Manager (software), 334
fund of funds, 106
FundAlarm (Web site), 138–139
fundamental analysis
 description, 147–148, 283
 on IPO, 283
 online tools for, 148–149
 value investing, 153–154
 Value Point Analysis Model, 149–153

• *G* •

GainsKeeper (Web site), 357
games, online investment simulation, 44–45
Gay Financial Network (Web site), 29
GDP (gross domestic product), 366
GE Center for Financial Learning (Web
  site), 51
general obligation bonds, 236
GILS (Government Information Locator
  Service) (Web site), 25
Ginnie Mae (Web site), 101, 235
Global Value Investing with Stock Valuation
  (Web site), 148
glossaries, 34–35
goals, setting profit-taking, 358
Gomez (Web site), 65
Good Till Canceled (GTC) order, 85

Google (search engine)
 content, 18
 international news, 268
 IPO of, 282, 288
 News, 200
 newsgroups, searching, 21–22
government bonds
 agency bonds, 235
 municipal bonds, 235–238
 savings bonds, 250–253, 255–256
 Treasury securities, 233–234, 253–262
Government Information Locator Service
  (GILS) (Web site), 25
gross domestic product (GDP), 366
growth and income funds, 105
growth funds, 105
growth stocks, 144, 167–168
GSA Government Information Locator
  Service (Web site), 204
GTC (Good Till Canceled) order, 85
guaranteed high returns frauds, 345–346

• *H* •

Harley Hahn (Web site), 21
Harris*direct* (brokerage)
 for beginning investors, 68
 extended-hours trading, 89–90
 initial account minimum, 74
 IPOs, 287
 option commission rates, 311
 stock screen, 172
 wireless trading, 95, 96
Harvard Business School (Web site), 208
Herald Tribune (Web site), 268
Highbeam Research (Web site), 26
Historical Stock Data (Web site), 214
hoaxes, investment, 344
hold recommendation, 209
Hoover's (Web site), 201, 286
Huron Consulting Group (Web site), 176

• *I* •

IBM Financial Guide (Web site), 186–187
icons, used in book, 7
IDBs (industrial development bonds), 237

income stocks, 144, 168, 369
Independent Means (Web site), 27
index funds, 107–108
The Index Investor (Web site), 108
IndexFunds.com (Web site), 108, 109
individual retirement account (IRA)
  bogus IRA-approved investment
    schemes, 345
  comparison calculators, 53–54
  description, 51
  Roth, 52–53
  Traditional, 52
industrial development bonds (IDBs), 237
industry leaders, investing in, 369–370
inflation-indexed notes and bonds, 254
information overload, avoiding, 32
information system, building online
  analyzing investment candidates, 13–14
  identifying new investments, 12–13
  monitoring investments, 15
  purchasing investments, 14
  selling investments, 15–16
initial public offering (IPO)
  description, 282
  Google, 282, 288
  limitations of, 284
  mutual funds and, 285
  selecting, guidelines for, 283–284
  speculative nature of, 145
  super-sites, 285–288
  timetable for participation in, 288–289
INO.com (Web site), 305
Insider TA (Web site), 156
insider trading, 192–193, 356, 360–361
InsiderScoop (Web site), 193
Instruments of the Money Market (Web
  site), 232
interest, compound, 48–50
interest coverage ratio, 191
interest rates, 359–360
International Economics Study Center
  (Web site), 269
international funds, 105
International Herald Tribune (Web site), 268
international investing
  ADR (American Depository Receipt),
    274–276

advantages, 266–267
company information, 270–271
diversification, 266–267, 277–278
emerging markets, 272–273
indirect, 276–278
mutual funds, 277–279
news and research, 268–270
online trading, 271–272
problems, 272–273, 273–274
quotes and indexes, 267–268
risk, 275
international stocks, 144
The Internet For Dummies (John R. Levine,
  Carol Baroudi, and Margaret Levine
  Young), 4, 32
intrinsic value, option, 308, 309
Intuit
  Quicken, 55, 322, 332–333
  TurboTax, 333
Investing Basics (Web site), 33
Investing In Bonds.com (Web site), 224,
  226, 260
Investing Online Resource Center (Web
  site), 4, 85
Investing Simulator Center (Web site), 347
investment club, 43–44
Investment Company Institute (Web site),
  102, 110
The Investment FAQ (Web site), 224, 233
investment strategies, 196
Investopedia (Web site)
  bond ladders, 262
  company information, 187
  stock information, 142
  tutorials, 232
Investor Home (Web site), 61, 359
Investor Relations Asia Pacific (Web
  site), 276
Investor Relations Information Network
  (Web site), 177–178
Investor Responsibility Research Center
  (Web site), 28
InvestorGuide (Web site), 44, 297, 363, 371
Investor's Business Daily (Web site),
  39, 367
Investor's Guide to Municipal Bonds (Web
  site), 227

InvestorWords (Web site), 34, 35
Investrade (brokerage), 75
Investtech.com (Web site), 155
IPO. *See* initial public offering
IPO Daily Report (Web site), 286
IPO Data Systems (Web site), 287
IPO Monitor (Web site), 286
IPOhome (Web site), 286
IRA. *See* individual retirement account
IRIN Annual Report Resource Center (Web site), 297
IRS Tax Tips for Capital Gains and Losses (Web site), 363
iShares (Web site), 110
ISI Emerging Markets (Web site), 272
iVillage MoneyLife Personal Finance for Women (Web site), 29

• *J* •

J. D. Power (Web site), 2
JaxWorks (Web site), 191
The Journal of Finance (Web site), 40

• *K* •

KeepMedia, 200
Kelmoore Strategy Funds (Web site), 137
Key Bank (Web site), bond calculator, 248
Keynote Web Broker Trading Index (Web site), 77
keyword, 16
Kiplinger.com (Web site)
  content, 40
  financial planning, 49
  IRA information, 53
  online brokerage ratings, 77
  zero-coupon bonds, 240

• *L* •

Lambert, Drexel Burnham (investment banker), 192
LatinFocus (Web site), 269
LatInvestor (Web site), 269
Lay, Kenneth (Enron chairman), 192

Leading Economic Indicators (Web site) 205
Lebenthal.com (Web site), 237
Level I stock quotes, 91, 215–217
Level II stock quotes, 91, 217–218
leverage, 302
Levine, John R.
  Fighting Spam For Dummies, 343
  The Internet For Dummies, 4, 32
Lexis-Nexis (Web site), 26, 171
limit orders, 68, 85
Lipper (Web site), 100, 127, 128, 131
liquidation value, 169–170
loads, 103, 133
loser, selling, 358–359

• *M* •

magazines, online versions, 39–40
MagPortal.com (Web site), 200
mailing lists, 23–24
Manufacturing and Trade Inventories and Sales (Web site), 203
market capitalization, 161, 164
market information, 206
market makers, NASDAQ, 86–88, 218
market orders, 68, 85
market timing, 157
Marketocracy (Web site)
  simulations, 45
  stock alerts, 329
  stock-picking communities, 57
maturity date, bond, 222, 223
MAXfunds.com (Web site), 106
Merrill Lynch (brokerage)
  for affluent investors, 71
  HOLDRs, 324
  initial account minimum, 75
  services, 65–66
message boards, 22–23
Metacrawler (metasearch engine), 16
metasearch engines, 16–17
MicroCap 50, 147
Microsoft
  Excel software program, 246
  MS Money, 55, 322, 331–332

Microsoft Network (Web site), as portal, 19
Milken, Michael (insider trader), 192
mission statement, 283
Momma (metasearch engine), 16
Money Fund Basics (Web site), 232
Money & Investing (Web site), 28
money market accounts (MMAs), 230
money market certificates, 229
Money Market Deposit Accounts (MMDAs),
    231–232
money market funds, 101
money-rates.com (Web site), 230–231
monitoring investments, 15. *See also*
    portfolio management
Moody's Investors Service (Web site), 227
Morgan Stanley (Web site), 268, 270
Morningstar (Web site)
    international stock funds, 279
    IRA comparison calculator, 54
    mutual fund information, 116, 117, 125
    mutual fund ratings, 119, 128, 130
    mutual fund screens, 112
    mutual fund search engine, 113
    portfolio tracking, 357
    Premium Portfolio X-Ray tool, 129, 138,
        320–321
The Motley Fool (Web site)
    investment clubs, 44
    IRA information, 53
    message board, 23
MS Excel software program, 246
MS Money (Microsoft)
    accessing data on the Internet, 332
    budgeting, 55
    portfolio management, 322, 331–332
MSN Money (Web site)
    accessing MS Money program, 332
    alerts, 329–330
    analyst evaluations, 209
    bond information, 227
    earning forecasts, 368
    international indexes, 268
    international news, 268
    mutual fund screens, 112
    new investor information, 34
    portfolio management programs, 325–326

Power Search, 162, 163
    stock quotes, 219
    stock screen, 166, 167, 369
    upgrade and downgrade information, 210
MSN (search engine), 18
MSNBC (Web site), 19, 361
multilevel marketing plans, 340–341
multimedia investment news, 41
multinational companies, 278
Muni Direct (Web site), 249–250
municipal bond funds, 101
municipal bonds, 235–238
Muriel Siebert & Co. (brokerage), 74, 134
Mutual Fund Education Alliance (Web site),
    117, 135
mutual funds
    analyzing, 116–119
    asset allocation, 121–124
    automatic investment program (AIP),
        126, 135
    broker, using, 132–135
    buying online, 132–133, 136–137
    categories, 101
    checklist, 125–126
    choosing, 124–128
    closed-end, 102
    commission-free, 133–135
    exchange-traded funds, 108–110
    expenses, 116
    fees, 103–104, 117, 125
    foreign funds, 277–279
    fund of funds, 106
    index funds, 107–108
    information sources, 106–107
    IPOs and, 285
    listing, online, 126–127
    loads, 103
    minimum initial deposit, 135
    NAV (net asset value), 100
    open-end, 102
    performance, 127–128
    prospectus, 113–116
    rating, 128–132
    returns and costs, 117–118
    risk and, 110–111, 118–119, 122, 123, 128
    screening, 111–113

selling, 137–139
share classes, 103–104
types, 105
Mutual of Omaha (Web site), 55
My Excite (Web site), 18
My Yahoo! (Web site), 18
MyBookmarks.com (Web site), 37
MyStockFund (Web site), 293
myStockOptions.com (Web site), 309–310

• *N* •

NAIC. *See* National Association of Investors
     Corporation
NASD Investor Education (Web site), 33
NASDAQ (stock market)
  Level II quotes, 91
  market makers, 86–88, 218
NASDAQ (Web site)
  ADRs, 275
  extended-hours stock information, 89
  IPOs, 287
  NASDAQ-100 Dynamic Heatmap, 206
  SharpScreen, 166
National Association of Home Builders
     (Web site), 203
National Association of Investors
     Corporation (NAIC)
  company information, 187
  DRIPs, 298, 299
  Personal Record Keeper 3.0, 334
  portfolio management program, 331
National Association of Securities Dealers
     Regulation (Web site), 67
National Association of Securities Dealers
     (Web site), 33, 348
National Bureau of Economic Research
     (NBER), 366
National Fraud Information Center (Web
     site), 352
National Futures Association (Web site), 350
NAVPS (net asset value per share), 126
negotiable order of withdrawal (NOW),
     231–232
net asset value (NAV), 100
NetBank (bankerage), 78

NETirement (Web site), 318–319
NetstockDirect (Web site), 275, 293, 295
New York Stock Exchange, 67, 86–87, 275
The New York Times (Web site), 39, 327
news sources
  international, 268–270
  magazines, 39–40
  multimedia, 41
  news organizations, 38
  newsletters, 41–43
  newspapers, 38–39
  scholarly journals, 40
  search engines, 200
  uses of, 37–38
  Web sites for, 199
newsgroups
  description, 20
  finding perfect, 21
  names, 20
  searching with Google, 21–22
  subscribing to, 20
Newsletter Access (Web site), 42
newsletters
  bogus, 342–343
  electronic, 41–43
newspapers, online editions, 38–39
Newsville (Web site), 21
Nigerian investment scam, 344
no-load funds, 104, 133
no-load stock plans, 293
North American Securities Administrators
     Association, 79
NOW (negotiable order of withdrawal),
     231–232

• *O* •

Oak Associates (mutual fund company), 137
odd lots, 85
Oklahoma Securities Commission, 67
123Jump (Web site), 287, 368
Online Investor (Web site), 359
open-end mutual fund, 102
optional cash payment plans (OCPs),
     297, 298
Optionetics (Web site), 304, 312

options
  call, 303, 311
  description, 302
  education and data sources, 304–306
  exercising, 302–303
  expiration, 303, 308, 309, 311
  out-of-the-money, 311
  premium, 302, 309, 310
  put, 303–304, 311
  screeners and calculators, 307–308
  software tools, 312–313
  strategies, 314
  strike price, 302, 308, 311
  types of contracts, 302
  value determination, 308–312
  virtual trading, 309
Options Industry Council (Web site),
    305, 306, 307, 314
OptionSmart (Web site), 306
optionsXpress (Web site), 307, 309, 312, 314
order specifications, 84–85
ordinary income, 81–83
overlap, stock, 129

• P •

par value, 143, 222, 247
passively managed funds, 107
Patriot Bonds, 250
pattern day traders, 93–94
PC Trader (Web site), 260
PCAOB (Public Company Accounting
    Oversight Board), 181
P/E ratio. *See* price/earnings (P/E) ratio
performance
  measuring portfolio, 321–322
  mutual fund, 115–116
personal digital assistant (PDA), 94, 95
personal finance software, for portfolio
    management, 331–333
Personal StockMonitor (Web site), 334–335
PersonalFund.com (Web site), 117–118, 138
Pew Internet (Web site), 1
Philadelphia Stock Exchange (Web site), 305
phishing, 343
PIMCO (Web site), 262
PitNews.com (Web site), 306

planning, financial
  analysts, investment, 56–59
  budgeting, 55
  expectations, realistic, 60
  goals, investing for, 55
  importance of, 47
  IRAs, 51–54
  personalized plan, building, 60–61
  portfolio management, 59–60
  risk assessment, 54–55
  savings need to reach goals, 48–49
  savings versus investments, 50–51
  Web sites for, 51
Polson Enterprises (Web site), 199
Ponzi schemes, 341
portals, 19. *See also* search engines
portfolio management
  alerts, 329–330
  asset allocation tools, 318–319
  data needed for tracking, 317
  importance of, 316
  information resources and tools for, 15
  online news and portfolio tracking,
    327–330
  options for, 322–323
  PC-based programs, 330–335
  performance measurement, 321–322
  portal use, 328–329
  prebuilt portfolios, 323–324
  rebalancing, 357
  risk assessment, 319–321
  Web-based programs, 324–326
Portfolio Systems Inc. (software), 333
PowerOptions (Web site), 307
PR Newswire (Web site), 199
Precision Information (Web site), 235
preferred stocks, 143
premium
  bond, 221
  option, 302, 309, 310
Premium Portfolio X-Rays (Morningstar),
    320–321
price fluctuations, stock, 155
price/book value, 154, 164, 168
price/earnings (P/E) ratio, 167
  buying strategy and, 370–371
  description, 164

mutual fund, 128
  performance measurement and, 321–322
  spurts, 359
  as stock screen criteria, 161, 168, 170–171
  value investing and, 154
principal, bond, 221, 222
Principal (Web site), 135
Private Securities Litigation Reform Act of
  1995, 342
Producer Price Indexes (Web site), 203
profit wipe-outs, 361–363
Profusion (metasearch engine), 17
ProphetNet (Web site), 155
prospectus
  IPO, 283
  mutual fund, 113–116
Prudential's Glossary of Terms (Web
  site), 34
Public Company Accounting Oversight
  Board (PCAOB), 181
Public Register's Annual Report Service
  (Web site), 178
pump-and-dump schemes, 346–347
put option, 303–304, 311
pyramid schemes, 340–341

• Q •

quick ratios, 168
Quick & Reilly (brokerage), 72–73
Quicken (Intuit), 55, 322, 332–333
quotes. *See* stock quotes

• R •

Raging Bull (Web site), 23
ratios, financial, 188–189, 190
RealPlayer, 41, 211
Realtor.org (Web site), 202
rebalancing your portfolio, 357
recession, 366
red herring, 283
relative strength, company, 355
Remember icon, 5
research report, bogus, 342–343
return on assets (ROA), 168
return on equity (ROE), 164, 356
returns, calculating, 59–60

Reuters (Web site)
  Alerts, 59
  company information, 169
  portfolio management program, 326
  portfolio tracking, 357
  Power Screener stock screen, 167
  ratio analysis, 190
  stock quotes, 367
  stock screen, 368, 369
revenue bonds, 236–237
Righteous Rockets, 162, 163
risk
  beta as measure of, 162
  exchange rate, 275
  of international investments, 275
  mutual funds and, 110–111, 118–119, 122,
    123, 128
  online analysis, 319–321
  tolerance, assessment of, 54–55
  watching out for investment risks, 165
risk premium, 148
Risk Tolerance Assessor (Web site), 55
RiskGrades (Web site), 111, 118, 319–320,
  357
ROA (return on assets), 168
Robot Wisdom Newsgroup Finder (Web
  site), 21
ROE (return on equity), 164, 356
Roth IRA Web Site Home Page (Web site),
  53
Roth IRAs, 52–53
Royce Funds (Web site), 137
RS Investments (Web site), 137
Rule 12b-1 fees, 103–104

• S •

Sarbanes-Oxley Act, 180–181
savings, 50–51
Savings Bond Wizard, 252–253
savings bonds
  advantages, 251
  buying online, 234, 255–256
  redeeming online, 256
  Series EE, 250
  Treasury Direct account, 255–256
  types, 250–251
  value, calculating, 252–253

SavingsBonds.com (Web site), 251
scaling out, 354
SchaeffersResearch.com (Web site), 306, 308, 314
scholarly journals, online, 40
SCOR Report (Web site), 291–292
Scottrade (brokerage)
  for active investors, 70, 92
  commission structure, 74
  initial account minimum, 74
  Scottrade ELITE trading platform, 92
screeners, option, 307–308
search engines
  business news, 200
  description, 16
  hierarchical indexes, 16
  metasearch engines, 16–17
  newsgroup searches, 21–22
  personalized, 18
  popular, 17–18
  Securities and Exchange Commission (SEC), 182–183
  selecting best, 19
seasonal stocks, 144
SEC Info (Web site), 183
Securities and Exchange Commission (SEC)
  annual reports, 368
  company information, 169, 176
  complaining to, 352
  cyberfraud and, 339, 342, 345, 348–349
  downloading filings, 181–182
  educational materials, 165
  electronic communications networks (ECNs), 86
  filings, 15
  mutual fund NAV, 102
  pattern day traders, 94
  search engines, 182–183
  sting, 345
Securities Industry Association (Web site), 365
Securities Investor Protection Corporation (SIPC), 67
Select Net system, 88
Sell Direct, 259–260
selling
  goals, setting profit-taking, 358
  information resources for, 15
  losers, 358–359
  personal rules for, 353–356
  profit wipe-outs, avoiding, 361–363
  rebalancing portfolios, 357
  when changes occur, 361
  when insiders sell, 356, 360–361
seminars, investment, 346
senior investors, Web sites for, 28
Series EE savings bonds, 250
Series HH bonds, 250
Series I bonds, 251
7 and 7 approach, 371
ShareBuilder (Web site), 295–296, 366
shareholder investment programs (SIPs), 296
shares outstanding, 164
Shareware.com (Web site), 313
ShibuiMarkets.com (Web site), 271
Siebert (brokerage). *See* Muriel Siebert & Co.
Silicon Investor (Web site), 22
simulations, 44–45, 85
Sindell, Kathleen (author's Web site), 7
SIPC (Securities Investor Protection Corporation), 67
SIPs (shareholder investment programs), 296
Site-by-Site! (Web site), 279
SLS Reference Service (Web site), 215
small-saver certificates, 229
Smart Money (Web site)
  alerts, 330
  Bond Calculator, 249
  brokerage comparison tool, 71
  Capital Gains Guide, 15
  Capital Gains Tax Estimator, 363
  earnings estimates, 212
  mutual fund information, 116
  mutual fund screen, 113
  online brokerage ratings, 77
  Smart Money University, 34
  Treasury securities, 260
  yield curves, 246
Smith Barney Access (Web site), 237, 248
Smith Barney Municipal bond Inventory (Web site), 225
Social Investment Forum (Web site), 28
SocialFunds.com (Web site), 28
socially responsible investors, Web sites for, 28

software
  active trading, 91–93
  personal finance, 331–333
  portfolio management, 333–335
  technical analysis, 156–157
  tools for options trading, 312–313
spam, 342–343
speculative stocks, 145
spiders
  search engine, 17
  Standard & Poor's Deposit Receipts, 109
spread, 87–88
Spreadware (Web site), 188–189
SPREDGAR (Web site), 189
Stable Technical Graphs (Web site), 156
standard deviation, 116, 119, 321
Standard & Poor's Deposit Receipts
    (spiders), 109
Standard & Poor's 500 Index, 145, 267
Standard & Poor's Fund Services (Web
    site), 106, 279
Standard & Poor's Index Services (Web
    site), 268
Standard & Poor's (Web site)
  analyst evaluations, 209
  bond rates, 228
StarMine (Web site), 59
STAT-USA (Web site), 26, 171, 207
Stock Alerts (Web site), 330
stock analysis
  active stock, 206
  analyst evaluations, 209–210
  business economic indicators, 202–204
  company analysis, 197
  company profiles, 200–201
  consumer economic indicators, 204
  earnings conference calls, 210–211
  earnings estimates, 211–212
  economic analysis, 196–197
  financial market data, 205–206
  forecasting earnings, 212
  industry analysis, 197
  investment strategies, 196–198
  Level I stock quotes, 215–217
  Level II stock quotes, 217–218
  market indices, 206
  market research Web sites, 207–208
  news and press releases, 199–200

  officers, researching background of,
    213–214
  prices, historic, 214–215
  stock quotes, 215–220
  valuation analysis, 197
stock order, 84–85
stock overlap, 129
stock quotes
  extended-hours, 89
  fee-based, 220
  free delayed, 218–219
  free real-time, 219
  free wireless, 219
  Level I, 91, 215–217
  Level II, 91, 217–218
stock screening
  for bargains, 169–173
  brokerage screeners, 172–173
  for companies reporting deficits, 171
  criteria for first stock screen, 160–161
  criteria terminology, 162–164
  description, 159–160
  fine-tuning, 161
  for growth stocks, 167–168
  for income stocks, 168
  prebuilt screens, 162, 165–167, 172–173
  quick, 165–166
  for stocks selling below book value, 169
  for stocks selling below liquidation value,
    169–170
  for stocks with low P/E ratio, 170–171
  for turnaround candidates, 171–172
  using results of, 161
  for value stocks, 168
stock splits, 83
Stock Wiz Links (Web site), 368
stock-picking communities, 57–58
stocks
  capital appreciation, 141–142
  capitalization, 146
  common, 142–143
  market index, 145–147
  market timing, 157
  preferred, 143
  technical analysis, 154–157
  types, 144
  valuation, 147–154
StockSelector (Web site), 326
Stockworm (Web site), 148–149

Stone & Youngberg (Web site), 237, 238
stop market order, 354
stop order, 85
stop-limit order, 85
stop-loss order, 354
TheStreet.com (Web site), 106–107
strike price, 302, 308, 311
SurfWax (metasearch engine), 17
sweep account programs, 78

• T •

T. Rowe Price (mutual fund company),
    106, 137, 153
taxes
    capital gains and, 82–84, 362–363
    international investing and, 273
tax-exempt commercial paper, 237
TD Waterhouse (brokerage)
    commission structure, 74
    fees, 72–73
    initial account minimum, 75
    for mainstream investors, 69
    mutual fund purchases, 133, 134
    services, 66
    wireless trading, 95
technical analysis
    description, 154–155
    Dow Theory, 155–156
    software, 156–157
    Web sites for, 155
Technical Stuff icon, 5
TechWeb News (Web site), 287
TeenAnalyst (Web site), 28
10-K Wizard (Web site), 182
ThirdAge (Web site), 28
thread, 23
3DStockCharts (Web site), 219
TIAA-CREF Mutual Funds (Web site), 137
ticker symbol, 218
Tile.net (Web site), 23
time values, option, 308
Tip icon, 5
TIPS (Treasury Inflation-Protection
    Securities), 255, 256
TradeBonds.com (Web site), 250

trading
    abroad, 271–272
    day, 86, 87, 91–94
    electronic communications networks
        (ECNs), 86–87
    extended-hours, 88–90
    insider, 192–193, 356, 360–361
    order specifications, 84–85
    wireless, 94–96
Trading Direct (brokerage), 74
trading platforms, 91–93
trading range, 354
Treasury Direct (Web site)
    buying online, 257–259
    as information source, 233
    opening an account, 250, 254–257
    savings bond account, 234, 255–256
    Sell Direct program, 259–260
Treasury Inflation-Protection Securities
    (TIPS), 255, 256
Treasury securities
    buying online, 257–259
    competitive and noncompetitive bids,
        257–258, 259
    description, 233
    fraud, 261
    inflation-indexed, 254
    information resources, 233–234, 260
    ladder, 261–262
    savings bonds, 234, 250–253, 255–256
    selling, 259–260
    Treasury Direct program, 233, 234,
        254–260
    types, 253–254
    yield curve, 246–247
Treasury strips, 240
TurboTax (Intuit), 333
turnaround candidates, screening for,
    171–172
turnover ratio, 116
tutorials, online investor, 32–33

• U •

underlying stock, 302, 303, 308
underwriter, 282, 283

Unemployed Insurance Weekly Claims Report (Web site), 204
unit investment trust, 108
U.S. Business Reporter (Web site), 201
U.S. Census Bureau (Web site), 203, 204
U.S. Futures & Options (Web site), 305
U.S. State Department (Web site), 344
Usenet, 21

• *V* •

value funds, 105
value investing, 153–154
Value Line (Web site)
  industry surveys, 370
  mutual fund asset allocation, 122, 123
  mutual fund ratings, 128, 131–132
Value Point Analysis Model, 149–153
Value Point Analysis Stock Forum (Web site), 149–150
value stocks, 145, 168
ValueInvestorsClub.com (Web site), 57–58
ValuEngine.com (Web site), 149
ValuePro (Web site), 149
Vanguard Index Participation Equity Receipts (Vipers), 109
Vanguard (mutual fund company)
  buying funds, 136
  fund of funds, 106
  index funds, 108
  IRA calculator, 53
  mutual funds, 137
  Online Planner, 51
  Vipers, 109
variable-rate demand obligations, 237
variable-rate note, 222
VectorVest (Web site), 157
VentureWire Alert (Web site), 199
Vickers Stock Research (Web site), 193
Vipers (Vanguard Index Participation Equity Receipts), 109
Virtual Stock Exchange (Web site), 45
virtual trading, at optionsXpress Web site, 309
Vivisimo (metasearch engine), 17

• *W* •

The Wall Street Journal (Web site)
  alerts and newsletters, 42
  annual report service, 178
  breaking news, 199
  earnings estimates, 212
  mutual fund rankings, 130
  mutual fund ratings, 128
  as news source, 39, 42, 199, 367
  portfolio management program, 326
  stock quotes, 215–217
Warning! icon, 5
Web sites
  analyst, 58–59, 209–210
  annual reports, 177–178
  for asset allocation, 318
  bond brokerages, 244–250
  bond calculators, 248–249
  bond information, 224–228, 233–235, 237, 239–241
  bookmark management services, 36–37
  brokerages, 65–66, 68–71, 78, 91–96
  business news, 327
  Chicago Board of Trade, 314
  Chicago Board Options Exchange, 304
  company information, 182–183, 186–190
  compound interest calculators, 49
  corporate officer information, 213
  databases, 24–26
  DPO information, 291–292
  DPP information, 293
  DRIP information, 297, 298, 299
  earnings forecasts, 368
  earnings information, 211–212
  economic indicator information, 202–206
  financial planning information, 51
  glossaries, 34–35
  industry information, 207–208
  investment clubs, 44
  investment simulations, 45
  IPO information, 285–288
  IPO online super-sites, 285–288
  IRA comparison calculators, 53–54
  IRA information, 53
  market information, 206

Web sites *(continued)*
  message boards, 22–23
  MMDA information, 232
  mutual fund information, 106, 108, 110,
    112–113
  mutual fund ratings, 128, 130
  mutual fund sources, 137
  for new investors, 34
  news, 38–42, 199–200, 367
  newsgroup information, 21
  option information, 304–309, 312, 314
  Optionetics, 304
  Options Industry Council, 314
  optionsXpress, 314
  personal finance software, 331–332
  portals, 19, 328–329
  portfolio management alerts, 329–330
  portfolio management software, 333–335
  portfolio tracking, 327–330
  prepackaged portfolios, 323–324
  risk analysis, 319–321
  SchaeffersResearch.com, 314
  search engines, 16–18
  special interest, 28–29
  stock analysis, 148–149, 155–157
  stock quotes, 219–220
  stock screens, 165–167, 172–173
  stock-picking communities, 57–58
  technical analysis, 155, 156–157
  Treasury securities information, 260
  tutorials, 33
  yield curve resources, 246–247
  for young investors, 27–28
Web100 (Web site), 179
Wells Fargo Bank (bankerage), 78
WIFE.org (Web site), 29
William Blair Funds (mutual funds
    company), 137
Wilshire 5000, 145
Windows Media Player, 41, 211
wireless stock quotes, 219
WorldNews Network (Web site), 270
WR Hambrecht + Co (Web site), 288
Wright Investors' Service (Web site), 271

• *Y* •

Yahoo! (Web site)
  agency bonds, 235
  broker listings, 71
  conference call calendar, 211
  earnings estimates, 212
  Financial Glossary, 34
  Groups, 21
  Industry News, 208
  insider trading information, 361
  international indexes, 268
  IPO News, 286
  news, 361
  portfolio management, 328–329
  ratio analysis, 190
  screening bonds, 239
  as search engine, 18
  stock quotes, 219
  stock screen, 166
  Treasury securities, 233
yield
  bond, 223, 244–248
  dividend yield, 163, 168
yield curve, 245–247
yield to maturity, 223, 247–248
The Young Investor Web site (Web site), 27
young investors, Web sites for, 27–28
Young, Margaret Levine
  Fighting Spam For Dummies, 343
  The Internet For Dummies, 4, 32

• *Z* •

Zacks (Web site)
  analyst evaluations, 209
  ratio analysis, 190
  stock screen, 166, 167
zero-coupon bonds, 240
Ziff Davis Publications (Web site), 42
Z-Score, 191